RURAL TRANSFORMATIONS IN INDUSTRIALIZING SOUTH AFRICA

Rural Transformations in Industrializing South Africa

The Southern Highveld to 1914

Timothy J. Keegan

Research Officer, African Studies Research Institute
University of the Witwatersrand, Johannesburg

RAVAN PRESS

First impression 1986

First published by **Ravan Press (Pty) Ltd**
P.O. Box 31134, Braamfontein 2017, South Africa

Typeset by Vine & Gorfin Ltd, Exmouth, Devon
Cover design: Jeffrey Lok

Printed by Galvin and Sales, Cape Town

ISBN 0 86975 310 X

Contents

Map	vii
Preface	viii
Abbreviations	x
Introduction	xii

1 The Nineteenth-century Political Economy of the Southern Highveld — 1
Land, labour and capital before 1870 — 1
Economic growth and agrarian change after 1870 — 9

2 Transformations in Boer Society — 20
White rural impoverishment: chronology and processes — 20
The *bywoner* as labourer and as producer — 29
Strategies of survival and the experience of urbanization — 33
Landownership, loan capital and the trap of indebtedness — 38

3 Black Tenant Production and White Accumulation — 51
The evolution of a sharecropping economy — 51
Absentee landlords, poor whites and black sharecroppers — 64
The black household economy — 74
Black productive resources and white accumulation: forms
of partnership on the land — 86°

4 Interventions of the Capitalist State and the Development of the Arable Highveld — 96
Marketing, railways and the emergence of the grain belt — 96
Origins of the interventionist state — 110
The dynamics of white capitalization — 113

5 The Making of a Servile Tenantry — 121
Labour tenancy: the constraints of capital and the resistant
peasantry — 121
Conflict, control and the process of law — 130
Policing the labour market: tenant mobility and the pass
laws — 149
Violence, paternalism and the working compromise:
sustaining productive relationships — 156
Organization and resistance — 160

6 Years of Crisis, 1908–14   **166**
  Financial boom   166
  The dimensions of the rural crisis   169
  The Natives Land Act and the great dispersal of 1913   182

  Conclusion   **196**

Statistical Appendix   208

Notes and References   219

Bibliography   272

Index   292

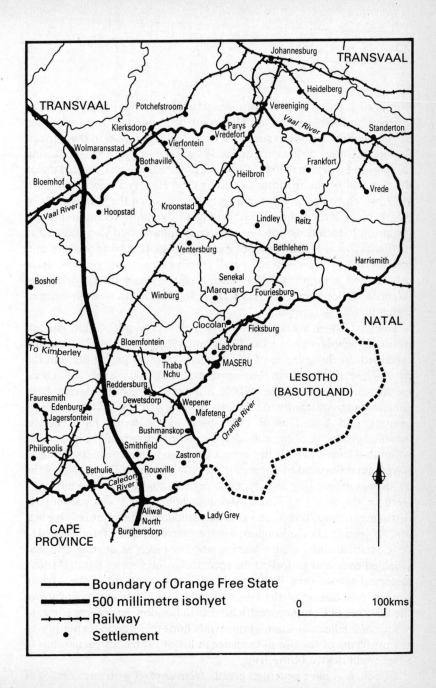

TRANSVAAL

Johannesburg

Heidelberg

Potchefstroom

Vereeniging

Vaal River

Standerton

Klerksdorp

Parys
Vredefort

Vierfontein

Wolmaransstad

Bothaville

Heilbron

Frankfort

Bloemhof

Vaal River

Heilbron

Vrede

Hoopstad

Kroonstad

Lindley

Reitz

Ventersburg

Bethlehem

Boshof

Senekal

Harrismith

Winburg

Marquard

Fouriesburg

Clocolan

Ficksburg

NATAL

To Kimberley

Bloemfontein

Ladybrand

Thaba
Nchu

MASERU

LESOTHO
(BASUTOLAND)

Fauresmith
Edenburg
Jagersfontein

Reddersdorp

Dewetsdorp

Wepener

Mafeteng

Orange River

Philippolis

Bushmanskop

Smithfield

Zastron

Bethulie

Rouxville

Caledon
River

Aliwal
North

Lady Grey

CAPE
PROVINCE

Burghersdorp

Boundary of Orange Free State

500 millimetre isohyet

Railway

Settlement

0   100kms

Preface

This book is based on a doctoral dissertation presented at the School of Oriental and African Studies, University of London. It was revised for publication during the tenure of a Research Fellowship in the African Studies Institute, University of the Witwatersrand, in 1983–4. During this period I was able to make extensive use of interviews collected under the auspices of the Institute's ongoing Oral History Project, started in 1979, which has concentrated largely on collecting the life histories of elderly black farm tenants from the Highveld region. Access to this oral testimony, which constitutes a resource of unparalleled value, as well as further archival research in, for example, district correspondence and the surviving transcripts of local criminal court proceedings, have necessitated a more radical rewriting of the thesis than I originally intended. Indeed, much of this book bears little relation to the thesis of which it is an outgrowth.

The past fifteen years have witnessed an explosion of South African historical scholarship. In the 1950s and 1960s, South African studies remained on the margins of the dramatic changes taking place in the field of historical research in universities throughout the world, not least in Africa. But since the 1960s, historians of South Africa have contributed significantly to scholarly debates well beyond the country's borders, and historians of other parts of the world have become increasingly aware of the considerable comparative treasure house that is South Africa's past. It has been a privilege to have witnessed and to have been influenced by some of these developments. The decade of the 1970s was an exciting and dynamic period in which to have cut one's teeth in the world of South African scholarship. I was particularly fortunate to have studied as a graduate student at the School of Oriental and African Studies in London, a nerve-centre of African studies, and to have studied under Shula Marks, who, as much as anyone else, has presided over and propelled the spectacular advance of South African historical scholarship. Professor Marks, past president of the African Studies Association of the United Kingdom and currently Director of the Institute of Commonwealth Studies in London, has been a constant source of intellectual stimulation. I only hope that her close attention to the problems of the use of evidence in historical reconstruction has in some small degree borne fruit.

Of course, I have benefited greatly from contact with any number of others whose own research interests have impinged on mine in greater or lesser degree. During the course of research one accumulates a host of debts, intellectual and otherwise. It would be an indulgence even to try to enumerate them here. But there are a few which should be mentioned. Colin Bundy and Terry Byres made thoughtful criticisms of the thesis and offered suggestions which proved invaluable in rewriting it. I also learned a great deal during a year spent at Yale University. Professor Charles van Onselen, Director of the African Studies Institute at the University of the Witwatersrand, not only offered me a Research Fellowship in order to prepare this book, but subsequently offered me a longer-term post as Research Officer in the Institute. I have benefited immeasurably from his own experience of rural research and his sharp intuitive insights into the nature of rural society. His scholarly standards and productivity have inevitably provided a constant model; and his keen and impatient interest in the progress of my own work has provided a constant spur. Finally, my wife, Margaret Kinsman Keegan, has taken on the roles of editor, proof-reader and typist, and has willingly put up with countless working weekends and holidays spent in libraries and archives. Moreover, her own extensive research experience has made her a shrewd and dependable critic of my work.

TIMOTHY J. KEEGAN

Abbreviations

ANA	Advisor for Native Affairs, ORC
BBNA, 1910	UG 17–1911, *Blue Book on Native Affairs*, 1910
BPP	British Parliamentary Papers
CO	Public Record Office, London, Colonial Office Archives
CS	Orange Free State Archives, ORC Colonial Secretary series
DA	Orange Free State Archives, ORC Department of Agriculture series
FA	The *Farmer's Advocate*
FSP	Orange Free State Archive, South African Police
FW	The *Farmer's Weekly*
G	Orange Free State Archives, ORC Governor series
GS	Orange Free State Archives, Government Secretary series
ISAA	Imperial South Africa Association
JUS	Union Archives, Pretoria, Department of Justice series
KRS	Orange Free State Archives, Kroonstad district files
LBD	Orange Free State Archives, Bothaville district files
LFI	Orange Free State Archives, Ficksburg district files
LHS	Orange Free State Archives, Harrismith district files
LIN	Orange Free State Archives, Lindley district files
LLA	Orange Free State Archives, Ladybrand district files
LPA	Orange Free State Archives, Parys district files
MLA	Member of the Legislative Assembly
NA	Union Archives, Pretoria, Department of Native Affairs series
NAB	Orange Free State Archives, ORC Native Affairs Branch series
NLC	UG 22–1916, *Natives Land Commission*, Minutes of Evidence
ORC	Orange River Colony
P	Archives of the State President, Orange Free State
RM	Resident Magistrate
SAC	South African Constabulary
SAIRR	South African Institute of Race Relations
SANAC	*South African Native Affairs Commission*, 1903–5, 5 vols (Cape Town, 1905)
SC	Select Committee Report

SBA	Standard Bank Archives, Johannesburg
SJP	Special Justice of the Peace
TG	Transvaal Government publication
UG	Union Government publication
VR	Orange Free State Archives, *Volksraad* series

Introduction

This book investigates the origins of the capitalist agricultural economy on the interior Highveld in the early decades of South Africa's industrial revolution. It starts from the premise that South Africa has undergone a capitalist transformation unique in Africa which needs to be explained. It seeks to examine the origins and early development of the dual process whereby indigenous whites were able to monopolize and accumulate rural capital resources at the expense of the blacks on the land, and were able to forge and control a black labour force. This book argues that these rural transformations were crucial to our understanding of the South African economic revolution over the past hundred years and especially the racially exclusive nature of the industrial order that emerged.

In South Africa's colonial economy, enclaves of export-oriented settler production arose in different areas at various times in the pre-industrial past: first, in the wheat and wine farms of the southwestern Cape, based on imported slave labour from the seventeenth century onward. Commercial wool and ostrich farming, based on various forms of semi-servile and migrant labour, spread through the dry expanses of the eastern Cape interior in the mid-nineteenth century; and on the sugar plantations of the Natal lowlands, indentured Indians were employed from the 1860s. The focus of this book, however, is on the arable Highveld, settled from the 1840s by Boers who practised extensive pastoralism and hunting. For this was the region which spawned South Africa's industrial revolution and which was radically transformed by the rise of internal urban markets for agricultural produce from the late nineteenth century onward. By focusing on the Highveld, the agricultural heartland of twentieth-century South Africa, we can best explore the conditions under which it was possible for a capitalist transformation of rural society to take place.

The rural Highveld is not a region with readily definable boundaries. Broadly, one can identify it as the highland savannah plain, bisected by the Vaal River, which forms the arable heartland of the South African interior plateau.[1] But any rigid definition based on topography or climate would be inadequate. For our purposes the Highveld is best defined in agro-economic terms. For the patterns of economic activity in large part determined the characteristic structures of productive relationships and the processes of social change. The concentration on grain production which increasingly characterized the arable Highveld implied certain patterns of relationships on the land and particular processes of change in those relationships. Of course, this is not to suggest that there has been a consistent homogeneity throughout the Highveld region. Indeed, there have been very considerable regional variations not only in periodization but also in the processes of social change. Furthermore, the boundaries of the grain districts have changed over time, as intensive arable production has expanded from the heartland of the Highveld outward, and as the centre of gravity of grain farming has shifted, most notably to the western Transvaal. We may very loosely envisage the arable Highveld as the area encompassed by what the school textbooks call the 'maize triangle', with its vertices at Zeerust, Ermelo and Zastron in the south.

This study is concerned with the arable Highveld as an agro-economic region, forming the agricultural hinterland of contemporary South Africa's industrial hub, the Witwatersrand. But it is also about a particular state with its own specific structure, set of laws, and hierarchy of actors and group interests. State structure and legal systems provide the essential context in which social and economic changes take place. Hence, although the book considers social and economic processes and transformations which cross state boundaries, it is nonetheless primarily concerned with the Highveld south of the Vaal River (falling within the Orange Free State) rather than north of the Vaal (falling within the South African Republic or Transvaal). To have attempted a wider geographical scale would have meant falling into the trap of over-abstraction; or else it would have meant considerable and ponderous duplication not only of research, but also of explanation and interpretation. So while I have not hesitated to draw on evidence from north of the Vaal in support of my analysis of social and economic change common to the arable Highveld region as a whole, consideration of state activities and interventions on various levels is by and large restricted to the Orange Free State. Further, the great bulk of the documentary evidence is drawn from Orange Free State sources. This focus is easily justified, given the fact that the most immediate and dramatic impact of industrialization and urban growth on rural areas was felt in the Orange Free State grain districts. It was here that the productive base of the rural economy developed most quickly. It was here that conflict over access to rural resources and control over productive enterprise crystallized earliest. And it was here that the processes of class formation, capitalization and dispossession were initially most starkly manifested.

Of course, political realities were themselves changing. The Orange Free State and Transvaal republics of the nineteenth century passed away with the turning of the century. As a result of the Anglo-Boer War (1899–1902) the Boer republics were annexed to the British Empire as crown colonies. After their white inhabitants had received self-government in 1907–8, they were incorporated as provinces in the Union of South Africa (in common with the long-established Cape and Natal colonies) in 1910. But even after 1910 the different provinces continued to differ markedly in their laws and local government structures and in the perspectives and preoccupations which their representatives brought with them into Union.

*   *   *

The book starts by exploring the nature of pre-industrial relationships and rural accumulation on the Highveld. It then examines the impact of internal urban development on rural economy and society. It investigates the social dislocations and the processes of class formation in indigenous white society, confronted with the decline of older productive activities, with the penetration of rural areas by speculative and loan capital, and the growing productive strength of the black rural economy. It explores the emerging productive relationships on white-owned land, particularly sharecropping, which became not only a major means of surplus extraction on the land of (often corporate) absentee landowners, but also very importantly a means of survival and accumulation for indigenous whites. Making use of oral evidence from elderly blacks, the book examines the nature and dynamics of sharecropping relationships, the social origins, changing family structures and forms of accumulation and of labour organization within sharecropping communities. The relationship between black share-cropping enterprise and the undercapitalized and dependant condition of white landholders is also analysed.

The book investigates the dynamics of white capitalization on the land. Changing forms of accumulation and state interventions in the promotion of white capitalist farming are discussed. The complex process whereby black rural production was undermined as white farming gathered momentum under the auspices of a paternalist state is examined. Particular attention is paid to the oral contract of tenancy as the locus of conflict and resistance. Use is made of transcripts from local criminal courts to investigate the role played by the legal system in promoting the interests and the economic leverage of white landlords; the struggles of black tenant households to maintain their independent productive base and the forms of resistance they adopted are examined; and the racial perceptions and stereotypes which emerged out of and shaped these struggles are discussed. The book then examines more closely a particularly dramatic period of rural crisis and rural change, the few years leading up to 1913, a year of legislative intervention in the subversion of sharecropping tenants (in the shape of the seminal Natives Land Act) and also a year of mass dispersal of tenants who declined to submit to the radically more stringent conditions of tenure which their landlords were attempting to impose on them. The cyclical dynamics of the process whereby white control was extended over black productive resources, the relationship of this process to white capitalization and the problematical nature and consequences of state intervention in this process are examined. Finally the complex of reasons for the drive to extend white supremacy at the point of production are analysed, as are its consequences for the nature of the industrial order as a whole.

*   *   *

The image of the countryside in South African historiography has changed significantly in recent years. Earlier writers like C. W. de Kiewiet and W. M. Macmillan stressed the backwardness and stagnation of the South African countryside. The image of the isolated, introspective frontier as the *fons et origo* both of impoverishment (black and white) and of racial exclusiveness and animosity, dominates de Kiewiet's writing in particular. Equally, black tenancy or the 'squatting system' was in his view an index of backwardness and lack of enterprise. De Kiewiet draws a stark contrast between town and countryside: the former progressive, competitive and prosperous, the latter mostly 'semi-feudal', unchanging and poverty-stricken. These images dominated a generation of liberal thinking.[2]

More recent writers, writing from a more radical, materialistic perspective, and faced with very changed circumstances, have stressed, first, the initial success of black tenant commercial production; and second, the vigour and strength of white agriculture, the rapidity of its development under the auspices of a modern, industrial state, and the brutality of the suppression of the once prosperous black rural economy. In this process, the 1913 Natives Land Act is given pride of place as the single most devastating blow aimed at black peasant production. Earlier writers stressed the rather more negative function of the act in the demarcation of reserves and the entrenchment of territorial segregation. More recently, the significance of the act has been seen more centrally in terms of its decisive role in the emergence of a white-dominated capitalist agriculture at the expense of the black peasantry.[3]

The more recent interpretations reflect to a far greater degree than did the inter-war generation of liberals, the perceptions of those who were involved in the agitations of the years before 1913. In the view of contemporary whites, there was nothing stagnant or decaying about the black rural economy. To those who forged the 'public opinion' of the day, the 'squatting system' was no moribund anachronism. As far as they were concerned, whites on the land were engaged in a life-or-death struggle for social and economic dominance.

The strength of the recent revisionist literature is its attempt to identify large-scale processes and transformations. But the megaview not only conceals as much as it reveals; it can often result in a distortion of vision. What has been missing from much (but not all) of this writing is a sense of the dynamics of change and an awareness of local specificity. When the focus is narrowed, what emerges is less a unilinear, homogeneous transition to capitalism, taking place in readily definable stages, but a far more complex, ambiguous and multifaceted process of change. In particular, it seems that the relationship between state initiatives (inevitably the primary focus of scholars who prefer the megaview) and local tranformations, is far from being an unproblematical one. Those whose methodological horizons are largely confined to a scrutiny of official publications commonly assume quite wrongly that parliamentary debates, commission reports and legislative enactments precisely reflect as well as shape social reality in rural areas. After all, it is altogether simpler to examine the details of laws and the professed intentions of their progenitors, than to try to unravel the complex social reality of which they are a product. But legislative initiatives often bear little relationship to what is practically possible for the state to accomplish. Further, much public perception of rural social reality as reflected in political agitation and debate is so encrusted with ideology as to be highly problematical as historical evidence.

Narrative, event-oriented history can raise wholly new questions for consideration, or can point to new dimensions of old issues. Consideration of the life experiences of individual people and communities can quickly reveal inadequacies in the prevailing interpretations of historical change. Microstudies can open up whole terrains of human experience, which previously lay hidden from history. Of course, this is not to suggest that the megaview is invalid, only that without constant interaction with detailed and parochial empirical research (which often entails enormously complex problems of evidence) it is sadly impoverished. The smaller the scale of investigation the more likely it is that the intricacies and complexities of social interaction will stand revealed, stripped of schematic abstractions. True comparative insight and meaningful generalization is only valid on the basis of detailed and often difficult empirical investigation.

While much of the more structuralist work tends to sacrifice empirical induction for large-scale schematization, much of the existing historiography relating specifically to the region with which this book is concerned – almost exclusively in Afrikaans – is devoid of any sense of the dynamics or of the totality and interconnectedness of social and economic life. While the structuralists are often concerned with the past as a terrain for the construction of social theory, the Afrikaans historiography is usually uninformed by any recognizable interpretive framework for the analysis of the past. In much of this writing, the nature of the readily available archival evidence dictates the focus of the research. The result is a largely mechanical kind of methodology, which allows for little interpolation of the historian's creative imagination. There is very little sense here of the nature and direction of the research being dictated by the historian's informed questioning. Rather, the standard sources of evidence (which are themselves highly problematical) are for the most part uncritically gathered and regurgitated.

These methodological deficiencies are related to intellectual limitations. Social analysis is apparently regarded in many South African universities as outside the scope of the historian's craft. Such limitations are particularly apparent when historians venture into the terrain of socio-economic studies. 'Agricultural history' becomes a catalogue of fencing legislation, irrigation projects and white farmers' associations. 'Local history' becomes a directory of local government, white religious and educational institutions and cultural organizations.[4] '*Verhouding-studies*' or studies of inter-group relations – a currently popular genre amongst Afrikaans historians – becomes a catalogue of government policies towards blacks. Thus, van Aswegen's monumental work on the 'relations between white and non-white' in the Orange Free State tends to resemble an uncritical index of legislative debate, (white) petitions to the government and letters to the press reflecting in minute and confused detail the distorted world of white racial perceptions. This scissors-and-paste historiography leaves no room for any decoding of the evidence, nor for any investigation of the complex reality of social relationships lying beneath the rhetoric.[5] Again, in Eloff's study of relations between the Orange Free State and Basutoland there is little systematic attempt to unravel the ways in which different social and economic systems interacted, conflicted and meshed, and how social and economic relationships changed over time. Rather, the author is largely preoccupied with official relationships as reflected in official correspondence (which also happens to have been largely penned by whites in the period of his study).[6] The exclusive concern with official sources and official perceptions results from a distinct preoccupation with the white community as a monolithic and discrete entity, embodied and represented in the white state. Other levels of stratification, cleavage and interdependence are disregarded. These historians also demonstrate highly culture-bound perceptions, manifested in anthropologically uninformed attitudes toward African history and social structure. Hence many (like van Aswegen) implicitly accept that it is natural and beneficial that blacks should have been transformed into a labouring force for whites.[7]

But these methodological and intellectual limitations are most sharply apparent in precisely the area of greatest scholarly awareness – the historical experiences of Afrikaners themselves. Afrikaners have undergone just about as dramatic a social revolution over the past century as any part of the African continent has seen. And yet for all the nationalist-oriented research which has been generated in the field of Afrikaner history, the actual dimensions of this experience are still remarkably little understood.[8] Despite the welter of biographical and institutional studies inspired by the nationalist movement, the complex processes of social change have never been investigated with any degree of sophistication. Indeed, no systematic and informed attempt has been undertaken to collect oral testimony from elderly Afrikaners (other than the political elite) – as is now being done for elderly black peasants in the Highveld region with remarkably gratifying results in terms of our understanding of the past. Yet if we are to make any progress in deciphering the totality of past human experience, such new sources of evidence are likely to prove indispensable, whatever difficulties of collection and interpretation they may present.

This book aims to make sense of the social transformation of the rural Highveld in the early decades of South Africa's industrial revolution. Ideally it is concerned to illuminate the integrated processes of social and economic change. On the other hand, I hope that it is also concerned with local specificity and with the diversity of individual experience. Without claiming to be a microstudy, it tries to avoid the temptation of reducing historical reality to a set of schematic generalities. If this book has succeeded in illuminating large-scale patterns of change while preserving a sense of the variety and unpredictability of social and economic experience, then it will have met its author's objectives.

1 The Nineteenth-century Political Economy of the Southern Highveld

LAND, LABOUR AND CAPITAL BEFORE 1870*

By the mid-nineteenth century, Boer pastoralists had been expanding into the interior of South Africa for almost two centuries, displacing and incorporating as labourers the indigenous Khoisan peoples. During the early decades of the nineteenth century the vanguard of the Boer frontiersmen began crossing the Orange River in search of grazing and hunting, and some settled permanently along the waterways and at the springs in what was to become the southern Orange Free State.[1] They had been preceded by the various Griqua or Bastard groups who had been thrown up and ejected by Cape colonial society, and who were to be swept aside in the process of white accumulation and state formation which were set in train from the mid-century onward.[2] The mass emigration of Boers from the eastern districts of the Cape from 1836 in the enigmatic and still little understood movement known as the Great Trek enormously expanded the frontiers of white settlement at a stroke. The *Voortrekkers*, after an unsuccessful attempt to colonize Natal and thus establish direct access to the sea free of British control, fanned out and sparsely peopled the interior Highveld. There they set about reconstructing their labour and productive systems in a new environment, and new forms of political authority began to coalesce.[3] The various centres of *Voortrekker* settlement were not entirely homogeneous. Those between the Vaal and Orange rivers remained more or less integrated into the loan, credit and exchange relations radiating out from the Cape colonial ports, which were themselves outposts of the international capitalist economy at the centre of which lay Britain. Those further afield on the eastern and northern peripheries of the Highveld and beyond were more tenuously linked to the larger

---

Note on measurement: The units 'morgen' and 'acre' are both used here according to the usage employed in the relevant source cited. No attempt has been made to standardize them. One morgen equals 2.12 acres. A bag of grain commonly contained a muid, weighing 203 lb.

economic networks, and were involved largely in ivory-hunting and raiding.[4]

Black chiefdoms had for centuries been expanding and fragmenting across the Highveld. To an extent white settlement on the Highveld was facilitated by the crisis of indigenous political authority attendant on the *Difaqane* of the 1820s and 1830s. This period of widespread disruption was caused in large part by Nguni fragments and successor states such as the Ndebele and Swazi moving on to the Highveld following the rise of Zulu power in the coastal lowlands to the east. While the extent of depopulation occasioned by these developments has no doubt been exaggerated,[5] nonetheless a number of substantial Sotho chiefdoms were disrupted and new foci of Sotho power developed out of the refugee bands which were scattered across the Highveld. The most significant of these in the southern Highveld was Moshoeshoe's kingdom, pressed against the mountain fastnesses of the Drakensberg and Malutis and with its nucleus in the Caledon River valley, which today maintains its much truncated independent statehood as Lesotho.[6] Other refugee groups on the southern Highveld coalesced around surviving pre-*Difaqane* rulers, such as the Tlokoa chief, Sekonyela, the Rolong chief, Moroka, and the Taung chief, Moletsane, amongst whom only Moroka's Rolong maintained an independent existence in the face of the expansion of Moshoeshoe's power on the one hand and Boer settlement on the other.[7] Moroka's territory, centred on Thaba Nchu, maintained its independence as an enclave client chiefdom within the Boer republic until 1884 when it was incorporated and partially dismembered.[8] For the rest, the early Boer settlers of the region found Griqua and Korana bands occupying river sites in the west (often sites abandoned by Sotho cultivators during the *Difaqane*). These settlements were interspersed by remaining San communities and impoverished Sotho refugees. Throughout most of the extensive flats of what became the Orange Free State and southern Transvaal, there was only intermittent and ineffective opposition to white settlement and land alienation, once the Ndebele had moved northwards from the Transvaal across the Limpopo River.[9]

In 1848 Sir Harry Smith, British governor at the Cape, extended the Cape Colony's boundaries to incorporate the whole area between the Orange and Vaal rivers, spurred by land speculators and by coastal merchants who saw the trading frontier rapidly advancing beyond the political control of the Cape colonial authorities. Fiscal exigencies and the efficacy of informal empire soon persuaded wiser administrators than Sir Harry to concede Boer sovereignty over the far interior, and in

1852 the British government recognized the independence of the Transvaal Boers. In 1854 the British withdrew their administration from Bloemfontein and handed over power to the president of the newly created Orange Free State Republic, situated between the Orange River in the south and the Vaal River in the north (although the British had difficulty in persuading many of the leading white inhabitants to take on the task of administration, as they were not all convinced of the benefits of independence).[10]

The new Boer republic thus created was singularly lacking in bureaucratic muscle. The popularly elected *Volksraad* or parliament was a largely ineffective body. Power and patronage were exercised informally and locally by the landowning and commercial elite. Apart from appointed *landdrosts* (magistrates) in the small commercial centres, policing and judicial functions at a more local level in the districts were exercised by prominent local notables – the elected *veldcornets* and appointed *vrederechters*. The military system was based on local burgher militias, whose elected commandants were also local notables.[11]

The Orange Free State economy was initially based on the provision of wool and hides for the international market. The southern Orange Free State in particular participated in the great wool boom which so radically changed the Cape economy from the 1840s.[12] The establishment of mercantile houses at the ports with agencies in all the inland towns,[13] the rapid spread of mortgage capital and credit,[14] the capitalization of land as a source of speculative investment and its consequent rise in value:[15] these are aspects of the qualitative change in the nature of the colonial economy which occurred not only in the Cape but also in the Orange Free State. In the 1850s towns like Harrismith, Bloemfontein, Fauresmith and Smithfield were centres of trade, and in the 1860s of banking activity too.[16]

Until well into the second half of the nineteenth century, much inland trade was in the hands of the Boers themselves. It was not uncommon for Boers to undertake trading expeditions with produce down to the coast to Durban or to transport wares for traders. They would also travel into the further interior with merchandise they had bought, or with wagons and livestock, which they bartered for other trade goods, skins or ivory – or slaves. The ownership of a wagon and oxen was as important as a gun and ammunition in the accumulation of capital amongst Boers seeking to establish themselves as independent pastoralists and landowners.[17]

Thus, Boer pastoralists were deeply involved in exchange and dependent on merchants for the maintenance of their economy.[18] For many on the Highveld, trade was based more on hunting than on anything else until at least the 1870s. During the 1860s, in particular, the price of skins ruled high, leading to indiscriminate and irreparable destruction of game. During the year 1866, for example, a single firm in Kroonstad exported 152000 blesbok and wildebeest hides.[19] Another source of income for those with firearms was the sale of ostrich feathers. The first feather boom began in 1860, and resulted in the rapid decimation of the wild ostriches which had once been so numerous. A good male bird fetched a profit of £10–15, and this trade added substantially to the commercial boom of the early 1860s.[20]

The Orange Free State quickly developed a typically colonial elite which consisted of the mercantile, financial and legal bourgeoisie of the trading towns, as well as the wealthier of the Boer stockowners. What all these had in common was a tendency to accumulate land as the major route to status and the exercise of patronage in the Boer state. The towns of the Highveld were overwhelmingly English-speaking until the twentieth century. The republic's popularly elected president between 1864 and 1888 was a British-educated lawyer, J. H. Brand, son of a Speaker of the Cape colonial parliament.

From the very beginning of land alienation by the early land commissions in the 1840s and 1850s, much land on the Highveld was owned by speculators – the mercantile and professional bourgeoisie living in the coastal ports or in the internal centres of trade and administration. Much land also fell into the hands of British administrators. From the start the conditions of alienation (six months' residence in the state and occupation of the land) were a dead letter, and in practice huge tracts of land – dozens of farms in some cases – were concentrated in the hands of individual speculators. What was more, individual farms could sometimes reach an extent of some 40000 or 50000 morgen, despite the official standard of 3000 morgen.[21]

The prevalence of colonial market relations and merchant and speculative capital in shaping the political economy of the republican state did not preclude forms of accumulation amongst Boer notables in the early years (before 1870 in the Orange Free State) which involved tributary and clientage relations with indigenous peoples. In areas where black chiefs had patronage of their own to dispense (such as in the northeastern Orange Free State) Boer notables with control over land were able to enter alliances with African chiefs enabling them to draw off surpluses from black production in the form of tribute, tax, rent or labour service. Boer notables had access to wealth in their capacity as military commanders as well. In the absence of any full-time military or police force, much initiative in raiding African peoples lay with the *veldcornets* and the burgher militias. The acquisition of influence and wealth through livestock booty, however, was no longer possible in the Orange Free State after the end of the 1860s, when defined borders were established between the Orange Free State and Basutoland, and the incessant warfare between the two was ended by British annexation of the latter territory.

It was quite common for Boer notables to combine great wealth derived from stock-rearing, trading and speculation, with elective political and military office and considerable accumulation of land. C. J. de Villiers from the Harrismith district is an instructive case in point: a large stockowner, speculator, financial manipulator, land baron with a penchant for fraudulent dealings, *veldcornet*, member of the *Volksraad* and commandant of the local militia. De Villiers enjoyed a lucrative, semi-official relationship with the local Sotho chiefs, who lived on land which he owned or for which he claimed to be an agent, and to whom he issued passes so that they could hunt game through the district on condition that he be given a half-share of the skins so obtained. However, by the 1870s the increasing settlement and exploitation of the land by white farmers undermined the basis of de Villiers' local dominance.[22] In the Transvaal on the other hand, where the Boers were weaker in relationship to the various black chiefdoms within the state's borders, and where land alienation and white settlement (at least on the margins of the Highveld and beyond) were less intensive, these pre-industrial forms of accumulation based on the exercise of patronage and military adventurism endured to the end of the century.[23]

* * *

The Boers were in some degree reliant on acculturated dependants of non-European descent for their labour in the early years of settlement. In the approximate census of 1856 it was estimated that the white population of the Orange Free State was just under 13 000 while there were 7454 'coloured' *dienstboden* or servants.[24] Many of these dependants were Afrikaans-speakers of Khoisan or slave ancestry, who had accompanied white families on the trek northwards. They were supplemented by the purchase of 'apprenticed' children acquired by Boer military forces in warfare or by trade with African peoples, mostly north of the Vaal.[25] 'Bushman hunts' were common sport in the 1840s and 1850s, in which parties of Boers, according to a Wesleyan missionary, attacked 'every kraal they can find, kill the parents and lead the children into hopeless captivity'. During the period of British rule of the territory north of the Orange (1848–54) *veldcornets* were authorised to disperse 'Bushman *kraals*' and place their residents 'under contract' to local Boers.[26]

The apprenticeship system was a form of slavery designed to tie African workers to the Boer household by capturing them young, and bringing them up as forcibly deculturated dependants.[27] An elderly informant remembers her grandmother, captured by a Boer commando as a child, telling her that they were whipped if they were caught speaking Tswana.[28] The system was regulated in the Orange Free State by means of an ordinance passed in 1856, which provided for release at the age of twenty-one for males, eighteen for females. But in reality, once apprenticed, the 'apprentices' were tied to the colonial economy for life. As they reached maturity and married, they were granted a degree of independence and might be loaned stock. The farmer was thus not burdened with the expense of maintaining adult dependants.

From the 1860s onward, the more explicitly dependent work force became less important in the agrarian economy, as the sources of supply of apprentices dried up and as the Boers became more and more reliant on tenant labour, particularly, as we shall see, in the aftermath of the Sotho wars.[29] Nevertheless, some later observers distinguished between the Afrikaans-speaking *'oorlamsches'* and the 'raw *naturellen*' on the farms.[30] It seems likely that the former, divorced from African society, were largely products of the apprenticeship system, many born on the farms, and linked by economic and cultural ties to Boer families. Many house servants and overseers came from this stratum, as did many of the more skilled of the black town dwellers.

Further, refugees from neighbouring African societies – or further afield – settled for shorter or longer periods on the farms. This movement of individuals or family groups of Africans into the areas of white settlement was a common source of labour in the Cape as far back as the eighteenth century, and was considerably boosted from the early nineteenth century as a direct consequence of the dispersal attendant on the *Difaqane*.[31] There were always – because of drought or war – numbers of impoverished Africans for whom service on the farms was a not dissimilar alternative to entering client relations with a chief. Such Africans might be offered a piece of arable land for household cultivation, and a heifer for a year's service was a common wage.[32] Seasonal migrations of labour, most notably for sheep-shearing, were also common from an early date at a rate of perhaps a penny a sheep.[33]

Movements of Africans into temporary wage employment were regulated and controlled to some extent by their chiefs. The fact that chiefs were officially empowered by the white authorities to issue passes enabled them to assert some degree of control over labour migration. Chiefs were generally able, it seems, to exact a proportion of migrant earnings, hence the significance not only of cattle and sheep but also of firearms as wage items, long before the opening of the diamond fields.[34] Missionaries also urged their followers to earn wages in the employ of white farmers. Residents on mission stations such as Carmel, Beersheba and Bethulie were frequently engaged as 'day labourers' amongst the Boers in the 1850s, from whom they obtained wagons, ploughs and wooled sheep.[35]

Increasing numbers of Africans found themselves willy-nilly on white-owned land, as white graziers encroached on their settlements and as title deeds were issued to white land claimants, or as large chunks of land were arbitrarily incorporated in the settler territory. Thus the 1849 Warden line robbed Moshoeshoe, as he put it, of 'thousands of my people'.[36] Although much formally alienated land was not at first effectively occupied by whites, nevertheless the extension of colonial law had potentially disruptive effects on indigenous African settlements. The fact that many Sotho resident on the farms still regarded themselves as falling under the jurisdiction of the Sotho paramount is suggested by the fact that many deserted farms in 1852 'at the call of their chief' in anticipation of the eruption of hostilities.[37]

The flurry of legislative activity from the 1850s onward provides evidence that from the earliest days there was a considerable African population living relatively independently within the settler territory. As early as 1854 a pass law was introduced which sought to control movement into and within the state by means of a pass system. The following year an amendment added that an African 'without an honest livelihood' – that is, one who was not in the employ of a white burgher (citizen) – was liable to criminal prosecution. The law also empowered *veldcornets* to disperse black 'squatter' communities on white-owned land if they inconvenienced neighbouring whites. Efforts were also made to restrict 'squatting' on state lands. Popular agitation for the control of *landlopery* (vagrancy) and *plakkery* (squatting) continued throughout the 1850s and 1860s, and a more stringent law was passed in 1860.[38] This type of legislation – which was concerned with security as well as with labour supply – was more a statement of burgher ideals than an operative and effective system of labour coercion and control. The state was rudimentary and lacked the capacity for systematic coercion.

The frequency with which laws relating to the mobility and settlement of Africans were amended in subsequent decades indicates their relative ineffectiveness. Nevertheless, the activities of the legislature do illuminate in some degree the realities of racial conflict and interdependence in areas of common settlement.

However, the Sotho were not only potential labourers in Boer eyes. It is apparent that in the early decades of Boer settlement on the Highveld, they were largely reliant for their grain supplies on their Sotho neighbours,[39] who were producing substantial surpluses of maize and wheat, as well as wool and mohair for colonial markets. As early as 1842, the missionaries working with the Sotho reported that they 'have strenuously applied themselves to the cultivation of European corn; they sell it to the farmers who barter it for cattle, clothes, soap, salt, etc.'[40] In 1846 the *Grahamstown Journal*, referring to the Sotho, noted that 'corn in great abundance has been brought to our markets from beyond the border. . . . At present the colony obtains its principal supplies of meal from that quarter'.[41] H. Green, the British resident in Bloemfontein, reported to Governor Cathcart in 1852 that white farmers in the plains without access to water supplies for irrigation were 'in the habit of exchanging cattle for corn with the kaffirs in the hill country'.[42] Grain was also bartered from Basutoland and the Transvaal in exchange for merino sheep.[43] In this way wool production spread to African and the more northerly Boer communities. During the 1863 drought, Boers transported sheep no longer able to walk to Basutoland by wagon in order to buy Sotho grain.[44]

A major element in the relationship between autonomous black and white societies on the southern Highveld was the process of alienation of African land, which reached a peak in the wars of the 1860s. These wars culminated in the occupation of the 'Conquered Territory' by the Boers, and the annexation by Britain of the remaining Sotho territory beyond the Caledon River in 1868, thereby obstructing Boer ambitions of an even more extensive occupation – much to the anger of the burghers. The seizure of Sotho land was probably related to the collapse of the wool trade and the commercial depression which set in the late 1850s. As an editorial in the Bloemfontein newspaper, *The Friend*, urged in December 1864, 'Let us endeavour to repair the past by looking to other sources than wool and sheepskins'.[45] One way of doing this was by pre-empting the profitable Sotho wheat trade with the Cape Colony. Seizing Sotho land for Orange Free State farmers became a major goal of Orange Free State policy.

Gaining access to Sotho labour was also a paramount consideration in the wars. In 1865 the French missionary, E. Casalis, suggested that the aim of the Boers was to force the Sotho 'to live within such narrow limits that it becomes impossible to subsist on the produce of agriculture and livestock and to be compelled to offer their services to the farmers in the capacity of domestic servants and labourers'.[46] The 1866 treaties entered into by Moshoeshoe were far more advantageous to the Boers than were the final borders as defined in 1868. 'Locations' were to be established, ruled over by *landdrosts*, and a hut tax was to be levied.[47] It was the British intervention – together with the resistance of the Sotho themselves – which stymied the efforts of the Free State burghers to dismember the Sotho state and shake free even more Sotho labour for use on the Boer farms.

However, the wars did result in a considerable influx of impoverished Sotho onto white-owned farms. The commandant over Molapo's territory (included in the Free State by the 1866 settlement) reported that he was being 'plagued' by requests for passes. Thirteen Sotho families a day (presumably entire patrilineal homesteads or extended settlement groups) were reportedly entering the Winburg district in June 1866.[48] Further, the Sotho were able to remain on the alienated lands in considerable numbers, where they hoped to enter relationships with white landlords which would enable them to re-establish the homestead base of their economy, albeit at the cost of producing a surplus as rent or of rendering intermittent labour service. *The Friend* reported in October 1869: 'Many Basotho seem not to have moved . . . . Some are anxious to enrol as servants to avoid leaving their old ground'. For many, service on the farms with the prospect of payment in stock was a means of re-establishing homestead production. Sotho in the new Ladybrand district were reportedly of the opinion that 'as all their cattle and sheep have been captured, they preferred remaining and working for more, to going into their own country to starve'.[49]

ECONOMIC GROWTH AND AGRARIAN CHANGE AFTER 1870

The relations of production in the arable Highveld were to be profoundly affected by events in the thornveld to the west of the Orange Free State, where by 1871 a large extractive industry had sprung up with remarkable rapidity. The diamond fields of Griqualand West were the first enclave of industrial capitalism in the interior of southern Africa, and as such had a profound impact on the agrarian societies, both white and black, over a very wide area.

One effect of the economic boom of the 1870s which accompanied the development of the diamond industry was a considerable rise in wages – 30*s* or 40*s* per month being common at the diggings by 1872.[50] The competitive conditions at the diamond fields were such that recruitment was unorganized and employers of labour found it difficult to combine to keep wages low. The provision of arms and ammunition to migrants from Basutoland became necessary to attract them to Kimberley, despite official attempts to halt this trade. Throughout the Cape Colony, wages were forced upward as public works, rail construction and commercial wheat and wool farmers competed for what labour was available.[51] The independent African peoples, such as the Sotho, did not yet need to send out labourers in any great numbers in order to sustain their homestead economy. Generally, those who went out to labour from Basutoland did so under the auspices of the royal lineage, anxious to maintain its own authority and independence by utilizing the age regiments in order specifically to acquire guns and livestock.[52] However, the relative self-sufficiency of the Sotho and their preference for agricultural production as a means of entering the colonial economy meant that the amount of labour provided was never adequate for the requirements of whites. It was under these circumstances of severe labour shortage at a time of economic boom that schemes of federation between the white-ruled colonies and republics and pressures for imperial intervention became evident. It was also under these circumstances that rigorous efforts were made, militarily and otherwise, to subvert independent African societies throughout southern Africa in the interests of an embryonic industrial capitalism.[53]

But the Sotho did respond vigorously to opportunities for producing agricultural surpluses for the expanding markets at the diggings and elsewhere, despite the recent war devastation and land alienation. One missionary wrote in 1871:

> Every part of the country is once more under cultivation; their old villages have been rebuilt; others have sprung up, which will be separated by smaller distances as the frontiers have contracted. The ploughs will soon be as numerous as before. The wagons are still rare, as they are more difficult to procure since the discovery of diamonds, but their numbers are increasing. Export of grain is taking place by the thousand bags to feed the mining camps, the Free State and some districts of the Colony.[54]

In 1873 alone, 600 ploughs were imported. According to the 1875 census, the African farmers of Basutoland owned 2749 ploughs, 238 harrows and 299 wagons. Moreover, by 1875, close on fifty trading stations were operating in Basutoland as against a half dozen before, according to Commissioner Griffith:

> Today, hundreds of wagons penetrate and traverse it [Basutoland] in every direction, collecting the grain which the country produces and exporting it to the Free State and diamond mines. The cultivation of cereals has markedly increased and the plough has almost everywhere replaced the native hoe. In every direction we meet herds of cattle and sheep which had completely disappeared during the war.[55]

Exports from Basutoland in 1875 amounted to 2000 bales of wool, 100000 muid bags of grain and a considerable number of cattle and horses. The *Volksraad* was told that the annual payment for grain imported from Basutoland amounted to 14000 sheep and £30000 in cash.[56] The greater proportion of this produce was resold on the diamond fields. By 1879 Sotho commercial production had increased to the point that between 200000 and 400000 bags of cereals were officially reported as having been exported, as well as £75000 worth of wool and other produce. By the end of the decade, the number of trading stations in the country had reached seventy, some of them 'requiring capital from £15–20000 to carry on'.[57]

As a result of the opening of the diamond field markets from 1860, the Orange Free State Boers turned in large numbers to the lucrative activity of transport-riding. *The Friend* reported in 1883 that many burghers 'made ... most of their money up to recently by speculating in grain or by carrying the produce of British Basutoland to Bloemfontein, Jagersfontein and Kimberley'.[58] The profits to be gained as middlemen were initially more attractive than market production for Boer landholders.[59] In August 1876 a correspondent from the Conquered Territory wrote:

> mealies are not sown to any great extent on this side of the Caledon; farmers can get them cheaper from the Kaffir [black] trading stations than they can grow them, as a rule.... According to what most farmers said at the end of the last wheat harvest, they would not sow any more. 'It didn't pay, when Kaffir wheat could be bought at seven shillings a muid', they said.[60]

Some burghers even established mills inside Basutoland in order to export flour to the diamond fields, according to the *landdros* of Ladybrand in 1875.[61] The provision of wood for fuel was another entrepreneurial activity which not only led to rapid deforestation, but also brought huge returns to those with wagons and oxen.[62] And the transport of coal by wagon from the coal mines in the northern Orange Free State and southern Transvaal provided much employment and income after 1879.[63]

So the carrying trade was a very important occupation for many Boers, including landowners or their sons, and their activities as middlemen brought a return which they could not derive from their land, given the prohibitive labour costs involved and the shortage of capital. Indeed, the surveyor K. J. de Kok wrote in his reminiscences of young Boers going to Kimberley with one or more wagonloads of produce, and returning with £200–£300 in their pockets; and several young men from the Edenburg district bought farms with the income derived from a few transport-riding trips.[64] It is in this light that we should understand the staunch opposition from so many allegedly 'conservative' burghers to the extension of the railway lines into the Free State.

On the other hand there were increasing numbers of white farmers, many of them newer settlers of British origin, or from the coastal colonies, who sought to turn their own arable land to profit.[65] From the mid-1870s onward, as the military threat posed by the Sotho kingdom began to recede, white landowners in the newly acquired rich grainlands of the Conquered Territory gradually began to settle on their land and invest capital acquired through trade or by mortgaging their land, in permanent improvements. Many of them were able to establish labour relationships with their black tenants whereby the tenants ploughed, sowed and cultivated lands for their landlords, enabling the latter to enter produce markets on their own account. It was during these years that sharecropping first made an appearance in these districts – a relationship which was to become gradually entrenched as arable production became more intensive. The proximity of Basutoland meant that there was temporary labour available for peak seasonal activities such as reaping.

Because of the threat of competition from Basutoland, petitions to the *Volksraad* complaining that the Sotho grain trade 'is holding our burghers back from cultivating the land and is enriching the Kaffirs' were common in the 1870s.[66] In 1875 the *Raad* imposed a licence for the import or through-carriage of grain or flour from Basutoland. The licence fee for a wagon was 10*s*, 1*s* 6*d* for every pack animal, or 6*d* for each bag transported individually over the Caledon.[67] Nevertheless, the import licence does not seem to have had much effect on the viability of

Sotho production. It provided little income for the state treasury, and it was scrapped in 1887 despite considerable protest from capitalizing white farmers in the Conquered Territory.[68]

The question of labour supply was intensified by the rise of arable production on white farms. Africans moving through the white-settled areas were subjected to harassment, abuse and violence from white farmers who were frustrated by their inability to attract adequate labour supplies. Guns earned in employment on the diamond fields or in the Cape were confiscated.[69] In 1874 a shilling pass was imposed on all Africans passing through or leaving the Free State, eliciting strong protest from the Sotho.[70] The farm labour problem was particularly critical for the white farmers not only because of closer land settlement in the Conquered Territory and the rapidly emerging market for arable produce, but also because the pre-existing tenancy relations were undermined by the emergence of relatively highly paid wage labour in the burgeoning capitalist sectors of the regional economy. Farmers repeatedly complained that 'all our best servants – poor even at the best – are being drawn from us by the superior attractions of the diamond fields'.[71] The most serviceable young men in tenant families were drawn off by the supposed lure of adventure and high wages, leaving behind women and children, older men and stock.

The problem confronting white farmers was largely one of drawing labour from African tenant communities unwilling to render it. The African population on the farms in the arable districts had become quite substantial since the wars of the 1860s and the alienation of the Conquered Territory. An upsurge of agitation against the independence of African communities on the farms was evident in the 1870s. It was under these pressures that a masters-and-servants law was enacted for the first time in 1873. The purpose was to ensure the employer swift and effective access to the criminal courts for the prevention of desertion, insubordinate behaviour or dereliction of duty. To this end contracts of service were made mandatory for the first time, backed up by the force of criminal law.[72] An indication of dominant feeling was the meeting of sixty to seventy 'influential' farmers of the Ladybrand and Winburg districts in March 1876, which complained of unoccupied farms being let out to Africans, of stock theft and beer-drinking, and of the unwillingness of the state to come to the aid of the labour-starved burghers.[73] In 1880 fifteen petitions containing over 700 signatures urged the *Volksraad* to act against the *plakkersplase* ('squatter farms').[74]

It was under these circumstances that the Labour Commission appointed in 1878 recommended that a statutory limit be placed on the number of African tenant families permitted on a farm. Ordinance 7 of 1881 laid down that no landholder was to allow more than five families on his farm, or two if the farm was unoccupied by a white man (a family being unrealistically defined as a married male and his unmarried dependants). Permission could be granted for the limit to be exceeded up to a maximum of fifteen families on application to a commission of three to be elected in each *wyk*, or sub-district.[75] Those who welcomed the law most vociferously spoke of the greater availability of labourers which would follow the dispersal of 'squatter' communities; they looked forward to the day when white children would be able to go to school instead of having to work in the fields; they promised an end to stock theft and the other supposed evils resulting from the independence of black tenants. Enthusiastic support for this legislation came from the non-arable southern and western districts where there were no 'squatter' communities, and the white farmers were dependent on contracted wage labour. Clearly any measure which sought to disperse Africans was likely to win support from that quarter. In the Highveld arable districts, on the other hand, the law and the principles it represented promoted considerable antagonism and conflicts, for there were strong forces in the white community which were antagonistic to any attempt to undermine the tenant peasantry. Large absentee landlords who derived profit from exacting rent from tenants were opposed to it, as were many of the more capitalized and wealthy white farmers. For well-to-do farmers were almost always large landholders, too. Under these circumstances, African peasant families could cultivate the land and graze their stock without too much harassment. If the land was extensive and the African communities large, labour could be provided for the white farmer without unduly interrupting the productive cycle in the peasant economy. The smaller the African community, the more disruptive the labour demands of the landowner or lessee were likely to be, and the greater the degree of conflict and resistance implicit in the relationship.

On the whole, the more land a particular farmer controlled, the more likely he was to oppose anti-squatting measures.[76] The social engineers, on the other hand, those who sought an 'equitable distribution' of black families, were more concerned with the problems confronting poorer whites, who had to compete with blacks for control over rural resources and whose access to land was increasingly limited. Many of the Boer pastoralists, after all, did not own land. In the event anti-squatting legislation was never vigorously implemented, given the state's lack of coercive muscle. But the legislation of 1881 and the responses it elicited reveal some of the emerging strains and tensions within the burgher community. No other issue was to dominate *Volksraad* proceedings, popular petitions or the columns of newspapers in the last two decades of the nineteenth century to the same extent as the issue of black peasant producers on the farms and demands for their suppression.[77]

This issue also throws light on the nature of the republican state and the role of the *Volksraad* in mediating the different and conflicting interests amongst the burghers. The social-engineering proclivities of the populist masses in Boer society were mirrored in *Volksraad* debates and legislation in the final decades of the nineteenth century, although a prominent minority of *Raad* members represented the interests of the economically dominant urban bourgeoisie (such as Sir John Fraser, Speaker of the *Volksraad* and Bloemfontein attorney).[78] But the legislature was largely divorced from the realities of power on the local level. The activities of the *Volksraad* bore little relationship to practical realities. Andries Burger of Ladybrand declared in the ORC legislature in 1908 that there had been 'leading men' in the republic who 'used to count the Kaffirs on their property by the hundred and even thousand; and under the influence of *mooi praatjies* [sweet talk], the executive did not enforce the law'[79]. The laissez-faire interests of the landed notables, both English- and Afrikaans-speaking, prevailed, whatever policies the law mandated.

*　　*　　*

The process of rural capitalization was by no means uniform or unilinear. For after a period of sustained capital formation – in both black and white agriculture – the middle years of the 1880s saw the onset of economic depression.[80] After the wild financial and commercial speculation that characterized the year 1881, markets slumped. The diamond mining industry entered a phase of consolidation and concentration, accompanied by a slowdown in production. For the white farmers, the depression of the 1880s had severe repercussions.[81] In March 1883 *The Friend* reported of the landowners in the Conquered Territory:

> They have mortgaged their lands to buy machinery or to build with, or as often occurs, to pay off instalments of purchase amounts. It has been calculated that unless things mend in Kimberley before twelve months have expired, nine out of ten of the farmers in some of the districts of the Conquered Territory will have to succumb. . . . Now we hear of rich farmers who own farms valued at £5000 to £7000 and large flocks and herds, who are now hard-up for £50 to £100.[82]

Further, the construction of railways linking coastal ports with internal markets was a major new factor in the developing political economy of the region. From 1885, when the railway from Port Elizabeth reached Kimberley, wheat imports began to compete with Highveld producers on local markets. The missionary P. Germond wrote in 1888,

> Basutoland has become impoverished.... The Diamond Fields, the Free State and the Colony which formerly provided an outlet for Basutoland, are henceforth closed to her. The railway line from the Cape to Kimberley is throwing foreign wheat on the market at a low price, and the products of Basutoland which would have to be brought at great cost in ox-wagons, cannot compete.[83]

The result was a massive drop in grain prices. In 1886 a muid of wheat in Basutoland fetched 6*d*.[84]

All this changed dramatically with the discovery in 1886 of the gold reefs of the Witwatersrand.[85] An enclave of advanced industrial capitalism sprang up in the centre of the agrarian Boer republic north of the Vaal River. One important consequence of the mineral revolution and the financial boom that followed in its wake was the amount of speculative capital which swept through the rural Highveld. This resulted not only from the direct sale of land at high prices to speculators, individual and corporate, but also, more commonly, from the granting of prospecting rights and options on land to prospective buyers.[86] Most important, the mortgaging of land was becoming widespread, and the speculative inflation of land prices was increasing greatly the amount of money which could be borrowed against the security of land. Such was the amount of speculative money entering the country, that individuals and companies were only too willing to loan large sums of money to landowners against mortgage bonds. Although many capitalist farming enterprises were emerging, the position of most resident landowners did not necessarily improve as a result of the accumulation of indebtedness; as often as not loan capital was not expended on permanent productive improvements but on speculation.[87]

Nevertheless, the consequence of the opening of the Rand gold fields for the rural hinterland was the emergence of the arable districts of the northern Orange Free State and southern Transvaal as an area of more intensive grain production. Here a commercialized sharecropping economy based on black peasant production quickly emerged. This was not only the case on many Boer farms but also on the considerable stretches of land bought up by mining companies, for the mid-Vaal districts particularly were rich in coal deposits. An example was the Vereeniging Estates Limited, owned by the Lewis and Marks group.

Under the Potchefstroom Convention of 1889 the Orange Free State farmers were given free access to the Rand markets across the Vaal River.[88] This was an important concession for the arable producers south of the Vaal, for foodstuffs from outside the borders of the two republics were heavily taxed. But given the relative backwardness of commercial grain production on the Transvaal Highveld, this reliance on the farmers of the Free State was inevitable if the burgeoning consumption needs of the gold fields and the new adjacent towns were to be met.

In 1888 it was estimated that 75 per cent of the produce sold on the Rand came from the Orange Free State. In 1892 some two-thirds of the proceeds of sales on the Johannesburg produce market went to the Free State – over £200 000 in that year. According to *The Star* of Johannesburg, the 'Free State loads consist of the best and most valuable kind of produce such as grain, forage, etc.'. Official figures indicated that in 1893 £303 000 worth of produce was exported from the Orange Free State into the Transvaal. In 1894 the figure was £454 000 and in 1895 £931 860 (the latter was a year in which yields were considerably less than in previous years and the increase reflects price rises more than anything else). In 1896, again a year of scarcity, Orange Free State exports to the Transvaal averaged nearly £100 000 a month. Nearly all imported maize and sorghum (over 200 000 bags) and 60 per cent of Rand cereal and flour imports came from the Orange Free State.[89]

Much of the produce arriving on the Rand from south of the Vaal in the 1890s was still in fact the produce of Basutoland. Considerable quantities of Sotho grain were sold as Orange Free State produce in the Transvaal, and hence free of duty. During the bumper crop years of 1893 and 1894 an agitation went up against the proposed branch railway line to the grain districts of the eastern Orange Free State, as this would allegedly be of greater benefit to Sotho farmers, whose production costs were lower and whose terms of trade were deteriorating,[90] and whose grain in consequence was invariably cheaper than that reaped on the white-owned farms.[91] One petition from Winburg in 1894 warned that the consequence of railway construction would be that farmers would have to give their produce away for virtually nothing 'in order to enrich the owners and shareholders of gold and other mining companies'.[92] A flood of petitions in 1894, prompted by the good harvests of that year, demanded that urgent steps be taken to put a stop to the illicit influx of

Sotho grain into the Transvaal as Free State produce. Petitioners expressed the fear that Orange Free Staters' privileged access to the markets of the South African Republic (Transvaal) would be abrogated if the abuse were not stopped.[93] White farmers complained that they barely made a profit at the depressed prices ruling, given the many costs involved in marketing their produce. Prices of 4s on the Bloemfontein market were intolerably low.[94] As one petitioner put it: 'Just as much grain is imported from Basutoland as is produced in the Free State, and it is a certain fact that we honest burghers cannot compete with natives by producing grain as cheaply as they.'[95] New efforts to impose a tax on Sotho grain were, however, in vain. The opposition of the mercantile interests and the advantages to the Orange Free State of membership of the Customs Union with the Cape Colony (whereby the republic received a proportion of all duties levied at the ports, and of which Basutoland was a member) ensured that free trade with Basutoland continued.[96]

By the 1890s, much more so than in the 1870s, the peasant producers of Basutoland had become a serious threat in the eyes of the burghers. Capitalized merchants and mill owners (many of them wealthy farmers too) were squeezing out the mass of Boer middlemen who had dominated the grain trade in the early years of the diamond fields. Transport-riding, too, had by the 1890s become a far less lucrative entrepreneurial activity than in the 1870s, and was largely a means of survival for poorer men, working intermittently under contract to merchants and mill owners at rates which varied with the seasons.[97]

The 1890s saw a renewed upsurge of agitation amongst Boers for state intervention in the social transformation of the countryside. The rise of Boer populism, more urgent and militant than before, was a marked feature of the 1890s in the republics.[98] By the end of the nineteenth century it had by no means been established that white capitalism rather than black peasant production was eventually to dominate the countryside. For, while some white farmers were capitalizing, many others were increasingly dependent on the peasant production of their black tenants. Most alarmingly, Boer society was already spawning its own impoverished 'dangerous classes',[99] at the same time that many blacks seemed to be taking control of the rural economy.

Once the initial boom associated with the rise of internal markets had receded, Boer society seemed increasingly vulnerable in the face both of foreign capital seeking investment in the land, and of the accumulation of resources in the black rural economy. It became increasingly apparent to many in the 1890s that either the Boers were going to seize control of and monopolize rural resources and forge a white-supremacist political economy, or else they were going to become increasingly marginalized in an economy dominated by foreign capital and black peasant production.

2 Transformations in Boer Society

WHITE RURAL IMPOVERISHMENT: CHRONOLOGY AND PROCESSES

As the extensive hunting and pastoral economy began to give way to intensive grain production in the late nineteenth and early twentieth centuries, economic and social relationships within Boer society changed dramatically. Landless Boers were increasingly marginalized and impoverished. Many Boer landowners were increasingly vulnerable to dispossession. The drift of the 'poor white' to the towns had begun. An overwhelmingly rural, pastoral people, living in the outskirts of the international economy, the erstwhile Boers were by the 1930s and 1940s in large degree town dwellers, having undergone as traumatic a social revolution as industrial capitalism has wrought anywhere.

By no means all Boers were landowners in the nineteenth century, or wished to be, given the fluidity of the pastoral and hunting economy. Non-landownership was not necessarily an economically disadvantageous condition while the Boer economy required and allowed great mobility and an ill-defined sense of proprietary right. Land was always a highly desirable commodity in speculative terms, and land accumulation was a road to status and office in the Boer state, but absentee proprietorship was extensive, farms were ill-defined and unsurveyed, and fencing was non-existent before the final decade or two of the nineteenth century. Non-landownership did not initially entail any disabling economic disadvantages. It was only later – toward the end of the century – that landlessness became a decisive determining factor in the process of class differentiation in Boer society.[1]

There were also great differences in the extent of landownership amongst Boers. Some Boers were able to accumulate large stretches of land and with it influence and patronage. Others owned subdivisions of farms that by themselves were insufficient to ensure families their independence. But here again, in the nineteenth century grazing land was readily to be had, either by the system of hiring grazing by the hundred head of stock, or simply by the utilization of land as required irrespective of formal ownership – especially since so much land was owned by absentees.[2]

Perhaps over half the white rural families of the Highveld were non-landowners in the nineteenth century.[3] The term *bywoner* for a non-landowning white living on the land of another does not seem to have had any pejorative connotation before the age of the mineral revolutions. Grosskopf found in his investigations in the 1920s that old, non-landowning Transvalers objected to the use of the word *bywoner* in this connection; they insisted that they had obtained a *vergunning*, or concession, on the land of others. Some such individuals might be wealthier than the landowner in early years.[4] Often *bywoners* were landowners' own sons – married or unmarried – or sons-in-law, who did not yet own their own land, although operating as independent farmers with their own flocks and herds.[5] The *bywoner* might render a share of income and of the increase of livestock to the landowner – who might have loaned them to him in the first place.[6] A small share of the *bywoner's* crop might also be handed over, although cultivation was a marginal activity in earlier days.

It was only after the mineral revolutions and the opening up of large internal markets for arable produce that a regular rent in the form of a share of the crop from *bywoners* became central to such relationships. By the turn of the century most *bywoners* in arable districts were settled cultivators, as well as stockowners. Sharecropping had become a usual condition of residence for landless whites on the farms of others.[7] Further, the notion that a *bywoner* should render his own or his family's labour to the landlord seems to have been rare before the final decades of the century.[8] Grosskopf concluded:

> In course of time, however, when land became scarcer and dearer, and produce had a market value, the *bywoner* was expected to give some service in consideration of what he received. In cases where the *bywoner* ploughed, and had used the owner's water supply for irrigating, he was expected to give up a share of the crops.[9]

It is clear that stratification within Boer society ran deep and had always done so. The earliest evidence from the pre-Trek Cape indicates that there were not only landed and landless in Boer society, but also rich and poor, patrons and clients, even masters and servants. Some owned large flocks and herds, commanded large numbers of unfree 'coloured' labourers and traded extensively. Others lacked the wherewithal to live independently. The system of loaning out livestock to poorer men on half shares of the increase was commonly practised in the republics as it had been in the Cape earlier.[10] But upward mobility was probably fairly common prior to the mineral discoveries and few young men could not aspire to independence. Grosskopf discovered that among the most prosperous Boers of the republics in the nineteenth century there were many who had been landless *bywoners* in the Cape Colony.[11]

But by the 1890s the differentiation in status and wealth which had always characterized Boer society was rapidly crystallizing out into sharp class divisions. Formal property relations were becoming economically determinant. The 'poor white' problem became a major issue throughout South Africa for the first time in these years.[12] Indeed in the 1890s it was discovered that many of the oldest and longest-settled burghers in the Boer republics were severely impoverished, having never been landowners.[13] The survey, fencing and occupation of the land, the decimation of game and the coming of the railways all served to create a depressed class which was already in transition to lumpenproletarian status. Those who has a wagon and oxen could still 'ride transport' in the 1890s and 1900s, and many could survive as small sharecroppers, stockowners and labour tenants on the farms of others. But this was an inherently unstable status. Drought and disease, war devastation and the growing hostility of the capitalizing landholding class gradually combined to strip many of the *bywoners* of their tenuous access to land.[14] Moreover, the construction of railways reduced the opportunities for transport-riding, which in the 1870s had been for many Boers the major means of capital formation and of acquiring land.[15] *The Friend*'s correspondent in Frankfort wrote in 1907 that many of the farmers were against the building of a line from Tigerskloof (on the Bethlehem–Harrismith line) through Reitz and Frankfort to the Transvaal, on the grounds that many of them were dependent on transport-riding between Harrismith, Frankfort and Heilbron for their living. 'Although the railways are said to open up the country', he wrote, 'yet there seems to be absolutely no need for the proposed line, except for the convenience of a few.'[16]

Moreover, the number of merchant firms established in the small towns of the Highveld increased rapidly from the 1870s, and the Boer transport riders had become dependent on the traders and agents for shorter-distance work – where railways had not already rendered them expendable. So what we see from the 1870s into the early twentieth century was the brief flaring and then the gradual dousing of a trading and carrying economy dominated by non-specialist Boer pastoralists. By the end of the century transport-riding had ceased to be an independent means of accumulation amongst Boers, and had largely become a means of survival for the poorer members of Boer society, dependent for work on merchants and wealthy wagon owners (although it was not to be entirely displaced until the coming of the motor lorry in the 1920s).[17]

The rapid spread of fencing and veterinary regulations made the *trekboer* economy – the regular seasonal migration of graziers who often did not themselves own land – less and less viable. Travelling with stock became a hazardous enterprise. The subdivision of land meant that landholders became more jealous of their own grazing resources and the *trekboer* was restricted to fenced roadways. Crown lands were also being cut up and sold in the 1890s. Grosskopf tells us that in the 1890s stockholders would still drive their herds into the scrub veld in the northwestern Orange Free State for the dry winters, and then move to the new sweet grass of the Ladybrand district after the veld had been burnt in the spring. This soon became very difficult, particularly after the turn of the century. Although trekking by landowners in search of pasture at times of severe drought did not disappear, the *trekboer* economy could not survive the changes of these years. Grazing was no longer a free resource.[18]

Impoverishment was greatly aggravated by the paucity of formal education amongst the Boers. It was estimated in 1889 that only 2200 white children of school-going age were receiving formal education as against 10500 who were growing up without seeing the inside of a classroom.[19] Further, in the 1890s the extent of deskilling amongst Boers was becoming a cause of some alarm. Attention was repeatedly drawn to the inability of the younger generation to use tools, build houses, make and mend wheeled vehicles, make clothes and boots, and repair machinery.[20] Under these circumstances the collapse of the hunting/trading/trekking economy left little alternative to a slow, bumpy slide into a new, white, industrial lumpenproletariat.

Within the same family a considerable degree of stratification was often increasingly evident as the redistributive characteristics of the Boer economy declined. Many a *bywoner* lived on the land of more fortunate relatives – an uncle, cousin or in-law. In earlier years this was of no great moment, for land was not a scarce resource, and in any event the *bywoner* was generally able, if he wished, to occupy new land beyond the reaches of settlement. But by the 1890s many families were being splintered along the lines of class;[21] and while there was considerable mobility 'downwards', there was now precious little opportunity for upward mobility once the axe of expropriation had fallen. By the turn of the century those who wished to buy land on which to farm had to have access to substantial capital resources.

Anxiety about these widening fractures in the burgher community was reflected in populist agitation against foreign capitalists and black tenant farmers, who together were supposedly taking over the land and ousting the whites. While similar agitation against black rural production had occurred earlier in Boer history, it reached a peak in the 1890s, taking on a whole range of new symbols and meanings. An upsurge of moral anxiety about the consequences of allowing whites to 'sink' in status to the point where independent and prosperous black peasants began to dominate them went hand in hand with antagonism against speculators whose hunger for land was allegedly insatiable, and who settled their land with black tenants.[22] Fears of displacement mounted as capitalization proceeded, pressures were exerted on *bywoners*, and white rural distress became widespread. It was repeatedly asserted that blacks were becoming richer than the whites, and that the whites were having to 'make way' to black *indringing* and *oorheersing* (infiltration and domination).

Agitation against independent black peasant producers was concerned not only with narrowly economic considerations of labour supply and market competition, but with the forging of a white-supremacist political economy at all levels. There were recurrent crescendos of resentment against the *plakkersplase* ('squatter' farms) and the apparent independence and prosperity of African tenant communities. The general indignation at the vision of whites having to compete with successful black farmers for access to resources and for patronage from landowners, was a constant theme in the agitation against the black tenant communities.[23]

Boer populism was espoused most vociferously not by the impoverished themselves, but by those who saw themselves as the guardians of the moral order. The 'petty bourgeois' intelligentsia, most notably the teachers and churchmen, some lawyers, literati and many of the politicians of the new generation (such as President Steyn), were concerned to mobilize popular support for interventionist policies. One of the most controversial issues of the 1890s in the burgher community was that of compulsory education, a proposal which was resisted by many of the poorer burghers for whom it was intended. Over a number of years petitions repeatedly rejected compulsory education as an act of enslavement intolerable to a free people which would provoke rebellion in the land.[24] Many objected that they relied on the labour of their children as herders and workers in the fields for their survival.[25] The upholders of racial standards and racial supremacy did not always see eye to eye with the intended beneficiaries of their cultural initiatives.

Indeed, the resentment of the Boer underclass could not easily be dissipated. The warning by the editor of *The Friend* in 1892 that the burgher community was rapidly breeding its own 'dangerous classes' seemed increasingly justified as the 1890s progressed.[26]

Another manifestation of disaffection amongst the *bywoner* class was their disinclination during the 1890s to attend the *wapenschouwingen* – the military camps which all burghers were obliged to attend annually, according to the law of 1890.[27] There was a long tradition of protest against the performance of commando duty without pay amongst Boers who could not afford to equip themselves with guns and ammunition, and whose families were hard-pressed to subsist in their absence.[28] Revolt against the demands of the burgher militia system became a cause for concern in the 1890s. Repeated demands were made in petitions for the state to provide needy burghers with guns as increasing numbers ceased to be able or willing to provide for themselves, especially since hunting had largely ceased to be a viable element of the Boer economy. A good 10 per cent of the burghers, it was estimated (2400 in another estimate) were not armed;[29] and, as will be seen, the Anglo-Boer War which began in 1899 partially confirmed fears about the unwillingness of the *bywoner* class to take up arms in defence of republican independence.

The process of impoverishment within Boer society was greatly accelerated by the crippling rinderpest epizootic of 1896–7, followed in the latter year by a severe drought. Widespread destitution was the inevitable result: 'the poorer classes of our farmers are now finding themselves in very straitened circumstances', commented an editorial in *The Friend* in August 1897:

> The living of so many of them depended on the riding of transport and the tilling of a small piece of land, that the want of draught cattle is being severely felt....we fear the tenants and *bywoners*, many of them, will have a hard time of it.[30]

The drought of 1897 was for many the last straw, killing off much of the surviving livestock and decimating crops. 'The last few years of drought and disease...have crushed the very lifeblood out of many of the people of this country who were fairly well-off ten or twenty years ago', commented *The Friend*'s editor in December 1897. 'It is not to be wondered at, then, that the army of Poor Whites has...increased to an alarming extent.'[31]

One result was a critical influx of destitute into the towns in the region. Many moved to Johannesburg in search of work.[32] But smaller centres like Bloemfontein also faced unprecedented problems as parts of the town turned into slums seemingly overnight. The secretary of the Bloemfontein Benevolent Society reported that up to twenty people were commonly living in single rooms by the end of 1897. When mayor Sowden suggested land be set aside with water laid on where newly destitute could build their own temporary homes, several councillors objected that this would only aggravate the influx. A school for poor white children started by the Dutch Reformed Church attracted 130 scholars, a number which, according to Reverend Kriel, did not nearly represent the numbers of destitute children in town.[33] In small rural towns, such as Ficksburg, where starvation was reported, the situation in the summer of 1897–8 was also critical.[34]

Many urged public works, such as railway construction, as an urgent means of relief. The *Volksraad* in 1898 considered at great length the possibility of establishing irrigation settlements, building dams on the major rivers and subsidizing the acquisition of drills and pumps by individual landowners who were prepared to take on white tenants on irrigated plots.[35] In January 1898 in response to several petitions, the government reduced the rail rate on seed wheat and maize to 1*s* 3*d* per ton per mile, and customs duties on grain for seed purposes were abolished.[36] This was intended to assist white farmers who had suffered crop failure as a result of drought to acquire seed. (However private merchant such as Charles Newberry and Co. of Ladybrand were also concerned to use the opportunity to improve the standard of wheat produced in the country by importing seed to sell on credit.)[37] An indication of the degree of impoverishment is provided by the avalanche of petitions from lessees of state-owned land begging the government to grant relief from rent payments in 1898 and 1899.[38]

The rinderpest and drought proved to be the prelude to the Anglo-Boer War of 1899–1902, which devastated the entire countryside. Those without landed security found it difficult to recoup losses. P. J. Blignaut, former state secretary, found many ex-*bywoners* in the concentration camps in 1902 who before the war had been:

> in possession of a fair amount of property, such as waggons and oxen, ploughs, etc., by means of which they were able to earn a living, and who had also some cattle and sheep, but who have through the war been deprived of everything, and are now quite destitute.[39]

The magistrate in Vredefort, echoing many others, reported in 1903:

> The pinch is felt keenest by those who are not landowners, and whose wealth before the war consisted of stock with which they tilled

sufficient land to maintain their families and pay the landowner his share of the crop. Owing to their animals now being gone, their means of livelihood is in this sense also gone.[40]

Before the war most people had had cows to milk, but 'except among the better class of farmers milk is now an unknown quantity'.[41]

Antagonisms within Boer society were reflected in the fact that large numbers of Boers refused to heed commando call-ups during the war,[42] and even more dramatically in the large-scale desertion of Boers from the republican forces, considerable numbers of them enlisting on the imperial side. Thomas Pakenham estimates that as many as a fifth of the Boer fighting men were fighting on the British side by the end of the war.[43] A. M. Grundlingh has shown that the National Scouts, ORC Volunteers and other burghers who entered the service of the British were on the whole the poorest in Boer society.[44]

Boer politics in the post-war years were characterized by extreme bitterness between the *bittereinders* – the irreconcilables who had fought to the end of the war – and the *hensoppers* – those burghers who had betrayed their country's cause. But underlying the rhetorical form there was another reality at work. For the grass-roots division coincided by and large with that between landed and landless. This deep hostility running through Boer society was apparent to all who had first-hand experience of the new colonies in these years. Joseph Chamberlain, for example, wrote in 1903 of the Orange River Colony: 'It is perfectly obvious that there are serious divisions among the people of this colony...and I myself fear that feeling runs even higher than it does in the Transvaal'.[45]

Many *bywoners*, relying on the new administration to improve their lot, found themselves in a difficult situation. E. F. Knight reported:

The one grievance of the *bywoners* whom I met on the road was the appointment of Dutchmen as compensation and repatriation officers. It was maintained that Dutch officials would favour their own friends, whereas British officers would be impartial, and do their utmost to be absolutely fair.[46]

And indeed, it seems that these fears were by no means exaggerated. The repatriation commissioners, most of whom were Boer landowners, often did not scruple to discriminate against the *bywoners* in the distribution of plough oxen and seed. A petition of February 1903, for example, asked that money allotted for the compensation of the 'loyal Dutch' (those who had fought for the British) should be apportioned by special commissioners entirely independent of the repatriation commissions.[47]

The Repatriation Department set up by the new administration made every effort to induce landowners to provide land and/or employment for the newly and increasingly destitute. Thus plough oxen were lent to *bywoners* and seed given to them in order to ensure the re-establishment of pre-existing social relations. Further, the landless were given free rations.[48] But many landowners were no longer willing to provide land for impoverished and unproductive white tenants, many of whom had been less than willing to defend their country's independence.[49] This was especially so since they often refused to submit to labour, and their capacity to provide their own subsistence in times of drought, such as the two years following the war, was dubious. Magistrates reported that landowners had refused to take on landless white families on the grounds that they could not maintain them.[50] The magistrate in Hoopstad, commenting on the shortage of labour in the district in 1903, wrote: 'I have always urged upon them [the farmers] to employ poor whites but the reply I invariably get is "where will you find one that will work?"'[51] Other magistrates reported cases where landowners had told their *bywoners* that unless they or their children rendered labour they would have to go.[52] Many of the indigent whites in towns such as Bloemfontein after the war were found to be ex-*bywoners* who had not been allowed back on the farms on which they had previously lived, since war injury, ill health or old age had rendered them unfit for farm work.[53] Further, many more were reported to have no land to return to because of the death of relatives or friends on whose land they had previously lived.[54]

In order to deal with the problem of *bywoners* excluded from the land and the related problem of emptying the concentration camps, the Relief Works Department was established after the end of the war. Its function was to provide employment for indigent burghers, mainly on dam construction and other irrigation works on government-owned farms. Indigent white labourers were also used on the Bloemfontein–Ladybrand railway. In July 1903 some 3139 people were dependent on the relief works, which paid at a rate of 4s 6d per day.[55] However, there was a general prejudice against entering the relief work camps, partly it seems because it was feared that it would mean irrevocably sacrificing all rights to land.[56] Some 6000 white indigents were dependent on the government for rations in January 1904, despite efforts to end ration payments altogether and to persuade the recipients to move into camps where they could learn the 'dignity of labour'.[57]

The British administration also sought longer-term solutions to the problems of white impoverishment. The social-engineering proclivities of the Milner regime were well to the fore in the proposals for 'Burgher Land Settlements'.[58] In order to strenghthen the 'pro-British tendency' of the *bywoner* class, the latter were to be settled on the farms of politically safe landlords. These landlords were to be assisted financially to lease farms and to take selected white tenants, 'under proper supervision and checks'. Major Legget, director of Burgher Land Settlements, wrote to Lieutenant Governor Goold-Adams that such a system:

> will lead to the enhancement of wealth, and thus of power, of selected lessees, and with the backing which such men will get from tenants bound to them by ties of self-interest, we should perhaps create a new class of veld leaders, whom it should be more easy for Government to influence than the individual tenants of lower intelligence and less strong individual ties.[59]

Piet de Wet, brother of General Christiaan de Wet, and a leader of the pro-British National Scouts during the war, was one such whom the sanguine Legget hoped would be suitable for installation as a landed notable. However, the scheme, revealing though it is as an indication of British intentions, never really got off the ground in the ORC. However, its failure did not deter subsequent governments from pursuing the chimera of a regenerated white tenantry.[60]

THE BYWONER AS LABOURER AND AS PRODUCER

Bywoners did not disappear from the farms in the aftermath of the Anglo-Boer War. Their transformation was altogether more gradual. Many were able to reaccumulate some stock and implements and in general those with the means of arable production could still find land to plough in the early years of the twentieth century. But there is no doubt that their status was deteriorating sharply. Many moved from farm to farm at quite regular intervals. Restrictions on the number of stock that a *bywoner* could graze was often the cause of their eviction and the general insecurity of their position. For the *bywoners*, as for the black tenants, stockownership was the major form of capital accumulation. Again and again, *bywoners* preferred to leave a farm on which they were living rather than dispose of their animals.[61] A *bywoner* who had lived on five farms since the Anglo-Boer War was reported to have told a traveller in 1913 that 'my stock is my capital, and the farmers won't have us now the size of the farms has decreased. They have the Kaffirs, stock-owning Kaffirs, but not white men'.[62] The MLA for Heilbron, P. J. G. Theron, summed up the *bywoner's* dilemma in 1913:

> The *bywoner* as soon as he gets ahead a bit after being helped by the man on whose ground he lives, is not helped any further by that man, especially if he has a fair quantity of stock and the ground is pretty small. Then the man tells him he must make some other plan for himself.[63]

Another cause of the insecurity of the *bywoners* was the transfer of land. Death or the sale of land by the owner (often a relation) could mean the eviction of the *bywoners*.[64]

Moreover, *bywoners* had to compete with blacks as cash-crop tenants and as labourers on the farms. This was an increasingly precarious existence, for landowners had sound reasons for preferring black sharecropping tenants to whites. The Boer economy was essentially pastoral and extensive in the nineteenth century. Grazing, hunting, and trading were the basic elements of the Boers' economy until late in the century. They had long been partly reliant on African-produced grain, and the first reaction of many to the opening of internal arable markets was to turn to trade and transport-riding. Even on the white-owned farms it was initially the Africans who had the arable skills, did most of the work, and as often as not owned all or some of the means of production – hence the prevalence of sharecropping relationships between white and black. The poorer, landless Boers were the least likely to have had direct experience of cultivation. Many of them had been transport riders, *trekboers* or hunters when these had been more viable activities, and the transition to commercial crop production as a settled tenantry was a painful one for many.

One advantage of black tenants was their greater density of settlement and greater intensity of cultivation. A farmer writing in the *Farmer's Weekly* spelled this out:

> A native ploughing on the halves is quite satisfied with, say, thirty acres of land, and if you have 200 acres to let on the halves you can get six families on to work for you when they have finished ploughing, whereas a white man wants at least 100 acres to keep him alive.[65]

The main reason for this lay in the settlement patterns of the Sotho cultivators, who lived in extended homesteads or small villages, usually comprised of kindred groups, pooling their grazing resources.

But the most important aspect of the failure to adapt to intensive cash-crop production was the *bywoners'* unwillingness to make intensive use of family labour. They often expected to have access to a number of black labourers for agricultural and perhaps household work. This was in marked contrast to black tenants. Emelia Pooe remembers her family competing as sharecroppers with white *bywoners* on a farm on the Vaal River some time during the First World War. The Pooes were so successful, she tells us, that the *bywoners* had to leave the farm in the second year after their arrival. The Pooes moved into the house vacated by the white family. Another white *bywoner* lasted for only a year:

> With us blacks, I would go out into the fields with my husband and perhaps with my children if they were already old enough. With the Boers as '*bywoners*' it was different. Normally their wives could not go out into the fields to hoe. The husband would have to do the hoeing alone. Or sometimes he would take out money to pay for whomever he could hire. With us we would hoe together with Naphtali [her husband] or organize a work party.[66]

For black sharecroppers the labour of household members was the foundation of all productive activities, frequently supplemented with the communal labour of kin and neighbours, organized on the basis of reciprocity.[67] Whites were generally reluctant to employ female family members in the fields, although they sometimes might have been obliged to do so. They certainly employed their children in agricultural labour, but this was increasingly contrary to the dominant social ethic and was regarded by populist opinion as a moral evil resulting from shortage of black labour. Maybe of greater importance, whites did not employ the network of co-operative labour arrangements that characterized the black household economy; and inevitably landlords were reluctant to allow *bywoners* access to valuable black labour resources.

Further, as we have seen, the *bywoners* were generally reluctant to place themselves under the control and authority of landlords. Labour for general work on the farm as well as the regular labour service of unmarried sons and daughters were often provided by the black sharecropping families. *Bywoners* often fiercely resisted subservient status, and often conflict was the result of landlords' attempts to extract labour.[68] Whites generally expected payment for work performed. Black tenants rendered labour service free of money as a rule in the early years of the century. Moreover, blacks were consiodered far more self-sufficient in the acquisition of productive resources and of articles of consumption than whites – not without justification, for in large degree a redistributive economy still functioned amongst Africans, particularly between kin, whereas whites were far more dependent on the patronage of their landlords when times were hard.[69]

In general, Africans were, in the eyes of the landlords, more profitable and tractable tenants than whites, especially since the latter generally demanded a larger share of the crops – usually two-thirds in the early years of the century.[70] Alfred Barlow of Heilbron district wrote in the *Farmer's Weekly* in 1911 that 'I plough on the shares with the natives, and so do hundreds and thousands of farmers'. The reason, he added, was that it paid him to do so:

> I would be glad to plough on shares with white men tomorrow if I could get them to come with their own ploughs and oxen, and give me the share that I want, and if they would put themselves under my orders as the native does.[71]

The 1908 ORC Natives Administration Commission concluded from the evidence of farmer witnesses in the Orange River Colony that:

> The majority prefer to work with blacks rather than with whites, first because the latter demand a larger share of the profits, and secondly because they are more independent and less amenable to discipline and cannot be set to perform the same work as the natives.[72]

It was repeatedly asserted by employers and by government officials that poor whites refused to perform what in the terminology of the day was described as 'Kaffir work'. It was a constant source of wonder and annoyance to the emergent bourgeoisie that the 'demoralized' stratum refused to allow their sons to take up farm work or their daughters to enter domestic employment. 'There is unfortunately a foolish pride to be met with which prevents parents from allowing their children to work', the ORC Minister of Public Works told the legislature in 1908.[73] There is of course a certain contradiction between these prescriptions on the one hand and those of the Afrikaans intelligentsia, who were concerned to get Boer children out of the fields and into schools, on the other. These latter populist culture brokers were concerned with mobilizing Afrikanerdom to counteract the supposed morally and materially depressing effects of foreign capitalism. As often as not those who sought to inculcate proletarian work discipline and subservience into poorer Boers – especially the children – had very different perceptions and visions of the future from those of the Afrikaner populists with their concern with education. Often they were newly arrived British settlers, whose imperial-race ideology stopped short of embracing the mass of Boers as members of the ruling class. However, the contradictions between the two should not be overemphasized; after all, it was clear to imperialist bourgeoisie and anti-imperialist petty bourgeoisie alike that the 'demoralized poor' posed great dangers to social stability and control in a racially ordered society.

But, contrary to the image of the lazy and dissolute landless Boer who was worthless as a labourer, it seems that there was little objection to manual toil amongst most. Many were only too willing to show initiative as transport riders, or as self-employed workers at the salt pans or diamond diggings. Moreover, those who had no alternative to the alienation of their labour were no less adaptable to proletarian status than any other agrarian people undergoing the transition to industrialism. This is indicated by a petition signed by twelve landless Boers of Trompsburg district in 1908, asking for employment in public works or railway construction. They complained that landowners much preferred black labourers, who were given arable ground as pay, while the landless whites could no longer find employment on the farms.[74]

On the other hand, it does seem that many did resist and resent proletarian status. There appears to have been a strongly rooted objection to rendering labour at the behest of and under the control of their landlords.[75] A perceptive observer noted in 1908:

> In speaking of the poor whites I notice that they are all classed as unwilling to work. Now this is absolutely contrary to my experience. There is a fault common alike to the natives... and the poor white, and that is the unwillingness to sacrifice freedom to routine, especially for small remuneration.[76]

This resistance may have been particularly marked amongst the newly impoverished, whose major concern was the re-establishment of their productive independence.

STRATEGIES OF SURVIVAL AND THE EXPERIENCE OF URBANIZATION

Right up to the 1930s the answer to impoverishment was seen in terms of a 'return to the land'. The farmers' congress in Bloemfontein in 1906 resolved that 'considering the appalling decadence and the daily increasing poverty of a large portion of the white inhabitants of this Colony, including a large number of born farmers, seeing that these are fast deteriorating into a class of farm paupers', the government should set up 'industrial and farming settlements' for such white indigents.

Over the years much effort was expended in trying to establish indigent white families on agricultural settlements. One of the most important resulted from the recommendations of the Poor Whites Commission in 1908, which persuaded the ORC government to grant the Dutch Reformed Church £30 000 for the establishment of agricultural settlements. Also as a result of the commission's report, a government land bank was established, with one of its specific purposes the re-establishment on the land of landless whites as sharecropping tenants.[77]

The report of the commission and the establishment of the land bank were accompanied by much debate on how best the impoverished whites could be helped to get back to the land. G. J. van Riet, a Thaba Nchu lawyer, suggested in a letter to *The Friend* in August 1908 a system of loaning livestock and equipment to poor whites to the value of £100 each:

> Under this scheme, men assisted in the above manner would to a great extent take the place of numbers of natives who can and only do oust the whites by virtue of their possession of stock for ploughing and agricultural purposes. In this manner the squatting of natives on farms and the ruinous system of ploughing on the halves with them would be to a great extent circumvented.[78]

During the debate on the Poor White Commission's report in the ORC Legislative Assembly in 1908, several speakers urged that a sizeable chunk of the £75 000 proposed as the capital necessary to launch the land bank should be earmarked for just such a purpose as van Riet had in mind, such as the distribution of breeding stock and farming requirements to the heads of poor white families on a 'hire-purchase' system.[79]

In the event these pleas did not fall on deaf ears. For the ORC Land Bank, established in 1909, was unique amongst similar institutions in other South African colonies in that it made provision for loans to non-landowners of up to £200 against the security of promissory notes. Such loans were only made if endorsed by two landowners as sureties and co-principal debtors. Between the establishment of the ORC Land Bank and its replacement by the Union bank in 1913, 884 individuals were aided against the security of promissory notes to a total of £124 555 (on the average £141 each).[80]

But the landless whites do not seem to have derived much lasting benefit from the ORC Land Bank's operation. Not surprisingly landowners were reluctant to provide surety, except for their own sons or sons-in-law. The loans granted seem more often than not to have been abused by the sureties, who used ignorant *bywoners* to raise money to which they were not entitled and which the *bywoners* never saw.[81] Indeed, far from the loans promoting a stable and prosperous tenant class, most of the debtors proved extremely difficult to trace after a year or two.[82] Despite pleas from populist Orange Free State members of the Union parliament, the 1912 Land Bank Act deleted all provision for loans to non-landowners.[83] All such schemes to rehabilitate landless whites as a viable tenantry were doomed to failure, as they flew in the face of the harsh realities of capitalization and accumulation in the rural economy. As was so often the case in these years of rapid change and social crisis, populist perceptions and anxieties conflicted with the individual interests of members of the rural bourgeoisie.

The Boer 'dangerous classes' continued to evoke a deep social anxiety within the white community as a whole. It was precisely their resistance to the cultural interventions of the purveyors of education and improvement and their refusal to be transformed into a subservient working class (at least without a struggle) that lay at the root of this anxiety. Afrikaner populists seeking to use language and culture as weapons in struggle were frustrated by their inability to instil a sense of ethnic consciousness in the emergent Boer lumpenproletariat.[84] Imperial social reformers in the towns battled to propagate their ideology of domesticity on recalcitrant poor whites.[85] In 1914 an armed rebellion against the government's decision to join the war against Germany drew many Boers spontaneously to arms throughout the former republics, posing a real threat for a time to the maintenance of order. In 1913 the burgher commandoes had been mobilized to deal with a threatened strike of mine workers on the Rand, and this reactivation of the military network clearly paved the way for the mobilization of anti-government rebels the following year. The rebels seem overwhelmingly to have been landless and poor – a cross-section of the dispossessed in Boer society.[86]

But eventually, despite the 'back-to-the-land' schemes pursued by successive governments (none more vigorously than Hertzog's Pact government in the 1920s),[87] most of the landless whites, unsuccessful both as a cash-crop peasantry and as an agrarian proletariat, were to end up as wage earners in the rising industrial towns of South Africa. But it should not be inferred that the process of proletarianization amongst the landless in Boer society was sudden, uniform or irreversible. Like the process of capitalization itself, the formation of a white proletariat came in cyclical waves. There were always – right up to the present day – newcomers to the ranks of the landless as working farmers succumbed to mortgage indebtedness, overextensions of credit, and the innumerable plagues to which agriculture is heir. And there were – at certain times more than at others – ways in which white men and women right up to the mid-century and beyond, could eke out a living in the countryside. One individual could move intermittently or seasonally between petty commodity producer, small-scale entrepreneur, and wage earner. Many were able to survive as sharecroppers and lessees of marginal land owned by absentees. Survival in the countryside for the 'poor whites' required considerable geographical mobility, often remarked on by contemporaries and explained in mystical terms as the 'trek spirit'.[88]

One important way in which landless whites were able to maintain their independence from proletarian status in the countryside was to enter relationships of dependence on prosperous black peasants. For the whites had one valuable right which the law denied blacks: they could legally hire land. The poor whites thus served as a conduit whereby black households were able surreptitiously to gain access to land. The Africans would then undertake cash-crop production, perhaps on shares, and the white lessee would subsist and pay the rent on the basis of the peasants' enterprise. Or else a poor white was used by an absentee landlord as a 'front', while black sharecroppers worked the land independently of any supervision. Such opportunities for poor whites to survive as parasites on black production might even have increased during the Great Depression. This crucial subject will be examined in greater depth later.[89]

Riding transport for small-town traders or farmers in the interstices of the spreading railway network remained a major non-agricultural activity until well into the 1920s, when the advent of the motor lorry began to put the final quietus on this activity. Many were also able to utilize skills in fencing, dam-building and masonry. Hawking wood or fruit was an intermittent possibility for the poor rural whites. The fortunate few who could break free from a marginal existence and accumulate some capital sometimes set up as small contractors with threshing machines, borehole drills, or – later in the 1920s – motor lorries. Alluvial diamond-prospecting on proclaimed diggings too extensive, accessible and quickly exhausted to allow for concentrations of capital were for long a resort for members of rural society during slack periods on the farms or in dry seasons. The very fluctuating population on the diggings contained only a minority who could be called professional diggers. For the most part they were *bywoners* or poor farmers, who could not survive on the farms throughout the year.[90]

The loss of an independent base in rural production was often separate from and prior to the experience of urbanization; but once the one had occurred, the other was bound to follow sooner or later – sometimes much later. The transition to urban proletariat was rarely a quantum leap; it was more often a gradual, erratic slide. Many were able to keep one foot in the countryside for long periods, buoyed up perhaps by periodic trips of individual family members to larger urban centres in search of temporary employment. A common feature of small rural towns (or *dorps*) in the early decades of this century was the large and fluctuating community of impoverished and destitute white families, who oscillated between casual town employment and seasonal labour on the farms when crops were good. These depressed urban communities were continually being supplemented by families who were unable to survive permanently on the land, and there was a constant movement from small towns to larger industrial centres.[91]

On the other hand, Boers did not always arrive in towns like Johannesburg as a ready-made lumpenproletariat, to await their call into the ranks of the working class. Charles van Onselen has shown that for many urban Afrikaners in the early years on the Rand, there was great scope for petty commodity production and entrepreneurial activities. He argues that the Boers were dispossessed twice – once in the countryside and again in the towns, as large capital encroached on Afrikaner urban enterprise and squeezed them into the working class. Wherever larger concentrations of capital had not swept it aside, small-scale Afrikaner capital outside agriculture played a significant role in the South African industrial revolution.[92] Indeed, for many Boers, more particularly in the early years, the trek to the towns was an escape from poverty and hopelessness rather than a final humiliation and defeat.

Often the male head of the family would move to the Rand or smaller centres in search of work, leaving his family on the farm or in the *dorp*. But it was frequently the unmarried female members of the family who first moved permanently to urban centres. The difference in this regard between Boer and African urbanization may be partly explained by the different sexual division of labour in Boer and African families.[93] Control over the labour of black women within African societies (through, for example, the bridewealth system) meant that when labour migrancy by males became widespread, rural production (to a large degree) was maintained and the household economy endured. In sharp contrast, the Boer household economy proved far more brittle in the face of an emergent industrialism. The spread of exchange relations very quickly robbed Boer women of their economic functions. The unmarried younger generation was able and often obliged to take up urban employment, and in many cases they sent back remittances to their families. Female heads of families rarely stayed in the rural areas. The consequence was that by the 1920s, the proportion of the Afrikaans female population living in the urban areas was substantially higher than the proportion of Afrikaans menfolk.[94]

Over the long term the efflux of white families from the countryside to the rising industrial towns was gradual and cumulative. The process of white depopulation of the rural areas, already apparent in the long-settled sheep districts of the Cape in the final decades of the nineteenth century, was clearly to be seen in certain of the Highveld maize districts during the second decade of the twentieth century (at the same time as the black population was increasing rapidly). Up to the 1920s there was still land on the barren peripheries of white settlement where the mobile pastoralist could find succour. However, those moving into un-developed areas had to have substantial amounts of capital available if they were not simply to delay the final fateful day of proletarianization. Moreover, most of the dispossessed simply did not have the wherewithal to trek to pastures new. For many, the only route to survival lay along the railway line to the urban centres.

By 1930 it had become clear that opportunities to settle relatively undeveloped areas were no longer available, and the net flow of whites was massively from the rural areas to the towns and cities. It was thus in the 1930s that a fully urbanized Afrikaner nationalism set about mobilizing the Afrikaner working class for the purposes of ethnic capital formation.[95]

LANDOWNERSHIP, LOAN CAPITAL AND THE TRAP OF INDEBTEDNESS

By the end of the nineteenth century, not only were sources of income and accumulation for the landless receding rapidly, but many propertied Boers were entering the ranks of the dispossessed. The process of class differentiation within the ranks of rural whites was not simply a function of the changing status of the non-landowning *trekboer* or *bywoner*. Landownership itself was very insecure. First, Boer testamentary practice and the prevalence of land fragmentation were factors tending to the impoverishment of landed families. Second, and no doubt more important, the incapacity of Boer farmers to generate and accumulate capital through their own productive effort and their tendency to indebtedness frequently resulted in the loss of land.

There was a considerable degree of fluidity and unpredictability in the process of class formation. Emergent class divisions were not monolithic or static. Relatively well-off landowners could very quickly become impoverished. Landed wealth and status were no guarantee against precipitate impoverishment. 'The affluent independent land-owner of one generation easily becomes in this country, the *bywoner* of the second, and the "poor white" of the third', wrote the editor of *The Friend* in 1906.[96] Frans Schimper, a wealthy farmer in the Winburg district, wrote in 1893:

> I knew people when I came to the Free State in 1863 who owned 60 000 morgen of ground which they got for a mere song, and their children are without a single inch of ground at present... many of the wealthier farmers in this district, who did not value the education of their children, if still alive, would see them... occupying the lowest position imaginable.[97]

A farmer in Frankfort in the north of the Orange Free State similarly wrote in 1912 that he knew personally about a dozen *bywoners* who, when he arrived in the district some thirty years previously, had owned farms and a good deal of stock.[98]

Under the Roman–Dutch law of inheritance, each child of a testator was entitled to what was known as the 'legitimate portion'. Parents were formally obliged to leave their children a defined minimum share of the estate. In the Cape Colony, this stipulation was legally abolished in 1874, but in the republics it survived until the British conquest at the turn of the century. But even after the introduction of the principle of liberty of testation, the convention of equal shares persisted in practice. As a consequence, the subdivision of farms was a widespread, ongoing process. Often the convention of equal shares entailed the mortgaging of land and consequent chronic debt contraction, as daughters (and younger sons as often as not) were paid out their shares in cash which had to be raised on the security of the land. More commonly the entire estate was sold off and the proceeds divided. In practice many younger sons became *bywoners*, and there was a constant northward drain (and westward into the dryer areas) throughout the nineteenth century from the Cape as well as the Orange Free State as landless young men moved off into new areas of settlement where land was still cheap.[99]

In the early 1890s with the opening-up of Rhodesia for white settlement under the auspices of the British South Africa Company, a number of treks northward into the new territory were mooted; and many Boers from arable districts joined the treks. Amongst the participants were members of long-established and prominent land-owning families in such arable districts as Ladybrand and Bethlehem. A number of newspaper reports in 1891 and 1892 told of meetings of farmers in these districts organizing treks into the new territory. In May 1892 it was reported that 200 applications for farms had been received from Orange Free State farmers. This movement was in large part related to the fact that young men saw little opportunity for setting up independently on parental land.[100] Similarly, a correspondent from Vryburg in the sparsely settled northern Cape beyond the Orange River wrote in 1892 that many Orange Free Staters were settling in the district. Their reported reasons were that the farms in the Orange Free State were becoming 'too full', two or three generations occupying one farm.[101]

Orange Free State farm registers indicate that most farms in the arable districts had been subdivided a number of times. But formal registration of subdivision of land was often avoided, because of the need to pay survey fees and transfer duties. The land registers for the period are full of examples of farms with a number of co-owners, not necessarily related.[102] Very often newspapers advertised sales of undivided portions of farms. Thus many landowners owned a half, third or quarter share of a larger farm, and the shares had never been formally registered as separate farms.

Yet unless the landholder had substantial capital resources available there was a limit beyond which land could not be further subdivided without its ceasing to be economically viable. Land subdivision could sometimes reach the stage where it became impossible for all co-owners to earn a living from the land.[103] Some or all had to move off in search of alternative land or employment. Indeed, many an impoverished white man or woman living in the towns was the legal owner of an undivided share of a farm somewhere.[104] The subdivision of large landholdings on the arable Highveld was still very much on the upswing in the early years of the twentieth century; but by the 1890s many individual farms had ceased to be able to provide a living for those who had a legal claim to them, because of the lack of capital required to adapt to more intensive arable farming.

The incidence of excessive fragmentation and 'overcrowding' of land was related perhaps to the nature of the patriarchal family.[105] In the earlier days there seems often to have been a tension between the patriarch's wish to retain his extended family on the farm and the will of sons to move off in search of new land. The custom of entailing property

– that is, placing a testamentary injunction in a will restraining legatees from alienating the fixed property, sometimes in perpetuity – was fairly common.[106] One effect of such entails was that land could not easily be mortgaged, since land which could not be alienated was unwelcome as security (although creditors could take over the usufruct for life). The land often became useless to the co-owners, who might be numerous by the third generation, and most of whom were very widely scattered. It was not unknown for the *Volksraad* to set aside the provisions of wills in this regard, and a trickle of petitions over the years begged the legislators to relieve the petitioners of such servitudes.[107] In 1896 the Orange Free State *Volksraad* made provision in law for release from burdensome dispositions by application to the Supreme Court (Law 24–1896) – a provision which was extended to the whole Union in 1915.

In a petition of 1897, L. J. Botha revealed the extent of the constraints imposed by entails on property. He had inherited from his father a quarter of the farm, Claudius, in the Rouxville district. These 487 morgen were all that Botha possessed, except for two horses. He had at one time owned sixty head of cattle, 1200 sheep and ten or fifteen horses. Most of these animals had perished in 1891 and 1892 as a result of *hartwater* and *kapok*. His crops had repeatedly failed. The traders refused to give him credit as he could offer no security. He had been offered £2 a morgen for the ground and a firm in Rouxville had undertaken to lend him £300 at 6 per cent interest for five years should he succeed in having the servitude on the property removed.[108] This story was not an altogether atypical one, and reveals some of the pressures which drove landowners, confronted with the alternative of impoverishment, to accumulate debts against the security of their land.

Debt itself was a major cause of land loss. The purchase of land in the arable districts – most particularly at times of inflated land values – generally meant incurring considerable mortgage debt; and, as we have seen, raising money to pay off co-heirs had the same effect. The experience of land loss was not a new one. As long as the Boers had been involved in exchange and credit relations (as they always had been in some degree) the threat posed by mercantile capital to landownership was a real one. From the 1840s onward in the sheep districts, increasing land values, the penetration of the interior by mortgage and speculative capital and the widespread contractions of debt that these entailed, combined to render landownership a precarious status for many, particularly during commercial depressions. The depression of the 1860s, together with the Sotho wars, meant that when the Orange Free State courts were reopened in 1869 at the close of the wars, a spate of insolvencies amongst landowners followed.[109] The mineral revolution on the Highveld and the unprecedented influx of speculative capital which accompanied it quickly provided new opportunities for Highveld landowners to gain access to funds on the security of their land. As land values rose, so did the extent to which land was encumbered with mortgage debt.

By the 1890s the old colonial finance and trust companies based in the coastal ports were seeking new outlets for surplus funds beyond the borders of the colonies, where the mortgaging of land had reached an advanced stage. 'Latterly insurance companies and other corporations' reported *The Friend* in 1892, 'which have lately experienced more difficulty in finding safe and suitable investments than in increasing their funds, have turned their attention to the comparatively virgin ground of the Free State.' Orange Free State landowners were soon following in the footsteps of Cape landowners mortgaging their land in order to take advantage of the new influx of funds seeking profitable investments. Between 1888–9 and 1892–3, new bonds passed on land per year increased from £271 655 to £607 976. Forty per cent of new bonds passed on land in the Orange Free State in 1892–3 was in the hands of foreign investors. Although no earlier figures were available, *The Friend*'s editor had no doubt that this proportion had been increasing rapidly in the foregoing five years: 'the landed property of the State is gradually becoming bonded to foreign investors, and this fact will eventually make money very tight here as the interest will all have to be paid to the foreigners.' The editor warned that as a result 'in course of time many who are now the proud possessors of their own farms might find them so encumbered that they will be only too glad to sell off and trek to other places. This is a class of men the State can ill afford to lose.'[110]

In 1894 a spate of petitions reached the *Volksraad* asking that interest rates on government funds be lowered so as to allow landowners to take advantage of state loans rather than relying on funds from outside the state – especially as government funds were allegedly lying idle.[111] One petition signed by twenty-six burghers from Winburg complained that landowners were cancelling their bonds in favour of the government's school fund and taking out new bonds in favour of capitalists and companies in the Cape and elsewhere at an interest of 5 per cent, 1 or 2 per cent less than they had been paying. The petitioners asked that interest on loans from the school fund be lowered to 4 per cent in order to 'avert the serious consequences which will result if the land of the Orange Free State is bonded exclusively by capital of foreign institutions and investors'.[112]

There were other ways in which foreign capital was eating away at the self-sufficiency and ultimately the security of Boer landowners. In the great speculative boom year of 1895 it was reported that prospecting rights over 'nearly the whole' of the districts of Heilbron and Kroonstad had been granted to speculators. There was reportedly a 'great deal of excitement among farmers and landowners generally all over the Northern districts right now, for syndicates and speculators are offering very exciting terms for the right to prospect properties'. In Heilbron representatives of a Johannesburg firm were securing options to buy farms for 25s to 40s per morgen, with a view to securing some 60 000 morgen. L. V. Emanuel and H. Vecht, representatives of 'some Johannesburg people', had secured options on 294 606 acres of land. There were 'any number of speculators roaming all over the country pretending to prospect', reported *The Friend*, 'but who are in reality doing nothing but securing options on all the farms they can'. When, after the abortive Jameson Raid at the end of 1895, many leading Johannesburg capitalists found themselves in Transvaal prisons, petitions were hastily circulated amongst Boer landowners praying for amnesty because of the sudden cessation of their option annuities.[113] The value of some of these options on mineral-rich land is illustrated by the fact that Tom Minter, a well-known speculator in the Orange Free State, received £30 000 in 1898 for his half-option for the purchase of the farm Rietgat. The farm was diamondiferous and was only six miles from the Kaalvallei diamond mines in the Kroonstad district.[114] No doubt many Boers gained a substantial income from such sources, but such income was not necessarily converted into productive capital. The ready availability of speculative funds promoted the conviction that merely owning land would bring a greater return than agricultural enterprise could ever pay.[115]

It was under these circumstances that the populist anti-capitalist rhetoric of the 1890s should be understood. The fear that imperial interests were engaged in establishing a stranglehold over the economic resources of the country, most importantly the land itself, became the basis for a populist agitation which was expressed increasingly in terms of the symbols of cultural nationalism and economic self-reliance. 'We have to fight against the capitalists', declared President Steyn in March 1898, when laying the foundation stone of a home for indigent white youths. If the burghers did not take up arms 'then we will deserve to become slaves of the capitalists, and our labour will no longer bring freedom and happiness, but enslavement and misery'. In the *Volksraad* debate of 1896 on limiting the franchise so as to guard against an influx of *uitlanders*, Steyn suggested that citizenship of the Orange Free State

Republic should be made a condition for the acquisition of property.[116]

The Bloemfontein newspaper, *De Express*, under its German editor, Carl Borckenhagen, was the major disseminator of anti-capitalist ideas, repeatedly warning of the dangers posed to the independence of the burgher community and its access to land by 'foreign bloodsuckers', and constantly giving publicity to efforts by burghers to forge alternative economic networks to those provided by foreign capitalists and merchants dependent on foreign credit. These local initiatives (which were recurrently mooted in republican days) were given a boost by the Jameson Raid at the end of 1895 and the rinderpest of 1896–7, which accelerated the impoverishment of the Boers and the expropriation of their land. Various plans were formulated by farmers' associations to establish co-operative stores and loan banks controlled by the farmers in an attempt to undermine the alleged stranglehold of foreign speculative and mortgage capital. None was more ambitious than the *Help Mekaar*, organized in Ficksburg in 1898 with an initial capital of £50 000.[117] But none of these schemes got off the ground – partly because of the outbreak of war in 1899.

It is not at all clear how widespread or significant the accumulation of land by foreign capitalist interests was in the 1890s. There can be no doubt that this was happening, for example in the coal-rich northern Orange Free State where companies like Lewis and Marks were consolidating their landholdings over large areas.[118] But the populist rhetoric of wholesale dispossession needs to be regarded with scepticism. The prevalent assumption that all the land in the republics had at some stage in the past – before the influx of foreign capital – been owned by the burghers, was a myth. As we have seen, landownership had always been very concentrated, much of it in the hands of aliens, from the earliest days of the republics; and there had never been a classless democracy amongst the Boers such as the rhetoric of the 1890s (and much subsequent Afrikaner historiography) has implied. Nevertheless, by the industrializing 1890s the scale of the perceived threat to the Boer landowners' relative self-sufficiency was much greater than at any previous period.[119]

As a result of the unrelenting pressures on landowners with heavy mortgage debts to meet, there was a strong resistance amongst many Boer farmers to bonding their property. The grip of mortgage capital was an irksome burden, and farmers were deeply conscious of the greatly unequal exchange relations that their own dependence on the credit of others imposed. In Lindley, for instance, after the war, when political sensibilities were particularly aroused, several farmers whose land was unmortgaged were 'extremely short of the necessities of life by way of food and clothing, and...yet are unwilling to raise money on their properties'. In Frankfort it was reported that landowners, big and small, were so loath to bond their farms that they had no cash with which to rebuild. The magistrate in Bethulie in 1910 wrote that 'farmers as a rule do not wish to bond their properties' and would 'rather undergo hardships than have bonds on their farms'.[120]

However, the doubtful capacity of farmers to generate capital through their own productive endeavour meant that they were reliant on supplies of capital from outside the farming economy. It was hardly surprising, given the vicissitudes of agriculture, drought, stock disease, pests and war, that wherever loan capital penetrated, it could potentially reduce the landowner to a state of dependence. The high incidence of bonding of property on the Highveld after the Anglo-Boer War reflected the landowners' vulnerability to debt contraction; but many returned to their farms after the war with no hope of raising funds for debt payment and rebuilding, since their land was already so heavily mortgaged as to be of no value as security to creditors, and they could not persuade the government to take over their debts on easy terms. It was these landowners, reported the magistrates, who were in a particularly bad way.[121] The magistrate at Smithfield reported in February 1904: 'Many farmers have neither purchasing or borrowing power to make a fresh start. A great number of farms have consequently been sold to Dutch Colonial farmers and old residents are leaving the district.'[122] Many others in the arable districts sold off portions of their farms. There was no shortage of buyers: large numbers of capitalized farmers from the coastal colonies – not to mention the new British land settlers – were moving into the interior.

Land prices ruled high immediately after the war. The new administration sought land for its land settlement scheme. Land companies, speculators and option hunters were no less active. When J. A. Sugden visited the concentration camps on behalf of the new administration with an eye to acquiring property for land settlement,[123] he came across the representatives of at least a dozen syndicates trying to get options on Boer farms and was himself offered free shares in two syndicates provided he acquired options for them.[124] The significance of all this was a steady process of land loss amongst Boer landed families. Either voluntarily or under duress, many were becoming landless.

The loss of land accelerated from 1904, as the drought intensified and the post-war commercial boom was succeeded by a deep depression as a result of overtrading, overspeculation, and overextension of mercantile credit. One consequence was a collapse in the land market. According to the editor of *The Friend*, 'The values of farm property went up higher than was justifiable soon after the war, and in the present state of the money market have now sunk to the opposite extreme.'[12.] This was partly due to the amount of land thrown on the market by indebted owners, and partly due to the unavailability of loan capital for prospective buyers. 'The outcome' wrote Governor Goold-Adams in 1908, 'is that land is being freely put in the market, purchasers are not obtained and consequently land values have depreciated considerably.'[126] In Heilbron, for instance, land bought in 1904 for little less than 60*s* per morgen was resold in July 1908 for 33*s*.[127] The slump also meant that the inflow of option money into rural districts was checked.[128]

Particularly, between 1904 and 1908 the ready availability of credit and loans to farmers gave way to a tightness of cash which raised interest rates, and most banks insisted on prompt repayments. Creditors generally began to put pressure on farmers for the return of loans and to refuse renewals. The government needed funds too, and banks were called upon to supply them, increasing the pressure on banks' debtors. The magistrates at Vrede and Rouxville reported in 1904 that the local banks were not advancing more money, even on the best security.[129] In the same year the magistrate in Bloemfontein reported that there was evidence that 'the need of money is now more felt than at any other time since the war'. The banks had:

> stopped all advances and even men who have good security to offer have either to agree to the exorbitant terms of the local money-lender and the horrible tenacity of his grasp once it has fastened on the land or go without practically the necessities of life.[130]

As a result of all this, a unanimous resolution of the ORC Central Farmers' Union called for easy government loans to farmers; otherwise many 'will be compelled to sell their farms at prices much below their value'.[131] 'War, drought and disease have played their sorry part in draining resources and impoverishing individuals' wrote the editor of the *Farmer's Advocate* in 1906. 'Money has been borrowed at the usual ruinous rate of interest and mortgage has been piled upon mortgage to tide over incessant crisis.' In 1908 the ORC Poor Whites Commission estimated that mortgage bonds on farms in that colony amounted to £3 580 000.[132]

The result of this financial depression was an acceleration of the process of impoverishment amongst the less capitalized Boer landowners. The weight of indebtedness which hung over their heads was in many cases grossly disproportionate to the productivity of their enterprise and their financial returns from it. The excessive mortgaging of land to make good the ravages of stock disease and war could prove fatal unless the farmer was able to intensify his use of the land, and unless he had ready access to markets and was able to earn a reliable income out of which debt and interest payments could be met. Economic depressions, coupled with poor seasons, low prices, and a depleted stock population, combined to ensure that for many farmers, debts were mounting steadily and ominously during the half-dozen years after the end of the war.

One can illustrate this process with reference to the Pienaars, two farmers of the Winburg district. W. J. Pienaar owned Nooitgedacht, 1070 morgen in extent. The first bond on the farm, for £1000 was in favour of the Funds Department of the government. The second, for £350, was to an E. B. Rosslein. A third bond had been passed in favour of William Fendick for £135. We can speculate that this was passed to secure a debt to Fendick which Pienaar was unable immediately to pay. But then we find that a fourth bond, again to E. B. Rosslein, had been passed for the amount of £73. This last bond was probably interest accrued on the earlier bond, and Rosslein had extracted yet another bond to that amount in the hope that the estate, when dissolved, would yield sufficient funds to cover it. By this time, bonds to the amount of £1558 had been passed on the farm, and clearly Pienaar had virtually exhausted his creditworthiness and was sliding toward a state of insolvency. J. Pienaar, a relative, owned Mazelspruit of 1169 morgen, and Elsidore of 489 morgen. The former was bonded to widow Schnehage to the amount of £600 and to the Repatriation Department for £400; on the latter, bonds had been passed in favour of the South African Mutual Trust Company of Cape Town (£400), and the same E. B. Rosslein (who by now must have been a very worried creditor indeed) to the tune of £537. The bonds on these farms added up to £1937. The Pienaars were desperate men, for they offered the farms to the government for the amounts of the bonds and interest due, suggesting that the government then allow them to remain on the farms under the land settlement scheme. The government declined, and we can conclude that the farms were probably sold off in settlement of accounts.[133]

This was the story of a great number of farmers – a gathering weight of indebtedness, relieved only by entering ever more onerous debt obligations, until all creditworthiness was exhausted, and their property and livelihood had to be sacrificed to the baying pack of creditors. F. T.

Nicholson, secretary of the Transvaal Agricultural Union, wrote in 1906 that the war, stock disease and drought had:

> led farmers in all parts of the country to borrow money upon the security of their farms, and many having found themselves unable to continue the payment of interest on their loans, have been compelled to part with their holdings, and are daily becoming more and more impoverished. Others have, with the greatest difficulty, managed to meet their liabilities, at the expense of their own personal comfort and that of their dependent families. Here and there a wealthy farmer is still to be found, but their numbers are being continuously reduced. It is safe to say that, for many years past, the farming community has never been in a position so precarious as that which it now occupies.[134]

In July 1908 the editor of *The Friend* noted that Boer farmers were gradually selling their farms or allowing them to be sold, and were migrating to the towns:

> The sales of farms are in many instances due to sheer inability to meet liabilities owing to the badness of the times and the utter absence of the means of earning money. In many instances the heavy interest on mortgage took more than a good year's crop, so that with bad seasons like the last two years, the farmers were unable to meet the interest, and foreclosures resulted.[135]

Again, such impressionistic generalizations as those of the editor need to be treated with caution in the absence of statistics. A degree of exaggeration was especially to be expected from the Afrikaner populist intelligentsia. Rev. J. D. Kestell was a prominent exponent of cultural mobilization in the early years of the new century. At a 'Day of the Covenant' meeting in 1912, this leading figure in the Dutch Reformed Church expressed alarm at the sight of the Boers selling off their farms. There was hardly a single Boer farm within two hours' journey from Ficksburg, according to Kestell. The farms near the town now belonged to people 'not of our own blood', while the Boers left their homes and trekked further inland. 'Must the Boer be nothing but the tamer of the desert which others are to inhabit?' he asked.[136]

But despite the polemical nature of some of the evidence, it seems clear that particularly during periods of depression such as the years 1904–8, farms frequently fell into the hands of non-farmers, many of them foreign (colonial and metropolitan) companies, syndicates and individuals, others members of the local urban bourgeoisie, merchants, lawyers, auctioneers and moneylenders. It was not at all unusual, W. M.

Macmillan discovered some years later, for the former owner of a farm to stay on as a *bywoner*, perhaps tending the absentee landlord's stock, or as a fully fledged lessee paying a rent, perhaps in the form of a share of the crop.[137]

Mortgage capital was clearly a mixed blessing. Although some farmers were capitalizing and expanding their productive capacity, many were not. For many resident landowners, increased indebtedness meant increased vulnerability, given the tendency peculiar to agriculture for productive capital to be wiped out in years of drought, of infestation or epizootic. Moreover, there was a tendency, widely noted in later years when agricultural economists began to examine these matters, for loan capital to be expended on items of consumption or on speculation such as land purchase – or to pay off earlier debts to merchants – rather than on expanding productivity.[138]

However, although it is probable that during periods of economic depression the process of land alienation by non-farmers was cumulative, it was not sustained indefinitely. For when land prices were rising and mortgage capital was once again readily available, such as in the years after Union, absentee landowners sought to realize their assets by selling off their land to farmers with capital and/or access to mortgage loans. In the second decade of the century, once the land bank had been set up, state succour to white farmers not only increasingly cushioned them against the vagaries of the market, but also facilitated the acquisition of land by new settlers. This subject will be examined in chapter 6 where the years of financial boom after Union are examined. What can be said with certainty is that when statistics became available from 1918, the proportion of farms occupied by resident landowners in the Orange Free State was climbing, from 63.9 per cent of all farming units to 68.5 per cent in 1925, at the same time as the number of registered farms on the Highveld was climbing as well.[139]

Indeed, during the second decade of this century, the influx of new settlers into the rural maize districts (from other parts of South Africa as well as from overseas) was still larger than the efflux of the impoverished out of them. This was particularly the case in the Transvaal Highveld districts, where the decade 1911–21 showed 'abnormal' increase of the white population according to the 1921 census report. In the words of the director of the census this was due to 'recognition of the agricultural possibilities of the country, and the subdivision of farms into smaller but workable holdings which have been taken up by numerous settlers from other parts of the Union and elsewhere'.[140] While the size of Karoo sheep farms was increasing in the early twentieth century for economic and ecological reasons,[141] the trend in the Highveld maize districts was in the opposite direction until the 1930s at least (when a process of consolidation began under the impact of the Depression and mechanization). Subdivision of land in the maize belt into smaller productive units was general in the first three decades of this century. The declining white population in certain parts of the rural Highveld (starting in the earlier developing Orange Free State) in the 1910s and 1920s reflects the efflux of the landless and not any decrease in the number of farms.[142] There was also clearly a steady increase in the numbers of English-speakers in the white rural population, both absolutely and relative to the older Boer population.[143]

3 Black Tenant Production and White Accumulation

THE EVOLUTION OF A SHARECROPPING ECONOMY

The kinds of loose tenancy arrangements on which the Boers depended for part of their labour supplies when extensive pastoralism and hunting were the foundation stone of their economy, no longer served their purpose once large internal urban markets for foodstuffs had emerged. In a land-extensive economy, alliances between white landholders and seniors in black communities could only function when the landlord's demands were unintrusive and did not interfere with the productive activities of the tenant homesteads. Such arrangements were not suitable for commercial crop production, which was rapidly becoming indispensable to the viability of the white rural economy toward the end of the nineteenth century. Alternative sources of labour supply were not readily forthcoming, especially given the considerable competitive disadvantages of agricultural employers in the rapidly emerging capitalist labour market from the 1870s onward. From the 1870s, too, the seepage of the most serviceable young black men from the farms into temporary employment elsewhere undermined the farmers' position. Add to this shortage of labour for arable production, a severe shortage of capital on the part of white farmers, as well as their widespread lack of experience in the skills required for cultivation, and it is not surprising that whites in large numbers chose to batten on to and exploit the one resource to which they did have access by virtue of their control over land – the productive potential of independent black farmers.

It is quite possible that the bulk of grain produced on the arable Highveld in the early twentieth century was produced by relatively independent black tenant farmers – an impression which if anything is confirmed in the sample of black experience represented by the oral evidence collected in recent years. Sharecropping was the typical form taken by this dependence on black tenant production, and can schematically be seen as transitional to a more explicitly capitalist type of enterprise under the control of white farmers.

Sharing arrangements were by no means new. Stock-loan systems involving sharing of the increase were integral features of both Boer and black societies. Crop-sharing by Sotho cultivators existed on Griqua lands in the 1860s, and it is possible that arrangements of this sort emerged, for example, in Basutoland and in the pre-Trek Cape midlands long before the emergence of large urban markets in the interior of South Africa.[1] However, these arrangements would have differed greatly in intensity, in commercial orientation and in scale to the sharecropping associated with the rise of capitalist farming between the 1870s and 1910s.

From the early 1890s in particular, white landowners and lessees, many of them absentees, were increasingly inclined to take advantage of the boom conditions by entering sharecropping agreements, particularly in the arable districts of the Free State and southern Transvaal.[2] And at a time when the rich lowlands of Basutoland were feeling the effects of two decades or more of intensive exploitation and population growth, many Sotho were inclined to take advantage of the opportunities offered over the Caledon River in the less populated Orange Free State, where they were also able to escape the exactions of chiefs who wished to reserve for themselves the profits to be made by trading enterprise.[3]

In the 1880s and 1890s there were increasing numbers of extended kindred groups – whole homesteads usually – edging their way deeper into the Orange Free State seeking to establish alliances of patronage with white landholders. These large settlement groups, with substantial productive resources and skills as cultivators, were to evolve into the sharecroppers of the arable Highveld. The Makumes, of Taung origin, left the Matsieng district of Basutoland some years before the Anglo-Boer War. In their party were Motetesi, his sons, Mohlakala, Gafa and Mosimane, plus five daughters, and Motetesi's younger brother Sefako, with his three sons, Mese, Koeranta and Tebellong, plus their own children: three (eventually four) generations in all. Their purpose, according to Mohlakala's grandson, Ndae Makume, was to find land which they could cultivate. They brought with them not only their cattle, horses, sheep and goats, but their scissors and sickles, so as to find piece-work on Boer farms as shearers of sheep at a penny per animal, or as reapers of wheat and barley. 'They left Lesotho without any positive destination in mind. They did not at first have any place where they could stay and graze their stock; they moved from farm to farm looking for a place where they could settle.' Anxious to find a place where they could sharecrop, they eventually settled in Lindley district, where they found various forms of sharecropping contracts in operation. Early in the new century the group split up, with Motetesi and Sefako each going their own way.[4]

This process of fission, an inevitable consequence of wage labour and the independent access of juniors to productive resources and bridewealth cattle, was ubiquitous amongst such extended settlement groups on the farms. Motiapi Chebase's family originated in Zululand, fled Shaka's wrath, settled amongst the Mpondo and then amongst the Xhosa (perhaps the Mfengu), subsequently attaching themselves to Moshoeshoe as Phuthing. Motiapi was then given land in Thaba Nchu by the Rolong chief, Moroka, and after the Anglo-Boer War when so much of Moroka's territory was settled by whites, moved on to a farm near Senekal. Motiapi had three wives, eight sons and eleven daughters, as well as grandchildren with him. Another informant, Chebase Manaba, born during the war, was the last-born son of the third wife. His father, he tells us, hardly knew how to inspan an ox, as he had grown up at a time when only the hand hoe was used: he sowed skin blankets and looked after the sheep while his sons worked the soil. So big was the group and so many animals did they own, that they were obliged to split up. The senior wife and her sons moved off with 200 sheep and over fifty beasts, while the remaining two houses with 400 sheep and seventy beasts, moved to a farm in the Lindley district, under the patriarchal authority of Moweng, son of the second wife.[5]

Another example is that of the Phalimes. Kodisang Phalime's grandfather, father and uncles emigrated from Witsieshoek on to the farms of the northern Orange Free State (apparently in the 1880s) 'because they needed more land for cultivation. They came for sharecropping'. Kodisang, who was born in the Orange Free State on the farm he remembers as 'Tsaile', recalls that as a small boy his extended family commanded three spans of oxen of some sixteen animals each and sold the wool of perhaps 300 sheep.[6]

Many of the people moving into the Orange Free State in these years seem to have originated initially in the western Transvaal, having sought protection in Moshoeshoe's emergent kingdom during the Ndebele wars of the 1820s and 1830s. It is possible that many of these, Koena and others, had been forging a new identity in Basutoland. In the early twentieth century many sharecroppers in the mid-Vaal region seem to have been such refugees from the *Difaqane* who had spent many years in Basutoland, and perhaps because of their distinct identity, were particularly susceptible to new ideas, Christian influences, and a desire to escape from chiefly control.[7]

Emigré groups intending to move permanently away from the Sotho kingdom usually moved beyond the Conquered Territory into the north-central Orange Free State and the southern Transvaal. It was also fairly common for inhabitants of Basutoland to cross the border into the Orange Free State with their oxen and equipment at ploughing time to take advantage of the conditions of relative land abundance existing there, and then to return to their homesteads across the river until the harvest, when they would return with the requisite labour to clear the crop and claim their half-shares. Small offshoots of larger homesteads in Basutoland might settle on border farms, and draw resources of seed, oxen, equipment or labour as required from their larger homesteads of agnatic kin in Basutoland to work the land. Whites complained that many Sotho, including chiefs, made use of farms across the border to graze their cattle under the care of tenants on the farms.[8]

Others amongst the sharecroppers were the overflow population of Rolong from Thaba Nchu, an enclave chiefdom in the eastern Orange Free State which lost its independence in 1884. Many of the Rolong, who for long had produced commercial crops, found their way on to white-owned land outside the district, and much land privately owned by individual Rolong notables fell into the hands of whites. As a result of the annexation of Rolong territory, in the words of the editor of *The Friend*, 'an unusually large number of well-trained, Christian natives, ready and willing to occupy and till the soil on shares or for a certain consideration' was dispersed onto white-owned land. He described these '*oorlams*' Rolong as 'generally well-clothed, civil, law-abiding and skilled in farming' and 'exceedingly useful to the farmer in dam-making and in fencing'. Such comments cannot be dismissed, coming as they do from so negrophobe a source.[9]

Opportunities for maize production under sharecropping contracts in the mid-Vaal region in particular were opening up in the 1890s and many Sotho were finding their way thither. Much land in this coal-rich area had been bought up by individual speculators, syndicates or land companies, often based in Johannesburg, such as the twenty-two farms of the Vereeniging Estates.[10] These speculative landowners were intent on realizing the commercial potential of this land by drawing rent from share tenants. Many were also concerned secondarily to draw a labour supply for their mines, manufactories or plantations. There were many Africans with the skills and means to take advantage of the opportunities for profit in this less densely populated area, suited to dry-land maize and sorghum cultivation and close to the industrial heartland of the region.

Many who had emigrated from Basutoland much earlier came to the mid-Vaal region at this time from white-owned farms in other parts of the Orange Free State, much to the chagrin of the white farmers. In

Volksraad debates the absentee estates south of the Vaal were often described as a major grievance amongst the burghers (but C. R. de Wet, member for Boven Modderriver, Bloemfontein district, was no doubt exaggerating when he claimed in 1895 that 'most' Africans in his district were moving to the northern districts, especially the coal mining estates).[11] One such was Tloaele Mokale, a Koena who had moved from a Boer farm in the Magaliesberg into Basutoland and then settled on one Wessels' farm in the Lindley district, where he lived for many years accumulating stock before moving to the Vereeniging Estates to sharecrop in the mid-1890s – as, according to his grandson, he had access to too little arable land to grow food for his horses.[12]

Perhaps more revealing of the motive forces pushing such people into sharecropping relationships is the story of Rankwane Molefe, who traces his origins to the Ngwato of the western Transvaal. His family had some time in the nineteenth century taken up residence in Basutoland, but left the country in the 1880s, moving to the vicinity of Heilbron. Immediately after the rinderpest epizootic and a severe drought seriously affected the area, Molefe took to sharecropping on the farm Zaaiplaas in 1897. His daughter remembers the circumstances and the family disputes surrounding the move to Zaaiplaas with a clarity that suggests that the decision was a step of major significance in the family history and was perceived as such at the time. She tells us that many people had not ploughed and that there was little food available. In order to get a ploughing team together, her father had to borrow young bullocks and heifers from neighbours, probably kin. He reaped 70 bags of sorghum and 100 bags of maize. So what might have led him to commercial sharecropping was the promise of seed on credit from the landlord (whites had access to seed loans at this time from merchants anxious to secure custom), and the prospect of pooling plough oxen with kindred sharecroppers, thereby recovering his stockholdings with the proceeds from his enterprise.[13]

Similarly, Johannes Moiloa's father went sharecropping on the farm Rooibult the year after rinderpest, which killed his whole span save for two oxen. His previous landlord, Roelf Reineke of Boomplaas near Ladybrand, had demanded that he hand over the animals on the grounds that he, Reineke, had supplied the medicine which saved them from the disease. Moiloa left the farm on which he and his children had been born and was able to start sharecropping for the first time by collecting together oxen from his kin. Johannes testifies that his father entered sharecropping arrangements in 1898 rather than live as a labour tenant without his own means of production. Sharecropping, which provided opportunities for reaccumulation, was the only alternative Moiloa was prepared to consider. 'He did not like the way these people were exploited – he saw no gain from that type of tenancy.... He then realized that it could be profitable for him if his children worked for him under sharecropping arrangements.'[14]

Sharecroppers would presumably usually have had access to extensive good ploughing lands; indeed, their acceptability to landlords would have depended on their willingness to maximize the crop. Under these circumstances, and given the reliance on markets for many items of productive and personal consumption, as well as credit relations and tax demands which were already part and parcel of the African rural economy, economic survival as independent producers meant for many families a decision to throw in their lot with a white landlord who had both land and, increasingly, access to state aid and mercantile credit – most importantly after the rinderpest and drought of 1896–8 in the form of seed. It is also likely that many of the sharecroppers were helped to set up as commercial producers from the earnings of migrant wage labour, for example in the mines of the region or in towns. In these ways many black tenant households were drawn more fully into the rural capitalist economy as sharecroppers producing for markets and supplying the accumulating landlords with a substantial income.

Available testimony suggests an element of choice and individual initiative in the decision to begin sharecropping. Emelia Molefe's father's brother refused to follow her father into sharecropping:

> He said we plough and work in the field only to share the harvest with a man who has not helped to produce it. He felt it was better simply to work on the farms. He did this until he was very elderly – until his daughters had to substitute for him in order to keep the family's place on the farm.[15]

Further, such testimony indicates that landlords of the area were actively enticing black families with skills and resources on to their land as sharecropping tenants. It is also possible that there were strong pressures building up from white farmers jealous of black access to capital resources and who resented the numbers of stock which Africans owned – at least before the rinderpest – and who were attempting to increase labour services from their tenants. This would certainly have been the case during the boom years of 1893 to 1895. These pressures would have increased the advantages of settling on absentee-owned land as share tenants.

*   *   *

Antagonism toward sharecropping arrangements was widespread amongst rural whites in the 1890s. It was the more explicit sharecropping arrangements on absentee-owned land where the black producers were largely independent from white control or supervision that petitioners, determined to forge a white-supremacist political economy, railed against. The litany of complaint against the '*los kaffirs*' and '*leegleggers*' included the assumed denial to poor whites of the opportunity of finding a place on the land for themselves, the demand that black labour was urgently required on the land of white farmers rather than being expended to their own benefit and that of capitalist absentee landlords, the supposedly deflating effect which black producers had on market prices for produce, their alleged propensity for stock theft, and the 'bad example' which they set to the servants of neighbouring white farmers who were intent on controlling the lives and labour of their black tenants.[16]

These sentiments were most widely and urgently expressed at times of heavy crop yields, such as those of 1893 and 1894. The latter year especially was one of very large winter cereal harvests in the eastern districts and in Basutoland, when prices were depressed, wagon transport at a premium, and labour for reaping very scarce. Not only were the many burghers who signed petitions in 1894 (and who thereby secured the enactment of the anti-squatting law of 1895) motivated by the spectre of Sotho competition for scarce transport resources and competition on inelastic urban markets, but they were also enraged at the great surge of African peasant prosperity and blacks' increased independence from the need to render labour for whites. It was at such times of accelerated accumulation amongst black producers, when they were able to consolidate and extend their control over productive resources, that the spectre of long-term economic decline and increasing dependence amongst whites was most vivid. Without state intervention in the protection and promotion of white-controlled production and white accumulation, and in the suppression of the black rural economy, many considered that white authority and control were in danger of collapse. The alien land speculators and absentee landlords whose interests seemed to be opposed or indifferent to indigenous white capital formation, were not to be trusted. The political economy of white supremacy could not be simply assumed; it had to be fought for and actively forged under the new conditions of industrial capitalism. The populist petty bourgeoisie who were at the forefront of this struggle saw the dominance of foreign capital and black control of market production as the twin-edged sword which was threatening to overwhelm them.

One can see in the agitation of 1893–5 the incipient perception amongst whites of a potential watershed in the relative fortunes of black and white on the land. For it was at such times of boom and productive expansion (to be repeated with even more dramatic results in the similar boom years of 1908–13) that whites saw most clearly that their fate as a ruling race depended on their control and manipulation of the state's resources. In consequence, in both periods intense pressures were brought to bear on the state to intervene. The anti-squatting laws of 1895 (enacted in both the Free State and the Transvaal) grew out of a set of circumstances similar to those prevailing in 1913 when the more far-reaching Natives Land Act was enacted.[17]

The law of 1895 was designed to restate and tighten up the provisions of the law of 1881, [18] restricting the number of tenant families (defined as nuclear families) allowed per farm to five. The law was very much the product of those seeking to protect the landless 'little men' in Boer society from the consequences of allowing prosperous independent black peasant communities to accumulate on the land of large landowners at the expense of the poor burghers.[19] I. S. Ferreira, the representative for Korannaberg (Ladybrand district) in the *Volksraad* and a spokesman for populist sentiment warned in 1897 that the 'needy burghers' would be oppressed as the landowners would simply fill their land with African sharecroppers. 'Many foreign capitalists will then also buy land in this country for that purpose, and the result will be that within thirty years only a few burghers will be in possession of their own land.'[20] Petitions from arable districts in these years of deteriorating conditions for the 'needy burghers', particularly after the rinderpest of 1896–7 destroyed the insubstantial economic base of many, called for the tightening-up and stringent application of the anti-squatting law of 1895, so that no landowner, no matter how much land he owned, would be allowed to provide land for more than five heads of black families, as, in the popular perception, 'the poor whites are being wholly oppressed by the accumulation of too many loose Kaffirs'.[21]

There was seldom any real attempt to implement the law in the face of opposition from the big grain farmers, who relied on larger, relatively self-sufficient tenant communities for labour supplies.[22] But like the 1913 Land Act several years later and other such rural social-engineering legislation, the activities of the legislators were designed to fulfil a symbolic, mobilizing function, rather than produce a practical code capable of regulating real relationships.

It is not coincidental that the rise of sharecropping coincided with the rise of a public anxiety about the problem of white impoverishment.

There can be little doubt that the influx of Sotho commercial producers onto white-owned land greatly undermined the position of the landless whites, *bywoners* and small herd owners, whose lack of expertise and resources for arable farming was in marked contrast to many of the Sotho. As we have seen, white tenants were not profitable for their landlords; it was customary for the *bywoner* to hand over only a small remuneration for the use of land, originally no more than a tenth of the crop.[23] If it was rural crises, such as the crucial rinderpest, which ruined many of the poor whites and created a massive welfare problem for the republican governments, it was in the boom times, such as the years 1893–5, that their insecurity of status and of tenure, and their lack of utility for the landowners, became painfully obvious. Hence the way that petitions of the times harped on the fact that poor whites were being denied access to land by the rise of black peasant farming on white-owned farms in the arable districts.[24]

In 1893 111 burghers in the vicinity of the Vereeniging Estates petitioned the *Volksraad* to prohibit sharecropping arrangements, for 'by allowing natives to plough and sow on such a large scale, the poor burghers of the state are greatly disadvantaged'. This refrain from the farmers of Kromellenboog ward was a constant for the next twenty years, and reflected antagonism toward the absentee owners of so much land south of the Vaal.[25] Petitioners in the neighbouring Vechtkop ward were even more explicit in their anxieties. In 1894 they complained that no servants were to be found anywhere:

> and thus we cannot send our children to school because they must be used as servants; the result is that the Kaffirs are generally better off or rather richer than the whites, and do not need to hire themselves to whites, and yearly more land is sown and grain reaped by the Kaffirs than by the whites. Meanwhile the poor farmer has no servants to watch his cattle or to work his land, although encircled with Kaffir villages.[26]

A member of the *Volksraad*, W. J. Badenhorst from Taaiboschspruit, echoed these sentiments when he said in the same year that the blacks would gradually 'outfarm' the whites and that they were by degrees becoming richer than the latter. 'We must come to the aid of the burghers', he declared.[27]

* * *

It was in large part the status of black commercial producers, most obviously the sharecroppers working the soil without interference or supervision, which riled white populist opinion. However, it is likely that many of those who signed petitions objecting to such sharecropping arrangements were themselves increasingly dependent in some degree or another on black-owned and black-controlled means of production and black productive initiative, even if the white farmer was in command of the operation – albeit often in a largely nominal sense. Before the mineral revolution on the Highveld, it was possible for most of the Boer landholders to survive on the land with little or no cultivation of the soil. Farms were often quite large and the burden of mortgage debt not yet so overwhelming as it was to become. Non-landowners had little difficulty in finding land under easy terms of tenancy. Livestock, wool, skins, transporting, perhaps growing some fruit or tobacco, usually provided sufficient income for the cash requirements of the Boer household. After the mineral discoveries of the 1880s, many derived some extra income from option payments and prospecting fees. What changed this situation of relative self-sufficiency and made the Boers so vulnerable in the face of the influx of foreign capital was a series of crises which progressively and cumulatively ate away at the resources of the farmers: drought, locusts, and foot-and-mouth disease in 1891, 1892 and 1893, rinderpest and drought in 1896–8, and finally and most catastrophically, the Anglo-Boer War. The self-sufficiency of many rural people eroded as their stock dwindled and their debts mounted. For more and more, cultivation of the soil became the prerequisite for survival. Grain farming spread rapidly in consequence through districts where previously it had been negligible; and for many, arable production meant dependence on the instruments, the oxen and the labour and skills of whatever black families with these resources they could attract on to their land. So, many of those who lamented the enrichment of the blacks were themselves being sucked into the vortex of dependence in one or another form on these same resented competitors.

The rinderpest epizootic of 1896–7 was a major spur to sharecropping for white landholders as well as for blacks. African-owned stock was in greater demand than ever before. Although Africans were likely to have suffered as severely as whites from the deprivations of the disease, they were able to plug into the networks of kindred reciprocity which enabled them to maintain productive independence far more effectively. When in 1898 sixty-three burghers from the border districts of Ficksburg and Ladybrand petitioned the *Volksraad* to suppress sharecropping on the grounds that it would further undermine the position of the poor whites, C. can der Wath from Moroka (Thaba Nchu) and C. R. de Wet from Boven Modderrivier (Dewetsdorp) urged the *Raad* to consider the positions of their constituents who would be ruined if they were prevented from making use of the plough oxen of black tenants at that time of rural crisis. The majority of their colleagues agreed with them.[28] The unenforceability of legislation certainly did not deter the legislators, who were well-practised in passing unenforceable laws when it suited them and their constituents to pin their colours to the mast. But those who had been outraged during the boom times by the intolerable vision of landowners, often absentees and frequently men of means, profiting from black peasant enterprise, found that at times of crisis it was black productive resources and initiative which were maintaining many a Boer family on the land. Hence the unlikely sight of the usually interventionist *Volksraad* backing away from calls for action against sharecroppers on the land of foreign capitalists, for fear of the consequences for the poorer landholders amongst their burgher constituents.

However, the rinderpest also had devastating effects on the stock population of Basutoland, and many Sotho families were reduced to hoe culture and the use of horses and mules for ploughing. The sudden reduction in pressure on grazing resources in Basutoland meant that the pressures pushing Sotho farmers into the relatively land-abundant Orange Free State subsided for a time, and some Sotho even returned across the Caledon to their homesteads.[29] In contrast, after the Anglo-Boer War, the black farmers were able to take advantage of white impoverishment and dependence on an unprecedented scale.

The Anglo-Boer War was the most devastating blow yet to the rural economy. While its effect throughout the Highveld was destructive of the capital resources of black and white alike, it did have important implications for the struggle for control of resources between black and white on the land. Although the picture inevitably is very uneven, most white landholders came out of the war more vulnerable and dependent on black productive enterprise than before; while very many blacks, particularly those who had sought refuge in Basutoland and elsewhere with their stock, and who had been enriched by the war, were able to take advantage of the new situation to forge favourable tenancy agreements on white-owned land. It was reported from Mohale's Hoek in Basutoland that the cattle population had doubled as a result of wartime influx. From Maseru district came a report that such was the increase in the cattle population that overstocking had become a serious problem, and the mortality rate had increased as a result.[30] But not all cattle which found their way into Basutoland during the war belonged to the Africans. The assistant resident magistrate in Mafeteng noted:

Some Boer stock was found in this District in the possession of Natives; some had been sent over for safety by the Boers under arms; others brought in by Free State natives who stole the stock on their masters' farms, and others were looted by Basotho living in Mafeteng District.[31]

Much stock was channelled through southern Basutoland into the Cape, where it was sold off; and a report from Mafeteng complained of the damage done to pasturage and cultivated lands by the use of the district as a 'safe highway' to the Cape. Indeed, it seems that the British troops sometimes even encouraged looting in the border districts, in order to deny commandoes access to foodstuffs and facilities. Accumulation of cammandeered stock in African hands was partly the result of payment by the military for Sotho horses and ponies. In the year 1900–1, some 20 000 horses were exported from the territory, valued at nearly £263 000. Indeed, in Leribe district it was reported that the remounts were buying ponies for four or five head of cattle apiece, in value some £28 to £35. The grain trade was also lucrative for the Sotho during the war, as was the demand for labour by the military at relatively high wages – as much as three times pre-war levels.[32]

On the other hand, many Africans, perhaps most of the pre-war inhabitants of the Orange Free State farms, had much less beneficial experiences of the war. Many thousands of blacks found themselves in concentrated agricultural locations near the line of rail, where they were expected to grow their own food (although they were reduced to hoe cultivation for the most part) and provide war service to the British military as carriers, scouts and guards. By the end of the war, the population of the camps in the Orange Free State had exceeded 52 000, and shortly thereafter, as a result of the return of Africans from surrounding territories, reached 60 000. No less than 31 000 acres in all were cultivated, and in December 1901 the total produce was estimated at £44 000. While many prospered from the sale of grain and from the high wages offered, many more lost everything, including their lives from disease.[33] After the war many former black tenants in these camps proved very reluctant to return to the farms, especially since most impoverished Boers were unable to pay wages, certainly at the war-induced boom-time rates prevailing elsewhere. But perhaps more important than the impoverishment of the white farmers and the alternative employment opportunities in explaining the reluctance of blacks to re-enter tenancy agreements was the fact that so many thousands in the camps had lost their stock and equipment. For many, the land simply did not offer the possibilities of a livelihood available elsewhere.

Nevertheless, those thousands of blacks who had found refuge for themselves and their stock in Basutoland, in the Thaba Nchu reserves or in Natal, and others who had benefited from the war-time opportunities for accumulation, were quick to take advantage of this situation. A renewed wave of colonization of Orange Free State farms began. Deforestation and overgrazing in Basutoland, after a temporary reprieve caused by the deprivations of the rinderpest, were greatly accelerated by the considerable influx of population and stock during the war.[34] The consequence was that once peace had returned, the ravaged Orange Free State, denuded of stock and crops, seemed once again to many well-to-do Sotho farmers to be the natural area for expansion. These Africans had far greater economic leverage in the striking of tenancy agreements than before the war. Many white landholders welcomed with open arms any black tenant with stock and equipment who could plough and sow.[35]

Unlike many blacks, the Boers had been uniformly impoverished. Given the collapse of the stock population and the dramatic increase in the level of indebtedness amongst most Boer landowners, dependence on arable production increased greatly. To an even greater extent than the rinderpest, the war undermined the traditional Boer economy and thrust the Boers into the new world of cash-crop production, and for many this meant reliance on black tenant production or the loss of their land. Most impoverished Boers returning to their farms found themselves at first largely dependent on rations and repatriation loans from the new administration. Their position was aggravated by the drought that followed the peace.[36]

Sharecropping – or similar relationships – thus became more entrenched than ever before as a dominant relationship in the arable districts; and it was those Boer farmers who had been most vociferous in their condemnation of independent black tenant enterprise in the boom years of the mid-1890s who at this time of crisis found their survival as landed members of a ruling class dependent on cultivation by – or in partnership with – blacks. Many of these landlords, of course, regarded these forms of dependence as a temporary expedient in the wake of the conflict. Nevertheless, most must have realized that if white-controlled capitalist agriculture was to emerge victorious from the ashes of war, it would have to be on the back of a state committed to a white-supremacist political economy. And, as in the mid-1890s, this realization was to translate into another fierce populist agitation against the black farmers, once the drought had broken and the post-war depression had lifted, not much more than half a dozen years after peace had been signed.

Furthermore, new elements in the rural economy were the 700 – 800 land settlers introduced into the Orange Free State under Lord Milner's regime. These undercapitalized settlers, too, were reduced in large numbers to dependence on black tenant farmers for survival once their initial expectations of brave yeoman self-reliance had been shattered by drought, locusts and the baking African sun. The forms of 'partnership' emerging on the farms of undercapitalized, working white farmers, newcomers and old burghers alike, were often somewhat different from the largely independent and unsupervised tenant production to be found on the land of absentee landholders, and will be examined in greater detail in the final section of this chapter.

The sharecroppers, however, did not maintain their ascendancy. The balance of power undoubtedly shifted over time against them, and their terms of tenure were in time to deteriorate. The degree of dominance which they exercised over many impoverished landholders immediately after the war was not to be sustained.[37]

ABSENTEE LANDLORDS, POOR WHITES AND BLACK SHARECROPPERS

Throughout the arable Highveld, there was a great deal of absentee-owned land, whether under lease to whites or not, on which black tenants were able to farm independently and without too much interference from landlords. Increasingly toward the end of the nineteenth century, particularly during the 1890s when many Sotho and Rolong with control over productive capital were taking advantage of the land-abundant conditions on Orange Free State farms, this absentee-owned land was being turned to sharecropping purposes.

It was common for town-based members of the commercial and professional strata to invest in land as a source of income and in anticipation of a rise in value – or for land to fall into their hands in settlement of debts. Many notables had managed to accumulate numbers of farms at earlier times of low land prices – J. G. Keyter, lawyer and moneylender of Ficksburg, being one example; Charles Newberry, who had made his money at Kimberley before settling near Clocolan, another.[38] Sir John Swinburne, member of the British parliament, owned 9368 acres near Harrismith.[39] Mrs G. W. Peeters (born Voigt) of Johannesburg, owned the farms Roseberry Plain and

Saltberry Plain in the Vredefort district in the north of the territory, comprising 6333 morgen or 21 square miles. In 1900 over 5000 bags of grain were reaped by the African sharecroppers on her farms. The list of examples is endless.[40] But the most prominent of the absentee landlords were the speculative land companies, usually closely linked with mining capital, whose major purpose in land accumulation was to take advantage of the inevitable appreciation in land values, and to exploit whatever mineral wealth might lie under the earth. On the whole these speculative and mining interests were not concerned with capital investment in the improvement of such land.

In the Orange Free State, mining capital was not nearly so important in landownership as in the Transvaal. By 1900 almost one fifth of the land area in the Transvaal was claimed by speculative corporate landowners, most of it away from the arable Highveld in the as yet sparsely settled and underexploited (by whites) Middle and Lowveld regions, where many of the indigenous black peoples had only recently been subjugated.[41] In these areas the possibility of earning a profit from rent-paying black farmers was a secondary consideration – as was the possibility of securing labour for mines from tenant households. But in the Highveld areas, such as the coal-rich mid-Vaal region, where land speculators managed to accumulate property, they invariably did seize the opportunity to turn their land to profit by peopling it with sharecropping tenants.

The Orange Free State districts of Heilbron, Vredefort, Bothaville, and Kroonstad were heavily infiltrated by speculative landowners with connections with mining capital. O. W. Staten, magistrate in Heidelberg, just north of the Vaal, a district which was much affected by speculative and corporate landownership as a result of its suspected mineral wealth,[42] described the origins of the system:

> A lot of companies bought land in the Heidelberg district for their mineral values only; they had no thought for the agricultural value. Their agents found that by allowing natives to go on to the land with their ploughing implements these farms returned with the least possible trouble hundreds even thousands of bags of mealies and a very large revenue.... The most profitable thing then was to let the natives work these large areas on a share system; it was the least trouble and involved the least expenditure of capital to the large landowner and companies.[43]

Not only did rent-paying tenants provide substantial revenue, but also large quantities of grain crops necessary for feeding the large mine labour force.

Nearer the Witwatersrand gold fields, the value of sharecropping tenancy on land owned by mining companies as a means of providing subsistence for the labour force was very considerable. Thousands of Africans lived on company farms within ten or twenty miles of the gold fields, sowing land on shares and providing the mining companies with thousands of bags of maize for the compounds. So profitable was this activity for the Africans, that they also commonly paid cash rents of £6 or £7, sometimes even £10 or more in addition to the share of the crop. These locations also provided services for town and mine employees, for example, as manufacturers and sellers of liquor at weekend beer-drinking sessions.[44]

The best-known and perhaps the largest such absentee-owned estate in the mid-Vaal region was the group of twenty-two farms on either side of the Vaal River, known as the Vereeniging Estates, owned by the Lewis and Marks partnership, and which Stanley Trapido has described.[45] The tenants on these farms were aided and cushioned against loss to some extent by the provision of loans for the purchase of oxen, ploughs and seed after rinderpest and especially after the Anglo-Boer War. Indeed, the Estates, backed by a large and profitable business partnership involved in a whole range of capitalist enterprises in the fields of mining and manufacture, might have been more willing to invest in the productivity of their tenants than most such landlords. The company had a distillery and bottling factory near Pretoria which required large supplies of grain,[46] and the company's coal mines needed ready supplies of labour.

Lewis and Marks made their first acquisitions in the area in 1879 with a view to exploiting the coal resources already apparent there. The partnership, which had accumulated its capital in the eastern Transvaal gold fields and before that at the Kimberley diamond diggings, was, Trapido concludes, a rare early example of indigenous industrial capitalism, concerned to invest in every field of enterprise in which they could expect to make profits – except, before 1902, Rand gold mining. Samuel Marks in particular, in Trapido's view, was an integral member of the republican ruling class in ways in which the Randlords never were.[47]

When Marks requested permission from the Orange River Colony government to allow the exiled Rolong chief from Thaba Nchu, Samuel Moroka, and his following of about 100 families, then living in Francistown, Bechuanaland, to move on to Vereeniging Company land, he considered that they could be adequately settled on three or four of his farms. The 'usual' conditions would apply, he wrote – half the crop and a supply of labourers for the company's mines.[48] This intensity of exploitation of the ground, and the alternative possibility of drawing labour supplies, made African tenant production a major source of profit for such landowning capitalists. However, it seems that share tenants who had the wherewithal – or the network of kin – to produce reasonable crops were able to avoid mine labour.

White sharecropping tenants were by no means unknown on absentee-owned land, of course. There were a number on the Vereeniging Estates. Seven of the fourteen share tenants on Fanie Cronje's farm, Vlakplaas, near Vereeniging, were white. The Pooes found white share tenants on Oorbietjiesfontein on the banks of the Vaal in 1913.[49] But it seems clear that the white *bywoners* were almost invariably outperformed by the blacks, for reasons elaborated earlier: they needed much more land as they did not graze their animals communally or live in small kindred villages as blacks often did; they required access to tenant or wage labour and did not use family labour and reciprocal work teams; they did not have access to the web of mutual help and co-operation which cushioned blacks against flux in availability of oxen or seed; and very likely they lacked the productive skills and commitment to hard labour in the fields.[50]

The ubiquity of sharecropping relationships as opposed to fixed rentals on absentee-owned land farmed by blacks throughout the Highveld can be explained in terms of mutual advantage. Sharecropping had the great benefit for both parties that it implied a sharing of risks and rewards. The uncertainties of arable production and of markets were such that the tenants were reluctant to commit themselves to a fixed money rent in case of crop failure, stock loss, or market depression. The capitalist landlords, who could generally sell in the best markets and ride above market fluctuations, were reluctant to forego a share in the successes of their tenants in bumper years, especially if they had invested capital in improving the productivity of tenant enterprise. Grain in hand collected after the harvest was far more profitable than trying to collect cash rents of a similar value from individual African tenants who did not have the same privileged access to markets, and who often did not sell for cash and rarely kept substantial cash reserves, preferring to accumulate livestock as the major form of liquid asset. What made sharecropping a viable alternative to fixed rentals was the fact that the black sharecroppers on the whole were skilled cultivators intent upon commercial production, and the landlords could rely on intensive exploitation of the land by their tenants.

This is not to say that sharecropping relations were uniformly harmonious. Indeed, they inevitably involved conflict. The exact size of the crop which was to be distributed in predetermined shares was subject to manipulation. The African producer had plenty of opportunity to minimize the actual quantity which the absentee landlord received. Generally, there was little supervision of the sharecropper's activities and the landlords often suspected that they were being deceived.[51] One source of dissension was the African practice of picking off the ripening cobs and consuming the green maize from about January through to the harvest in June or July. This practice was commonplace and served to diminish reliance on stored grain.[52]

Landlords tried to insure themselves as far as possible against manipulation by insisting that they (or their agents) had first choice of the reaped and bagged crop. Thus the tenant could not neglect half the fields in the knowledge that that half constituted the landlord's share, nor could he separate off the poor quality grain after harvest and hand it over to the landlord. As a Wepener landlord put it, the African 'must not know what he is going to get before it is in the sack'.[53] This physical control over the crop that landlords exercised once it was in the bag no doubt enabled them to exercise some manipulation too. The provision of credit might also have enabled absentee landlords of means to exact extra produce in repayment.[54] Landlords generally attempted to extract a larger than usual share where they had some leverage over the means of production: for example, if the tenant borrowed the landlord's oxen, or if he had considerable stockholdings and required large acreages for grazing. Landlord's costs were commonly deducted from the tenant's share, and also perhaps the threshing costs.[55]

In this section we have primarily been discussing sharecropping on absentee-owned land, where the financial strength of landlords and the independence of tenants were far greater than on the land of resident white landholders. As we shall see in the final section of this chapter, very different conditions prevailed in relationships between under-capitalized white farmers and their black tenants. But first we should explore the ways in which white lessees of absentee-owned land (who could in no way be termed farmers) were able to intervene between absentee landowners and black tenants to their own advantage.

*   *   *

There were many absentee-owned farms available on lease to white farmers paying an annual rent. Many speculative landowners, particularly those living far away, were not able or willing to organize sharecropping arrangements with black peasants on their land, and were content to receive a fixed annual sum in rent from one or more white lessees. But many an impoverished white lessee of absentee-owned land was rather more enterprising in his pursuit of black-generated wealth than was the landowner. Many of those profiting from black sharecropping were not themselves landowners, but lessees of land. There were a variety of ways in which such whites could batten on to black production. It was common for three or more whites to hire a farm and then induce Africans to settle on the land to sow it for them on shares, wrote indignant petitioners to the authorities: 'the Kaffirs plough as much for themselves as they want, do nothing else, and thereby not only are markets spoilt for us, but whites are robbed of labour'. The Africans, they wrote, settled densely on such empty farms wherever they had the opportunity.[56] Clearly one means by which many whites without capital resources were able to survive on the land was by entering a partnership of this sort with black peasant producers. Such an arrangement enabled many a non-landowning Boer to maintain a foothold in rural areas while many of their brethren were moving into towns as unskilled workers.

Referring to the widespread occurrence of sharecropping by black tenants, Acting Governor R. D. Allason wrote in 1908:

> This unsatisfactory condition arises from the fact that there are very many indigent white persons who for years have been sinking in the social scale and are prepared to do anything possible to earn a livelihood as long as they are not compelled by necessity to do any manual labour. These persons act as intermediaries between the wealthy natives and the white owners of farms. They lease farms in their own names, reside on them but allow the well-to-do natives to make use of the farm and in fact become servants of the native. The native is really the lessee of the farm and the white man is simply kept for the sake of appearance. They get as many natives on the farm as possible and they simply live on the proceeds of the natives' labour.[57]

Allason's observations were supported by F. A. S. Schimper, a wealthy farmer of Winburg, who noted in 1911 that Africans 'who are today ruling the roost, are getting white men to hire farms for them, and employing white men to superintend their ploughing'.[58] Schimper wrote in 1905:

> Where the white man lost everything he possessed during the war, the native made capital out of it and as a rule a good many natives have wagons and oxen, whereas the poorer farmers have only their families

and nothing wherewith to support them, under these circumstances the poor farmer hires a piece of ground the rent of which is paid by the native and the farmer lives with the native as *Bywoner*.

There was an example of this on a farm neighbouring his own, testified Schimper.[59] Such relationships flourished as long as there was absentee-owned land which propertyless whites could exploit. Partnerships of convenience between poor whites and black sharecroppers were commented on at a meeting of the Petrus Steyn Farmers' Association in the Orange Free State maize belt in 1924. P. Olivier reportedly 'lamented' the 'prevailing custom among farmers, mostly of the lessee type with insufficient draught animals, to allow natives owning trek oxen, practically to plough farms on half shares of the mealie crop'. Olivier urged members of the association 'to take a lead in fighting this evil'.[60] Corroborative oral testimony comes from Kodisang Phalime who explains the origins of sharecropping in these terms:

> Whites who moved to towns hired out their farms. Those who leased them were poor and they wanted our livestock to work for them . . . . That is how sharing . . . came about. A span and the plough were mine. The landlord who leased the land did not spend anything.[61]

But there were also possibilities for profit by very different white lessees of absentee-owned land. Petitioners from Hoopstad pointed to men who lived outside the state altogether, who hired five or ten farms and then allowed blacks to cultivate them on halves. Such absentee lessees were presumably often men of means living in towns who were indulging in some profitable speculation as a sideline.[62] Jameson Molete remembers sharecropping in the second decade of the century near Koppies in the northern Orange Free State on a farm hired by a man named Bloch who lived elsewhere. 'There were these Jews who hired farms especially for farming with blacks', recalls Molete. The turnover of such speculative lessees of land could be quite high, it seems, some hiring land for a year or two in order to make a quick profit.[63] This phenomenon perhaps explains the folklore found in more than one informant's recollections from that part of the world that black tenants prospered as long as 'Jews' (a reference, perhaps, also to Samuel Marks) were in charge of the 'government', and that they began to suffer when the 'Boers' took over.

The provision that only two black heads of nuclear families could live on any farm uninhabited by whites, first included in the anti-squatting law of 1881 and repeated in the 1895 law, was intended to undermine the viability of tenancy agreements on absentee-owned land. But the provision was easy enough to circumvent (although, of course, these laws were never effectively implemented). In deference to the anti-squatting law, such landlords often induced a landless white to live on the farm by offering him land for his own use, or else by nominally letting their land to a poor white, who would then act as a front while the independent black farmers cultivated the soil and handed over the rent. A Frankfort justice of the peace and farmer described a common arrangement:

> There are a class of people in this Colony – I cannot call them farmers – who do not think it beneath them to go in with natives. Some live and have businesses in town, buy or rent a farm, squat a poor white on it to say it is occupied by a white man. Then they put five heads of natives on and get them to cultivate on shares. Of course, the native is practically his own master.[64]

Many land companies were increasingly inclined to place nominal white lessees on their land on the Highveld to avoid the stigma attached to 'Kaffir farming'. The intervention of poor white middlemen became increasingly common on absentee-owned land as white opinion became more and more sensitized to the social and economic threat posed by independent black tenant production, especially in the years immediately before 1913.[65]

No doubt in such cases the white *bywoner* often filled the role of representative of the landowner in his dealings with the tenants, and perhaps acted as a 'spy' to ensure that the landlord was not cheated of his share of the yield by keeping a watch over the growing crops. They might also have acted as witnesses of the reaping and bagging on the landlord's behalf. But, as the Kromellenboog Farmers' Association complained in 1904: 'as the *bywoners* who in some cases also reside on these farms have no right to exercise any control over these natives they (the natives) are in reality lessees of the ground they occupy'.[66] Jameson Molete remembers that on Bloch's farm on which he sharecropped there lived an Afrikaner who was hired to watch the farm. He was 'just a peasant', recalls Molete, and the black tenants were under no obligation to provide him with labour.[67]

Indeed, it seems that on occasion the black farmers took the initiative and persuaded a poor and landless white man to hire land on their behalf, while they paid the rent. This was risky though, as Ndae Makume found out at a later date when he hired a government farm near Lindley for £360 per annum, the best in the area, he maintained, yielding some 2000 bags of maize in good seasons. Surrounding whites became suspicious as the white man to whom Makume gave the money to pay the rent (one Loot-Jan Graaff) was known to be penniless. Even the two cows he milked were lent him by Makume. The local farmers hired a lawyer, de Wet, who applied to the court and had the contract cancelled. That such arrangements were not uncommon emerges perhaps from the fact that de Wet expressed his sympathy and suggested that Makume should have leased the farm through him, as nobody would then have questioned the arrangement. Lawyers were notorious absentee landlords, after all. The magistrate too was sympathetic, and told Makume that his mistake had been to form a partnership with a poor white. This apparently was too brazen a display of black enterprise for local whites to stomach. Absentee landlords, whether lessees or landowners, could perform the same function as this poor white man, but at a greater profit to themselves than poor whites were able to elicit.[68] As was observed earlier, populist outrage at such examples of black economic independence and prosperity was unlikely to be shared by the most marginalized in Boer society; and the private behaviour of individual entrepreneurs often conflicted with public perceptions of morality.[69]

*   *   *

The guerilla struggle which raged between the absentee landlords and the new colonial administration after the Anglo-Boer War is revealing as to both the interests of the corporate and speculative landowners, and the perceptions and priorities of the new British rulers. From the start the British under Lord Milner's social-imperialist leadership tackled their task of rural social engineering with determination. If they were to create a class of small-scale cash-crop producers on the land to feed the internal markets, and if these cultivators were to be state-subsidized British settlers rather than a black peasantry, then a labour force had to be provided for them. So an important aspect of British policy in the Orange Free State was the dispersal of the black locations and 'squatter' communities which were assembling after the conclusion of the war, and the forced creation of a black working class. The arable belt of the Orange Free State was seen as the most promising region for the emergence of an intensive capitalist agriculture. It was in the Orange Free State, therefore, that the British set about vigorously enforcing the republican anti-squatting legislation, which placed a limit of five on the number of black families allowed on any one farm, and which, as we have seen, had never been effectively implemented before. The new class of British yeoman farmers were not intended to be so self-reliant as to do without the services of a complement of black workers on their land. The British even went so far as to interpret the law as stating that only if the white man living on a farm were a *bona fide* lessee would the farm be deemed to be 'occupied' and therefore entitled to the full complement of five nuclear households instead of only two.

With the optimism of the uninitiated, the British set about attempting to disperse and distribute African tenant families in keeping with the supposed needs of progressive English-speaking arable farmers, who, they hoped, would soon people the Highveld.[70] However, they soon came up against the dissent of the vested interests, in the form, amongst others, of the Vereeniging Estates Company, which had quickly re-established its operations at the end of the war, making liberal loans and grants for restocking.[71]

The reconstruction administration very quickly proved a threat to these arrangements. Before the war the company had what the magistrate in Heilbron called a 'tacit understanding' with the republican government that the anti-squatting law would not be enforced. In September 1902 the magistrate enquired of the new authorities in Bloemfontein whether the company should be allowed to take back its old tenants, thereby enabling the Taaibosch refugee camp to close down. He asked whether the company's 'method of farming, which makes a virtual native reserve of a valuable piece of country, should be encouraged'. The reply reflected the administration's first flush of enthusiasm to re-order the colonial economy: 'the alleged "tacit understanding" with the late Government should be not recognized', and the terms of the law 'should be enforced in the case of the Vereeniging Estates Company as in the case of any other'. This attitude contrasted sharply with that of the Transvaal authorities, whose primary concern was to re-establish the mining industry rather than with the rural order, and who from the very first were prepared to allow the old order to be re-established on the company's farms north of the Vaal.[72]

Despite the administration's determination to undermine the black tenantry once and for all, there was little that they could practically do short of large-scale demographic engineering based on systematic coercion. Eventually in September 1904 the authorities in Bloemfontein informed the magistrate that no action should be taken against the company no matter how many Africans were settled on its land, as a relaxation of the law with regard to its farms had been authorized.[73]

This amounted in effect to an admission of defeat by the colonial administration. It had had to learn an old lesson anew: that it was impossible to restructure productive relations in the countryside by mere legislative edict or administrative fiat.[74] Black sharecropping on absentee-owned land endured as long as landlords profited from the greater relative productivity and lesser relative risk of black enterprise.

THE BLACK HOUSEHOLD ECONOMY

Sharecropping relationships, especially on absentee-owned land where supervision was minimal, depended not on coercion, but on a balance of interests. The viability and profitability of sharecropping for the landlord depended on the willingness of the tenant household to maximize its output. Investment in advanced implements, the mobilization of family labour resources and a commercial orientation to productive activities were preconditions of successful sharecropping.[75] Not surprisingly, as we shall see, the most productive sharecropping families seem to have been Christian, for in Christianity were to be found the cultural values required for the adoption of entrepreneurial attitudes.

Intensive sharecropping implied an immersion in the colonial economy and a subservience to market relationships. Many of the Sotho migrating out of Basutoland by the 1890s had been producing grain for markets for at least a couple of decades, and had accumulated the capital, acquired the technology and adopted the new attitudes toward labour, production and exchange which were the prerequisites of sharecropping over the border on the farms of the Orange Free State, where they were free of chiefly exactions and constraints. We are dealing here with people very different from the herders and subsistence cultivators of an earlier era. A number of informants describe harvests of several hundred bags of maize in a season (even 800 or 900) as not unusual for a single sharecropping household.[76] Sharecroppers who ploughed 40 or 60 acres, produced 300 or 400 bags of maize or more a year (as well as sorghum for consumption and – in the better-watered areas – wheat), owned a few spans of oxen and a flock of sheep, as well as advanced implements such as double-furrow ploughs, planters and harrows, were not at all uncommon.[77]

But by no means were all sharecroppers equally prosperous or productive. No doubt a large proportion of tenant families led an altogether more precarious existence, mixing sharecropping with labour tenancy, and possibly drifting in and out of sharecropping relations as shifting family fortunes and circumstances permitted. The extent of flux undoubtedly experienced by families should not be underestimated.[78] Sharecropping agreements might include the supply of a male adolescent throughout the year for work such as herding the landlord's stock, as well as a woman for housework or washing. It was quite usual for no wages to be paid for such services, although many of the better-off and more independent sharecropping families refused to provide labour services. Indeed, many families experienced a bewildering succession of contracts of tenancy as they moved from farm to farm, some involving crop-sharing, some labour service, and others a combination of the two. Apart from the Christian elite, who perhaps enjoyed a greater off-farm income, sharecroppers did not necessarily constitute a discrete stratum of farm tenants.

In the eastern districts, the major commercial crop from the opening of the diamond fields in the 1870s was wheat. In the drier northern districts wheat cultivation was rare, except on river banks and under irrigation. Sharecroppers in general seem to have grown much more maize than sorghum, although the latter was their staple from which sour porridge was made. For many, maize was not yet a major item of diet at the beginning of the century. Petrus Pooe remembers that maize meal became the staple only when they got to Johannesburg. Abraham Mokale ate it first in the Boer War camps. From the earliest days maize was used in the mine compounds. The more labour-intensive and less productive sorghum did not lend itself to commercial production on a large scale, although it generally fetched a far higher price than maize. When in 1906 the Vereeniging Estates manager tried to take the higher-priced sorghum instead of maize as the company's share of the crop, the tenants protested so strongly that the board had to step in. Sorghum, a crop grown only by blacks for the most part, required far greater care throughout the growing season than did maize. 'A sorghum producer had to trim his field, put up scarecrows, and be there in person every morning and every evening to drive the birds away' explains Petrus Pooe.[79]

A certain degree of investment in improved implements and methods was necessary if the sharecropper was to produce large surpluses. Steel ploughs and good seed were required. Two-share ploughs (known as *mmadiketane*) were fairly common amongst the sharecroppers. Large spans of fourteen or sixteen oxen were commonly used in the fields. Planters were not uncommon, though broadcast sowing was still the rule; wealthy sharecroppers like the Ngakanes at Vlakplaas had planters and never scattered their seed by hand. Harrows were also commonly used by sharecroppers. The Pooes used an itinerant maize-threshing machine for the first time on the farm Oorbietjiesfontein during or after the First World War and paid 9*d* a bag to the owner of the machine. The Ngakanes used steam threshers at the same time, taking two or three weeks to complete the work on the farm.[80]

Sharecroppers disposed of their often considerable surpluses to local storekeepers, merchants or millers.[81] Riding crops to market required access to wagons, and those who owned wagons controlled a valuable resource from which they could earn a profit, either by hiring them out or by riding transport themselves, apart from the advantages of being able to seek out the best market for their produce. Kodisang Phalime at Donderskop in Vrede district remembers that the tenants 'formed companies' for the transport of produce to the railway station.[82] The poorer labour tenants who did not sharecrop or produce commercially and lacked access to transport facilities would dispose of their small surpluses to the nearest small storekeeper or dealer – often itinerant – who would buy a basketful at a time and then bag the grain himself.[83]

Work on the fields amongst the black sharecroppers (unlike that amongst the white *bywoners*) was a joint effort in which women and children participated. Women in sharecropping families (which seem to have been overwhelmingly monogamous)[84] did the hoeing and weeding and played a major role in the reaping and threshing. Quite young boys and girls aided in these activities. Men were responsible for the heavy work, and were indispensable to successful ploughing of the land and transporting the crop. The success and the resilience of many black tenant farmers is explained by their use of household labour, supplemented by their access to communal work teams, especially amongst kin. The mutual help and support provided by kinship networks survived the fragmenting of large settlement groups which was the usual consequence of their settling on the farms.

But although the potential for fission was clearly very considerable under sharecropping arrangements, it also seems to have been still common for married sons to remain under the authority of their fathers in tenant families, forming extended homesteads. When Tloaele Mokale settled on the Vereeniging Estates before the Anglo-Boer War, his adult children still felt obliged to work for him, although they had children of their own. They had to plough his land first, and he controlled the family's stock, allocating each year's lambs to each son in turn.[85] On Gert Muller's farm in the northern Orange Free State in the 1890s, Kodisang Phalime's father and uncles sharecropped under the authority of their father. They had some three spans of sixteen oxen each, as well as perhaps 300 sheep, goats and horses, most of which belonged to Kodisang's grandfather. Kodisang, the eldest of his father's sons, worked for Muller as a shepherd, while his brothers stayed at home helping in the family fields.[86] Ndae Makume remembers that:

> children of olden days used not to leave their parents immediately after getting married, they were supposed to stay on and work under their parents. Even your wife was supposed to stay with your parents and cook for them. We had a separate hut where I slept with my wife but during the day she had to work at my parents' home. In those days my wife was regarded as my parents' wife, not mine. The old man had authority over us.[87]

All the stock was also under his father's (or grandfather's) control, no matter that a junior member had earned them. This prosperous family of tenant farmers was perhaps unusually cohesive, but their capacity for accumulation is undoubted.

Often several sharecropping households who were of the same patrilineage or related by marriage – brothers-in-law, cousins – would stay close to each other, often on the same farm, perhaps forming a small village settlement, and would pool their labour resources, even though farming separate productive units. This was especially the case where the heads of the separate households were of the same generation without the controlling influence of a senior generation. If a household moved, they often sought tenancy on land already occupied by kinsmen. On Fanie Cronje's farm, Vlakplaas near Vereeniging, the seven black tenant families consisted of Paulus Ngakane, his brothers and cousins. Naphtali Pooe and his two brothers held tenancies on one of the Vereeniging Estates farms. Petrus Pooe's parental family lived side by side with his father's two brothers' families on the farm Arcadia, Heilbron. When a sharecropping family moved on to a farm, it was common for them to invite brothers or cousins to join them. This was a crucial factor in the successes of these households as peasant producers. The labour resources at the disposal of such sharecropping families were considerable, and the degree of reciprocity they practised insured them against deprivation in the event of the failure of a crop or the loss of oxen.[88]

It was possible to exploit kinship networks to enter sharecropping, even though one did not have the requisite plough oxen or equipment. Usually those without the resources to work the land themselves entered labour-tenancy agreements, but it was possible for households with ties of kinship to established sharecropping communities to establish themselves as independent producers in their own right. Oxen for ploughing were frequently loaned to those who did not have enough. In such instances they 'would borrow additional cattle from neighbours especially during the fallowing season when there was need to get the cattle used to being inspanned'.[89]

Abraham Mokale recalls of the Vereeniging Estates that those who had no oxen would have their lands ploughed by those who had a span, although they balked at providing seed for their neighbours, as lack of seed apparently implied improvidence. When Morobane Ngakane's father settled on Fanie Cronje's farm, Vlakplaas, after the Anglo-Boer War, he had no cattle. Since all the other black tenants were brothers or cousins of his, he was able in no time to establish himself as a successful and well-off farmer. Ngakane had reason to believe that he could enter sharecropping by exploiting the resources of his kinsfolk, and so to establish productive viability.[90]

Inevitably perhaps, informants' memories of labour co-operation during the heyday of the sharecropping economy are coloured by romanticism. Dinah Molope Pooe, looking back over seventy years or more, remembers the mutual aid in the fields amongst sharecropping communities of the northern Orange Free State with self-confessed amazement. But, she adds:

> If you had had your sister, brother or neighbour helping you on a certain day, it was a matter of custom that they should go home with baskets full of maize, sorghum or whatever you were handling on that day. Or if it so happened that he or she had been with you for a few days, you would have no option but to give a bag or bags for him to take away.[91]

When the harvest on Zaaiplaas failed in 1895, Emelia Molefe and her mother paid an extended visit to her aunt in Rustenburg district in the Transvaal, assisting in the harvest and threshing of wheat. At the end of the season, her aunt gave them ten bags of sorghum.[92] At harvest time especially kinship networks were activated, sometimes over fairly long distances.

However, it is likely that these somewhat idyllic accounts of reciprocity and co-operation obscure part of the picture. For new social relationships seem to have been emerging as well. Clearly reciprocal labour between sharecropping households was general, especially when ties of kinship were present, as was often the case. But it is probable that very much less equal relationships also flourished. The labour tenants on the farms – those who did not have the resources for independent production – provided labour for the sharecroppers, especially during the hoeing, harvesting and threshing seasons. They participated in the work parties (*matsema*) where beer and slaughtered sheep were served to the workers.[93]

It seems that amongst wealthier sharecroppers, such arrangements between tenant farmer and labour tenants were indicative of a considerable degree of class differentiation. The differentiation between the sharecropper with 60 acres and the capital to cultivate them and the labour tenant with inadequate productive resources and little more than his labour power to sell suggests that the relations between them were asymmetrical to the point at which they began to seem like class relations, whatever form remuneration took. Indeed a number of informants remember labour being hired for wages in cash or kind.[94]

Further, it was unlikely that new or disadvantaged households without supports of kinship could very easily establish independent tenant production by tapping communal resources. It may be significant that families immigrating from the eastern Cape were often regarded as more exploitable and poorer than most tenants.[95] The efficacy of neighbourliness between strangers was being undermined as a social force. One can perhaps detect in some of the oral evidence, such as that of Emelia Pooe, a nascent class consciousness in their relations with the poorer tenants, although it might be the product of hindsight. Significantly, the Pooes were always in a position to refuse terms which included the rendering of labour service to white landlords.[96]

The process of class formation which was giving birth to a sharecropping elite very likely had much to do with the adoption of Christianity. It is unclear whether their Christianity was a consequence of their economic status or vice versa. Either way, Christianity implied not only a concern for accumulation, improvement, and material achievement, but also a commitment to education.[97] Despite the demands on family labour and family wages for productive purposes, many of these sharecropping families were concerned to ensure that their children were fitted for better things than a life of work in the fields. Many were clearly sufficiently well-to-do to form an embryonic educated elite. It was their commitment to education as much as their material success which marked them as an elite. The link between the two was very likely their greater access to off-farm income.

Christianity and education were important elements in the lives of many of the sharecroppers. When in 1913–14 many sharecroppers from the northern Orange Free State moved on to their recently bought farm,

Swartrand, near Ventersdorp in the Transvaal, they petitioned to have their Presbyterian minister, Abraham Poho of Heilbron, transferred to their new home.[98] Poho, like so many of these sharecroppers, emanated from a family which took refuge in Basutoland during the *Difaqane* and left the territory toward the end of the nineteenth century.[99] What seems to emerge from this evidence is an extensive network of sharecroppers and tenant farmers throughout the northern Orange Free State bound together in part by kinship and partly by adherence to Christianity, consisting of emigrés from Moshoeshoe's kingdom, many of whom originated in the western Transvaal before the disruption caused by the Ndebele wars (and therefore constituted perhaps a distinct alien identity in what was in any event a very disparate Sotho state). Indeed, their status in Basutoland probably inclined them to conversion before the diaspora on to the farms.

Naphtali Pooe, one of the purchasers of Swartrand, learnt to write Afrikaans with the white farmer's sons and taught at the schools on the farms where he sharecropped. 'After the harvest', his wife remembers, 'when the schools were on he used to get somebody to replace him in his fields so that he could go back to school.'[100] Schools seem to have been common on the farms in the sharecropping districts – often built on the initiative of the tenant communities themselves. Barney Ngakane remembers that the tenant community on the farm Vlakplaas on which he grew up near Vereeniging built the school, made the benches and approached the Methodist Church to provide a teacher, one Mashabani. The success of the school and the fact that the teacher produced better results than those achieved in the local white school was a cause of great resentment, and eventually the school was forcibly closed in about 1912. Nevertheless, young Barney went on to school in the Evaton township (staying with relatives) and the Methodists' Kilnerton Training Institute near Pretoria (where the boarding fees were £10 per year). Peasant farming and rural accumulation were clearly an important base for the emergence of a black political elite in twentieth-century South Africa, of which Barney Ngakane is an outstanding example.[101]

The fact that both these extended families, the Pooes and Ngakanes were settled in close proximity undoubtedly facilitated the provision of labour in the fields and increased their capacity to accumulate. But there seems still to have been some tension between the educational imperative and the requirements of labour in the fields. Petrus Pooe recalls that:

in those days schools were not run the way they are now. The major job for boys was looking after cattle. A boy did not have the full week to himself or for schooling. Each of the boys went to school in turn. That is why we never became really educated.

Pooe, unlike Ngakane, ended up working at the Johannesburg fresh produce market for twenty-two years and his son entered domestic service.[102] Petrus' uncle Naphtali Pooe, the teacher, naturally wanted to provide an education for his own children. He offered Rantshawe, his son, the proceeds of a plot especially set aside so that he could continue his schooling elsewhere. But none of Naphtali's children got very far at school. His wife, when pressed for an explanation, said that 'in those times...much time was spent in looking after cattle and milking cows'.[103]

But other sharecroppers had not imbibed the Christian ethic and did not care much for the white man's teaching. Jameson Molete, who was born in 1904 and grew up in the northern Orange Free State, had to struggle with his father in order to attend school:

> My father had a lot of livestock and cared little about school, but I liked it. I would go to school and the following day look after the cattle, just like that. It was because I was determined, otherwise I would not have gone to school.

His parents, recalls Molete, 'did not realize that education does not decay and that it is not destroyed by sun, drought and starvation. What they wanted was land and animals; they did not realize that education is important'. Molete, who in later years became a local township politician of some importance in Kroonstad, was the last-born in his family. His brothers received no education at all, as they were too busy helping with the farming. It is possible that parental control over the last-born was commonly looser than over his elder siblings, and that the youngest was most inclined to seek alternative avenues of accumulation and improvement to those offered by the land, given the fact that much parental wealth might already have been distributed by the time he reached marriageable age. But when the young Jameson left the farm (Doringspruit, near Kroonstad) permanently after the Great War to work in town and to further his education (against his father's wishes), the 9*s* he earned per week went into buying grain bags for his father. 'Now the little money I tried to save for my education was taken by him, when he bought the empty bags for his crops.' Jameson could not completely break his ties with his kin group, and the battle for control over his wages was won by his father.[104]

Indeed, conflict over the proceeds of wage labour performed by household members seems to have been common. Tensions seem often to have arisen from competing demands on wages, between family heads concerned with maintaining rural production, and juniors with new consumption requirements. Petrus Pooe reveals some of the pressures at work in explaining why he abandoned peasant farming for town employment:

> We wanted to be gentlemen.... We wanted to wash, be clean and well-dressed. Guys would come back from Johannesburg with these trousers on. We would think to ourselves that we could be like them if we went to Johannesburg. We looked down on young men who walked barefooted and had cracked feet covered with red soil all the time.[105]

For many homestead heads, maintaining control over the labour as well as the wages of household members was critical to their continued success as sharecroppers. Crises arose within individual homesteads as dependent children grew to adulthood and were confronted with the possibilities of escaping from the authority of the seniors. Indeed, it is clear that eventually young men and women became increasingly inclined to move into economic activities more promising than peasant farming, more particularly once the boom period of sharecropping prosperity had ended. The eventual decline of the black rural economy was due not only to the double squeeze of state pressures and white capitalization, but also to the break-up of the family as a productive unit.[106] Wage labour no doubt enabled many juniors to accumulate independently of parental control, and was a major factor in the hiving-off of young married couples from parental authority. A more egalitarian distribution of resources, particularly stock, was most certainly not in the interests of the older homestead heads.

Whatever the dangers of loss of control over the labour and wages of juniors, wage labour in towns was an important form of accumulation for many sharecropping families. The reinvestment of proceeds in rural production was essential for many in order to maintain the viability of the household economy in bad years, or simply in order to pay taxes or debts to storekeepers. Many tenant families were not sufficiently well-off to survive on the proceeds of tenant production alone year in and year out (especially since labour service of tenants was not usually paid for). When in 1914 Johannes Moiloa returned to his family on Theuns Wessels' farm near Winburg after two years on the railways at Bloemfontein and on the mines at Kimberley, he handed over £30 to his father, much to the latter's joy. Kodisang Phalime, whose family lived on farms in the northern Orange Free State, remembers that migrants saved their money and rather than send it home, which was risky, they would hide it and on their return to the farms would secrete it in an armband on the upper arm.[107] The wage earners' labour was only seasonally required in parental fields, and during periods of low labour intensity in the annual cycle, there was probably a disproportionate number of adolescents, women and older members of peasant families employed in productive activities on the land.

The importance of wage-earning for the viability and expansion of rural production is perhaps reflected in the common complaint amongst white farmers that the stock grazing on their farms included the animals of tenants' relatives who worked in the towns. R. Seggie of Holfontein wrote of an African tenant in his neighbourhood whose herd of cattle had swollen from eight to seventy-five since moving on to the farm four years previously:

> The fact is this, the native has several brothers working on the Rand, and all their wages go into stock, and the native ploughing on shares puts this stock on his 'boss's' farm, without even asking liberty to do so.[108]

The extended family network so vital to the success of the sharecropping enterprise is clearly discerned in this distribution of stock into the care of relatives on the farms. 'The custom of the native' said one white farmer, 'is to divide his cattle amongst his family: he does not lose the ownership.'[109] Townward migration with the explicit intention to restock after the rinderpest epizootic or the Anglo-Boer War was particularly common.

But notwithstanding access to wage income, there were substantial obstacles to accumulation for most tenant families. Insecurity of tenure on the farms was one major inhibiting factor. Permanent improvements or soil conservation were seldom worthwhile under these circumstances. Even houses regularly had to be abandoned. The fact that accumulation in tenant families generally took the form of investment in stock itself made incremental accumulation over the long term difficult. Moving from one farm to another usually took a toll on stock, especially as it took place after the harvest in the middle of winter.[110] Stock was also vulnerable to natural disasters such as rinderpest or drought. Animal disease was widespread and difficult to control given the nature of the state's resources. Thus a natural check was maintained on African herds and flocks and black accumulation of wealth, quite apart from the limitations placed on tenants' stock by landlords. Stockholdings collapsed after the rinderpest outbreak of 1896–7, followed by the devastation accompanying the Anglo-Boer War of 1899–1902. The rapid recovery of the stock population in the post-war decade presented the black tenants with new insecurities. A very common cause of tenant evictions was the unwillingness of landlords to cater for large stock numbers and the refusal of tenants to dispose of their flocks and herds. During the period of financial boom after 1908 for instance, when more and more land was being turned to maize cultivation and arable land was becoming a valuable resource for black and white alike, evictions of wealthy stockowning tenants reached alarming proportions.[111] In the long run, of course, no one was immune from the blows of dispossession and subjugation. The large multi-generational settlement group declined with the declining capacity of the seniors to control the accumulation and deployment of productive resources under landlord pressure, as well as their declining capacity to control the labour and wage income of juniors.

Redistributive aspects of the black rural economy were a further factor inhibiting individual accumulation. A degree of class formation was indeed taking place. The sharecropping elite, more specifically the Christians, were forging a new identity, as we have seen. But even though relatively considerable productive capacity was concentrated in the hands of individual households, kinship obligations still remained intact. Even where the extended homestead had given way to the nuclear household (as was generally the case with the Christian elite) there still seems to have been a sense in which the patrilineage had a claim on the accumulated capital, particularly the livestock, as well as labour resources, should these be required to commence or re-establish tenant farming.[112]

One aspect of the levelling tendencies of the redistributive economy was bridewealth, an important social institution amongst farm tenants, including the Christians.[113] Kodisang Phalime paid eighteen oxen and cows when he got married in the Vrede district before the First World War – the standard number at the time apparently. He maintains that his family's wealth declined as a result of this and also the loss of cattle incurred while trekking from farm to farm. On the other hand, Johannes Moiloa, who was left with only a calf after his father died on Theuns Wessels' farm near Winburg (his half-brother having removed the rest of the stock) became an independent producer when his eldest sister married. 'God came to my rescue as . . . I came into possession of her *lobola* cattle. Those were the cattle that made me a man.' His haul comprised eighteen animals – fifteen cattle plus a horse and sheep. However, Johannes in his turn had to hand over a large herd on his own marriage.[114]

It is not clear to what extent indebtedness was a major aspect of the sharecropping economy. The Vereeniging Estates certainly made loans to their tenants, and credit from landlords, deducted from the tenants' shares, was a widespread arrangement. There is little evidence to suggest that debt peonage was ever an important aspect of the system. But the vulnerability of some Africans was noted in 1911 by the magistrate in Fouriesburg, who wrote that Africans were becoming 'far too fond' of borrowing from white men and in many cases had to pay very high rates of interest, such as 2*s* per £1 per month.[115] This usurious rate is evidence of the weak financial position of Africans who were unable to borrow from banks or other financial institutions and were thrown at the mercy of the local moneylenders, who then presumably expropriated the crop after harvest at a price which was highly advantageous to themselves.

If the African producer found that he had sold a greater proportion of his crop than he could afford as a result of large debts or a poor harvest, he might have to buy back again later in the season at a much higher price than he had received. This predicament, which was common to black and white producers alike, was widely noted. The Bothaville magistrate tells us that Africans bought seed at from 15*s* to 20*s* per bag, yet they sold their maize at from 5*s* 6*d* to 7*s* 9*d* per bag and their sorghum at 12*s*. Several magistrates reported in 1910 that Africans kept only enough for their own subsistence after harvest. This financial vulnerability was noted by the magistrate in Winburg when he wrote that 'unless the Native has a reserve of cash or foodstuffs (a remote contingency) he must either run into debt with his "partner", the farmer, or resort to questionable means of subsistence pending the marketable stage of his crops'.[116] In these cases, wage labour away from the farm by members of tenant households became an essential means of maintaining rural production. However, we are not dealing here with the wealthier sharecropping elite, but probably with those caught in far more servile relationships.

The nature of the sharecropping community can perhaps be better understood if we compare the Highveld sharecropping districts which are the focus of our attention, with other regions where sharecropping was conspicuous by its absence despite the ubiquity of absentee-owned land. After the Anglo-Boer War, Africans in the northeast of the Orange Free State (Harrismith/Vrede districts) were reported to be paying rents of £5 per 'hut' (a unit of payment which implied that individual women in polygymous households still had some organizational control over arable production). In this area of dense settlement and advanced state formation before the *Difaqane*, the slow process of white settlement on the large tracts of absentee-owned land was to an extent superimposed on independent black communities which had re-established themselves after the *Difaqane*. Whites moving in, particularly from the 1870s and 1880s on, had met with fierce resistance and a determination to protect communal resources by the local Sotho and Zulu. Polygyny and large patrilineal village communities were the norm here. The tradition of chiefly rule and the reality of chiefly authority were still strong at the end of the nineteenth century, and in the political campaign to reclaim the land after the Anglo-Boer War, the Tlokoa and Kholokoe chiefly families were in the forefront as representatives of popular struggle, even going to London in deputation in 1907 to press their cause. The refusal to enter sharecropping relationships here (and also the absence of such arrangements in adjacent Natal and in the Middleveld and Lowveld of the Transvaal where similar conditions of chiefly authority prevailed) should be seen as part of the larger history of resistance to the alienation of resources such as land and labour, by Africans who had never committed themselves to the colonial economy in the ways that the Sotho emigrés of the sharecropping Highveld had.[117]

BLACK PRODUCTIVE RESOURCES AND WHITE ACCUMULATION: FORMS OF PARTNERSHIP ON THE LAND

It should now be apparent that black commercial producers thrived on white-owned farms of the arable Highveld at a time of unprecedentedly rapid capitalization in the rural economy of the region. This was not only because they fed expanding urban markets in foodstuffs and enriched speculative and corporate landowners. In the transition to capitalist farming the productive resources, the capital and the organizational skills of black tenants played an important role in white capitalization on the land. It is this crucial aspect of the sharecropping economy – the dialectic between the undercapitalized condition of white farmers and the relatively considerable productive resources of many black cultivators – that we now address.

Despite the importance of the absentee landlord in the political economy of the arable Highveld, the bulk of the land was under the formal control of resident white landholders (lessees as well as owners)[118] whose sole source of income was from the land, either worked under their own direct control using black labour, or worked by independent surplus-producing black tenants – or some combination of the two. Many of the white farmers had black sharecroppers on their land at one time or another, and most benefited from the productive resources – the implements, oxen and know-how – of their tenants. White landholders who were essentially farmers themselves turned to sharecropping arrangements with black tenants in fairly large numbers, as a result largely of their own lack of capital resources. Those white farmers who were most dependent on the surplus production of their black tenants were generally the poorer and less capitalized, who were therefore the most vulnerable to land loss and expropriation at a time when more and more private capital was seeking lucrative investment in the land against mortgage bonds, when mercantile credit was easily obtainable and the relative self-sufficiency of the Boer family was eroding.[119] And, as we have seen, the relative vulnerability and dependence of the white arable farmers increased substantially as a result of the devastation caused by drought, rinderpest and war.

The significance of the capital constraints blocking capitalist agriculture can best be understood by examining the productive processes involved. A one-share plough drawn by oxen can turn no more than about two or three acres of ground per day. Climatic conditions on the South African Highveld dictate that ploughing be completed in as short a period as possible, since rain comes in sharp, intense thundershowers, and the soil is wet enough for easy ploughing only for relatively short periods. Before the age of motor traction, farmers who were dependent on arable production for their survival were hard-pressed to get a large acreage under crops.

Thus by the late 1890s some capitalized white farmers in the Orange Free State used more than twenty ploughs simultaneously.[120] This might require the labour of up to sixty workers (including children as leaders of the span) plus 120 or 160 head of oxen at the least. Not surprisingly, given the labour and capital constraints experienced by white farmers, most were simply incapable of mobilizing resources on this scale. J. H. Oberholzer, *Volksraad* member for Ladybrand, complained in 1897 that burghers in his ward had had to curtail their ploughing many times as a result of a lack of servants.[121] Under these circumstances, it was a more viable proposition to draw off a surplus from a number of individual peasant households working with their own implements and oxen. Hence the partiality for sharecropping arrangements amongst so many white farmers. George Tylden, a farmer of Ladybrand district, defended sharecropping relationships in the following terms in 1908:

> Very few of us Boers ... can afford to keep more than one span of oxen to plough with ... it means too much capital locked up in

animals which do not increase. This means that in our extremely short ploughing seasons we cannot bring a sufficient proportion of our land under cultivation . . . . The farmer therefore gives one or more of these natives, who own perhaps three spans between them, a certain amount of land to plough. The boy finds the labour and often the seed, and gives the owner of the farm half the crop grown.[122]

Another Orange Free State farmer wrote in 1913 that in many parts the rainfall was 'so small and far between that a farmer considers himself lucky if he manages to get in a few bags of grain'. In consequence, he wrote, if blacks were prevented from ploughing on shares for their white landlords, the latter would ultimately be forced into bankruptcy. 'The rich man will perhaps be able to pull through, but the small farmer will suffer.'[123]

There was not necessarily a division between sharecropping landlords on the one hand, and those on the other who directly controlled productive activities on their land. Both types of relationship often coexisted on the same farm. As we have seen, there was a considerable degree of differentiation within the African tenantry, and while many tenants had the wherewithal to succeed as sharecroppers to their own as well as to their landlords' benefit, others were more dependent on rendering labour service. On the farm, Berlin, near Parys, where the Pooes settled in 1907, there were a few families, especially those who were long settled on the farm (the Lebona, Rampa, Ramakhana, Magatle and Lekima families) who had the resources for sharecropping. The poorer tenants who were unable to produce large surpluses provided labour for the landlord in return for rations and access to arable land and pasture. Jòhannes Moiloa tells a similar story of the farm on which his father sharecropped in the years after the rinderpest of 1896–7.[124] Many a landlord had limited means of production of their own, and they needed to supplement their own productive efforts (using tenant labour) with the independent enterprise of sharecropping tenants. Thus, many a white farmer would use tenant labour to work the employer's implements and oxen, while supplementing this production with the surplus production of sharecropping families using their own implements and oxen. It was further not unusual for junior members of sharecropping households to be called upon sometimes to provide labour in the landlord's fields, sometimes for a daily wage.

Sharecropping was especially indispensable to settlers who were newly established on the land. The Highveld was becoming more densely populated in the years following the Anglo-Boer War, and farms were rapidly being subdivided. The amount of capital required to buy up and settle on relatively unimproved land was often out of proportion to the productive capacity of the land, given the level of technology available. Thus new settlers, many of them introduced by the reconstruction administration, commonly lapsed into sharecropping relationships. The larger Boer landowners of an earlier date had managed to maintain themselves on the basis of extensive pastoralism. The smaller landowners (or lessees) who were becoming more and more a feature of the arable districts had to survive on the basis of grain production – supplemented by dairy and wool farming – or go under. Given high land values (pushed up by speculative buying and option-hunting immediately after the war and again after 1908) and the need to enter debt in order to establish basic improvements on the land, it is not surprising that these newer settlers very quickly became dependent on black tenant enterprise.

The significance of sharecropping in this context is illustrated by C. C. Chase of the farm Townley in the Heilbron district. In August 1913 he described the pattern of the 'many young, struggling and progressive farmers' like himself. He had been farming for two years, and had little capital but forty-three head of cattle. He could only afford to work one plough and one team of oxen. He held his farm on lease and hoped eventually to buy it. But with the value of land soaring, it was impossible for him to make enough money on the produce of but one team of oxen. Thus he had found it necessary to supplement his own efforts with those of two sharecropping families. In order to improve his finances, buy his farm and invest in stock and equipment for more intensive exploitation of the land, he wrote, he was dependent on the productive capacity of his sharecropping tenants.[125] Francis Carroll, who farmed 700 acres near Kroonstad, was another example. He started with sixteen cows, one bull, eight oxen and a plough. At the age of 26, after a year or two on the land, he had increased his stock and declared himself satisfied with the progress he had made: 'I put it down to ploughing on shares. . . . The half share system has been the salvation of the poor men like myself.'[126]

G. J. van Riet, lawyer of Thaba Nchu made a similar observation with regard to the post-war settlers of that district:

If you look round the country you will see some of our settlers who, were it not for the sowing on shares, could not stand today where they are now. The natives were planting and sowing under their supervision, and where settlers were not in a position to buy cattle those natives helped a lot. It is practised by nearly every farmer in the district and by new settlers.[127]

A correspondent in the *Farmer's Weekly* concurred when he wrote in 1911 that the settlers in the Thaba Nchu district 'could not get a quarter of the crops they do now were it not for having squatters who have oxen .... The settlers are not in a position to purchase much themselves as yet.'[128]

Finally, in 1913, J. O. Oberholzer of Bethlehem had five African tenant families on his 1000-acre farm, each with ten head of cattle, horses and ploughs, who cultivated on half shares and did all the 'loose work' on the farm, as well as supplying household servants who were paid a wage. There were many young beginners in his district who were in the same position, he said. 'The well-to-do farmers have their own oxen' noted W. Robertson, magistrate at Bethlehem in 1913, 'the farmers not well-to-do, if having only one span, get the natives' oxen, and perhaps cultivate three times as much ground as they otherwise could. In some instances the native is the better off of the two.'[129] The experience of these farmers suggests that the productive resources of the black sharecropping tenantry was keeping undercapitalized and often overindebted white farmers afloat.

Many white families became economically dependent on their more prosperous black tenants and neighbours. As an instance: a landowner returned to his farm after the Anglo-Boer War with no working capital, having to sell off some 4000 acres of his 10000-acre farm to pay off his debts. The Africans who had lived on his land returned from the town where they had been during the war. Within a year they had a herd of cattle and began ploughing on half-shares. By 1912 the tenants had about 160 head of cattle against the landowner's one hundred. The Africans also had some 500 head of small stock. They were reportedly far better off than the owner of the ground and declined to render service. The African-owned stock that year ate the fenced-off pasture veld, and the landowner had to wait for the tenants to reap their crops before he could feed his cattle on the arable fields.[130] The magistrate in Fouriesburg gave an instance in 1911 of a white landowning family in his district living entirely on the production of one African head of household resident upon the farm, who owned several spans of oxen and a couple of wagons. The African did all the ploughing as well as transport work. 'The owners do nothing', added the magistrate.[131]

Sharecropping was attractive to many on account of the risks involved in investment. One farmer wrote in the *Farmer's Weekly* in 1912 that, given the climatic conditions and the uncertainty of yields, the cost of production of cereal crops amounted on average to more than half the income from the crop (of course, in some years the crops failed

altogether). Under these circumstances, wrote the correspondent, it paid
the white farmer better to allow sharecroppers to bear the costs and the
risks and get half the crop, than to do the work with hired labour and
risk a loss on investment. 'Guarantee a farmer a fairly reasonable
prospect of a crop every year as a result of his labour' he wrote, 'and
Kaffir farming would be as dead as the dodo tomorrow.'[132]

In a situation in which agricultural technology in the peasant
economy was not very different from that in the landlord economy, the
direct subsumption of black labour under white capital did not have any
great advantage in terms of productivity or profitability.[133] Maize-
harvesting continued to be a labour-intensive activity well into the
twentieth century, involving as it did simply picking off the cobs (stalks
were left in the fields as winter feed). Where new technology brought
competitive advantages – as in the case of threshing machines (generally
owned by syndicates of whites who hired them out by the day in return
for a proportion of the crop threshed) – it was compatible with the
household organization of labour. For the white man who was unable or
unwilling to capitalize his production, the best course often was simply
to leave the black tenant in command and control of the means of
production and to live off the surplus generated. This was especially so
since the sharecropper was likely to devote more attention and care to a
crop of which half was to be his own than to a crop which was to be of
profit to the white farmer alone. A 1908 commission reported that
whites who defended sharecropping asserted that 'some natives are as
good or better farmers than some white men, and that unless the former
has a direct interest in the crop, he will not exert his best endeavours
towards its successful production'.[134]

There was another related reason why sharecropping was so
congenial to landlord and tenant household alike. It protected the
former against desertion and the latter against eviction, in an economy in
which town employment offered more remunerative opportunities for
younger family members than did farm work. The landlord knew that
even if the most productive workers went to town to earn the money
wages obtainable there, the crop would still be tended and reaped, for it
was in the tenant household's interest to see to it. And the household
knew that provided the crop was delivered, the landlord could not object
too strenuously to family members oscillating between farm and town.

But whatever the advantages of sharecropping arrangements in terms
of their relative productivity and relative risk for the white farmers, the
cultural pressures pushing whites to assert ever greater control over
productive activities on their land were considerable. Many white

farmers who had command of the necessary capital and labour to work the land themselves were concerned not only with considerations of economic advantage but also with their standing as a rural ruling class. Large-scale industrial interests were not as likely to be concerned with the maintenance of racial supremacy at the workplace. But white control over black labour was of profound symbolic importance to the Afrikaner populists as well as to the 'imperial-race' ideologues who so keenly supported British settlement schemes. Those who 'farmed with Kaffirs' were seen as actively undermining the dominance, psychological and moral as well as purely economic, of the dominant race. This antagonism was directed toward the more explicit forms of tenant enterprise where little or no supervision or control was exercised and where black producers were able to prosper free from any restraints imposed by landlords. Populist sentiment was particularly infuriated by the vision of white landlords being enriched by 'Kaffir farming' without exerting any direct coercive authority over their tenants. The result was that most white farmers felt pressure to subvert the productive independence of their tenants and to force them into servile relationships as far as their resources allowed. This was especially the case in periods of crisis and productive expansion, such as 1893–5, and in particular the years leading up to 1914.

Of course, there was often a world of difference between individual practice and public perception. As we have seen in the testimony of sharecropping landlords like Tylden and Chase, there were those, in private at least, who were prepared to rationalize their dependence on sharecroppers. But even those who were undercapitalized and dependent in some degree on tenant enterprise often attempted as far as they were able to disguise this dependence behind a façade of control and supervision. The essential point about sharecropping in this context as a form of accumulation amongst white farmers is that, in contrast to the seigneurial stereotype of sharecropping elsewhere, it was a partnership between parties who together could muster the resources to work the land and supply markets; but a partnership nonetheless in which one party, the white man, strove to maintain the putative status of master in his own eyes and those of his peers. Few such white farmers would have admitted, and some would not have even apprehended, that they were involved in forms of equal partnership with blacks.

But insofar as sharecropping implies the sharing-out of a common crop between the contracting parties, it was only one possible form of partnership between white 'master' and black 'servant'. Where the white farmer was actively present as a *master* at all stages of the productive process, there was often no need for the protective convention of a sharing ceremony of a common crop (designed to ensure that the direct producer did not neglect the landlord's share at any stage in the productive cycle). Rather the black tenant often produced his own crop on a separate field given him for his own arable operation – often ploughed and worked in tandem with the rest of the arable.[135] However, as long as the means of production were owned and set into motion by individual peasant households, the household remained the basic unit of production on the farms.

For the landlord who held the whip hand and was prepared to invest time in the supervision of productive activities, such arrangements could be profitable insofar as the tenants could be given marginal or worked-out land to plough for themselves. Alternatively, tenants could be given unimproved, stony ground to plough, which – once ploughed and fertilized – would then be taken over by the landlord after one season. The four-day/two-day convention (four days in landlord's fields and two days in tenant household's) became increasingly common from the 1910s, replacing sharecropping in many instances, as landlords were able to tighten up conditions of tenancy. However, in such cases the means of production still usually belonged to the tenant.

But even where relations of production were more explicitly capitalist, with the white farmer in control of productive resources, it was still common for him to supplement his own means of production (notably oxen) with some of those of his tenants. This relieved him of the need to acquire and maintain his own – especially since the means of arable production were only intermittently used and were unproductive for most of the year, during which time they had to be maintained in working order. This certainly applied to draught oxen, which had to be fed and maintained for long periods during which their services were only occasionally required. Tenants' oxen were used in order to finish the ploughing in as quick a time as possible during the short ploughing season and generally for transport and heavy-duty purposes. Again, this common practice was generally related to the relatively limited capital available to most white farmers.[136] The cost advantage for the undercapitalized white farmer in such arrangements was considerable, especially since oxen did not reproduce and were purely a capital outlay.

Indeed, ploughing and sowing was probably the last seasonal activity to fall under the control of landlords; for ploughing spans were still commonly controlled by tenant households after arable production in general had been taken under the control of the white farmer. And, unlike other activities in the productive cycle, ploughing and sowing did not readily lend themselves to the organization of traditional work parties or of work gangs. Often a money payment per acre ploughed, or a share of the crop, was paid to the owner of the ploughing span (who might not even be a tenant on the same farm)[137] or perhaps two bags of grain for each ox.[138] Such arrangements remained widespread until oxen were displaced by tractors in the 1930s, 1940s and 1950s. The spread of such 'ploughing-and-sowing' contracts for pay in place of explicit sharecropping arrangements usually went hand in hand with a squeeze on tenants' own arable production and economic independence.

Similar to the widespread exaction of 'oxen service', women might use their own hoes in weeding landlords' fields. A white farmer, complaining of the high prices of hoes in 1918, wrote to the *Farmer's Weekly*:

I have all my scuffling done by Kaffir maids, whose hoes, worn down to mere stumps, are no longer fit for the work, and they refuse to replace them at the price now asked. Rather than that the work should stop, I am now offering to share the cost of new hoes with them, but the majority refuse to pay even the half-crown.[139]

In all such instances, capital accumulation amongst whites was in part dependent on expropriation not only of black labour, but of black capital resources as well.

Thus the forms of dependence and partnership existing between undercapitalized white farmers and black tenants encompassed not only the more or less explicit sharecropping arrangements already discussed, but also a range of relationships in which formal black servility was combined with control by blacks of certain of the animals, instruments and organizational skills indispensable for landlord survival and accumulation. Such relationships encompassed varying degrees of organizational control exercised by the white farmers and varying proportions in which the landlord and tenant respectively owned the means of production. The distinction between sharecropper and labour tenant was thus often blurred. Many a landlord condemned 'Kaffir farming' while his lands were ploughed by his tenants using in part their own ploughs and oxen, albeit under his supervision and authority, for which they received in payment a share of the income from the crop or ploughing lands of their own. These complex forms of partnership between white and black on the land, facilitated by the fact that the means of production at the disposal of the white employer of labour were no different from those used by many independent black sharecropping households, were transitional to more explicitly capitalist farming, and indeed were often instrumental in white capital formation.

The bitter rivalry and antagonism of interests between white and black farmers in the period of primary industrialization was not without its ambiguities. For there was a parasitical quality to the relation between the emergent white rural bourgeoisie and the black tenants on the land. Once the capital base of white agriculture was sufficiently developed and once the possibility of escape became severely restricted as a result of the fairly rapid development of a land-scarce economy in the early twentieth century, no amount of resistance and struggle on the part of the blacks could stay the hand of dispossession and coercion as and when individual white farmers sought to assert their new economic and political power. Capitalization and mechanization of white agriculture on the basis of state supports were eventually to destroy the advantages of greater relative productivity and lesser relative risk which made black tenant production so attractive to white farmers in an earlier period. But this transition took several decades to work itself out.

4 Interventions of the Capitalist State and the Development of the Arable Highveld

MARKETING, RAILWAYS AND THE EMERGENCE OF THE GRAIN BELT

A capitalist farming economy can only emerge on the basis of developed transport and marketing facilities. Productive resources can only be turned to profit if markets (domestic or external) are readily to hand which are sufficiently elastic to absorb a growing output without serious logistical obstacles or prohibitive costs being incurred in reaching such markets. In colonial economies the requisite infrastructure of roads, railways and terminal storage and loading facilities are typically oriented toward export markets, and are directed toward coastal ports. In South Africa, however, as in other industrializing countries, there was in the late nineteenth and early twentieth centuries, a radical reorientation of trading networks toward internal centres of population growth, most notably on the Witwatersrand. This reorientation was accompanied by a dramatic development of the productive base of the rural economy on the Highveld, as well as the rapid rise of an advanced mercantile capitalism.

Considerable barriers to generalized commodity exchange and specialization existed at the end of the nineteenth century. These included the seasonal cycle of glut and famine and consequent price instability, as well as the difficulties of transportation and the sheer immobility of produce. In order to understand the obstacles to grain marketing, we need to examine the factors which shaped exchange relationships between producer and merchant.

In the middle decades of the nineteenth century much internal trade with coastal ports was in the hands of the itinerant *smous* who carried his wares from door to door and then returned to the coast several months after his departure, with wool, hides, livestock or feathers with which to pay off his creditors. Many merchant firms also had agencies in the small inland towns and mercantile capital was spreading through the sheep districts in the south. Much trade was in the hands of the Boers themselves. In the 1870s particularly, as we saw earlier, Boers acted as middlemen and speculators in the emerging produce market at Kimberley, buying directly from the Sotho producers. The number of fixed traders established in the small towns of the Orange Free State increased enormously from the 1870s too until by the end of the century virtually all trade was in the hands of a fixed professional trading class, and the Boer transport riders had become dependent on the traders for work on contract – where railways had not already rendered them expendable. As intensive grain production developed on the Highveld, so did the grain trade fall under the control of mercantile capital. The rural trading concerns were often very substantial, such as Frasers of Wepener, J. Robertson of Jammerberg Drift, C. Newberry of Leeuw River or C. Vincent of Clocolan. On the other hand, many smaller storekeepers lacked capital and were dependent on the credit of larger wholesalers and suppliers.[1]

The illiquidity and slow turnover of the agrarian economy inevitably meant that much agrarian trade was based on credit. Store supplies were brought by farmers 'on the book', to be paid off as and when the crops were reaped and the wool shorn. A Winburg farmer wrote in 1896:

> Some capitalists and storekeepers – I know of many instances – together octopus [sic] the farmers' prospective crop twelve months in advance, even two or three years in advance, crops that are not even sown yet. Written promises are extracted from the farmer, binding him to deliver produce at a fixed and ridiculously low price.[2]

A chain of debt leading to the wholesalers was at the basis of agrarian exchange relationships. The farmers' reliance on storekeepers' credit, and storekeepers' reliance on wholesalers' credit created a situation in which the large merchant with cash resources was able, through his control of the credit system, to dominate the marketing system to his own advantage. The illiquidity of agrarian commerce, and farmers' lack of working capital, meant that many of them had no control over marketing decisions, and that they had to sell produce at whatever price was ruling at harvest time. They could not hold back their crop in expectation of a rise in prices, since very likely their crop was bonded to the trader in payment of debt accrued during the many months when the farming enterprise was not earning any income. So the grip of merchant capital was an irksome burden for those involved in rural production, and farmers were well aware how heavily the terms of trade were weighted against them.[3] Most farmers could not hold their produce after harvesting for any length of time for other reasons too. Heat, moisture, frosts and pests all damaged stored grain. Weevils generally made their appearance by November, and without adequately insulated storage facilities, maize could become unsaleable very quickly. The more capitalized with storage facilities and cash resources could play the market by holding back grain until the price rose. But they were very few.[4]

A consequence of the illiquidity of agrarian commerce and of the credit system was the annual cycle of glut and famine, of low and high prices. Oversupply in the months after harvest generally gave way to higher prices, and sometimes the need to import from overseas.[5] So dealers and speculators (some of whom were also highly capitalized farmers) who were able to store large quantities of grain, were often able to make considerable profits at the expense of farmers selling in a chronically overloaded market. In the large markets such as Johannesburg prices did not slump very dramatically, for the dealers could regulate supplies to their own advantage. It was the farmer who suffered from low prices, and the middleman benefited. The period from the 1890s to the 1920s was pre-eminently the era of the speculator, and large fortunes were made by buying up large quantities of maize and holding them in anticipation of a rise in prices.[6]

*   *   *

Another structural obstacle to grain production and distribution was the sheer immobility of produce, given the generally primitive nature of transportation in many parts of the country. Local gluts and local famines often coincided. It was quite usual for maize to be imported to one part of the country from overseas at the same time as it was abundantly available in another part. During 1904–5, a year of glut, more maize was imported into the ORC than was exported from it.[7] A farmer observed in 1914 that in his experience:

> the markets in one part of the country might be glutted with some variety and practically unsaleable, or prices be so low that farmers lost by growing the particular commodity, while in another part it was unobtainable or so scarce that very few persons could afford to use it owing to the high prices asked for it.[8]

Although railways eased this situation in some areas, it was still true of much of the country well into the twentieth century.

The significance of this factor can be understood if we look at the extent of the operation involved in transporting the crop of the eastern

Orange Free State and Basutoland to the markets or to the railhead. In 1895 the *Volksraad* was told that millers of Wepener needed 1200 wagons to carry 66000 bags of grain, while Newberry and Co. of Ladybrand spent £16000 in transport costs in the same year. In 1896 more than 6000 wagons were needed to carry Messrs Newberry's 187000 bags and Messrs J. Robertson's 163000 bags.[9] Inevitably, the farmers of the Conquered Territory were severely affected by the collapse of transport in the late 1890s when rinderpest virtually put a stop to all ox-drawn traffic, as the millers and merchants were hesitant to buy their crops for fear that it would be impossible to convey them to markets. A delegation of farmers from Ficksburg and Wepener appealed to the state president in June 1897 to authorize the immediate construction of a railway line into the grain districts in order to ease the problem. They contended that unless means were found of getting their grain to market, half the farmers in the Conquered Territory would be ruined.[10] In 1899 5000 wagons were urgently required to transport grain from the border town of Ladybrand to the railhead at Bloemfontein. But the decimation of the trek oxen during the rinderpest epizootic meant that huge quantities of grain simply could not be shifted: 'all the mills are filled to the ceilings of their store rooms with grain and meal and flour; the millers cannot buy any more from shortage of space' wrote the *landdros*.[11] Well might inhabitants of Ficksburg assert in a petition in 1903 that it was common for 'thousands of bags of grain – badly wanted in the large towns – to remain in these, the producing districts, unsold and unused owing to want of transport'.[12]

But apart from animal disease, markets also became periodically inaccessible as a result of climatic conditions. Both drought and heavy rainfall could render roads impassable. Rivers, streams and sluits could become raging torrents after heavy thundershowers, entirely cutting off one part of the country from another. In his annual report for 1905–6 the Director of Public Works described the roads system thus:

> Our best roads are but fairly even natural tracks; in the very dry season they become over considerable distances mere masses of dust or sand...while during the period of heavy rains considerable portions become almost impassable from the depth of the mud, and it is quite an undertaking to make a short journey of thirty miles.[13]

Further, the comparative backwardness and thinness of permanent settlement in the northwestern Zandveld before the war – Hoopstad district for instance, which was later to become one of the major maize districts of the Highveld – is in part explained by the very sandy nature of the soil, which made road transport very difficult for much of the year.

Ox-wagon transport could become virtually unobtainable during the dry seasons, because of the difficulties of feeding and maintaining trek oxen. *The Friend* reported during the 1891 drought: 'Thousands of loads of wheat... are today lying... at our mills, quite useless on account of the prohibitive rates of transport'.[14] Again in October 1912 during the drought of that year, *The Friend* reported:

> Farmers cannot send things into railhead, because there is no grass for the oxen and no water at the outspans. In fact, it is reported everyday to the dealers in Johannesburg that cattle are dying for want of water, and that good supplies are thus 'held up'.[15]

Equally dependent on ox-drawn transport were the Orange Free State mines. In May 1891 100 wagonloads of goods destined for the Jagersfontein diamond mine were awaiting transport at the Jagersfontein Road station south of Bloemfontein. The roads were in such a wretched condition that no transport riders were offering their services, even though the distance to the mine was only some 27 miles. The merchants at Jagersfontein were offering 1*s* 6*d* per 100 lbs for this short trip, with no success. When the railhead was at Colesberg south of the Orange, the rate had been 2*s* 6*d* per 100 lbs.[16]

In January 1911 the Koffyfontein mine management was compelled to send out traction engines to fetch supplies at the railhead as no transport was available because of the dry weather and there was serious talk of the mine having to close down unless the veld improved and riders could return to the road. During the following year the mine was again almost brought to a standstill, and many men, black and white, were thrown out of employment because of the drought and the unprocurability of supplies.[17]

Moreover, as was generally the case with all who trekked with stock, transport riders found it increasingly difficult to find grazing on private land. Fencing, closer settlement and permanent occupation of land had much to do with this; and overstocking and the consequent effects of drought made landowners far less willing to allow others, for remuneration or not, to trample down their valuable veld.[18]

*   *   *

Transport was particularly scarce and expensive on the Highveld immediately after the Anglo-Boer War, as a result of the decimation of the stock population both by rinderpest and war devastation. The rate of carrying a bag of grain from southern Basutoland to Bloemfontein by ox wagon immediately after the war was 10*s*. A bag of grain or meal could be carried from Argentina or Australia to Johannesburg for considerably less. Railway petitioners from Ficksburg on the Basutoland border argued in 1903 that 'today it costs three times as much to put a bag of grain from Ficksburg on the rail, as it does to bring one from New York to South Africa'. The result was that foreign grain and meal were being consumed in Bloemfontein and Johannesburg whilst home-grown grain was immobile.[19]

Moreover, the war saw very considerable quantities of grain stockpiled in Basutoland. In December 1900 a petition from G. R. Hobson, chairman of the Basutoland Chamber of Commerce, urged the necessity of extending a railway line to Basutoland. He estimated that, excluding a large quantity still in the hands of the Sotho, traders had no less than 325 000 bags of grain awaiting carriage to the markets, 'and to this number will shortly be added the wheat crop now growing, followed by the new Mealie crop next season, as well as Wool, Mohair etc.'.[20] Thus Basutoland was in a congested state, with every road to every market blocked. Yet grain prices in the main urban centres were exceptionally high in the aftermath of war.[21] Thus the new administration gave priority to the construction of a 'grain line' extending eastwards from Bloemfontein through Thaba Nchu, passing by Ladybrand, to join the Natal line eventually at Bethlehem. To meet the immediate problem, however, a traction-engine service was instituted shortly after the peace was signed. Four engines were set to work transporting produce to Bloemfontein and not less than 400 tons of grain a month were thus off-loaded on to South African markets.[22] Moreover, £600 were set aside to build a road suitable for ox and steam transport from Wepener on the southern Basutoland border to the railhead at Thaba Nchu.[23]

So rail construction was a consideration of great importance in the years immediately following the Anglo-Boer War as a result of the shortage of trek oxen and farmers' increased reliance on producing crops.[24] In order to re-establish himself on the land, the landholder was in many cases obliged to mortgage his property or enter some other form of indebtedness. If he then could not market the crop, he could not meet his debt obligations. The Wepener Repatriation Board, for instance, in August 1902 urged that railway construction was vitally necessary if farmers were not to find themselves in an even more helpless plight than they were in already. 'There will be his crop, from which he must pay interest and wages and buy clothing and other necessities, and *there will be no means of profitably getting his grain to a market*.'[25] Ready income when needed to meet debt obligations or consumption needs had previously been available from the sale of stock or animal products. Rinderpest and the war had barred this option. More than ever before, farmers were dependent on the income derived from cultivation – often, as we have seen, their tenants' cultivation rather than their own – and the marketing of crops required far greater transport facilities than were then available in most areas.

A public meeting in Bethlehem in August 1902 warned that without rail communication with the main internal markets 'a very considerable proportion of the population will be unable to support themselves and will thus remain a source of expense and a burden to the Government'. Extension of the railway from Natal through Harrismith and Bethlehem to the main north–south line from Bloemfontein to Johannesburg would:

> be the best means of enabling the grain-producing farmers to devote all their attention and energy to the raising of crops without having to consider how such crops when raised could be got to market and by doing this would retain in South Africa large sums of money which otherwise would be sent away to pay for foodstuffs which can and ought to be grown locally.[26]

Railway construction was thus seen as an important element in the reconstruction of Highveld agriculture, enabling farmers to restock, reducing the relief-aid burden of the state and providing much needed labour for the greatly expanded impoverished and landless stratum in white rural society.[27]

The grain line through the eastern Orange Free State heralded a shift in emphasis in railway construction in the early twentieth century from a priority on import–export trade centred on the mining industry, to a greater preoccupation with the development of internal agricultural resources. This railway construction on the Highveld was heavily concentrated in arable districts,[28] and crop production responded readily to the stimulus. Railway construction was generally accompanied by an extension of cultivated acreages – especially after the post-war depression lifted from about 1908, bringing readier access to loan capital and credit for white farmers, at the same time as a succession of good years from about 1907 facilitated cultivation and ensured good yields.[29]

Furthermore, railways meant that farmers could survive economically on smaller holdings, and facilitated closer settlement by newcomers on the Highveld. In the rural economy of earlier days, there was a limit beyond which subdivision of the large farms of the nineteenth century could not go without the productive unit ceasing to be viable. The smaller the land at his disposal, the more reliant the landholder became on the cultivation of the soil and the sale of crops and dairy produce for his income. And these activities required not only markets but also good transport facilities. From Frankfort in 1908:

> Owing to the sub-division of the properties the farms are becoming so limited in extent that the owners are forced to depend on the production of cereals and, unless they have other transport than the ordinary 'ox-wagon', their means of existence will be exceedingly precarious.[30]

As farms got smaller, the proportion of land put under the plough increased. Railways were often the cause of closer settlement, or else they were a necessary consequence.

These considerations might be illustrated by closer empirical investigation into the northwestern Zandveld – Hoopstad and Bothaville districts. The Zandveld was potentially rich maize country, and was to become a major maize-producing region. However, very little cultivation took place there before the war. The sandy nature of the soil made road transport very difficult for much of the year, and made the marketing of grain on a large scale almost impossible.[31] Indeed, before the war, a Bothaville correspondent tells us, 'grain was often brought in from Klerksdorp and other districts, as enough could not be grown for local requirements, the country being practically a waste'.[32] A railway line was opened to the Vierfontein colliery up the Vaal River from Bothaville in 1905. In the following year the maize traffic forwarded from that terminus amounted to 210 tons. By 1910 it had climbed to 4500 tons.[33]

*   *   *

But the railway construction programme initiated by the administration after the Anglo-Boer War did not immediately solve the marketing problem; for urban markets contracted once the post-war boom receded and the military withdrew – and also because of the replacement of maize-eating Africans by indentured Chinese on the gold mines. The bumper 1904 summer grain crop demonstrated the limited nature of internal markets, which were quickly sated, given the quantity of grain still being imported from overseas and the farmers' greater dependence on cultivation of the soil for their survival after the war devastation. The 1904 crop brought maize prices tumbling. Farmers had been buying maize to sow (on credit mostly) at up to 25*s* a bag. But no sooner was the harvest in, than the price dropped to below 10*s* – and in some districts as low as 3*s* 6*d*. The trader Charles Stevens estimated that the new crop in Basutoland together with the balance of the old amounted to 200 000 bags. Yet, he added, the Rand market was fully provided for from the Transvaal districts of Potchefstroom and Marico.[34]

A year after the 1904 harvest, Stevens estimated that possibly two-thirds of the crop was still unsold in the hands of merchants. Further, because of the 'enormous quantities' grown in the Transvaal and Natal in the spring and summer of 1904, the 1905 crop in the ORC had 'absolutely no market'. The Rand had been the Orange Free State farmers' best customer before the war, wrote Stevens, but now Transvaal farmers grew more than sufficient for their own requirements.[35] Indeed, Lieutenant Governor Goold-Adams found on a tour of the colony toward the end of 1905 that in many places maize was only fetching about 5*s* per bag – considerably less than the cost of growing it.[36]

The problem of overproduction was eventually solved first by exportation, and second by easing access to non-producing regions of the country, such as much of the Cape, which were difficult to reach because of high rail rates. An agitation for subsidized export freight rates for maize was sparked off by the experience of 1904–5.[37] W. J. Palmer, the Director of Agriculture, asserted that 'unquestionably the great obstacle to good maize prices is the impossibility of getting cheap carriage for export of surplus stocks'.[38] *The Friend* echoed these sentiments: 'The main use of an export trade would be to create a better local market for stocks left in the country'.[39] H. F. Gill, chairman of the ORC Chamber of Commerce, pointed out that there were 200 000 bags of maize lying idle in one district alone in July 1904 and calculated that if they were exported at the modest sum of 7*s* 6*d* per bag they would bring in £75 000.[40]

In 1905, however, the price of maize in Britain was not sufficiently high to make exportation a paying proposition. The price for the ten years to 1906 hovered around 20*s* a quarter (480 lbs), or 8*s* 4*d* per muid bag (203 lbs). But in 1907 the price was higher than for many years past. In part this was the result of increased demand in Britain and the Continent for maize as a stock feed and for manufacturing purposes, as well as unfavourable reports of the crops in the three major producing regions – the USA, Argentina and southeastern Europe.[41] The increased price of maize in Europe coincided with a good maize crop in South Africa in 1907, and a considerable surplus came on to the market for sale at low internal prices. It was thought that the price would slump to 2*s* 6*d* to 3s.[42] These circumstances spurred Durban merchants to institute for the first time an organized export trade in maize. South African maize fetched good prices in London and established a reputation for quality. As a result of these initiatives, the colonial governments negotiated a low freight rate with the Conference lines of steamers (10s per ton) for the conveyance of maize, oats and citrus fruit to Southampton, London, Antwerp and Hamburg. Cheap rail rates to the coast for Highveld grain were also arranged; and a conference of the railway and agricultural representatives of all the colonies was held in Pretoria in January 1908 to hammer out the details of the scheme.[43] The *Natal Agricultural Journal* enthused over the significance of these innovations:

> In the old days, to extend the cultivation of a crop beyond a certain limit spelt loss: to a certain degree, the smaller the crop was, the greater was the gain. Now, however, with the limitless market that lies before us, we can safely put more and more land under mealies; and the extent of our income from this grain will only be bounded by our ability to produce.[44]

Furthermore, after no more than half a dozen years the export trade in maize was right at the centre of commercial life in the major port of Durban. The impending failure of the maize crop in 1914 was regarded as serious to the commercial prospects of the town, 'inasmuch as grain transactions provide a material amount of money in ready currency upon which business subsists in a centre such as Durban'.[45]

But the anomaly of export subsidization was that it became relatively cheaper and more profitable to export maize overseas than to transport it by rail to consuming centres within South Africa.[46] The cost of internal transport retarded distribution of produce from producing to non-producing regions. It seemed unsatisfactory to many at the time that while shiploads of maize were being sent to Europe, cargoes were being imported into South Africa from South America to supply the non-producing parts of the Cape. This situation was the result of high inland rail rates, combined with the cheap export rate introduced precisely in order to secure a viable and profitable market for the farmer. It was much cheaper to send maize to, say, Port Elizabeth for export, than to send it there for local consumption.[47] Maize from the Orange Free State would be sent to Durban by rail, thence by steamer to Cape Town, where it was distributed to inland areas where demand existed. This roundabout journey was cheaper than by rail transport over land, despite all the intermediaries through whose hands it passed. The result was that maize cost more in the Cape than it did in Europe – 15s or 16s a bag.[48] It was also an expensive undertaking to transport maize from an arable district to a pastoral one where it could be fed to livestock. In the words of the editor of *The Friend*, the rating structure 'led to the unsound position under which South Africa exported its maize overseas and purchased it back, at high figures, in the shape of bacon, ham, butter, cheese and meat'.[49] While access to external markets for surplus grain was of great importance in maintaining price levels during good seasons, nevertheless it was increasingly seen to be economically sounder to send, as far as possible, South Africa's own maize to local markets 'on four legs'; or, as Sir George Farrar said, it was far better to feed their stock and send their maize out of the country in the stomachs of their cattle, than to import frozen meat because their own cattle were starving.[50]

A very significant step toward shifting the balance was the change in taxation policy introduced soon after Union. For years the South African states' major revenue-raising mechanism was through the railway rating structure and customs duties. The first Union government after 1910 set about introducing an income tax for the first time, and simultaneously reduced railway rates until railway revenue covered the costs of railway administration and investment, leaving no surplus over for general purposes. This change, stretching over a four-year period, had a very considerable impact on the cost of transporting produce by rail within South Africa. One of the most important of the freight reductions was that of October 1911 when it was laid down that the maximum for the carriage of South African grain and forage between any two stations on the South African railways was to be 20*s* per ton.[51]

As an example of the effect the rate reduction had: at Graaff Reinet in the Cape, maize was fetching 15*s* a bag before the new rate was introduced. As a result of the new rate, a farmer was able to send 1000 bags from his farm on the Highveld direct to Graaff Reinet by rail, instead of shipping the cargo to Cape Town first, as had previously been the case. The price of a bag in Graaff Reinet immediately fell to 12*s*, while the farmer made a better profit on his produce. Thus, both producer and consumer benefited substantially.[52] The editor of *The Friend* wrote:

Up-country maize farmers will now find markets for their products in the Cape Province and farmers in the latter will be able to reciprocate by sending to northern markets that particular product that is in demand, and which hitherto has been imported from overseas in large quantities. South Africa is beginning to realize the benefits of the wise policy established with Union of running the railways in order to develop the resources of the country and not as a tax-raising machine.[53]

But by 1914 the marketing of grain was still in the hands of private dealers and speculators. The establishment of co-operative societies and the elevator system from the 1920s, under the auspices of the state, was dramatically to transform the marketing of grain. The former allowed the farmers themselves in their corporate capacity to control supply to markets. The latter provided for bulk handling, sorting and grading at depots in the maize districts themselves, storage in silos, and transportation in bulk rather than in bags. The 1930s saw the establishment of statutory marketing boards designed to stabilize prices by the bureaucratic regulation of supplies to markets. All the while, the extent of state subsidization of white farming was expanding.

* * *

Although much of the region which is the subject of this study was rapidly emerging as an area of specialized maize production in the early twentieth century with the results that have been described, in the early days wheat was the major crop of large parts of the 'Conquered Territory' and Basutoland.[54] However, the situation with regard to wheat production was very different from that of maize; for far from there being wheat gluts requiring exportation, South African wheat production was never sufficient to meet internal demand. Rarely in the first few decades of the century did wheat production provide much more than half the requirements. Wheat production on the Highveld entered a sharp decline in the second decade of the century – reversed temporarily by the very high prices caused by shortages in the immediate aftermath of the First World War. A departmental committee appointed in 1919 to investigate means of promoting wheat production and thus to reduce dependence on imports, found that the shortage of seasonal labour and the uncertainties of dryland wheat cultivation were the major reasons for the decrease in acreages in the Orange Free State.[55] In consequence, maize had for some years been ousting wheat as the primary crop of the eastern districts. The labour intensity of the maize harvest was considerably less than that in the harvesting of wheat. Wepener district, which ten years before had exported large surpluses of wheat, had to import wheat each year by 1919 to make up the balance of its requirements. In many of these districts rye had replaced wheat, as it was less susceptible to the depredations of the aphis and suitable for feeding stock. According to census statistics, the area sown with wheat in the Orange Free State dropped from 113 000 morgen in the bumper year of 1911 to 58 000 morgen in 1918.[56]

ORIGINS OF THE INTERVENTIONIST STATE

Any long-term breakthrough to capitalist agriculture amongst the white farmers required massive, sustained state support on two levels. First, a labour force had to be secured, which implied the undermining of black productive independence and, in the longer term, the suppression of the sharecropping economy. Effective initiatives on this level could only be undertaken when the conditions were propitious, that is when the capital base of white farming was sufficiently sturdy to contemplate punitive action against the black tenant farmers. The second form of state intervention was a precondition for effective intervention against independent black producers. This entailed the large-scale transfer of capital through the auspices of the state into the agricultural sector. Hence any consideration of white accumulation on the land requires first an assessment of the extent of state-sponsored capitalization.

Concentration of capital was not a significant feature of the rural economy. There was a limit to the extent to which accumulation could profitably take place in agriculture. Advantages of scale were limited in an age when mechanization was of peripheral importance. On the contrary, for most, the maintenance of productive viability in the face of the inexorable tendency toward indebtedness depended on continual state supports. Survival on the land was reliant on cushioning by the state against the destruction of capital resources. Unlike in industry, the capital base in agriculture is always vulnerable to destruction by natural causes – climate, disease or pests. Not only was the initial capitalization of white farming in general dependent on a high level of state interventionism, but the security of individual farmers required a continually increasing level of state involvement in every aspect of the agricultural economy from financing to marketing.

Systematic state action in support of the white rural economy had its origins in the 1890s, when the republican regimes were confronted with the stark realities of deprivation and impoverishment. The government's initial goal was to keep landholders on the land. One major aspect of state intervention was the search for water. From 1894 the *Volksraad* made provision for the purchase of eighteen diamond drills for loan to individual farmers for sinking wells. In 1898 provision was also made for subsidizing the purchase of drills by groups of farmers, the government providing 50 per cent of the purchase price. In 1899 £5000 was budgeted for the supply of pumps to farmers at cost price. Rudimentary veterinary services were introduced in the 1890s, and the compulsory dipping of sheep was enforced. A law regulating the fencing of farms was first passed in 1890.[57]

The reconstruction regimes after the war were much more activist than those that had gone before. The resources at the disposal of the new colonial administration and its predisposition toward intervention were much greater than in republican days.[58] State intervention to promote rural capitalization was from the beginning reserved for whites. Even the supposedly non-discriminatory compensation payments for losses during the Anglo-Boer War were seriously skewed in practice in favour of white rehabilitation at the expense of black tenant farmers. Tshwene Mmolotsi remembers this with a bitterness undimmed by nearly eighty intervening years:

> Whites robbed us of our compensation. They could write and we could not. Instead of us being compensated, they were compensated. Instead of writing that we blacks lost so many cattle, they instead wrote vice versa. That is how we were robbed.[59]

A major priority of the administration after the Anglo-Boer War was the lowering of labour costs on the Rand by lowering the cost of living. This meant first (and most important) ensuring the provision of a more dependable supply of agricultural produce than had previously been forthcoming. This was not simply a matter of providing greater and more efficient transport facilities – though this consideration weighed heavily. It was also seen initially and more fundamentally as a matter of transforming rural relationships in such a way as to promote the emergence and development of a specifically capitalist agriculture. This ideally entailed undermining the local dominance of the old Boer landowners, shaking land from their grasp, providing the *bywoners* with alternative foci of loyalty and patronage,[60] and providing a wage labour force by attacking independent black tenancy.[61] But most important, it entailed settling the land with progressive, model farmers loyal to Britain and the imperial cause.

The interventionist and social-engineering proclivities of the High Commissioner, Milner, and his acolytes were nowhere more apparent than in their efforts to mould the countryside in the image of yeoman Britain. It was a commonplace amongst the more sanguine of the British administrators immediately after the Anglo-Boer War that the Boers were characteristically a dull and backward people, whose stubborn and wasteful grip on the land had to be prized free by the infiltration of a vigorous and enterprising class of British settlers. This settlement scheme was to be coupled with an anglicization policy in education. It was universally accepted at first that the road to progressive agriculture lay, at the very least, in 'leavening' the indigenous white population with a substantial influx of more 'advanced' peoples.[62]

The new administration, generously funded by an imperial loan, spared no effort from the first to boost settler agriculture by a variety of means. Immediately after the war an agricutural department was set up, manned by experts recruited overseas. The department provided a full panoply of support services and experts, from a government entomologist and bacteriologist, to specialists in fruit farming, tobacco-growing, dairying, wool production. The department provided funds for restocking with better breeds of animals; it hired out stallions to service farmers' mares; it policed the mandatory dipping of sheep to eliminate scab; it issued arsenic and spray pumps for the elimination of *voetgangers* (young locusts); it provided loans for fencing and dam-building; it established experimental farms and dairies. In any number of ways the state was coming to the aid of white farming.[63]

In all, from the beginning of 1902 to the end of 1907 972 settlers were placed on the land by the ORC Settlement Board. Of these, 650 were still on their farms at the end of the period, and 154 had left their allotted farms but were still in the colony, many still farming. The majority of the settlers were British-born, though a substantial number were colonials. Apart from the special provision for settling Boers who had served the British during the war, the settlers were virtually exclusively English-speaking.[64] The land settlement scheme, which was far more purposefully implemented in the Orange River Colony than in the Transvaal, did not revolutionize the countryside in the way that was hoped. But it did have a substantial impact nonetheless. For each settler brought with him some £400–500 capital. Further, up to mid-1907, boundary fencing to the value of £48 000 had been advanced on loan to the settlers. Seventy thousand feet of drilling had been completed by government drills on land-settlement allotments. And between 1902 and 1909, £111 000 were advanced to settlers in cash and stock on easy terms of repayment.[65] All this amounted to an unprecedented degree of state aid for the promotion of a capitalist agriculture.

From the beginning, the intention of the land-settlement scheme was to settle the land as densely as possible. It was the policy to:

get as many men on to the land as could reasonably be expected to make a living on their holdings, and if some of these smaller plots were abandoned, such abandoned holdings should be divided between the successful men who remained.[66]

An important factor in closer settlement was the institution of irrigation schemes,[67] which served the further purpose of providing employment for indigent whites. The small size of the holdings, however, did prove the undoing of many settlers given the uncertainties of relying on arable farming in the post-war drought conditions.[68] But the fact that most settlers survived on the land can be attributed, first, to the adoption of sharecropping, a relationship which was particularly prevalent in districts of concentrated post-war British settlement, such as Thaba Nchu, Ladybrand and Heilbron. Second, good seasons, improved transport facilities and greatly enhanced opportunities for marketing grain after 1907 (as a result of the opening up of export markets) meant the settlers' lot gradually improved. No less important was the establishment of creameries, state-owned, co-operative and proprietary.

Post-war settlement schemes were not confined to the colonial administration. Colonel T. A. Hill's company, the British Settlement of South Africa Limited (initially the Scottish Sharpshooters' Association), was given 40 000 acres by the government in Heilbron and Thaba Nchu districts. The company enjoyed the financial support of 'several philanthropic gentlemen' in Great Britain who 'came forward time after time with considerable sums of money'. In the end the company proved a financial failure, but it did provide considerable funds for over 200 farmers whom it was responsible for settling in the colony.[69]

The role of the aristocratic entrepreneur in promoting improved farming methods amongst his tenants in the British countryside is well known. In the ORC the Duke of Westminster played a similar role on the large area of land bought in 1901 from Charles Newberry in what had been Moroka's territory east of Thaba Nchu. The Westminster Estate of some 9000 morgen (for which the Duke paid £31 700) was cut into sixteen small farms of 300 to 500 morgen each. To each tenant was allotted a house and an orchard paid for by the Duke himself. Boreholes were sunk and dams were constructed, and the tenants set to growing maize, potatoes, oathay and barley and providing cream to the local government dairy at the Tweespruit experimental farm. Small blocks of high quality sheep were introduced, and the Duke provided thoroughbred stallions from the Eaton Hall stud for the use of his tenants.[70]

Other private organizations and individuals were also involved in subsidized immigration and land settlement. The Imperial South Africa Association (of which the Duke of Westminster was president) envisaged settling up to a dozen families from East Anglia and Scotland on each of its farms, but in the event acquired no more than three farms for this purpose; and Lord Lovat raised a loan of £2500 from the government to start a settlement scheme in Lindley district.[71]

But the imperialists' initial optimistic visions of a new South Africa were hardly viable. Sooner or later more realistic bureaucrats realized the need to forge alliances with the old Boer landowning elite in the districts. Whereas the first wave of British administrators were not unwilling to preside over the ongoing economic decline of the Boer population, it soon became clear that it was beyond their power to create a new class of small-scale rural capitalists to replace the old burghers.[72] By 1904 the British had not only realized the futility of seeking to undermine and disperse the black tenant farmers to create a labour force, they had also recognized that the old burghers or their sons were going to be an important element in the future rural economy of the Highveld. This was not due so much to any comparative advantages enjoyed by the Boers, but to the failure of British settlement schemes. The ultimate significance of the land-settlement policy however lay in the extent of state subsidization of agriculture which it initiated, and the long-term commitment to the promotion of white capitalist production which it entailed.

Doubtless one of the most important and enduring interventions of the capitalist state was in the institutionalized provision of loan capital, thereby providing a more sympathetic, flexible and reliable alternative to resort to private capital. Land banks were established in the ORC and the Transvaal in 1907–8, and were superseded by the Union Land Bank in 1912.[73] The establishment of land banks whose facilities were available to whites only in the new colonies coincided with the transfer of responsible government to local whites. The ministries which came to power in 1907–8 were dominated by men who had commanded Boer forces in the Anglo-Boer War. Thus the imperial power confirmed not only its commitment to a capitalist and white-dominated rural economy, but also its realization that the recently conquered Boers were bound to be a major element in the state-sponsored rural capitalism which they envisaged emerging in the future.

THE DYNAMICS OF WHITE CAPITALIZATION

What enabled some white farmers to invest in implements and infrastructure and establish control over black labour power, when so many others remained reliant on extensive pastoralism, or where that was no longer viable, on black tenant production for their survival? Under what circumstances could individual accumulation from productive enterprise develop a momentum of its own? The answer must be in large part that many of the most successful farmers early on either had alternative sources of income (family finances or military pensions perhaps) or had accumulated capital from non-agricultural pursuits. Various forms of entrepreneurial activities commonly went hand in hand with capitalized farming. Many of the capitalized farmers at the end of the nineteenth century had been (or their fathers had been) full-time transport riders, traders and hunters in earlier years, with privileged access to exchange and credit networks. Much agrarian capital was derived from such sources. W. B. Gradwell, born of 1820-settler parents, hunted and traded in the Transvaal and beyond, probably in ivory, for many years from 1865 on, before settling down to the life of a farmer. By the turn of the century he owned 20000 morgen in Bloemfontein district, 3000 of which were regularly under crops irrigated from the Modder River, and he was the country's leading breeder of Afrikander cattle.[74]

Many of the wealthier farmers in the rich arable districts of the eastern Orange Free State (where capitalized arable farming emerged earlier than elsewhere) owned mills and steam threshing machines with which to service the crops of surrounding farmers.[75] Some owned fleets of transport wagons. Some combined farming enterprises with large-scale trading and speculation in the produce of Basutoland as well as the Orange Free State farms. One example of this combination of mercantile, processing and farming activities was the enterprise of David Scott of Rondeberg, who was known to reap 2000 bags of wheat on his land, and claimed to have introduced the first threshing machines and cream separator into the Orange Free State. In 1891 Scott's 'well-known' brand of flour produced in his mill reportedly fetched the same price as the best Australian brands on the Johannesburg market. Otto Jensen erected a mill on his farm Brandsdrift in 1891, on which he also had a store dealing in grain.[76] Other examples of the entrepreneur-farmer are Thomas Mitchell of Molenspruit, Charles Stevens of Schuttesdraai, James Robertson of Jammerberg Drift, J. Lloyd, Archibald Brothers and G. Stofberg.[77]

But the most impressive case from the wheat districts was that of the Newberrys, who made their initial fortune as claimholders on the diamond fields at Kimberley. Charles Newberry established a highly capitalized farming enterprise at Prynnsberg near Clocolan. He and his brother John, a director of De Beers, owned probably the biggest milling plant on the Highveld, on the Leeuw River, built in 1893. They also bought in the same year the mechanized mill built by T. H. Sephton on the farm Lovedale. The family business was one of the largest dealers in grain in the territory, sending large consignments of grain, meal and flour to the Johannesburg market. Charles Newberry also secured ownership of a large number of farms in Moroka's territory, previously the property of the Rolong elite, after that territory had been annexed to the Boer republic in 1884. It is very likely that he was able to do this by extending generous mortgage loans to the previous owners. In 1901 he sold much of this land to the British military administration for some £90 000. The Newberrys were amongst the earliest to experiment with large-scale fruit farming in the region – Mrs E. M. Newberry was responsible for planting an orchard of 14 000 trees at Wonderkop near Clocolan in 1907. She was also a member of a syndicate which established a pork factory in the town in the same year.[78]

Land speculation was a common form of primary enrichment. Many an early land accumulator was able to make massive profits later. Many landowners had been enriched by periodic speculative booms in land in the Cape as a result of the development of merino sheep farming from the 1840s, and more spectacularly in the intermittent ostrich-feather booms in the years between 1870 and 1914, and the related great demand for lucerne grown under irrigation. These speculative booms spread throughout the Cape midlands and into the Orange Free State, as capital derived by landownership in the districts at the epicentre was invested massively in further land purchases. The amount of productive potential thus generated amongst landowners and their descendants was considerable, and the eddies were felt far and wide as young men in search of new land to settle, moved northwards.[79] It was under circumstances such as these that the potential was created for the capitalization of farming on the Highveld. Indeed, it was a commonplace observation at the time that most progressive farmers in a district were the late arrivals, often colonial farmers from older areas of settlement in the Cape or Natal who had cashed in on the higher land values available there and in consequence were able to invest capital in improvements on newly acquired land on the Highveld.[80]

Furthermore, a number of examples can be given of industrially or commercially-generated wealth being invested in farming. Not all absentee-owned land was peopled by black sharecroppers. Some companies and wealthy inidividuals chose to take the riskier and perhaps less profitable course of investing directly in capitalized agriculture. Randlords like Henry Nourse, Sir Abe Bailey and Sir Percy Fitzpatrick, the Lewis and Marks Company, as well of course as the Newberrys from the diamond fields, were all involved in the development of highly capitalized farming operations on the Highveld.[81] Names that regularly recurred amongst the prizewinners at the big agricultural shows in Johannesburg, Bloemfontein and Kimberley included such representatives of big capital as Sir George Farrar, De Beers Consolidated Mines, the Smartt syndicate, as well as big merchant firms such as D. and D. H. Fraser of Wepener, who not only had a dozen trading stations in Basutoland, but were amongst the Orange Free State's leading sheep breeders.

The Pilgrims Mining, Estate and Exploration Company, owned by the Bourke family, was involved in capital-intensive and large-scale maize and dairy farming in the vicinity of Vierfontein in the northern Orange Free State. In 1904 the Bourkes had 500 morgen under grain and some £50000 invested in buildings and machinery on their lands. The Bourkes, who were known as amongst the most progressive farmers in the Orange Free State, had made their money initially in the eastern Transvaal gold fields, and were major shareholders in the Transvaal Gold Mining Estates Company. They also happened to have extensive coal-mining interests in the northern Orange Free State. They were the country's major breeders of pedigree South Devon cattle, and imported J. K. Evans from Britain to manage their stud herds after the Anglo-Boer War.[82]

Tom Minter provides another instance of capital derived from mining and speculation being invested in agricultural production. Minter, member of a syndicate which speculated very profitably in mineral-rich land in the Orange Free State, sold his half-option on the diamondiferous farm Rietgat for £30000 in 1898. Minter used his proceeds to order from England a twelve-furrow steam plough, weighing 200 tons. The machine cost £4000, plus £800 to convey it from the factory to Minter's farm. With his new steam plough, Minter predicted that he would raise 30000 bags of wheat, and he advertised for sale all his cattle (318 head) and a large assortment of implements. Whether Minter was ever able to prove the profitability of his investment is doubtful, given the outbreak of war in the following year.[83]

A singularly telling example of this process is provided by the mining magnate, Sir Percy Fitzpatrick. Fitzpatrick laid down a large extent of his estate Buckland Downs (bought in 1902) to pasture using imported grasses. His imported breeds of cattle, Persian sheep and horses were raised and fed on cultivated pastures. His scientific breeding for dairy production was widely admired. He planted 1000 fruit trees and tens of thousands of other varieties – oaks, conifers, gums. He also built a series of dams. The essential nature of the enterprise, however, is revealed by Fitzpatrick's biographer: 'the property was always a cheque-book farm, into which it was constantly necessary to pour large sums of money.... The returns from the farming operations were minimal, the costs prodigious.' Also revealing as to the nature of the enterprise is the fact that the estate was used for hunting. It was stocked with eland, wildebeest and springbok, and Fitzpatrick imported deer from England and Scotland. Farming for Fitzpatrick as for so many other wealthy men was an object of conspicuous consumption. Thus was the self-made capitalist entrepreneur transformed into a member of a new gentry. Here, as on much other land belonging to companies or wealthy men, hunting had been radically transformed from a major economic activity on which much rural accumulation was based, to a sport for gentlemen from Johannesburg or Kimberley. More practical and less wealthy landowners might have preferred stocking the land with black sharecroppers rather than red deer.[84]

Indeed, it seems to have been not uncommon for the best-known and most capitalized farming enterprises with access to abundant finance from non-agricultural sources to have been thoroughly uneconomic. The name of S. G. Vilonel, president of the Senekal Farmers' Association, was repeatedly to be found amongst the judges as well as the winners of prizes at local agricultural shows for his horses, his Rambouillet sheep and Friesland cattle. On his farm De Rust outside Senekal he cut 60 tons of lucerne hay a year, grown under irrigation with water from four boreholes which pumped 70 000 gallons a day into storage dams. But Vilonel was only a part-time farmer, for he had a very lucrative law practice and auctioneering business in Senekal, and was also mayor of the town. Indeed, De Rust (which was only 300 morgen in extent), seems not to have been a viable commercial proposition. It was a rich man's toy, a week-end pastime for one whose real sources of wealth lay outside agriculture.[85]

Another farmer famed for his imported stud flocks of sheep and feared at the local agricultural shows was G. McKechnie, who farmed a much larger property, Wildebeestfontein in the Winburg district, 3500 morgen in extent. But it comes as no surprise to discover that the property was in fact owned by African Farms Limited, a public company of which the Randlord Julius Jeppe was chairman, and McKechnie was the company's manager. McKechnie had a ready supply of corporate funds at his disposal to invest on the property. As Jeppe himself said, the company's goal was to make its farming operations self-supporting, and 'if possible' profitable. To this end the company not only provided capital but it gathered and indexed 'every kind of information which promises to eliminate the element of chance', in this way echoing the kind of entrepreneurial role in promoting scientific agriculture as was evident in the Duke of Westminster's activities. However, the company seems to have made no profit on its farming operations, but was essentially concerned to exploit speculative booms in land prices in order to earn a dividend for its shareholders. In 1908 sixty company farms were being worked by whites, either by managers employed by the company (such as Wildebeestfontein) or by tenants who hoped eventually to buy the land with the aid of mortgage loans; but as Jeppe complained, it was extremely difficult to find tenants with the requisite capital to be successful farmers.[86]

So not only was sustained accumulation from rural production alone atypical if not impossible, but even where capital was readily available for investment in farming, its availability did not guarantee profits. Capital-intensive enterprises did not invariably pay dividends corresponding to the level of capital investment. Tom Minter, despite his investment in a steam plough worth £4000 in 1898, ended up bankrupt. In 1904 J. A. McLaren, South African agent of the steam plough manufacturers, John Fowler and Company of Leeds, rented 2000 acres from the Vereeniging Estates. For ten years McLaren spent large sums of money to demonstrate the viability of steam ploughing under South African conditions. Nevertheless, despite high yields (40 000 bags of grain in 1910) the enterprise lost £35000 in all. Again, in 1915, Robert Seggie of Holfontein, Kroonstad, was involved in a suit against the sellers of a steam traction engine for ploughing which had been a 'complete failure'. The action cost Seggie some £2000.[87] It is perhaps ironic that Seggie had himself written some years earlier that:

The ox is the natural draught animal for South Africa, and, therefore, the horse, steam plough, or any other invention will never replace it. The price that we get for our produce is too low, and the product per acre is too small, that any ploughing which costs more than from 8*d* to 1*s* per English acre would be too high, with all the other drawbacks that we have, to leave a margin of profit.[88]

In the light of this estimate it is significant to note that steam ploughing on the Vereeniging Estates was computed to cost some 4s per acre, even with the ready availability of coal from the nearby collieries. Sir Percy Fitzpatrick was advised by the Director of Agriculture upon enquiry that 10s might be a more realistic estimate on Buckland Downs.[89]

Thus, heavy capital expenditure was as likely as not to undermine the profitability of the enterprise. However, the bulk of landholders did not have unlimited capital resources at their disposal for investment, and they had to make a profit over costs at least more often than not, in order to survive. For many, a proportion of the crop of sharecropping tenants was an important supplement to their own efforts. For many, access to black tenants' productive skills and resources, such as ploughing spans, was indispensable. Once again, it is in the context of the uncertainties and risks involved in capital investment and the unpredictable productivity of rural capital resources that the prevalence of sharecropping relationships should be seen.

No doubt many farmers were able to make judicious investments in, for example, implements such as three-share ploughs, planters and cultivators, in boreholes, dams, fencing and the dipping of animals, which enabled them to control the element of chance in some degree and thus to avoid the trap of indebtedness which sucked so many others under. But over the long term, survival as farmers (which did not necessarily mean consistent and cumulative profit-making) required access to fairly substantial funds from outside agricultural production, at least initially, and continual reliance on the state's resources as a cushion against climatic variations and market fluctuations. From the 1920s onward, state-subsidized farmers' co-operatives, price supports and statutory marketing monopolies greatly extended white farmers' dependence on the state.

Successful farming not only required continued cushioning by the state, but also a level of education which the bulk of the landed Boers did not initially possess. Access to skills and to information of a technical and scientific nature was increasingly indispensable for survival on the land as extensive pastoralism ceased to be a viable option. The agricultural journals of the day reveal something of the level of educational proficiency required by the progressive farmer. The semi-official *Farmer's Advocate and Home Journal* which was launched in Bloemfontein in 1904, was a bilingual publication which sought to disseminate information of a scientific and practical nature to farmers, from methods of cultivation to seed selection, fencing, water conservation,.prevention of soil erosion, the provision of ensilage and fodder crops, and the breeding of livestock for optimal yields of wool or meat or milk. It provided information on local climatic conditions, rainfall figures, market prices, agricultural shows, the activities of departmental demonstrators and advisers and the results of trials at the Grootvlei or Tweespruit experimental farms. The *Farmer's Weekly* was launched in 1911, also in Bloemfontein, by the Friend Publishing Company. Its extensive correspondence columns were filled with queries and advice on mechanical matters, on boring, irrigation, fencing and the construction of encampments, on stock breeds, beekeeping and the growing of fruit. The journal included also a women's supplement on matters such as housekeeping, childcare, growing vegetables, raising poultry, and making butter and soap.

The bulk of the progressive farmers early on seem to have been English-speaking, although this impression might be exaggerated by the English-speaker's greater public visibility, especially after the Anglo-Boer War. Farmers' associations generally conducted their affairs in English, although there were always a substantial minority of Afrikaans names represented; but these seem to have been generally proficient in English, having acquired a more advanced education than that available to the bulk of the old Boer population.[90] Investment in education was indispensable to survival on the land for the Boers by the early years of the twentieth century. Those who received only rudimentary schooling in the traditional fashion were likely eventually to join the urban exodus.[91]

Diversification of farming activities was a key to profit and security over the long term. Nevertheless, it is probable that most farmers continued to be reliant on credit for much of the time, and rarely made large profits over and above what was required for basic consumption needs and servicing of debts, except in unusually good years. Indebtedness and a shortage of working capital might explain the fact that through much of the arable Highveld, farmers continued to concentrate on maize farming at the expense of other branches of production. By the 1920s over 80 per cent of the maize transported by rail in South Africa was grown in the 'maize triangle' of the Highveld, although under 60 per cent of the maize grown in South Africa was produced there. Thus the major maize-producing districts of the Orange Free State and southern Transvaal had become specialized in the production of maize for markets, internal and external.

The almost exclusive reliance on maize by many farmers was in the 1920s increasingly a cause for concern amongst agricultural economists.[92] Maize monocropping not only made farmers very vulnerable and dependent on increasing doses of state aid as the century progressed, but also had detrimental effects on soil fertility and made erosion a major problem by the 1930s. In African folklore, the drought of 1932–3 is remembered as the 'great winds of red dust'.

The emergence and survival of a capitalist agriculture on the South African Highveld, despite the vicissitudes of climate and market fluctuation, has entailed not only the control and accumulation of capital under the auspices of a paternalistic state, but also the creation and control of a work force. It is with this latter aspect that the next chapter is concerned.

5 The Making of a Servile Tenantry

LABOUR TENANCY: THE CONSTRAINTS OF CAPITAL AND THE RESISTANT PEASANTRY

The proletarianization of blacks on the land was not in the interests of white farmers, whatever the populist rhetoric of many might suggest. A dependent, servile and malleable labour force they certainly wanted and agitated for, but not one without property. As we have seen, black-controlled productive resources were often indispensable for white survival and accumulation on the land.[1] The use of tenants' means of production, most importantly plough oxen, was of crucial importance to white farmers whose capital resources were limited. But for almost all capitalizing farmers, even if they did not use the productive resources of their tenants, tenant household labour was preferable to wage labour. White farmers had plenty of experience of the instability and fluctuating nature of temporary wage labour supplies, and much preferred to maintain labour tenancy as the primary source of labour power. The greater attraction of wage levels in towns and mines meant that farmers were at an enormous competitive disadvantage in the labour market. Cash wage payments were still by no means general for the labour services of tenants, who were bound to the soil for their subsistence. It was not cash which ensured their service, but the security of their tenure on the land, the crops they reaped and the stock they grazed. K. R. Macaskill of Ruilplaats, Clocolan, wrote to *The Friend* in 1911:

> To abolish squatters and to rely on hiring boys would render the greater majority of farmers helpless, while the mines are 50 000 boys short. Farmers in a large way, for estate work, pay from 20*s* to 25*s* per month, and cannot command the number they require.[2]

A Harrismith correspondent made the same point when he wrote that he and his neighbours were jeered at every time they went to Basutoland or Witsieshoek to hire workers. 'If you wish to work properly keep your natives on your farm, and then you know where to find them and make your arrangements accordingly.'[3] The advantage of stockowning tenants not only derived from the productive potential of their plough oxen, but also their stockholdings put a premium on stability of settlement, given their lack of ready mobility.[4]

Most farmers could not be sure of sufficient cash income throughout the year to be able to pay cash wages to a proletarian work force. If money was tight, loans being called in and crops in a poor way, farmers were very hard-pressed to pay wages as well. The rural economy was still largely based on credit in the early 1900s. It was under these circumstances that farmers with labour tenants were greatly advantaged. For in so far as the workers were able to feed themselves by the produce of their own fields, the white farmers' liquidity problems were eased. If the crops failed, the tenant family had to improvise as best it could, for the employer was under no obligation to pay a fixed wage irrespective of year-to-year fluctuations in the productivity of labour.

But the nature of arable production also needs to be examined if the capital constraints behind labour tenancy are to be fully understood. This was characterized by relatively short periods of 'labour time' contrasted with long periods of 'production time' – when crops were growing but little labour was required. In other words, a considerable labour effort was required for short periods at particular times in the annual cycle (most intensely at harvest time) interspersed with long periods when the work load was minimal. Thus the work force was inevitably underutilized for much of the year. Farmers were reluctant to rely on temporary wage labourers for relatively short periods of employment more than was absolutely necessary. The most efficient means of maintaining a dependable work force on stand-by during periods when natural processes took over from labour processes in the growth and maturation of crops was the maintenance of some form of tenancy, whereby the employer was freed from the necessity of paying a wage during periods when little labour was being expended in the fields.

A Thaba Nchu farmer defended 'squatting' in January 1913 by reference to this point:

> Owing to the erratic seasons there are months at a time when there is almost absolute stagnation, and a farmer must be a bit of a capitalist if he is going to keep in full pay a host of labourers who are only wanted at certain times.[5]

It was the intermittent, irregular and unpredictable nature of productive labour in agriculture to which Andries Burger, Member of the Legislative Assembly for Ladybrand, was referring when he expressed the interests of the undercapitalized farmers of the eastern districts in 1908: 'What is a man to do with his corn ripe, shearing time at hand, and, perhaps, the scab inspector on his track, if he were limited to the small number of servants that he could afford to hire?' 'Squatters' were an absolute necessity for farmers with arable lands, he said.[6]

But not only did tenancy lower labour costs for white farmers, it also potentially made available to farmers the labour of entire tenant households. Given the mostly non-mechanized nature of production, the labour of women and children was vital in the landlord's fields (not to mention in his home as well). Women used hoes to weed the young crop, and boys helped with ploughing and herding. Women and children were particularly valuable at the harvest, the most labour-intensive of seasonal activities.[7] They had the added advantage that their labour was cheaper than that of adult men (where wages were paid – such as at harvest time). They were also relatively dependent on household heads, who served a crucial function in the control and direction of family labour.[8]

In the absence of a cash wage, white farmers were not averse to members of tenant households migrating elsewhere for part of the year – despite the dangers of desertion by young men and women no longer willing to subsidize tenant income in this way – as it enabled them to pay their taxes, buy necessary items of consumption, and tide over bad crop years. Migrancy infused landlord–tenant relations with a degree of instability and uncertainty, for such relationships depended heavily on control by seniors in tenant households over the labour of junior members when required by the white farmer, as well as over their earnings when away from the farm. The temporary wage labourers on one farm were often members of permanent tenant households on another farm. However, it was generally only during unproductive seasons – mainly after the reaping and threshing – that tenants would be given leave to go out and earn cash. General Olivier of the Lindley district told the Transvaal Labour Commission in 1903 that on his 1500-morgen farm, from seven to ten Africans were continuously employed throughout the year. Sometimes a larger number was required:

At certain seasons, for instance, when we are sowing and when we are reaping, we require a larger number. When we do not require them, about half the Kaffirs on the farm go and seek work. So that continuously half of the Kaffirs on the farm are working out in other districts – in Johannesburg, or somewhere else – and the other half are at home.[9]

Visits to towns or rail construction sites where wages were higher than on the farms (£2–3 a month could be earned) were often preferred to temporary agricultural employments. But the amount of time which tenants could spend away from the land was restricted by the intermittent and unregulated nature of labour service on the farms. A tenant under a labour contract who worked for six months continuously could often then leave the farm for six months; but most contracted members of tenant families were allowed at most only two months' leave at a time, in which case they could not travel very far in search of employment.

White farmers' preference for a tenant labour force rather than a proletarian one partly explains the common method of wage payment in kind, increasingly common as the twentieth century progressed and white farming became more capitalized, whereby the produce of a particular portion of the arable land was designated as belonging to the African tenant. The land would usually be worked as part of the general arable operations or the tenant might be loaned the means of production for use himself.[10] This arrangement, again, was a natural outgrowth of the lack of ready liquid resources at the disposal of white farmers throughout the year which would enable them to pay regular wages. Like sharecropping, this form of wage payment had the great advantage that it lessened employers' risks. The white farmer would not have to foot a wage bill if the crops failed, and if the crops succeeded, all would benefit. The tenant was then primarily responsible for his own subsistence from the proceeds of his crop until the following harvest.[11] Thus, the mobility of farm workers was lessened too, as their service was assured until the harvest. Further, the white farmer could appropriate stalks and cobs as winter feeding for his own stock – an important consideration at a time when seasonal trekking was becoming increasingly difficult.[12] Many fully capitalized white farmers seem to have increasingly preferred such arrangements to allowing the tenants to produce their own crops independently using their own oxen in their own time; for employers could then maintain tighter control over the tenants' work time. In this way, the advantages of tenancy were maintained while control over the tenants' lives was tightened. Indeed, by the 1930s, when many farm tenants had lost the wherewithal to plough for themselves, the system of ploughing plots on behalf of tenant families became the dominant practice on the land of capitalized farmers.[13]

*   *   *

Although the tenant community composed the core of the labour force, most white arable farmers required some seasonal recourse to some temporary migrant wage labour, particularly during the harvest. The difficulty of procuring harvest labour from off the farm particularly in good seasons was a major obstacle to wheat and oat cultivation, which was more labour-intensive than the maize harvest and had to be completed much more quickly if the grain was not to be ruined. During the November–January wheat harvest 1s or 1s 6d per day or 1s 6d to 2s 6d per hundred sheaves might be paid, or a share of the crop reaped, such as a tenth.[14] Men and women were equally involved in harvesting. Where reaping machines were not in use, wheat was cut by sickle, then bound into sheaves, and placed in stooks for drying before being transported to the threshing stacks. Reaping by sickle was a tedious and time-consuming process, requiring three or five men to cut an acre of wheat a day.[15] Wealthier farmers often required up to a hundred labourers or more at such times. At least one highly capitalized Conquered Territory farmer, David Scott of Rondeberg, who often employed seventy black workers in his extensive fields and to work his mill and threshing machine, imported quantities of cheap Cape brandy in order to throw a party and thus ensure a ready supply of harvesters. Not surprisingly, he was indignant when the brandy was confiscated by the authorities at Bloemfontein while being transported from Kimberley on his ox wagon in January 1889.[16] In the eastern and northeastern wheat districts of the Orange Free State the seasonal supply of labour was met in large part by migrations over the border from Basutoland. For example, a farmer on the border hired no fewer than 300 Africans for two days to do his reaping in 1913, paying each one bag for every ten he reaped. J. M. van Reenen of Ladybrand commonly went himself to Maseru to find fifty, sixty or seventy men for reaping each year – as did any number of farmers. This seasonal labour force would generally bring their own sickles on to the employers' fields.[17] Harvesters generally seem to have been recruited through chiefs and heads of homesteads.[18] It was also usual for permanent farm tenants to be paid the same rates as temporary hirelings at harvest time. At these times, great movements of labour from farm to farm were usual.

Given the labour intensity of the wheat harvest, the supply of seasonal labour was never very satisfactory from the white farmer's point of view. Few farmers could rely on acquiring sufficient labour at the right time for their purposes. This difficulty was exacerbated by the fact that the seasonal workers were members of and had obligations to peasant households. When the crops were good in the white farmers' fields, they were also good in the African households' fields. So when the white farmer most needed ready labour, it was least forthcoming.[19] In 1897, when Orange Free State farmers appealed to villagers in Basutoland to help with their harvests, the *Volksraad* was told, the Sotho answered that they were willing to hire Orange Free State burghers for the same purpose.[20] This situation was exacerbated as the labour requirements of the industrial economy steadily encroached on the traditional areas of seasonal agricultural recruiting – such as Basutoland.

The Sotho reapers were undoubtedly skilled practitioners. A farmer on the Basutoland border was full of praise for them in 1893: 'Their style of reaping and binding would gladden the heart of a Highland or Irish crofter who has to look after every straw. For good workmanship they beat any reaping machine ever introduced into this country.' He supported his opinion with the fact that he had harvested and threshed 1150 muids of wheat besides a quantity of oats by early February, using only Sotho labour.[21] However, whatever skills Sotho reapers brought with them on to farms, the overwhelming experience of white farmers was of the unreliability of seasonal labour supplies. A Senekal correspondent urging farmers to band together to buy reaping machines in 1894 estimated that machines saved $10\frac{1}{2}d$ per muid in reaping costs:

> One of the greatest drawbacks at the present time is the difficulty of harvesting crops when ripe. Much corn is deteriorated several shillings per muid by being left too long uncut. It becomes overripe, the husk becomes thickened and serious loss is caused to the percentage of meal and flour. Another loss is the quantity shaken out by the wind which in some varieties is as much as 25 to 35 per cent of the whole crop. Further loss is caused by hailstorms.[22]

The enormous risks involved in relying on a ready and sufficient supply of reapers at the right time were a major spur to mechanization from quite early days. During years when bumper crops coincided with financial boom, such as 1893–4 and 1911, there was widespread demand for reaping machines in the wheat districts.[23] But although reaping machines eased the situation, they did not solve the farmers' harvest problems. Senator H. G. Stuart of Marquard district pinpointed one problem in September 1912:

> In these parts, last wheat season, when the crop was unexpectedly good and when there was a sudden, hopeless scarcity of hands for reaping, several men rushed to the nearest store in a sort of panic and ordered reaping machines. What was the result? In most cases the machines very soon came to grief through faulty handling, were sworn at for being no good, and left alone, and the enterprising buyers

had to scour the country for sickle hands. I believe I am within the mark if I say that thousands of pounds sterling were lost last season in wheat and machinery through ignorance and unpreparedness.[24]

It seems that labour-intensive methods during the harvest seasons remained an indispensable element of production for most farmers, especially given the meagre capital base of much settler agriculture, the unreliability of machinery and the difficulty of acquiring spare parts once boom conditions had subsided and credit became tighter. In fact, during the first two decades of the twentieth century, the more reliable (although less profitable) maize was ousting the winter cereals such as wheat as the major crop of the eastern Orange Free State, and a primary reason for this, as we have seen, was the difficulty of procuring sufficient seasonal labour at the right moment for harvesting.[25] Further, wheat production was restricted to districts adjacent to Basutoland until mechanization became more viable from the 1930s on, because of the unavailability of seasonal labour further afield.[26]

The maize harvest which began in June was a simpler and less labour-intensive process than the reaping of winter crops such as wheat, and thus posed far less of a seasonal labour problem. It entailed picking the cobs, removing the husks, placing them in sacks, and transporting them to the shelling machines. Women might be paid 1*d* per bag of unhusked maize and 3*d* per bag of husked maize.[27] This hand labour was not mechanized until much later in the century, as it was common practice to leave the maize plants standing in the fields for winter feeding of cattle once the grain had been picked. Indeed, in 1911, when wheat-reaping machines were being imported in large numbers, it was reported that no maize-harvesting machine was then available for sale in the country.[28]

A major difference between the maize harvest and the wheat harvest was that the latter had to be completed in a relatively short space of time, or else the grain began to fall out of the ears. In the Orange Free State, too, the wheat harvest took place in the middle of the rainy season (November–December) and standing cereal crops could be ruined by excessive rain once ripened.[29] The maize harvest was not so urgent a matter, taking place as it did in the dry winter months, and hence it was an activity that could be spread out, thereby reducing somewhat the pressure on available labour resources. Often the maize harvest on the larger farms lasted two or three months, until August or September or even later.[30] A farmer in the Heilbron district who reportedly grew 1800 bags in 1910 could not complete the reaping until December[31] (– but at this time such a yield was unusually large).[32]

Thus the maize harvest was not as dependent as the wheat harvest on the ready supplies of reserve labour at short notice. No matter how large the maize harvest, the question of harvest labour never seems to have become as debilitating an obstacle as was the case during seasons of bumper wheat crops such as 1911. However, maize demanded more attention during the growing stage than did wheat; it had to be weeded or harrowed in order to ensure a good growth. Hence in the maize districts the labour problem was more one of ensuring a satisfactory complement of tenant family labour sufficient for year-round farming activities.[33]

*   *   *

White farmers' predilection for tenant labour for as much of the farm work as possible, and the greater viability of crops which did not depend on large-scale recruitment of seasonal wage labour, can be understood in terms of such constraints as these. But equally important, African resistance to the alienation of their productive resources was a major factor in the ubiquity of tenancy relationships, even on the land of capitalized farmers. The resiliency of the peasant economy, its resistance to permanent dispossession, coincided in some degree with the interests of the white farmers. Some sense of the peasant consciousness of farm workers is provided by Tshwene Mmolotsi, whose family lived in the northern Orange Free State. He still remembers the shattering experience of his family losing its independent productive base in the aftermath of the Anglo-Boer War:

> We had to start cattle-rearing from scratch. We had no alternative but to go and beg the whites for work because we were going to die of hunger. We ploughed their fields with their cattle that they were given by the government. Having ploughed for them they would then give us small pieces of land to plough for ourselves. . . . Our standard of living became very low. We survived by borrowing and lending to each other. If you had no animal and suffered a great deal, a brother or relative or friend or neighbour would lend you his cow so that you could milk it and drink its milk. [The whites] did not care about us. We had to see to our own affairs and support ourselves. . . . The thing that helped us to survive these hard times was that we loved and helped each other. A group of us would club together and cultivate 3 or 4 strips of land for each of us. . . . At the end of the harvest one would be able to get a calf here and another there. [The white man]

would call us to come to his house and thereafter order us to go and chop the wood for him. On coming back in the evening he would give you small pieces of wood if he liked you. That is how we lived until such time that our cattle had multiplied again. A man would come and borrow your scotch cart and when returning it the following day he would voluntarily give a present in thanking you.[34]

There is little indication here of a resignation to the loss of productive resources or to working-class status. The reciprocal, redistributive economy which inhibited individual accumulation also insured households against permanent separation from the means of production.[35]

Few black workers in the early years of this century would have seen themselves as members of a rural proletariat. Those who found themselves unable to work land independently did not consider this an immutable condition, but sought to establish or re-establish their productive independence as peasants.[36] Most black workers on white-owned farms would have regarded themselves as essentially members of peasant households who were providing tenant labour as rent to the white holder of land on which they lived, or who were seeking to accumulate stock and other means of production by rendering labour. Many would have been young, unmarried men who had not yet established their own households, either individual migrants or members of tenant households working under the aegis of their senior male kin. Even household heads working for wages typically aimed to accumulate sufficient to work the land themselves as peasant producers, with the eventual goal of sending their children to work in their stead and reducing their own need to render labour. Other such households might have been fragmentary offshoots of larger homesteads in black territories such as Basutoland, who maintained membership of the homestead economy there.

This peasant consciousness and this accumulative urge amongst farm workers also partly explains the forms of wage payment in kind – by designation of part of the arable as belonging to the tenant household – described earlier. Black tenant households who were dependent on resources controlled by their landlords to produce a crop were generally concerned to make use of the opportunities to accumulate or reaccumulate sufficient resources of their own to break free from their dependence. Young unattached men or new households which had not yet accumulated sufficiently to work their own land themselves would be involved in such arrangements, which provided opportunities of profit by sale of surplus to itinerant traders or local shopkeepers. Edgar Webb of Tweespruit told in 1911 of an African herd who declined a cash wage, saying it would only suffice to feed his family. Instead, he wanted land ploughed for him and planted with maize and sorghum, the landlord supplying the plough and seed. When the man left the farm after a year's contract, he took with him twenty to thirty bags of grain.[37]

Further, wage labour in the towns or elsewhere by migrant members of tenant households no more implied proletarian status or proletarian consciousness than did labour service for white landlords. It too was a means of accumulation, either on the labourer's own account or on account of the larger patrilineal homestead to which he belonged, by a younger member of what was still essentially and subjectively a peasant society. Labour migracy, far from invariably being a function of rural dispossession, was often a means of shoring up the black rural economy. Despite the degree of differentiation evident amongst black tenants on the farms and the increasingly servile status of many, they were still far from being transformed into a working class.[38]

Tenants' resistance to proletarianization – the loss of productive resources and of access to land for cultivation – needs to be taken into account when considering the entrenchment of tenancy as the major form of labour relationship on the farms. It was, however, becoming more and more difficult in the early decades of the twentieth century for young men to establish their productive independence on the land. Capitalizing farmers preferred to plough land for tenants as part of the general arable operation (even when many of the oxen did not belong to the white farmer himself but to Africans) rather than to allow the dependent tenantry to continue controlling their own productive domain. Decreasing numbers of tenant households were able to retain control over rural production in the long term. Only the most adaptable, tenacious and mobile were able to defy the surging tide of white supremacy in the rural economy by mid-century.[39]

CONFLICT, CONTROL AND THE PROCESS OF LAW

During the boom periods in the development of white agriculture, the struggle to intensify the extraction of surplus from African tenants, to transform their status and undermine their independence, and the struggle to resist these pressures, were fought out in the context of the contract of tenancy. In periods of productive expansion and of heightened tension and conflict between black and white on the land (such as 1893–5 and 1908–13) the contract or *akkoord* became the flashpoint of struggle and resistance. Emelia Pooe, speaking of the Heilbron district in the 1890s, remembers:

> Winter time in the Orange Free State was the time for trekking . . . there was a lot of disagreement between the landlords and the tenant labourers because of the changed *akkoorde*. After harvesting the landlord would call a meeting and you would hear him say: *'Vandag sal ons weer 'n ander akkoord maak. Ons sal nie weer met daardie akkoord werk nie'*. [Today we shall draw up a new agreement. We shall not work under the old agreement any longer.] He would then proceed to explain what they would have to do in the new year. Under such arrangements, no sooner would the year be out than most people showed a lot of dissatisfaction. They would have no choice but to leave.[40]

The typical contract of tenancy was generally a loose verbal agreement that the household head and/or members of his family had to perform certain duties when called upon by the farmer. Seldom was a definite period agreed upon in the first instance, and such agreements often continued year after year without any formal renewal (provided there was no attempt to alter them to the advantage of one party – such as commonly happened in times of crisis) on the tacit understanding that they could be terminated by either party at the end of any reaping season. The confusion reigning in the matter of contracts made them difficult to enforce and resulted in endless wrangling.[41] Africans frequently had no very clear conception of what was entailed by the contract to which they had apparently agreed; and the white man's understanding of the arrangement very often reflected none too accurately the agreement to which the African thought he had been party. Contracts which were negotiated in a European tongue were wide open to abuse, especially since they were seldom written down. Farmers and their organizations repeatedly urged that written contracts be mandatory, but seldom acted on their own advice.[42]

The chief statutory instrument regulating labour relationships and enforcing contracts in republican days was the Masters and Servants Act of 1873. The law stipulated that oral contracts were to be witnessed by two persons. However, this provision was rarely heeded. The control functions of the law are evident in the provisions for criminal sanction against the breaking of contracts, carelessness or irresponsibility in the carrying out of duties, incapacity for work as a result of drunkenness, use for the servant's own purposes of his/her master's property, disobedience, the use of insubordinate language toward anyone in authority, and losing, damaging or enrisking the master's property as a result of dereliction. The criminalization of a potentially very wide range of acts of commission or omission by servants applied only to blacks, and laid no corresponding legal sanction on employers.[43]

The law was clearly a particularly powerful weapon in the enforcement of labour agreements and servile status. For example, it seems to have been quite common for contracts to define the working day as beginning at sunrise and ending at sunset. This time discipline which employers sought to impose was the source of much conflict. Again, it was quite common for servants to desert on the grounds that they had been ordered to perform certain work which had not been stipulated in contracts – most notably transport work which involved journeying away from home. These conflicts revolving around the terms of contracts were reflected in much criminal prosecution in local courts under the Masters and Servants Act.[44]

Tenancy agreements or contracts were entered into by household heads and bound the labour of family members (often including married sons) in return for rights of tenancy. Thus a number of elderly informants describe themselves as having had to work for white farmers when young in order to secure their fathers' tenancy, while their fathers were responsible for maintaining and organizing the family farming enterprise. Emelia Pooe remembers:

> most Boers wanted to know from any new tenant how many boys he had so that he could determine beforehand whether he had a shepherd for his sheep, a *handlanger* [assistant] on the ploughing span, and finally, a boy who would milk the cows. Only then would he consider entering into an agreement whereby the tenant would be allowed to stay on the farm.[45]

Jameson Molete recalls that

> In those days when you looked for a place, the Boers would ask you the number of children you had. . . . In order to find a place from a farmer, you had to have two children to work in his house. In other words, they were on contract, and that enabled you to stay on that farm with your cattle. . . . But if one of your children fought with him, you would get the sack and you would have to search for another place. . . . One would work in the kitchen, the other one would look after cattle. You would never find a place unless you had children.[46]

Even for temporary hiring of individual workers who did not live on the farm for a few months' labour, white farmers very often negotiated the contracts with seniors. This applied often to recruitment of seasonal workers for reaping. The local courts were even known to cancel contracts which were disputed by the hirelings' parents, who often insisted that their children (even those who were adults) had no independent contractual capacity. The courts tended to place their full weight behind parental authority.[47]

Moving on to a new farm often involved a good deal of negotiation over conditions of tenancy, especially if (as was still often the case before 1914) the black settlement group consisted of a large, multi-generational family. 'When the group intended moving, they sent out at least two members from amongst the group to go and negotiate for accommodation with landowners first; once this had been obtained they came back to the family', according to Ndae Makume. When the Makume family moved from Christiaan Rabie's farm in 1913, Ndae's father and uncle, Sefake, had already made arrangements with Danie du Brill for the whole family to settle on his land: the group included Ndae's great-grandfather (the family head), his grandfather, and his uncles and their families. Du Brill even provided a span and wagon to supplement the family's, so that they could transport their belongings to their new home.[48]

When tenants moved, they were sometimes given testimonials on their passes. Ndae Makume recalls:

> Yes, they would write you a pass and in it the work that you were capable of doing. If you were a thief, they would know and you would notice it by the fact that nobody would give you permission to stay on their farm, then you would know that the pass had told them that they may take you at their own risk.[49]

But this was probably the exception rather than the rule. It was often suggested that the mandatory writing of credentials for each worker at the expiration of contracts would help to lessen the uncertainty of hiring labour and also severely reduce the bargaining power of the prospective tenants in negotiating terms.[50]

Junior members of tenant households were not themselves party to such tenancy agreements, although they were at the cutting edge of master–servant relationships. As a consequence, strains were likely to be placed on relationships between elders and juniors in tenant households. R. J. Hall of Murphy's Rust near the Natal border wrote in 1909 to the magistrate in Harrismith, begging him to intervene to force an elderly tenant's family members to work for him. 'The old man is a good old sort, but his family are quite unmanageable and he cannot do anything with them himself.' He continued:

> Could you arrange to call him to Harrismith with his wives and children so I could come to some arrangement before you with them for the year 1910? I might be able to come to terms with them, but as it is now, the women refuse to come out when called upon but on account of the old man I don't want to kick him off if I can help it.[51]

The conflict here was not simply between father and his children, but between husband and his wives in a polygynous family. The wives apparently resisted attempts to force them to labour, and also protected their own children from such pressures. It seems that Hall was able, in some degree, to elicit the support of the household head in his attempts to force the women and children to labour.

The heads of black households were likely to be only too aware that their own survival and security as peasant producers relied on the exploitation of their offspring. Patriarchs of large families often developed alliances of interest with their landlords in the control and direction of family labour. There were great advantages in particular for the heads of large patrilineal settlement groups in placing themselves under the patronage of large landholders, who controlled valued land resources and who helped to shore up the relations of authority within the extended black family.

One factor which was likely to sour this relationship and lead to legal proceedings or ejection was the desertion of the children. They often had special reason to desert, not having any direct interest in the maintenance of contractual relations, and generally getting no more than a pittance, if anything, by way of compensation for their labour – both in household fields and in the service of the landlord. An Orange Free State farmer wrote in 1911, when white agriculture was expanding rapidly with predictable effects on farmers' labour demands on their tenants and at a time of boom in the urban economy, that within a year or two of a family settling on his farm:

> we were left with the old fathers and mothers and the small children, whereas the working boys and girls have gone to Johannesburg or other towns. When once they get there they do not like to leave. . . . The time has come for us to stand up for our rights. We have housed and fed the Kaffirs on our farms, not for our own benefit, but the benefit of Johannesburg and other towns.[52]

A Harrismith farmer complained in the same year:

> The children run away and will not work, and their parents are driven
> away because they are unable . . . to compel their children to return.
> The unfortunate parents appeal to the farmer: 'We do not wish to
> leave; let the police rather catch the children and bring them back.
> Why does the Government treat us so that our children are allowed to
> leave us?' This is a daily occurrence.[53]

However, household heads also had obligations toward their own
wives, sons and daughters, and were often prepared to take up the
cudgels on their behalf against a demanding landlord. Thus in 1912 at a
time of rapid development in white agriculture, Johannes Moiloa's
father moved off one Marais' farm near Marquard because his children
were being 'exploited and overworked' and his protests 'landed on deaf
ears' in the words of his son. It is perhaps no coincidence that Johannes
(then in his 21st year) had the previous year fled the farm, first for the
railway works in Bloemfontein, and then for the Kimberley mines,
without informing his family of his whereabouts. He returned in 1913
when the family had already moved to Theuns Wessels' farm near
Winburg. Johannes, two brothers and two sisters had together been
paid £2 10s a month by Marais for their labour. The new landlord by
contrast had two farms, one occupied only by blacks, who cultivated the
soil. Moiloa's three sons, including Johannes, worked the land with him,
and his two daughters worked for Wessels.[54] Household heads often
resented what they saw to be unfair or autocratic treatment by
employers, which they also perceived as undermining their own
authority.

So family heads typically found themselves seeking to mediate
struggles between landlords and family members, and being torn two
ways in the process. Two cases under the Masters and Servants Act
heard by the *vrederechter* (justice of the peace) in Bothaville in
November 1895 will demonstrate the variety of responses elicited by the
intermediate positions of household heads. In November one Jonas sent
his son Piet away from the farm Enkeldoorns on which they lived, as
the landlord J. J. A. Geldenhuis had not asked his permission to take
Piet with him on a trip to buy sheep. 'The *baas* should have come and
asked me nicely if he could take Piet with him and not just have taken
him', Jonas told the court. Although Jonas' sons were contracted by
their father to work for the landlord when required, Jonas expected
them to be paid for undertaking trips with their master. In the
altercation which followed Jonas' act of defiance, violence erupted, and

the hapless tenant was imprisoned for fourteen days and subjected to fifteen lashes for his attempt to assert some control over his son's conditions of labour.[55]

On the other hand, 'Ou Jan', who lived on the farm Dwaalfontein near Bothaville, followed his son, Armoed, to town when the latter absconded one night in October 1895 and personally brought him before the *vrederechter* to be punished for desertion from his master's service. Armoed and his brother were contracted to their landlord by their father, who had access to grazing and ploughing land in return. Armoed had been worked hard by the landlord, herding cattle in the dry months and reaping oats. Ou Jan felt unable to punish his son himself, as the latter was 23 years of age; and as Armoed had deserted before, Ou Jan felt a suitable punishment inflicted by the *vrederechter* would be in order. The *vrederechter* obliged, fining Armoed 40*s* or twelve strokes with the *kats* (cat-o'-nine-tails). The strokes were duly delivered, no doubt to the entire satisfaction of the miscreant's father. Ou Jan was not yet prepared to grant his 23-year-old son the contractual freedom befitting his years, as his own access to land depended on his ability to deliver his sons' labour to the landlord, entirely at the latter's discretion. And again, the local *vrederechter* was concerned to uphold the parental authority, even though Armoed was legally a major.[56]

Additional complications in generational conflict were provided when young children – valuable assets as future labourers – were the subject of rival claims between their paternal household and their mother's family. Given the fact that the arrangement of marriage was often a long-drawn-out process, corresponding to the transfer of bridewealth cattle, there was plenty of room for conflict over the extent of conjugal and paternal rights enjoyed by a husband or father. Reginald Luck of Rensburg's Kop, Harrismith district, appealed to the magistrate in 1909 to retrieve a 10-year-old child from the custody of his maternal grandparents who were refusing to give him up and who had raised the child since the age of 18 months. The boy's father (who might or might not have been his genitor) had, according to his landlord, Luck, 'twice offered *lobola* for his wife, but the old man refuses to part with the child'. The landlord's interest in this matter of three-generational conflict (to the point of calling the police) arose from the fact that this 10-year-old boy had been employed as a herd for his calves before he decided to move off with his grandparents.[57]

Conflicts were particularly likely to arise during periods of transition within tenant families, when children grew up, when sons were beginning to set up their own households, when daughters married and moved away, or when elders withdrew from the work force or died. Rebecca Mogoai, born in 1889, remembers vividly the explosive conflict on Andries Cronje's farm Kromdraai, north of the Vaal River in Potchefstroom district, in the late 1890s. Rebecca's extended family, including her cousins, lived in what she calls a *stat* – a large homestead or village – on the farm. When the junior members of the settlement group grew to maturity, a conflict arose over whether they were to be bound by the contract like their fathers:

> The white men wanted our young men to work for them on their farms. They did not want them to go and work in towns. The young men refused and said, 'No we have not entered any contract with you. That is the agreement you made with our parents. Even though we used to work on the farm, it was only to help them'. . . . The landlord threatened to put them in jail or kill us if we all left for Potchefstroom town, because he claimed we were bound by the *akkoorde* . . . . He said, 'You cannot let your grown-up sons go and work in town. I want them here on this farm'. And they said, 'No, when our fathers entered the contract, we were not there. They are the ones who are to come daily to work on your farm. They work for you'. The Boer started hating them.[58]

We do not know what the attitudes of the older men in the situation was, but it is clear that they too were caught in between two irreconcilable forces, and were ultimately held responsible for the failure of their juniors to enter the landlord's service.

Quite young children, even pre-adolescents, were also vulnerable to the determination of white farmers to extract greater and more consistent labour from their tenants. Thus, one farmer suggested in 1893 that the Masters and Servants Act should apply to girls as well as boys from the age of twelve. Another urged action to ensure that all *jongens en meiden* should be in service for at least nine months of the year from the age of eight. Young children were used to herd small stock, work in the home, and to help with lighter work at harvest. W. Burns-Thompson told the Legislative Council in 1906 that Harrismith farmers felt that 'a good deal of their most valuable labour' consisted of boys and girls under sixteen, and that to allow children 'to move about without passes is extremely detrimental to their interests as farmers'.[59]

The emergent black elite, with its preoccupation with education, was particularly incensed by the exploitation of child labour on the farms. African associations regarded the 'enslavement' of black children as a major grievance. In discussing a proposal to erect a high school for blacks, a meeting of 200 Africans in Vrede in 1912 deplored the practice of including the labour service of black children in labour contracts on the farms. 'For no Native man is allowed to live on a farm if he thinks he can do what he likes with his children.' No matter what age they were, they were regarded as belonging to the master, it was asserted.[60] The majority of Africans on the farms were unlikely to have the same preoccupation with schooling, but they probably shared the sentiment.

Similarly, demands for the labour of women, and the treatment of women, were major flash points in relationships between employers and tenant households, also reflected in domestic conflicts within tenant households. Johannes Moiloa's wife remembers that she was obliged to do the washing for the landlord's family on Fridays. Her children would accompany her and help dust the furniture. In winter she would be responsible for preparing a slaughtered cow for the labourers on the threshing machine. But if she had a new-born baby, she did not expect to have to work in the whites' home. The Moiloas eventually left the farms and moved to Koppies location in the 1930s, because of the tensions generated by the increased demands of the landlord, Jan Erasmus of Moriya, and his wife on Mrs Moiloa's labour. Clearly Moiloa felt bitterly frustrated by his efforts to mediate between the demands of his wife and the Erasmuses. 'The whole set-up just got my head saturated and I could not take it any more; so I decided to leave the farm life once and for all. I came to the urban areas where everyone would be free to sell his or her labour to a white of his or her choice.' The tensions between motherhood and domestic work were crucial here, for Mrs Moiloa had recently given birth and was in no mood to bow to Mrs Erasmus' unyielding claims on her time.[61] This episode from the 1930s undoubtedly throws light on domestic rivalries and conflicts in the earlier period as well, although by the 1930s the tenantry as a whole might have been far more willing to accept the proletarian alternative to farm life. Tenancy usually implied that family members were vulnerable to constant harassment of this sort – unlike the proletarianized life in the towns. However, many tenants were no doubt able to protect their wives from landlords' demands.

Although women had independent contractual power, they were generally considered to be bound by contracts entered into by their husbands. It was usually in white landlords' interests to uphold husbands' conjugal authority in tenant households, except where husbands sought to protect their wives against excessive demands.[62] There is little evidence of women entering independent contracts with landlords as heads of tenant households. Presumably white farmers were not prepared to entrust control over male workers to their female kin. There is also little evidence of widespread conjugal instability such as was to become so marked a feature of African life in the margins of the industrial economy later in the twentieth century.

Control over women's productive and reproductive capacities (partly for bridewealth income) was of crucial importance to their parental households. The movement of single women into towns – often to escape the labour demands made upon them – was a matter of critical concern to senior males in tenant families as well as to landlords.[63] It was not so much married women who posed the problem for white farmers, it was their daughters, whose labour was usually depended upon for housework in white homes and who were also more liable to abscond.[64] It was to prevent this 'social evil' that women in towns in the Orange Free State were obliged to carry passes – an issue which proved the flash point for mass demonstrations in Orange Free State towns in 1913.[65] In 1895, provision was made for the mandatory issuing of passes to black women over sixteen travelling alone in rural areas too, but only if conveying stock or produce.[66] Many of the respondents to the Labour Commission in 1892–3 urged that women be provided with passes, partly because they were supposedly responsible for much stock theft, but also because of their resistance to the demands of white farmers and their wives: 'even young girls run away from their parents, and the fathers sometimes must seek them for weeks and months, being away from their masters' service all this time', wrote one *vrederechter*, M. J. Beukes.[67] Here again the patriarchy of the black household was very likely reinforced, even brutalized, by the demands and pressures of white employers, and the responsibility of household heads to satisfy them. On the other hand, another *vrederechter* wrote that whites were often helpless in the face of black girls' refusal to work in the white homestead, because of the resistance of their fathers, who were too valuable as tenants or workers to be antagonized over access to their daughters' labour.[68] No doubt both perspectives were valid, depending on the individual circumstances and the relative balance of power between white and black.

Many farmers considered that black women should be explicitly subjected to the criminalization provisions in the Masters and Servants Act, that corporal punishment for black women who were 'disobedient' and 'aggressive' toward their 'madams' should be written into the law and that they should be forced to work in the white household when called upon to do so by the police under threat of criminal sanction.[69] Some whites, particularly near the Basutoland border, expressed opposition to traditional initiation schools for girls at which they were inducted into the rites of womanhood; as one *vrederechter* wrote, young girls in tenant families were just becoming serviceable when they were removed to these schools for three months, after which they were regarded as ripe to be 'sold' in marriage.[70] The 'slave trade' in black girls was a constant theme in white ideology.

*   *   *

The Masters and Servants Act as an instrument in masters' hands for enforcing contracts had its limitations for capitalizing white farmers, and not only in relation to women. The legal position of independent tenants was unclear, a failure of definition which became particularly problematic during the boom periods of rapid development and expansion in white and black agriculture alike. In the 1890s farmers pressed for the Masters and Servants Act to be applied to *all* blacks on white-owned land, whatever their terms of tenancy might be.[71] The higher courts (as opposed to the lower courts) tended to interpret the law as applying only to servants who had been contracted to provide regular labour in return for a prearranged wage, and not to members of tenant families or communities who were expected under a loose oral agreement to work for the landlord when called upon, and who were considered by some to be thus immune from criminal prosecution under the law.[72] This would, for example, have been the case with sharecroppers, whether or not they were also expected to provide labour service. As James Collins, *landdros* in Ladybrand, wrote, the agreements of tenancy were generally very unspecific and unclear, and it was doubtful whether many tenants would be formally culpable for refusal to work, if the law were to be strictly interpreted.[73]

In fact many of the local criminal courts gave such legal distinctions little credence, allowing themselves to become the instruments of the master class, particularly during republican days. Nonetheless the ambiguity of the legal position did cause uncertainty. There was always the possibility that the finding of a lower court would be overturned by a higher court.[74] This became an issue of great concern during such periods as the mid-1890s when rural production was expanding and struggle between black and white agriculturalists for control over productive resources was growing in intensity. For it was precisely at such times that white farmers were seeking to redefine contracts of tenancy in their own favour, and interpreting oral agreements more stringently. The frustrations of white farmers were referred to by a *vrederechter* from Bethlehem who wrote to the Labour Commission that 'as long as the Kaffirs are regarded as *bywoners* many farmers will be without servants'. A. P. Cronje, commandant of police in Winburg, told the Labour Commission in 1892 that the only solution to the problem was to write into the statute law the servile status of every black living on a white-owned farm.[75] The commissioners agreed, and in the anti-squatting law of 1895, all heads of tenant families who had access to land for cultivation or grazing on a farm, together with their families, were placed under the jurisdiction of the Masters and Servants Act.[76]

However, not for the first time, whites discovered that the law, while an adequate scapegoat for their frustrations, could not engineer the kinds of social transformations they required. Extending the scope of an already repressive law could provide individual landlords with a useful weapon, but it did not break the resistance of tenant farmers to the intensification of their labour-service obligations. Furthermore, within a couple of years of the passing of the law of 1895, rinderpest and drought had ensured that the issue had ceased to be a burning one, pressures on black resources and labour demands on black tenants had subsided, and many whites had become more dependent than ever on black tenant production.

After the Anglo-Boer War, the reconstruction regime replaced the old, loose Masters and Servants Act with a new one, more suited to an urban, industrial environment. The 1904 Masters and Servants Ordinance, based as it was on established British and colonial law, relating to societies in which the working class was white, proletarianized and organized and was paid money wages, defined the term 'servant' so as virtually to exclude tenants.[77] Thus, in a much-publicized test case, the conviction of one 'Doctor' Makiza for desertion was quashed upon judicial review as the judge considered that the relationship of master and servant did not exist. The verbal agreement (whereby Makiza was to perform certain farm work in return for which his employer was to plough land for him) was more nearly a 'bilateral contract', decided the judge:

> Further, the entire service and time of the accused was not at complainant's disposal; he could not be regarded as a servant within the meaning of the Ordinance. In fact, it would be difficult to decide which was master and which was servant.[78]

This interpretation posed an unsustainable challenge to the ubiquitous institutions of tenancy on the farms.

In a circular to magistrates in 1906 the attorney general sought to interpret this ruling widely so as not to emasculate the law altogether in its bearing on tenancy relations. Although it clearly did not apply to sharecropping arrangements or similar conditions of tenancy 'where no actual service is rendered to the farmer', he wrote, the law should apply where 'a native agrees to act say as herd, driver, horsetender, or the like to a farmer under his orders and the remuneration or *quid pro quo* is a right to plough certain land, or to run certain cattle'. Under these circumstances, advised the attorney general, it could be accepted that a contract of service existed.[79] But white farmers were continually frustrated in the face of this lack of definition of what consituted a valid contract of service; they wanted the courts to be invariably available to them in the enforcement of their authority.[80]

* * *

In practice, whatever the trained lawyers who manned the higher courts might decide, and however unpredictable some of the lower courts might be, proceedings in the local courts in which cases concerning labour relations were initially heard seem to have been heavily weighted in favour of the master class. From the criminal record books which survive from the 1890s it seems that *vrederechters* and small-town magistrates mostly saw themselves as the guardians of masters' interests, although some such functionaries were more malleable than others.[81] Indeed, in many local courts, black tenants or servants were seldom acquitted when brought up for petty matters of disobedience (*ongehoorzaamheid*), dereliction (*plichtverzuim*), breach of the peace (*rustverstoring*), impudence (*brutaliteit*), or desertion, all of which were defined as criminal acts in the Masters and Servants Act. Usually the white man's evidence was sufficient to secure criminal conviction, typically with a liberal resort to the *kats* (cat-o'-nine-tails). It was standard practice for corporal punishment to be imposed in masters-and-servants cases under the republican regime; and, as the perceptive reader will already have noted, Africans were never dignified with their own names in these courts, but were referred to by the names they had been given by whites – 'Zwartbooi', 'September' or 'Koos'. This practice constituted an extension of the master–servant relationship into the formal setting of the courts.

Blacks did not usually make use of the opportunity to state their own cases before the courts, so that the white interpretation of events was generally unchallenged, even where, as in the many cases of alleged assault by black servants, the allocation of culpability was highly subjective. Indeed, acts of assault by whites on blacks were often regarded as unexceptional, especially as the white man could probably secure a conviction for whatever offense of omission or commission had allegedly precipitated the assault.[82] It was not often that blacks initiated cases against their employers or landlords, especially since the criminal law was so structured (and liberally interpreted) as to provide a coercive support for white masters in their conflicts with black servants and tenants, while blacks were denied use of the criminal courts for any such purpose, except for specific complaints of, for example, unprovoked assault, such as were provided for in the common law. In practice, though, most Africans simply did not know how to utilize the courts for this purpose, except in the very few cases where they were able to make use of the services of a local law agent. Further, their cases as often as not had to be taken to higher courts – an expensive undertaking – before they received a fair hearing relatively free of the enormous weight of public hostility and judicial prejudice.[83]

But law agents were likely to be employed on behalf of a black where a white employer had an interest in the case, such as in the appeal against *vrederechter* J. C. Bothma's conviction of one September for desertion from J. C. Berry's employ in February 1897. The services of the agent A. J. B. de Villiers of Ladybrand were called in to appeal the case as September's father, backed by his landlord, L. de Jager of Morgenzon, insisted that he had authority over the boy and had not consented to his entering a contract with the aggrieved employer, Berry, in the first place. Arraigned blacks seem to have been more likely to gain a fair hearing when they were in the centre of disputes between landlords and alternative employers competing for their labour.[84] The courts were also usually committed, as in this case, to uphold parental authority even over adult sons – especially where parental authority coincided with the master's interests. The issue of whether Africans who were legally majors could be bound by parental contracts was repeatedly ignored in the lower courts under the republican regime.

The effectiveness of the local courts depended on the speed with which they dispensed their brand of justice. Delays and multiple trips to the district town or *vrederechter*'s farmstead were intolerable to farmers seeking to maintain a tight rein on their work force. P. W. A. Nel of Main Reef farm visited Bothaville on Sunday, 14 April 1895, to attend *Nachtmaal* service. At noon on the next day, his herdsman, Crisjan, arrived in town to inform him that his oxen had wandered. Before setting off back to the farm that same afternoon with his master, Crisjan had been subjected to ten strokes with the *kats* at the behest of the *vrederechter* as a result of his negligence.[85] Often the dispensing of judicial violence in this way seems to have embodied a symbolic assertion of the authority of the master class rather than being a formal punishment for a specific criminal act.

The dispatch of judicial process was facilitated by the provision in the law that masters could forcibly bring their servants with them when calling upon the authority of the local court, without the issuing of a warrant. Blacks on the other hand had to persuade the official concerned to summons the landlord or employer to appear in court. They also had to tackle the obstacle course provided by the pass laws to lay a complaint. J. M. Theunissen, member of the *Volksraad* for Hoopstad district, told in 1895 of cases in his district in which the police had been informed by farmers that their employees were on the way to town to lay complaints of denial of wages and had arrested them under the pass laws before they could get there.[86]

The dispensing of judicial violence was particularly valued as an alternative to imprisonment, which stretched the state's resources and robbed farmers of their servants' labour. Naturally the white farmers did not look kindly on the imprisonment of their own servants. One Johannes Bothma of Roodebult, Ladybrand, had two servants, Jacob and Afrika, prosecuted for stealing a sheep. They were sentenced in October 1890 to 15 months' hard labour and fifteen lashes each. Bothma appealed to the state president in January 1891 to have the two men released as they were the only able-bodied men in their families who could render labour and sow the lands for their dependants' subsistence.[87] Terms of imprisonment were not usually imposed, except for particularly serious crimes.

The local judicial officers also commonly took upon themselves the non-judicial functions of issuing warnings and moral injunctions about the worthiness of obedience and diligence to servants at the behest of their masters. The *landdros* in Ficksburg saw fit to hear a case in 1891 in which W. J. Odendaal and Kleingeld, a Sotho migrant, disagreed about the duration of a contract. Since Kleingeld had not left his work there was no question of any criminal charge being proved; but *landdros* de Villiers considered it his function to uphold Odendaal's authority and order Kleingeld back to work to complete his three months. This was the informal arm of the law – the criminal court in all its awing solemnity being called into session in order to intimidate a recalcitrant worker threatening to leave his master's employ, even where no criminal act had been committed.[88]

The legal bureaucracy at the centre, which was more concerned with the formal, clinical interpretation of the law than with the legitimation and mediation of productive relationships, did not greatly interfere with local judicial initiative during republican days. However, the post-war colonial regime, in its drive to modernize the ramshackle administrative structures of the old republics, undertook to centralize the administration of justice. The lawyers who manned the higher courts were usually trained in the Cape Colony or overseas and were steeped in a more formalist legal tradition than the local functionaries, most of whom had no legal training at all. Under the new administration, the review and routine alteration or quashing of the convictions and sentences of magistrates and Special Justices of the Peace (who replaced *landdrosts* and *vrederechters*) transformed the local courts.[89] Selected cases quashed or altered by the judges in Bloemfontein were annually published from 1903 onward. Magistrates and SJPs were constantly slapped down when they strayed from the strict letter of the law enshrined in the statute book, often on purely technical grounds, and were forced to pay much closer attention to legal nicety than their republican predecessors. One newly appointed SJP, unaware at first of the need to submit all convictions for review, sent in 150 cases in a batch on being informed of this regulation. Of these, three-quarters had to be quashed – an indication perhaps of the extent to which judicial review undermined the practice of local justice.[90] This watering-down of local judicial initiative in matters relating to labour relationships was commonly resented by farmers. The partial transfer of power to enforce the master's will away from the patronage of the local notable was one of the most far-reaching attacks on the old informal and decentralized authority structures.

At first the SJPs' judicial powers were severely curtailed in relation to those enjoyed by the old *vrederechters*. Initially they were confined to minor cases such as pass offences and police cases (such as disturbing the peace). They were only given jurisdiction in masters-and-servants cases in 1903 as a result of complaints from farmers of the impracticability of using magistrates' courts for petty prosecutions of servants. But the problem was not greatly alleviated since the SJPs were sparse on the ground, and few were to be found in rural areas.[91] The ordinary JPs who were unpaid and were often farmers had no judicial powers. Further, SJPs' powers of punishment were severely limited.[92] For a crucial change wrought by the British administration was that it denied SJPs the rights to impose lashes as a routine expression of white social dominance. Magistrates could only inflict lashes on a second conviction within two years – and then with stringent conditions. Corporal punishment was discouraged except in cases of extreme brutality, and the judges spent much time striking out provisions for lashes when reviewing magistrates' sentences. This prohibition more than anything else robbed the local courts of their efficacy for white masters.[93]

Repeatedly, in reviewing cases, judges struck down convictions under the masters-and-servants law on the grounds that there was no evidence of a contract, that a relationship of master and servant had not been proved, or that the contract was invalid since it had not been entered into before two witnesses – a provision in the republican law which had been largely ignored in the local courts under the old regime. It was common for the judges to send cases back to the SJPs' or magistrates' courts requiring further proof of proper contract.[94] The judges were also wont to quash convictions for assault on masters if there was evidence of provocation, or of violence committed by the master, or if there was evidence that the servant was acting in self-defence.[95]

Under the new regime the utility of lower courts as bastions of the authority of heads of black households over their adult children was undermined, too, much to the inconvenience of their landlords. As has been seen, the republican courts tended to deny the rights of adult sons and daughters in their conflicts with their seniors and their landlords. The colonial Masters and Servants Ordinance of 1904 fully legalized the contracting of children's labour by their parents together with their own, but explicitly restricted parental authority in this regard to children under the age of sixteen. Reaching this age, sons and daughters could no longer be legally bound by parental contracts. Children not explicitly included in the contract were also protected against being forced to render labour.[96] Of course, this legal enactment had little effect on family structure or on relationships of authority on the farms. But it did render the local court less amenable as a weapon for household heads and their landlords.

The 1904 ordinance also protected married women from arbitrary impressment. They had to be consenting parties to any contracts which included provision for their services. Again, the practical effects of such legislative interventions were limited, but they did serve to reduce the coercive structural supports for the enforcement of patriarchy on the farms. In a local SJP's court, Mamatabele and Maphosono, 'reputed' wives of August, were convicted of deserting from the service of William Bauman in about 1905. On review the conviction was quashed since the husband 'cannot bind his wife by contract for her services . . . and the case is still stronger when the parties stand to each other in the reputed relationship only'.[97]

The partial breakdown in the role of the law as an instrument of the master's will was forcibly impressed on the magistrate in Ficksburg who after a tour of his district in 1904 wrote:

> nearly every farmer had complained about their natives; when ordered to do certain work in the lands they point-blank refuse and say that they care neither for prison nor fines – and as thrashing is now done away with they will do as they please.

The magistrate reported that it had been:

> frequently suggested that JPs should be given their old power to deal with petty cases, as the farmers could not spare the time necessary to bring the defaulters into Ficksburg or Fouriesburg to have them tried as they are so far away from both centres.[98]

General Hertzog, attorney general, estimated in 1908 that:

> taking into consideration how far the majority of the farmers are from any judicial centre, in about 90 per cent of the cases in the colony the masters leave cases unrecorded and put up with a great deal rather than report the matter to the nearest magistrate or SJP.[99]

When the newly elected responsible government reintroduced the term *veldcornet* into the nomenclature of local administration in 1908, a number of representatives urged that these appointed officials be given judicial powers in master–servant disputes. General Hertzog replied that since these were to be paid no more than £75 a year for their services (in, for example, the eradication of noxious weeds) 'he would rather see the farmers put up with the troubles they undoubtedly have than to establish a state of things which is bound to be a real hardship and a real injustice to the servants'.[100] But Hertzog, a former judge, also had in mind the probability that the imperial government would veto the act providing for *veldcornets* in its entirety if it sought to impose their tyranny on black tenants and employees.[101]

The truth of the matter was that the authorities in London – who maintained veto powers over legislation in the ex-republics even after self-government had been instituted in 1907–8 – were unlikely to tolerate a proliferation of courts through the countryside, conducted by farmers with no legal qualifications, as instruments for the control of the rural black population. The Colonial Office officials did not object to the intention, but their commitment to legal propriety was inviolable. However, the problems posed by this inhibition were likely to decline as towns in maize districts proliferated, bringing more courts, shorter distances and better roads.

The changes wrought by the new regime after the Anglo-Boer War should not be overemphasized. Judicial review of the convictions of lower courts was likely to be less and less intrusive as the new judicial regime established its own inertia, and as the bureaucracy at the centre shed itself of its social imperialists. With the passing of the reconstruction administration systematic review faded away altogether. In practice SJPs and magistrates were able to continue exercising a good deal of discretion in their interpretation of conflicting evidence between masters and servants and of the contents of the contracts of tenancy or service. Further, the criminalization of a whole range of acts of omission and commission by black servants which characterized the republican law continued in force. The hegemonic function of the law remained undisturbed; only its more arbitrary manifestations were tempered. Furthermore, the informal channels of intimidation and coercion outside the formal proceedings of the judicial system were largely unaffected. Criminal prosecution was only the most visible part – the tip of the iceberg – of the whole structure of class power in this colonial society.

But whatever inadequacies the operation of the law might have had for white masters, it must have seemed mainly malevolent to most black farm tenants. However, rarely does the documentary evidence allow us a glimpse of black feeling and then only through the eyes of the educated elite. Much was said at the annual congress of the ORC Natives Association held in Winburg in February 1909 about the enforcement of the law relating to labour relations. While accepting explicitly the validity of the legislation, believing as they did that it was 'originally intended to secure the servant against arbitrary treatment', the delegates nonetheless considered that it was 'now so administered as to become a weapon of oppression in the hands of masters and police'. In the words of the correspondent of *The Friend*:

> Several natives spoke feelingly of the treatment of the natives on the farms. It was shown that barbarities were practised upon natives and no one intervened. Instances of suffering and considerable loss on the part of servants, breaches of contracts and deliberate contravention of laws on the part of masters, were related, and despite attempts to report to the police, the farmers continue to act as absolute despots.[102]

But the experience of blacks in the courts was not uniformly negative. The law could be a friend as well as an oppressor. There were limits to which it could be put to serve white interests. It could not uniformly be relied on by masters or landlords to support their case. Often it demanded more evidence than could be provided to sustain a prosecution. It could even be used – although not often – to secure justice for an unsophisticated African against a rapacious landlord. After all, the hegemonic function of the law required that it occasionally be more than simply an engine of oppression.

As in all colonial societies in which the colonized had an alternative cultural reference point to that provided by the colonizer, the creation and management of a working class required a larger degree of coercion and force than is required in circumstances where the invisible hand of 'market forces' can be left to do much of the work. But the local exercise of power, both formal and informal, had at times to be tempered by the disinterested neutrality of a benevolent law if the edifice of racial hegemony was not to be placed under intolerable strain. The law was there as a safety valve of last resort. And, as will be seen, Africans sometimes (but not often) organized in self-defence against landlords and employers, using the courts as a weapon to secure their rights.[103]

POLICING THE LABOUR MARKET: TENANT MOBILITY AND THE PASS LAWS

The capacity of the landlords to enforce their will on their tenants depended largely on their capacity to limit the latter's mobility. In so far as tenants' bargaining power was proportionate to their ability to move off the farm and seek better terms elsewhere, the nature and outcome of conflict was likely to be heavily influenced by the success with which landlords were able forcibly to restrain them from leaving, especially at the end of the annual contract period, when farmers often sought to redefine contracts to their own advantage – thus provoking resistance from the tenants. There was a variety of ways in which masters could obstruct tenants or temporary workers wishing to leave their farms. Refusal of wages or a trek pass was particularly common, and were important weapons in white hands.

Refusal of wages was particularly common in relation to the individual migrants contracted for three or six months' or a year's service. In February 1895, when crops were good and labour at a premium, it was reported from the eastern districts that feelings were running high among the Sotho over maltreatment by farmers, many having been cheated out of their wages. One claimed that he had been severely beaten for demanding payment of his wage (one heifer) at the end of his six-month contract.[104] The practice of many local officials and police officers of legitimating and enforcing the denial of wages under the pretext of indebtedness was formally illegal. Some servants were unable to escape from their alleged indebtedness to their employers and were effectively tied to them with the connivance of the authorities.

Often the alleged loss of livestock while in the care of a servant served as a pretext for keeping the servant on the farm. When an African woman, Caterina, complained at the police station in Harrismith in August 1907 that C. D. D. van Reenen of Boschkloof was forcibly restraining her son on his farm after the expiration of a six-month contract as a herdsman because he allegedly lost six of van Reenen's sheep, Caterina was informed that she had no redress in this situation. When Natalie Parry returned to the district from Natal in July 1911, he discovered a calf had been lost. His response was to send the herdsman to magistrate Leary with the request that the latter should:

> put the fear of death into him. I have told him he has to stay and work now for nothing till the calf is paid for and the expenses therewith, so please tell him the same. Will feed him and give him clothes as before.[105]

Parry clearly had reason to anticipate the magistrate's complicity in this arrangement.

There were intermittent efforts to secure greater protection for servants by those alarmed at the social consequences of reliance on force and intimidation to maintain a work force. A number of respondents to the Labour Commission in 1892–3 urged that the Masters and Servants Act be amended to incorporate such a provision in the law. Z. J. de Beer, a Harrismith lawyer, called in 1893 for stiff fines to be imposed on employers who withheld wages. Such instances were widespread, he alleged, and only one case in a hundred came to light.[106] Blacks only had recourse to the civil courts to demand their wages. The Labour Commission drew up a draft law making the withholding of wages liable to criminal proceedings. But the representatives of Boer farming interests, predicting all sorts of trivial and vindictive complaints by their servants, secured its defeat in the *Volksraad*. It was not until the republican government was replaced by the colonial administration that such a provision was incorporated into the masters-and-servants law. But its tangible benefits for blacks on the farms were limited, given the lack of incentive to institute proceedings.

The denial of wages was not the only weapon in the hands of white employers determined to restrain blacks from leaving their employ and thereby to reduce their bargaining power. The statute law also presented a host of obstacles to Africans moving through the countryside without the authorization of whites. The pass laws were at least of equal significance with masters-and-servants legislation in the regulation of labour relations on the farms. The 'trek pass' in particular, issued by an official on application from a white farmer and valid for forty days, was required by an African driving his own stock through the countryside. The trek pass was a powerful weapon in whites' hands, for without one, African tenant families leaving a farm to seek out new tenancies were very vulnerable to arrest and the confiscation of their stock.

A local SJP in Harrismith district, Harry Mundy, wrote in 1911 that complaints by black tenants about this practice were 'very frequent'.[107] One case that came to his notice was that of one Stoet, who complained that although his and his family's year was up, his master, Piet Grobelaar, had decided that 'they must first make a thousand bricks without payment before he will give them a trek pass'. In another case in August 1909, Kleinbooi was refused a trek pass by his employer, Paul du Preez of the farm Middelpunt, unless Kleinbooi paid £2 10s for his cattle's access to du Preez's maize stalks for feeding. Mundy reported:

> When the lands were reaped Du Preez told his natives all the cattle could run free in the stalks, Du Preez's cattle with them, it is only because the bearer Kleinbooi wishes to trek that Du Preez says he must first pay £2 10s. He is not charging the natives who are not trekking.[108]

As rights and obligations were none too rigorously defined in the loose verbal agreement which normally constituted the contract or *akkoord*, there was plenty of room for the employer to make all sorts of demands from his departing tenants for reimbursement of gifts or concessions extended to them during their period of tenancy, even though there was initially no intention of requiring repayment (as in the case of du Preez's maize stalks).[109] Even where landlords willingly provided a pass, many tried to make it as difficult as possible for their tenants to remove their livestock from their land by denying a pass for the herding of stock.[110]

In an attempt to prevent such abuses, the colonial administration in 1906 enacted a law (Ord. 30) requiring employers to give passes to their servants on the termination of a contract, as well as the requisite application for a trek pass to remove their stock. But again legislation of this kind was only useful as a protector of servants' rights in cases which reached the courts. Few Africans were able to penetrate the wall of hostility, prejudice and informal administrative connivance, even complicity. Such statutory protection was probably of limited direct efficacy, whatever indirect cautionary effect it might have had in curbing the worst excesses of landlord behaviour.

Refusal of a trek pass was most likely to come before a court as a result of conflict between farmers in their search for tenant labour. Appeals to authority on this score were as often as not made by prospective new landlords trying to attract tenant families to their land. G. Robinson of the farm Bosch Hoek, Harrismith district, complained to the magistrate in June 1908 that one Fagu had given his employer notice of his intention to leave his employ several weeks before and had been given permission to settle on his, Robinson's farm; but Fagu and his family had been refused a trek pass by their landlord who 'gives them extra pieces of work to do . . . unless he comes to me at once he will lose the opportunity of my farm'.[111] In many such conflicts, it was the Africans' prospective new landlords who called for the intervention of the law.

This competition between white farmers for labour tended to undermine the efficacy of the pass laws in restricting black mobility. Farmers were generally not concerned to enquire into the previous employment or place of residence of Africans without passes. Thus, 'deserters' were always assured of finding work. A farmers' congress called to discuss 'native affairs' in Bethlehem in November 1908 proposed that no one should be allowed to engage an African unless he be provided with a permit from his landlord, in no case for longer than the permit allowed, and that this permit be registered at the nearest police station. The 1908 commission reported that farmers throughout the colony 'strongly urged that no one should be entitled to engage a native who cannot show a discharge pass from his last master's service, nor to engage him for a longer period than that for which his pass allows him to be absent'. This failure to control the mobility of Africans allowed them to play one employer off against another. Conflict between white farmers was often the result.[112]

Thus, a major problem confronting farmers which the pass laws were intended to address was to ensure that members of tenant families who left the farm to work or visit elsewhere returned to the farm when their labour was required. Landlords issued passes for this purpose, specifying the period of absence granted. Typical of passes issued by landlords for the purpose of going out to earn wages is the following, signed by J. N. van der Bosch on 18 January 1904:

The bearer of this is a native of my farm Oudebergspruit by name Kalamaatje, is working for the military. I herewith make known, I shall be in want of this boy at the 1st of February 1904. Should he fail to come to my service I will have him run in by the Government.[113]

Farmers regularly complained about their lack of control over the movement of Africans once they had left the farms in search of temporary work elsewhere, and the general difficulty experienced in getting them to return. Petitioners condemned the practice by officials of giving passes for six months and extending passes issued by landlords.[114] In response to a Central Farmers' Union deputation in 1904, the Colonial Secretary issued a circular deploring the practice: 'the extension should be granted only in *bona fide* cases where the holder of the pass is clearly unable for some good and sufficient reason to return within the time specified'.[115]

Charges under the pass laws (generalized under the rubric *landlopery* or vagrancy) were the most common cases in the small courts. These cases were also apparently the most peremptorily disposed of. The implementation of the pass laws was arbitrary, brutal and a weapon of mass intimidation in the hands of whites. In republican days any burgher could arrest an African for not carrying a pass, for carrying an expired pass, for not heading in the direction of the destination noted on the pass, or for herding livestock not accounted for on the pass. A fine of £1–2 or a week or two in prison with hard labour was the typical punishment levied, and this mechanical justice in practice amounted to wholesale extortion. It was common for Africans to be fined all the money they had on their persons, and then turned loose with no money and no pass.[116]

Inevitably the pass system lent itself to labour impressment too. Barney Ngakane remembers:

It meant that if you were going to a farm, a village about a mile away, just on the other side of the border of the farm, and the boss was seven or eight miles away, you had first to go to him in order to get a pass to get to the other village. Yes, and the farmers exploited this. Whenever an African came along the road they all call to him, 'Come here. Where do you come from? Who is your boss? Will you come and chop some wood for me?' And you did that and he let you go.[117]

The bribe was probably a customary transaction too. Barney Ngakane remembers his father cycling into town to replace a spare part on his plough which had been broken in the fields. When a policeman accosted him, Ngakane handed over the 'fine' on the spot with the words, 'Look, I am working, have we got any time to be looking for passes?'. The clearly illegal practice of levying 'spot fines' was apparently widespread.[118]

Effective implementation of the pass laws required a police force. In earlier days the policing function was largely seen as a military one with the locally elected *veldcornet*, usually a landed notable with plenty of patronage, the arm of the burgher community in its relations with blacks living amongst and near them. But by the late 1880s, the need for a more satisfactory policing system had become apparent. The establishment of the *Rydende Diensmacht* or mounted force in 1889 arose in part from the problems posed by the very considerable movement through the state of groups of Africans heading for the diamond fields and more particularly now the Witwatersrand. At first the officers of the *Diensmacht* were stationed on the state's borders and along the railway line. But from the start their resources were too stretched to be of much value. The force was only thirty-eight strong in February 1890 and complaints were made that the officers were seldom seen in the rural areas. In 1894 their number was increased to eighty, and by 1898 they were 102 strong.[119]

Under colonial rule the loose, local authority structure of the republic was replaced by a more centralized bureaucracy. A Native Affairs Department was set up with wide powers to direct, regulate and mobilize labour resources. The South African Constabulary, which took over from the *Diensmacht*, was in origin a military occupying force, consisting of recruits from Britain and the dominions, ex-soldiers for the most part, and some Boer *hensoppers* (those who surrendered early in the war). At the war's end, they consisted of 9503 men in both new colonies, but the number declined rapidly. In the ORC in 1905, 1213 policemen manned 129 posts.[120] Few members of the constabulary could communicate with the Boer population, and they were hardly likely to be sympathetically regarded by Boer farmers. At the Brandfort Congress in 1904 when the representatives of Boer populism met to found the *Orangia Unie* as a platform for the political mobilization of the Boer population in the wake of the war, the constabulary was widely condemned. The force's alleged incapacity or unwillingness to control the black population on the farms was a major source of criticism.[121] The police were often not inclined to intervene in disputes between master and servant or landlord and tenant, given the degree of accountability for their activities.[122]

The British authorities after the war did away with the provision whereby burghers were paid a compensation for detention of passless Africans, and the rights of arrest vested in the *veldcornets* were repealed with the abolition of that office. Rights of arrest were now a police prerogative (facilitated by the greatly expanded police force). The British, with their greater sensitivity to the aspirations of educated blacks, also provided for exemption from pass laws 'for teachers, ministers of recognized churches and practitioners of certain skilled trades'.[123]

But, much more serious, general disillusionment with the

administration of the pass laws arose from a decision of the High Court in 1906 which made it difficult to prosecute an African travelling without a pass unless he were shown to be a vagrant. The fact that he had no pass raised a 'presumption' of vagrancy which he could rebut, thereby destroying the evidence of vagrancy supplied by his being passless.[124] Before the war, Orange Free State farmers told the Industries Commission in 1911, they could always demand an African's pass on the road, but now they did not trouble, as they knew an African could go anywhere without a pass.[125] Attempts to consolidate and tighten up the pass laws were continually stymied by the competing interests of urban and industrial employers who were not always sympathetic to farmers' demands in this regard, as well as by the fierceness of resistance to pass laws in the 1910s and 1920s, particularly in the towns.[126] But again, the extent to which judicial interpretations actually interfered with the informal, intimidatory function of the law at the level of personal relationships between white and black is open to doubt.

In various ways, the British administration after the Anglo-Boer War appeared to be undermining the informal institutions of control and coercion which had characterized the old regime in the countryside. The British certainly had no intention of subverting relationships of authority and of property (although, of course, Lord Milner's initial dreams for the reconstruction of the rural order were hardly concerned with the interests of the old Boer population). Republican statute law criminalizing breaches of labour contracts by black servants and restricting black mobility were taken over intact. But British administrators also brought with them an unshakeable faith in equality before the law, the inviolability of statute and of judicial process, and the essential neutrality of the police function. They also brought with them a belief in administrative efficiency and accountability. It was little wonder that farmers looked back on the republican period as a golden age.

However, it was perhaps inevitable that white farmers intent on asserting mastery over the rural economy and gaining control of productive resources should perpetually be dissatisfied at the efficacy of the instruments of control. Expressions of frustration at the ineffectiveness of the police and the pass laws were a reflection of a wider sense of frustration at the resistance of Africans to total domination. Agitation for a more effective police function was also a means of mobilizing white popular consciousness to the need for more concerted action in pursuit of white supremacy in the countryside.

Similarly, complaints against the shortcomings of the courts and the statutes which they enforced need to be seen in large part as a reflection of the inability of the court system or the legislature to intervene decisively in the reshaping of the countryside. The courts, the police and the law book were useful instruments in farmers' hands, but the struggle for control of rural production was largely fought out at the point of production itself. This proposition forms a central theme of the next chapter.

VIOLENCE, PATERNALISM AND THE WORKING COMPROMISE: SUSTAINING PRODUCTIVE RELATIONSHIPS

The formal agencies of control – the courts and the police – were only the most visible part of the structures of domination. The informal means of coercion and intimidation represented a daily reality of master–servant relationships. The republican state connived in personal violence, and through the often arbitrary dishing-out of corporal punishment by the lower courts provided a model which was eagerly followed. Whipping of recalcitrant workers by their masters was widespread and often caused conflict between landlords and heads of tenant households.[127] It was widely regarded by the authorities as an acceptable alternative to having a whipping administered at the behest of a local court, a procedure which entailed a long journey for many remote farmers. The extent to which violence pervaded productive relationships between black and white is revealed in a cursory reading of lower court minutes.

In Lindley district, Ndae Makume remembers, there were notorious *veldcornets*, the Wessels brothers and the Serfonteins, who made a name for themselves assaulting recalcitrant servants at their masters' request. 'Whenever a tenant or labourer had offended his master, he would be given a letter to take to the Wessels' farm where people were beaten up by the *veldcornets*.' The poor innocent would be set to work in the storeroom, where he would be accosted by a gang of perhaps four white men who would then tie him over a wine barrel and beat him senseless with a saddle strap. Ndae's great-uncle, Ditsebe, died after receiving such treatment.[128] Most informants tell stories of brutal treatment at the hands of white farmers. Extreme brutality was not confined to white masters and black male servants. When Nomwola Kamtombwe disappeared from work in the Odendaal farmhouse in Harrismith district for a week in March 1910, her female employer, Johanna Odendaal, ordered her to stand in a syrup tin as punishment. When Nomwola refused, Mrs Odendaal lashed her with her husband's sjambok. A little later, Nomwola was found dying in the cellar.[129]

However, arbitrary violence was not invariably efficacious. Blacks were not without their own means of resistance. Their mobility and the degree of discrimination they were able to employ in the choice of employer ensured that brutality by employers was often counter-productive. The formal intimidation of the law and the informal intimidation of threatened violence were never more than partially effective in shaping productive relationships as masters would ideally have wished. Resorting to the criminal courts or the police or the informal authority of *vrederechters* or *veldcornets*, while intermittently effective against individual servants or their families, could no more sustain working relationships than could brutality alone.

Violence and intimidation were tempered by the practice of paternalism, which was not a discrete phenomenon, but very often rested on an uneasy compromise in which violence was always present as a sanction. Paternalism as an ideology defined and shaped day-to-day interaction and conflict in the workplace, beyond the reaches of the law or the coercive state. It represented a compromise, a *modus vivendi*, which enabled masters and servants, landlords and tenants on the farms to sustain working relationships. Paternalism mediated conflict, coercion and resistance, defusing and displacing the more destructive and explicit manifestations of struggle. Employers were able to rationalize the 'irresponsibility' and 'inefficiency' of the African workers, thereby enabling Africans to place limits on white farmers' efforts to subvert their communal independence and to impose work discipline.

The white farmers were never able totally to control the labour processes on the farms, for they were never able totally to control the labourers. Farmers were constantly bemoaning their inability to impose regular working hours or a five- or six-day week on contracted workers from tenant families. Time and again they found it vexatious that household heads refused to be contracted for labour service but would only provide junior family members, and that landlords had little control over which family members turned up for work. Tenant labourers contracted for six months' service in the year often did not render it continuously, but intermittently as their own productive activities dictated. The beer party was a constant source of white complaint, too.[130]

The tacit conventions that governed labour relations were soon discovered by newcomers to the Highveld. J. D. Spence settled in the

Bethlehem district shortly after the Anglo-Boer War and tried to establish the same routine to which he had been accustomed in Natal: each man on the farm to work six months in the year, and each day during the six months from sunrise to sunset, at a wage of 10s per month plus ploughing land. The first thing he discovered was that the Africans would only turn out for work at 7 a.m., and furthermore expected to be provided with breakfast. He was then informed that the heads of families could not be expected to do the routine functions such as milking. The unmarried young men and boys were all that the landowner could expect by way of a regular supply of workers. The married men would only work for the landowner during peak periods in the productive cycle when a full complement of labour was necessary, for example at harvest time. After two of the four families had left the farm, Spence submitted:

> It was evident that steady daily labour could not be expected and I have since worked them on the lines they have been accustomed to. To say that the system is unsatisfactory is putting the case very mildly and most farmers who have come up here from Natal are of the same opinion, in fact I know of several who have given up local natives as hopeless and brought up their old Zulu natives for farm work.[131]

The white farmer rationalized his inability to bend black tenants to his will by portraying blacks as lacking the moral and intellectual capacity to work continuously and diligently or to show initiative. Farmers generally accepted that work would be done tardily and inefficiently, unless closely supervised, a perception which in part reflected a degree of passive resistance and deliberate carelessness on the part of servants whose direct remuneration (if members of tenant families) was minimal.[132] Constant themes in the ideology of the farmers included the complaint that black labour was an obstacle to improvement in productive methods; that blacks were unable to handle animals other than the toughest beasts of burden (a factor often mentioned as inhibiting the improvement of dairy cattle);[133] and that they broke all but the strongest and most basic of implements.[134] Proponents of progressive and scientific agriculture sometimes predicted that black labour would be ousted eventually by skilled white workers from Europe if South African agriculture were ever to reach its full potential.[135] Of course, much of this imagery bore very little relationship to reality, and indeed conflicted with farmers' own experiences. But the false caricature of the indolent and apathetic African, unable to master basic animal husbandry or the management of implements, served an important function in taking the edge off labour relationships; for whites were often able to convince themselves that black resistance and their own inability to coerce Africans were the result of a state of nature, rather than their own weakness and the weakness of the colonial state.

The failure of coercion and control had more emotional, symbolic implications in regard to housework, especially amongst the newer British settlers of the late nineteenth and early twentieth centuries, struggling to maintain pretensions to gentility on the outskirts of the empire.[136] Compromise over work discipline and methods could not be so easily forged in the home as in the fields. Housework implied wholly new skills – from making beds to making tea. What made the issue so sensitive was the prevailing ideology of white motherhood and domesticity, which was so much part of the motive idea of the 'imperial race'.[137] The exaggerated fears for the health and well-being of settler women, 'many of them sickly and delicate, doing menial work and washing clothes . . . whilst half a dozen strong and healthy native women are squatting on the farm in complete idleness' should be seen in this light.[138]

But on the whole, working relationships were sustained from day to day by means of a range of ideological compromises, whereby whites sought to legitimize their lack of total control over work and production. The image of the black man as a beast was a characteristic of the urban, industrializing economy, where the overwhelming coercion of such 'total institutions' as the mining compound were relied upon for the control of labour. The image of the black man (or woman) as a clumsy, stupid child, on the other hand, was more suited to life on the farms. The child-like caricature was rarely more than a veneer under which seethed dark suspicions and resentments which rose to the surface at times of rapid change and economic development. But from day to day these perceptions of the irresponsible and inefficient worker helped to defuse the conflicts that were always present.

The most explicitly paternalist imagery of the trusting and loyal retainer was not altogether missing on the Highveld; but it was usually applied only to a particular class of permanent farm servants, more acculturated and subservient than the bulk of the tenants, almost always Afrikaans-speaking and members of the Afrikaans mission churches, and who had no alternative cultural reference point to that provided by the white farmers and their families. It is possible that such people, the '*oorlamsches*' or descendants of the apprentices, shared their masters' perceptions to a large degree.[139] They were particularly prominent amongst farm residents in the pastoral districts where arable tenancy was rare. In the grain districts, however, where tenancy arrangements of one sort or another predominated, labour tenancy was as likely to be characterized by coercion and resistance, or an uneasy balance of interests, as by the more explicit expressions of paternalism. Most of the tenant families of the arable Highveld had fairly recently been subjects of independent black chiefs, and were determined to maintain their independence from white control as far as possible.

There was still room for alliances between wealthy, land-extensive landlords and heads of large homesteads in the early years of this century, and successful, independent commercial production by black peasant families was widespread, especially but not solely under sharecropping contracts. Nevertheless, relationships were often coercive and distant. Violence, or the threat thereof, often hovered in the background. This was particularly the case on the land of farmers without excessive landholdings who were trying to seize control of production, especially at times of economic boom and productive expansion, when the struggle for control of resources grew fiercest.

ORGANIZATION AND RESISTANCE

If violence and coercion were always hovering in the background to be called upon when paternalism failed or became an obstacle to the further development of white agriculture, explicit forms of resistance were equally omnipresent. Blacks who controlled their own productive resources only submitted to the labour demands of the whites so long as it suited them.

Resistance most obviously and most importantly took the form of removal from a farm on which the conditions of tenancy that the landlord was trying to enforce became unacceptable to the tenant household. Hence, the importance for whites of limiting the mobility of blacks by the use of pass laws or whatever less formal means were available to individual white landholders; but within the nexus of the individual master–servant or landlord–tenant relationship there was enormous potential for the exercise of manipulation and resistance by Africans. Resistance to work discipline and the tyranny of the clock was ubiquitous, as we have seen. Equally, the go-slows, deliberate carelessness, feigned ignorance or stupidity were very likely just as widespread.

But more explicit assertions of independence and defiance were common too. Assault and violence were not the prerogative solely of whites. Clandestine violence was less common than open assault, but the poisoner loomed large in the public imagination. Albert von Berg, 'one of the most enterprising and energetic farmers' in the Ficksburg district, who planted thousands of trees on his farm, died after poison had been placed in his porridge in 1897. An African was sentenced to three years' hard labour in about 1894 for pouring irritant poison in one van Niekerk's soup in Winburg district. And 'Jan' was sentenced to 10 years and twenty-five cuts in 1892 for attempting to murder C. J. du Plessis and his family of Dwarsberg, Ficksburg, by placing Cooper's Dip in their butter.[140] These cases were by no means isolated, and many such cases probably remained undetected and unreported.

The poisoning of stock was not unknown either. For example, in January 1909 ten head of cattle and five goats were poisoned with arsenic on D. Ballantine's farm, Hammonia, in the Ficksburg district. It appears that Ballantine had refused permission to some of his workers wishing to leave the farm, and that these tenants had previously worked on farms where arsenic had been used for the destruction of locusts.[141]

A grievance could be assuaged and vengeance wreaked by an exercise of ingenuity. When an African named Moses of the farm Roodekop near Luckhoff found a Martini-Henry rifle buried on the farm immediately after the war, he had good use for it. For the landowner, A. J. Weideman, had recently thrashed Moses for some misdemeanour, and the latter bore him a bitter grudge. So Moses hid the rifle in the chaff house and then reported its presence to the local police post. Weideman was fined £100 for having the rifle in his possession. The truth only subsequently emerged.[142]

Resistance and revenge were likely to take an individualistic and often anonymous form given the difficulties of organization. One way of settling a grievance was the destruction of property, such as wheat stacks. The phantom incendiarist was a not uncommon figure in the countryside, especially at harvest time, and particularly in years of bumper crops such as 1911. In February 1912 a correspondent drew attention to the frequency of fires among gathered wheat crops in the Bethlehem and Ficksburg districts. One farmer, after stacking his wheat, was about to retire for the night when he noticed a moving object near the stacks which he took to be a horse, and which moved away in the darkness as he approached. At about 9 p.m. he noticed a glare near one of the stacks and on going out to investigate found four large stacks of wheat alight. Soon, the entire crop was ablaze. In the period since December the previous year, no less than £1000 had been lost through such mysterious fires within a radius of 25 miles.[143] The wheat harvest of that season had been an unusually large one, and it is likely that as a consequence of the severe shortage of labour for reaping and threshing, inducements were held out to Africans which farmers were unwilling or unable to fulfil. This circumstance would account for these incidents, which bore the hallmarks of wilful incendiarism.

Another means of resistance was stock theft. The commandant of the constabulary in Ladybrand opined in 1907 that sheep thefts were often 'retaliatory', and committed by servants who considered themselves to be ill-used or defrauded by their employers.[144] A certain degree of stock theft might indeed have been accepted as intrinsic to the landlord–tenant relationship. Farmers seem to have resigned themselves on the whole to a certain degree of stock loss if it meant a stable labour force. Colonel Pilkington of the constabulary wrote in 1904 that many farmers would not report losses of sheep to the police because in most cases the theft was traced to Africans in their own employ. According to Pilkington, the farmer would much prefer losing a few sheep to forfeiting the labour of his African workers while they were in prison.[145] A farmer in the eastern Orange Free State wrote in 1920 that 'Our native brother has become so valuable in these parts that very little notice is being taken of the stealing'.[146] Tenants relying on the produce of the soil for compensation for their labour service were very likely to feel cheated when the harvest failed to materialize. In consequence, the farm tenants bore a reputation for habitual stock theft. A Winburg farmer wrote in 1911: 'A drought sets in, and consequently the native reaps nothing. Where does he obtain food for the next 12 months? Neighbouring farmers' sheep (stud ones for choice), you may depend upon that.'[147] Another wrote in 1916 that 'Much of the trouble of stock theft is due to the stinginess of certain farmers who do not feed their servants.'[148] A variation was the incidence of death of stock caused by pieces of wire stuck in the throat or pierced through the body – which might have been significant in light of the fact that the flesh of dead animals was generally given to African tenants.[149]

The picking of ripening grain from the fields – especially green maize, which was commonly consumed by blacks during the months before harvest – should also be seen in this context. One farmer saw fit to issue the following advice in print:

Any time you wake during the moonlight, fire into the lands, using a Martini for preference, as it makes a big noise. You run a very, very slight chance of bagging a boy, but you do prevent stealing. I've never ever heard of a boy being hit, and I once found an assegai and a sack in the land. Another time a hat and a sack.[150]

These manifestations of individual assertion, whether inspired by revenge or self-preservation, were essentially reactive. More sustained challenges to the will of the capitalizing farmer required a greater degree of organization. It seems that labour organization on the farms in any formal sense was, with rare exceptions, non-existent in the years before 1914. Nevertheless, channels of communication for the dissemination of information regarding employment and tenancy conditions, and the peculiarities and characteristics of individual farmers, seem to have been effective in enabling Africans to establish informal and rudimentary forms of concerted action and resistance.

Important considerations in determining where African temporary workers chose to seek employment or tenants chose to settle were the attitudes and reputation of the individual farmer. Farmers repeatedly asserted that the matter of "treatment' was of relevance in explaining why certain farmers suffered greater shortages of labour than others. It seems that Africans were fully aware of which farms to avoid. The picture drawn by a correspondent to the *Farmer's Weekly* shows Africans practising a considerable degree of discrimination in their choice of employment:

> The natives generally know the characters of the different masters, and if they do not they will make enquiries, and if they are not satisfied will not hire to the master. The consequence of this is that while one master in a neighbourhood is never short of labour, another is sometimes without servants, simply because he has a bad character amongst the natives.[151]

It was this latter group which continually complained of the scarcity of labour, added the correspondent.

A correspondent of *The Friend* wrote in 1905 that he had been told by officials in Basutoland that 'the natives resent any inhumanity practised on them, and go from village to village telling of the injustice suffered at the hands of any particular farmer'.[152] In other words, they exercised judgement in their choice of employment and demonstrated a degree of solidarity amongst themselves. There were ways of investigating the credentials of a prospective employer through the informal channels of oral communication.[153]

This 'latent tendency to labour organization, based solely on mutual understanding',[154] was occasionally manifested in rather more concrete ways. For example, in January 1912, during the bumper wheat harvest of that year, a meeting of Africans at Mooi Valley in the Orange Free State resolved that none should work for less than 5s a day on the farms.[155] And in April and May 1910 two meetings were held at

Wolwehoek station in the Heilbron district and one in Parys location with a view to the formation of a 'Union of Natives'. Each member paid a subscription of 5*s*, which entitled him to legal aid in the event of litigation arising from employment disputes. A. M. Baumann of Winburg was contracted to give his legal services when called upon, and his fees were to be paid from the Union's funds. One Slinger was the leader of the Union at Wolwehoek and John Rampa the leader in Parys.[156] John Rampa (presumably the same one) was a scion of a prosperous sharecropping family, members of the sharecropping elite in the district, who was not only a Christian, but taught in the local school on the farm next to Arcadia.[157] It seems likely that much of the political leadership on a local level was provided by members of this educated elite on the farms – the tenant-teachers or catechists. It is likely that it was such men who were able to gain access to lawyers and to local courts on behalf of less sophisticated farm tenants, and who on occasion were able to organize sporadic resistance to the exactions of the landlords across farm boundaries.

The same Baumann gave evidence before the 1917 Select Committee on Native Affairs, on behalf of the Native Vigilance Committee in Winburg. He spoke of the deep grievances of Africans on the farms, particularly in regard to the Masters and Servants Act, and said that he received correspondence from all over the province attesting to the bad conditions on the farms. The ex-magistrate in Winburg, J. F. van Iddekinge, who gave evidence to the committee after Baumann, suggested that there were (unnamed) lawyers in that town who had been paid retainers by the white farmers not to appear for Africans.[158]

In March 1921 Colonel P. S. J. Botha told a meeting of farmers at Platrand that an African had been travelling from farm to farm telling the labourers not to work unless the farmers were prepared to pay them more. H. B. Swart informed the meeting that on 7 January his labourers had gone on strike and more than two months later were still refusing to perform any work. They had been prosecuted under the Masters and Servants Act, but the case had been postponed so that the strikers could acquire the services of an African attorney from Johannesburg. The meeting approved a motion of protest to the local magistrate against Swart being subjected to cross-examination by a black lawyer.[159] These episodes suggest that black farm labourers were not without access to legal aid in their struggles against their masters and the law. The role of African organizations in organizing and defending farm workers is an important and underexplored theme.[160]

Resistance by black tenants primarily took the form of resistance to the stripping of resources and the alienation of labour time; but equally important were the ways in which African workers caught in servile relationships sought to shape productive processes, and to reformulate the conditions of tenancy and service. Resistance to the assaults on household independence or living standards could be random, unorganized and reactive. It could also indicate a degree of local collaboration and organization in defence of workers' or tenants' interests, including resort to legal processes. This section has inevitably surveyed the possibilities somewhat randomly and unsystematically. But it is clear that in any number of ways, big and small, Africans were able actively to shape productive relationships on the land, both materially and ideologically.

6 Years of Crisis, 1908–14

FINANCIAL BOOM

The half-dozen years leading up to 1914 constituted a period of financial boom and productive expansion in white agriculture, a period of rapid land division and of unprecedented state intervention in the promotion of white farming. Particularly, it was a period of crisis in labour supply and in productive relationships, when agitation and concerted action against the independent black tenant farmers reached a fever pitch. In this, these years were not unlike the mid-1890s, albeit on a grander scale. It was at such times that the ideological compromise of paternalism ceased to function as a mediating factor and was replaced by a much more explicit resort to force and state power. The purpose of this chapter, then, is to draw various levels of analysis together so as to uncover some of the motor forces behind rural change during one period when circumstances in the political economy at large and on the farms in particular conspired to spark heightened conflict, social anxiety and employer mobilization. These years were crucial to the longer-term triumph of capitalist agriculture over peasant production.

The intervention of the state in the provision of transport and marketing facilities, of capital and credit, and generally in the propagation of improved methods and techniques of production during the decade after the Anglo-Boer War was a necessary precondition for the advancement of white agricultural capitalism. But state intervention in colonial agriculture was slow in bearing fruit. The greater access to capital of white farmers as often as not meant greater financial vulnerability, and many landowners were hard-pressed to survive once the post-war depression had set in. This was accompanied by a tightness in government finance which forced a severe cutback in aid to farming.

Nevertheless, by 1908 the tide was turning, and by the time of Union in 1910, a financial boom was once again under way. State aid to agriculture increased correspondingly. The establishment of land banks in the various South African colonies in the years immediately preceding Union in 1910 offered opportunities for farmers to raise loans at low interest rates from the governments. By the time the ORC Land Bank was incorporated in the new Union Land and Agricultural Bank in 1912, it had granted 774 loans totalling £426 735 against mortgage bonds, and 884 loans totalling £124 555 on the security of promissory notes.[1]

In the years immediately after Union there was greater liquidity in agrarian commerce and more generous provision of private loan capital than had been the case in many years, perhaps ever. The magistrate in Bethlehem wrote in 1910: 'Business has shown more vitality, money has been more plentiful, old debts have been liquidated and financial corporations as well as individual capitalists have shown more readiness to advance money on good security.'[2] This is fairly typical of reports from the districts in these years. A sharp decline in the extent of land loss amongst landowners was a result, as well as a general rise in the extent of bonding of land.

Indeed, such was the availability of private finance in some districts after 1910 that the ORC Land Bank was bypassed. The magistrate in Fouriesburg reported that very little use was made of the Land Bank in 1911, since 'farmers can get as much money locally as they require at 6 per cent'. J. G. Keyter, a lawyer of Ficksburg, for example, held bonds on farm property to the value of some £70 000 in 1912. His brother-in-law, D. J. de Villiers, the town's leading auctioneer, also had large funds to lend on liberal terms. And the magistrate in Smithfield reported in 1910: 'in addition to the banks there are no less than three rich private gentlemen who always have large sums of money to lend at 6 per cent. Money is advanced on note-of-hand at 8 per cent or even 7 per cent.'[3]

The sudden influx of loan capital into the countryside after Union was followed by a boom in commercial activity. As was the case immediately after the Anglo-Boer War, the numbers of licensed dealers increased rapidly. In Thaba Nchu town in 1911 they had increased from twelve to sixteen, and in the district as a whole from twenty-six to thirty-two. From Kroonstad and Parys came reports that 'Jewish traders and hawkers' had increased considerably and were apparently thriving.[4] Commercial opportunities followed newly built lines of rail, which were spreading rapidly in these years. The Vrede magistrate wrote a few months before the railway reached the town in 1912: 'The fact of the approaching Railway . . . has brought about quite a revolution. A number of buildings are going up in town and at the station site.'[5]

The advance of commercial banking in the Orange Free State is shown by the extension of the activities of the Standard Bank. Its branches in that province increased from five to seventeen during the four years to 1914, and its loans from £88 000 to £728 000. G. T. Amphlett, an assistant general manager of the bank, wrote in 1914:

Considering how large a portion of this amount represents advances to farmers, it is safe to say that while the Bank's relations with the community generally in the Free State are of the best, by no section is its presence more appreciated than by the rural population.[6]

The National Bank was even more generous in its advances to farmers – amounting to £100 000 in Heilbron district alone in 1911.[7]

The creditworthiness of colonial agriculture in the eyes of the commercial banks had never been very considerable except in brief boom periods. The banks were generally reluctant, particularly during times of slump and tight money, to make loans against mortgage bonds to farmers, since this form of business was very illiquid and entailed locking up large sums of money for long periods of time. This was business that was more often the domain of trust and insurance companies, boards of executors and private individuals.[8] But the official historian of the Standard Bank tells us that after Union the government land banks 'were lending so freely to farmers that money previously provided by mortgage and insurance companies was flowing into the banking field at a time when advances were not in great demand, whereas interest-bearing deposits were a heavy load'.[9] Now the banks were anxious to accept long-term mortgage bonds as a source of investment in order to drain their coffers of otherwise uninvestable funds.

A result of the financial boom was a considerable rise in land prices.[10] Land accumulated by land companies, speculators and creditors during the slump was frequently sold off after 1910 at high prices to new settlers with ready access to mortgage capital.[11] It was invariably during periods of boom (such as immediately after the Anglo-Boer War and again after Union) that large landowners sought to capitalize their assets in this way. State-aided settlement of the land became an issue of great importance after Union, and the corporate landowners were the strongest supporters of such schemes. A select committee investigated the question of land settlement in 1910 and 1911, and a Land Settlement Act was passed in the following year, providing for large-scale state purchase of private land. Just as Milner's land settlement scheme after the Anglo-Boer War was partly fuelled by large landowning (including mining) interests, so the same interests were behind the schemes of the early 1910s.[12] In the same year as the Land Settlement Act was passed, a Union Land Bank was established, incorporating the pre-Union banks of the constituent provinces. Its effects were mainly felt in the inland provinces, especially the Transvaal. The reason for this was the unevenness of penetration of loan capital. Very little settled and improved land in the Cape was not already encumbered with private mortgage debt to the coastal insurance and trust companies by the end of the nineteenth century. The field of activities of the Land Bank was therefore concentrated in areas, notably in the Transvaal, where much land was relatively undeveloped and concentrated in corporate and speculative hands.[13] Here again the interests of the large landowners, seeking to cash in on the greatest land inflation the country had experienced by selling off to white land purchasers with access to land bank loans, are to be seen. The Land Settlement Act and the Land Bank Act, both of 1912, were closely related statutes.

In the following year the 1913 Natives Land Act was enacted. That law will be examined later. But it should be noted here that at least one of the converging forces leading to the passing of the Act was the land boom. The Act in part was aimed at the suppression of black sharecropping. The soaring cost of land and the ready availability of mortgage capital for potential settlers eroded the attractiveness of black sharecroppers for many corporate landowners. The sale of land to white farmers with capital became an attractive proposition to those who owned land as a speculative investment.[14] More important, in so far as the Land Act sought to define black reserves and release additional land for incorporation in reserves, the big land companies saw potential for profit in the less developed Middleveld and Lowveld Transvaal, where the bulk of the speculative landholdings was concentrated and where the greatest potential for the enlargement of reserves by land purchase (by Africans or by the state) existed.[15]

THE DIMENSIONS OF THE RURAL CRISIS

Although the capital base of white agriculture and the extent of cultivation of the land were expanding rapidly in the few years from about 1908, most of the surge of mortgage capital moving into the rural areas in these years was not being spent on productive resources. Such was the accumulation of debt during the preceding years, that the bulk of mortgage loans made by the ORC Land Bank established in 1909 were taken up for the discharge of existing liabilities in cases of financial pressure, such as onerous conditions of repayment or high interest rates.[16] The bank's major purpose was the stemming of the flood of land loss and impoverishment, which had hit so many landed families.[17] Secondarily, the bank was intended to enable newcomers to the Highveld, as well as established lessee farmers, to buy land of their own. By the time it was established it was less urgently needed than a few years previously, for by 1909 boom conditions were already emerging, mortgage capital readily obtainable, and interest rates dropping. But between the establishment of the ORC Land Bank in 1909 and its replacement by the Union Land Bank in 1912, 774 loans were made against the security of mortgage bonds, amounting to £426 735 (or an average of £551 each); £259 994 was raised from the bank to pay off existing liabilities, and another £98 405 for the purchase of land. In the first full year of operation of the Union Land Bank, £231 639 out of £615 335 granted to Orange Free State landowners was for liquidation of liabilities, a further £270 942 for land purchase. Of the remaining amount, the bulk went on overheads or 'improvements', like building or fencing (required under the Fencing Act of 1912), rather than on productive equipment and livestock.[18]

Certainly, many farmers were able to buy improved implements, such as wheat-reaping machines or planters. But there were also limits to the benefits to be derived from investing in productive resources while the technology at the disposal of whites was not substantially different from that used by black households, especially ploughing spans and equipment, and while the weeding and reaping of the most important crop (maize) remained labour-intensive activities. The financial boom in the rural areas did not mean the universal capitalization of white agriculture. The advantages of less relative risk and greater relative productivity associated with sharecropping did not disappear. In the absence of widespread opportunities and motivation to mechanize (such as existed a few decades later) there was little incentive to suppress the peasant economy entirely. So while the rate of capitalization amongst white farmers increased greatly, this should not be overemphasized.

But there was plenty of incentive in these boom times to attempt to reformulate terms of tenancy to the advantage of landlords. They sought to increase their claims on tenant household labour, to restrict tenants' access to grazing land, and to increase the surplus extracted from tenant production. As a consequence of surging land values and the greater marketing and transport opportunities available, white landholders were often concerned to maximize their profits from productive activity on their land, whether black tenants remained the direct producers or not. However, these *were* also years of unprecedented albeit uneven capitalization. As more and more capitalized farmers took up land on the Highveld, intent upon investing in capital resources and directly controlling production, demands on the labour of black tenants greatly increased. To a greater degree than ever before, the independent black tenantry was seen as obstructing the development of capitalist farming in so far as tenant production severely impeded the availability of labour to white farmers. Again, it was the sharecropping tenantry on absentee-owned land, where tenant households were free of supervision or control and had seemingly unlimited opportunity for accumulation, which elicited the strongest condemnation, especially as their enterprise was frequently enriching foreign capitalists. It was not so much tenants' ownership of productive resources against which propagandists railed – as long as they were harnessed to the profit of resident white farmers – but rather the more explicit manifestations of black independence and prosperity. White farming was no longer as vulnerable and dependent as in the post-war years, and populist opinion could again be effectively mobilized against the black rural economy.

This crisis in relationships between white and black was particularly intense as not only was the capital base in the white rural economy expanding; the black rural economy was expanding too. Good seasons and the opening of export markets for the increasingly predominant commercial crop, maize, created new opportunities for black producers as well as for whites. The rapid increase in the extent of land put to the plough not only implied an expansion of white capitalist production, but also of black peasant production, more especially on the still very extensive landholdings of absentees. In the post-war years of depression, the proportion of land in the hands of absentees, of creditors and speculators, had no doubt been growing as resident landowners succumbed to the pressures of indebtedness.[19]

The black sharecropping tenantry thus reached its high point of profit and accumulation at precisely the same time that white agriculture was capitalizing at a faster rate than ever before. The inevitable result was that competition for resources reached critical intensity. The crisis in relations between black and white on the land was a replay, on a larger stage and with more actors, of the drama played out in the previous phase of financial boom and productive expansion, that of the years 1893–5, before the drought, the rinderpest epizootic and the Anglo-Boer War combined to draw the sting from populist agitation against the independent black tenantry. This time, too, the rural crisis was heading toward a legislative catharsis.[20]

Attempts by landlords to reformulate contracts of tenancy to their own benefit evoked considerable resistance and a great deal of trekking from farm to farm, especially in the months following the winter harvest. J. A. Sugden of Bethlehem district noted this as early as 1907, a year in which rains were good and maize crops were heavy. He reported that complaints regarding the scarcity of labour were becoming more frequent and noted that:

> the increased amount of work, which the Native squatters are being called upon to do, is causing an unusual number of Natives to trek on to other farms, in the hope of finding farms, where there will be less work to do.[21]

These kinds of complaints were general in the years under consideration. The magistrate in Lindley reported in 1912 that several capitalized farmers in the district had resorted to hiring Zulu migrant labourers under contract from Natal labour agents after having tried unsuccessfully to introduce new conditions of tenancy which involved the payment of small wages to workers and in addition ploughing and sowing plots themselves for the tenants' benefit. Local Africans had resisted this transformation to servile status, often with a large degree of success.[22]

The crisis of labour supply was reflected in a furious agitation which found its chief expression in the correspondence columns of newspapers and journals, such as the *Farmers' Weekly*, a Bloemfontein publication launched in early 1911. J. A. Jorissen, writing from the eastern Orange Free State, provides a sample of the genre, replicated in any number of similarly exaggerated diatribes. 'The real master', Jorissen wrote:

> is the native. He is independent; his services not purchasable for money; won't hire himself out or bind himself to any contract whatsoever. The only course he is agreeable to is to sow on the half. Whether the owner likes it or not, he has to submit. . . . The natives' hold over the farmers down in these parts is absolute.[23]

Another wrote:

> A native will rather pay rent and squat, and do as he likes, than live rent-free and work. This is the root of our difficulty, and while we have men amongst us who will indulge the native in this propensity, we will never get labour to work our farms, with the result that our lands remain unploughed and the country is going back instead of forward.[24]

We need not take these expressions of concern as reflections of objective reality to realize that what was being described was a heightened level of racial tensions and hostilities in the countryside, as white farmers sought to harness black labour and capital resources more tightly to their own profit, and as black households sought to resist these transformations in productive relationships.

One consequence of this crisis was an upsurge in agitation against perceived shortcomings in the masters-and-servants legislation.[25] When H. S. Viljoen of Fouriesburg failed to find satisfaction from the local magistrate in 1911, he wrote to the newspaper in protest:

> If a native according to the usage of the country lives on my farm and sows, and fails to fulfil his contract, he is free. . . . Our former Magistrate in such cases used to protect the farmer, and now we have to learn to our astonishment: 'if a native has lands from you, he is his own master and not your servant'.[26]

As another farmer put it, 'in the event of any dispute between the "partners", the white man will find in nine cases out of ten that in a Court of Law he has not the slightest chance of proving that he has any authority whatsoever over his black partner'.[27] During this period of heightened tensions, white farmers regarded the extension of masters-and-servants legislation to cover all Africans on their land as a major priority if black resistance to the intensified exaction of tenant labour were to be overcome. But the truth remained that no matter how coercive were the laws, how politicized the court system and how pervasive the police function, they were unlikely ever to satisfy by themselves the demands of whites for a social revolution in the countryside.

*   *   *

If white determination to extract more and more black labour was one manifestation of intensified competition for resources in these years, competition for grazing land was another. The rapid increase in the numbers of stock (white- and black-owned) on the farms in the years after about 1905 was another aspect of this crisis in productive relations. As was seen in chapter 3, one of the pressures driving many African households into intensified market production and sharecropping relations was the rinderpest epizootic of the 1890s. By the same token, the recovery of herds and flocks and their rapid increase after 1905 – unprecedented probably since the opening up of large-scale internal markets – provided alternative or supplementary access to commodity markets for many African households. For stockownership implied opportunities for profit from sales of livestock, hides and skins and wool. This tended to diminish African dependence on other, more servile, means of access to cash incomes, and rendered them less susceptible to debt bondage. As long as grazing land was available to them, many African households loosened their dependence on rendering labour and on credit. Under these circumstances, many African households were able to resist landlords' pressures towards increased labour service.

The explosion in the stock population can be explained by natural factors. The half-dozen years after about 1905 saw good rainfall; and the virtual elimination of many animal diseases by the administration meant that the natural checks were no longer maintained, especially since the Orange Free State escaped East Coast fever completely at the very time that it was ravaging other parts of the subcontinent. Economic boom meant a flood of wage income into the black rural economy, which was generally invested in livestock. And given the overgrazed state of Basutoland, excess stock was commonly sent across the border into the relatively land-extensive Orange Free State in the care of kin.[28]

Not only did grazing rights greatly benefit the black tenant, but they also materially penalized the white landlord whose access to grazing land was correspondingly reduced.[29] The situation was made urgent by the subdivision and overstocking of farms throughout the arable districts. Ladybrand farmers were reported in 1909 to be seeking out stock farms in other parts of the colony because of overstocking. In 1913, breeding stock was reported to be unsaleable in Bethlehem for the same reason, and the price in consequence had fallen by 25 per cent.[30] The magistrate in Winburg, R. Harley, wrote that in the past when the land had been cheap, landowners had not minded having Africans who owned as much stock as they on their farms, but as the farms were getting smaller there was less and less inclination to enter tenancy agreements with Africans who grazed large herds and flocks.[31] Nevertheless, many landholders lacked muscle to enforce their will, as they needed the labour and often also the capital resources of black households.[32]

Many farmers were becoming increasingly conscious of stock breeds, too, partly as a result of the Department of Agriculture's large-scale importations of pure-bred animals for breeding. Many were unwilling to allow intermingling of their own stock with tenants' rams, bulls or stallions. An Orange Free State farmer wrote in 1911:

Look at the drawback to progressive farming while natives are allowed to graze and breed any kind of mongrel stock. . . . Our

Government is spending large sums on the importation of pedigree stock, but what real progress can be made until we have a law enforcing the castration of downright mongrels?[33]

In order to avoid the danger of interbreeding, many white farmers were obliged to allow African tenants on their land free access to their own rams, bulls or stallions, on condition that no African-owned male animals would be allowed on the farm unless castrated.[34] With the rising value of grazing land, fewer progressive stock farmers were willing to make this concession. It was still common at this time for all stock to graze together. But paddocking was becoming widespread, which made it possible to restrict tenants' stock to stony or overgrazed camps, while landlords' stock was rotated – a decisive innovation in many black peoples' memories.[35]

It was not African stockownership in general that whites railed against, however. One of the major advantages of labour tenancy, as has been seen, was the widespread use of the tenants' oxen during the ploughing season. The more draught oxen available to the farmer, the more land could be placed under cultivation. It was those animals which were of less utility to landlords which they resented. Thus, a number of informants remember these years as the time when goat-herding came to an end at the behest of their landlords, apparently because they were very destructive of grazing and damaged trees, notably fruit trees. Ndae Makume remembers that this happened in 1913. Their fifty goats were sold for 10*s* each to speculators travelling from farm to farm buying up the tenants' animals.[36]   Orders to tenants to reduce their livestock numbers caused much movement by households from farm to farm. The white landholders' determination to undermine blacks' independent access to wealth in livestock was often obstructed by the bargaining strength of tenant households with considerable labour resources and productive potential. Again, this struggle for control over grazing land was the cause of much hostility and bitterness between white and black on the land.[37]

* * *

An important index of the increasing insecurity felt by African tenants was the extent of black land purchase during these years in the Transvaal, where, unlike the Orange Free State, it was permitted by law up to 1913. Africans generally purchased land off the Highveld, in, for example, the Rustenburg Bushveld. For the most part, they acquired it through collective effort, under the leadership of a chief. Unlike whites, Africans did not generally have access to mortgage loans. A *veldcornet* from the Rustenburg Bushveld, where African landownership spread rapidly before and after 1910, told the Natives Land Commission that Africans found it much easier than whites to buy land. 'The chief gives the order for each man to bring up so much money. If he has a thousand natives and each brings a couple of pounds it soon makes the purchase price.'[38]

In such areas it was largely a question of securing title to land on which independent black communities had always been settled, but to which absentee whites owned title. The native commissioner in the Pilanesberg section of Rustenburg district wrote in 1911:

> Purchase of land goes on apace, new purchases being reported weekly. Certain farmers and speculators are now selling lots from twenty morgen upwards (undivided) to individuals and companies of Natives. In the latter case the transfers are registered in the name of one man. The insecurity of the method of procedure has been pointed out to the purchasers. Sellers are prepared to take cattle or money in settlement. Natives usually pay from ten to fifteen times as much as a European for land. Tribes are also endeavouring to purchase ground. In most cases, the ground purchased is already occupied by a portion of the tribe, who either give their services or pay for the right to reside there. Farmers are continually offering their farms to native Chiefs. In some cases obligations are entered into for the purchase of the farm, the first instalment is immediately paid, and when the second instalment becomes due, the purchasers are loth to part with their stock and a deadlock ensues.[39]

In the Hex River ward of the Rustenburg district many white landowners sold out at good prices to Africans in the four or five years before African land purchase was prohibited by the law in 1913. Many white landowners found Africans to be ideal buyers who paid high prices. And there was no shortage of potential African buyers, whose livestock wealth was considerable and whose access to grazing land becoming tenuous.[40]

Many of these land purchasers were members of the sharecropping elite in the heartland of the arable Highveld. A large group of perhaps a hundred or more Orange Free State sharecropping families bought a farm, Swartrand, later known as Mogopa, north of Ventersdorp. Petrus Pooe, whose family sharecropped on the farm Arcadia, near Vredefort in the northern Orange Free State, remembers that largely as a result of the pressures to sell their stock, a group of their elders, including his own father, went to Bethanie near Brits in the Transvaal to seek out the Koena chief, Mamogale. Their request for land in the chief's reserve was turned down as it was already overcrowded; but:

> Chief Mamogale wanted to know from them whether they had money to buy. They said they did not have money but they had cattle. This was around 1910. . . . in 1911 Phiri-ea-Feta [a representative of Chief Mamogale] came to the Free State to inform our parents that there was a place between Koster and Ventersdorp which could make a good buy. . . . In fact they wanted to buy a farm close to Bethanie. But as that was not possible they had to look further afield. He, however, pointed out that the farm did not have good water resources. Our parents, being desperate to settle on a property of their own, assured Phiri-ea-Feta that they would solve the water problem as soon as they were there. Phiri-ea-Feta then asked them to start collecting money. The collection took them three years. It was in 1912 that they finally paid up the price asked for this farm Swartrand. It had to take that long because their major source of money was their cattle – which were fetching a very low price at the time. A big ox would fetch only £5 or £6.[41]

Each household paid some £75 toward the purchase price according to Petrus Pooe. The farm was bought in the name of the chief, Mamogale, who appointed Chief Petrus More as headman of the settlement. Some of the purchasers, like Petrus Pooe's uncle, Naphtali, never settled at Mogopa, managing to maintain their farming enterprise on the farms of the Vaal region, but with a right of access to grazing and arable land in Mogopa should it become necessary.[42]

Within the Pooe family there is a tradition that many of the local Sotho in the northern Orange Free State and southern Transvaal, many of whom lived under Moshoeshoe's rule after the *Difaqane* before migrating on to the farms, had always recognized the chiefs at Bethanie. Petrus remembers his uncle, Nchawe, telling him that 'Those who were in the Free State, especially of Koena origin, would come together to discuss matters of common interest or to decide on sending a present to their chief, Mamogale'.[43] But it is likely that a degree of *ex-post facto* ethnicity-building was at work here, for the Pooes were in fact Phuthing, not Koena, as were other families at Mogopa. The village was organized by the chief according to clan, with the ruling Koena, the Mogopa, settled together, followed by Ramorola, Tlhaping, Tlase, Mpshe, and so on, and then came the Phuthing, including the Pooes. Petrus Pooe notes:

'In other words we were settled according to the royal lineage's patterns.
. . . Earlier on when the royal family at Bethanie still had full control of
the area, they used to arrange the village according to their traditional
seniority.'[44] It seems that what was occurring was a deliberate attempt to
reconstruct clans in order to legitimate the creation of a new
community. Indeed, Dina Molope Pooe remembers her father changing
his surname from Mpshe to Molope in order to gain affiliation to the
clan.[45] In short we are witnessing a degree of ethnicity-building, in
which people created an ethnic homogeneity and claimed clan affiliation
in order to gain access to land – at a time when allegiance to a chief
seemed the best defence against the forced alienation of resources and
profits on the white-owned farms. In the twentieth century it has been
common for Africans to extrapolate a history of ethnic allegiance and
identity backwards as a defence against dispossession.[46]

A similar communal land purchase in the same area near Boons at this
time involved the mobilization of a Tswana clan, the Bakubung, who
also seem to have spent some while under Moshoeshoe's patronage in
the mid-nineteenth century after the Ndebele invasion of the Highveld,
and before moving back on the farms of the Orange Free State and
southern Transvaal. Ezekiel Moloko, born near Parys on the Vaal River
and a grandson of Chief Ramoloko, remembers cattle, horses and money
being taken to Pretoria to pay for the farm known as Molote (later
known as Mathopestad). In this case it appears that the reality of
chiefship for the Bakubung endured even during their stay on the farms
in the mid-Vaal region, although Bakubung identity was probably just
as flexible and open to imaginative reconstruction as that of the 'Koena'
at Mogopa.[47]

Not all such land was bought under the auspices of a chief. One
network of kinsmen who bought a farm close to Mogopa were the
Ngakanes. Seven brothers and cousins sharecropped on Fanie Cronje's
farm near Vereeniging. When Cronje issued an ultimatum that they
should sell their 'excess' stock, the family heads were in a quandary.
Barney Ngakane remembers that quite unexpectedly a young man
arrived from Johannesburg and told them of a lawyer named Pixley
Seme who was acting as an agent on behalf of blacks seeking to buy
farms. Seme advised the Ngakanes to inspect a farm named Klipgat,
near Boons, which they bought in 1913 just before the Natives Land Act
prohibited black land purchases. Fourteen different families
contributed to the purchase price, according to Morobane Ngakane.
These included the Ngakane, Nape, Thekiso and Malefetse families, all
related. Although the Ngakanes of Vlakplaas did not move to their new

farm until 1919 or 1920, they were able to send their excess stock there. Similarly, the Motsuenyane family, also wealthy sharecroppers, bought the farm Wildebeespan, near Klerksdorp, at roughly the same period.[48]

Seme's activities as an agent for black land purchases were channelled mainly into the Native Farmers' Association of South Africa. The Association bought the farms Driefontein, Driepan and Daggakraal as well as some stock in the Wakkerstroom district from one Gouws and one Potgieter in about 1912 for £20 000. The Association also bought the farm Vlakpoort. These farms were cut into ten-morgen lots and apparently sold to Africans for some £70, although the land and stock had been bought from Gouws for some £3 a morgen. The titles were issued by the Realty Trust Company of Johannesburg, acting on behalf of the Association. The local magistrate, C. Griffith, expressed the fear in 1914 that many of the African purchasers would not be able to pay. Some from Harrismith district depended on their stock to pay the purchase price, he said, and their stock was in a wretched condition.[49]

Many farm Africans with resources bought smallholdings in the vicinity of towns in anticipation of difficult times ahead. One was Naphtali Pooe, who bought a lot in Top Location, a freehold area near Vereeniging where many of the successful sharecroppers of the northern Orange Free State bought land.[50] Many white entrepreneurs who owned farms in the outskirts of towns made large profits by selling such plots. At Evaton, near Vereeniging, owned by C. N. Easton, purchasers received one-acre plots plus grazing rights on the commonage for £17–20. These landlords who owned whole townships on the outskirts of municipal areas were halted by the 1913 Natives Land Act which prohibited the sale of land to Africans in rural areas; but the Act did not interfere with sales already made.[51]

Amongst those Orange Free State Africans who failed to secure land of their own in the Transvaal before the legislative axe fell in 1913 were a large group of Rolong who had been subscribing money for some years for the purpose of acquiring land on which to settle. The Secretary for Native Affairs, E. E. Dower, noted in 1914 that he had been approached by a number of these Rolong farm tenants shortly after Union and on various occasions subsequently with a view to finding a reserve in the southwestern Transvaal near to their original homeland on which they could settle. The existing Tswana reserves in the northern Cape and western Transvaal, they asserted, were already overcrowded.[52]

This viable and increasingly pursued alternative to life as tenants on white-owned farms was closed off by the 1913 Natives Land Act. Clearly the pursuit of white supremacy on the land was in jeopardy if black farmers could maintain their independence and increase their security by resorting to the land market as a weapon of resistance.

*   *   *

A very important way in which the economic crisis was manifested was in a generalized social anxiety about the fate of the 'poor white', an ill-defined malaise centred on the supposed consequences of white 'degeneration' for the whole system of racial domination and social control. The crystallizing and propagating of a sense of moral panic about the 'lapsed whites' – the flotsam and jetsam of white rural society being thrown up during this period of rapid social and economic change – intersected with the emergent crisis of race relations on the land. The most evocative strand in the populist agitation against independent black tenant farming was the assumption that the very success of black farming on white-owned land was responsible for the failure of so many whites to survive as rural producers. At this point the crisis in rural relations became part of a larger, less tangible, more subjective ideological crisis of racial survival and racial purity.[53]

In particular, landlords' preference for black tenants was a cause of increasing alarm and anxiety. D. J. van Zyl of Bethlehem district was representative of many when he wrote to the prime minister of the ORC, Abram Fischer, in January 1909, complaining in urgent terms that the white rural poor were being oppressed by landowners. He wrote that the landed would not take in landless whites as tenants, but would rather maintain fifteen or twenty African households, provide grazing for their hundreds of livestock, and plough five to eight bags of maize for them. 'Is this not the same as taking bread out of the mouths of the poor?' he asked. The poor had borne the brunt of the war effort, he declared, under the impression that they too would become landowners once the war was over. But they were worse off than ever.[54] Also typical was the complaint in *The Friend* against an Afrikaans minister who asked the farmers in his congregation to plough two acres of maize each to pay for a black church. The correspondent wrote in 1911:

> In the same district, a white *bywoner*, with a small amount of stock, cannot obtain lands on the half ploughing system, whereas nearly every farm has natives who plough on the half, and in many cases have more stock than the white man.[55]

A story told by Barney Ngakane, who grew up in a wealthy sharecropping family in the Vereeniging district just north of the Vaal

River, will illuminate the point. In about 1912 the prime minister, Louis Botha, addressed local farmers on Jan Muller's farm. Ngakane's father and uncles witnessed the proceedings:

> At the end of the meeting one farmer stood up and asked a question of General Botha, whether it was right that there should be black people who were living a life of comparative ease, when there were *hundreds* of poor whites, *bywoners*. And the answer from General Botha was 'No'. And then Cronje [the Ngakanes' landlord] got up and he asked, 'Well, gentlemen, I have seven *bywoners* on the farm and I've seven black families, and I get from one of those black families what I cannot get from the seven *bywoners* together. And so are you going to ask me to take food out of my mouth?' This was the way he put it.... The next thing that happened there was that the farmers all said *'Donner hom!'* ['Beat him up!'] They were going to assault Fanie Cronje for saying seven white farmers could not produce what one black farmer produced. And that was the beginning. Pressure was brought to bear upon Cronje after the meeting.[56]

The Ngakanes soon found the pressures brought to bear on them were such that in 1913 they bought their own farm in the western Transvaal. Of course their landlord, Cronje, might well have had his own reasons for tightening conditions of tenancy. But it does seem that widespread intimidation of sharecropping landlords who allowed their tenants too much independence and latitude for accumulation was taking place in these years. In the popular perception, the black tenant farmer was a major factor in the impoverishment and marginalization of large numbers of rural whites.

Younger Afrikaners, products of the emergent 'Christian-nationalist' education system under the auspices of the populist Afrikaans churches, were particularly likely to be sensitized to the dangers implicit in the impoverishment of masses of rural whites. The younger generation was often more susceptible than their elders to the need for radical social and political intervention, if white supremacy was to be secured in an industrializing economy, and if white rural accumulation was not to be crushed by imperial capital on the one hand and the black rural economy on the other. The cultural pressures being exerted on landholders to take greater control over production on their land and to exert their own mastery over members of black tenant households were growing rapidly.

A great deal of proselytizing and agitating against the dangers implicit in independent black accumulation and enrichment was conducted at specially convened farmers' meetings. In September 1912, a congress was held at Reitz, attended by fifty delegates from throughout the Orange Free State, with a view to establishing a *Boerenbond* to push for the destruction of the sharecropping economy, the enforcement of compulsory master–servant contracts on all tenants, and the stipulation of maximum remuneration for workers which no farmer would be allowed to exceed. N. W. Serfontein, member of the provincial council, captured the spirit of the occasion when he said that the aim of the congress was to ensure the 'natural rights' of white men and to make South Africa a 'white man's country'. A *Boerenbond* congress met in Kroonstad in February of the following year, attended by sixty-five delegates, with a view to pressuring the government to take action.[57] This mobilization of farming opinion was fairly typical of these years. Farmers' congresses were held in places such as Wepener and Bethlehem, where angry words were exchanged about the 'squatting evil' and the impossibility of saving or rehabilitating the mass of impoverished whites while sharecropping arrangements were allowed to persist.[58]

This mobilization of moral outrage was expressed in comments that whites who lived off black sharecroppers were 'morally and spiritually atrophied', and that the white race, like the ancient Romans in the days of their decline, was degenerating and had lost the will to rule. Just as the Romans had abandoned production in the hands of the slaves and had withdrawn to the debauched pleasures of the towns, so were the whites allowing blacks to gain control of the motors of economic life. General Hertzog and others repeatedly warned of the danger that the whites would go the way of previous supposed colonizers of Africa, such as the Phoenicians, unless they asserted their control over productive enterprise. Such was the rhetoric of the day, particularly apparent during times of heightened sensitization, such as marked the years leading up to 1913.[59]

THE NATIVES LAND ACT AND THE GREAT DISPERSAL OF 1913

It was into this arena of struggle and resistance and mounting social anxiety amongst whites that the 1913 Natives Land Act – far and away the most important legislative intervention in the process of rural change in these years – was launched. The five years leading up to 1913 saw an unprecedentedly rapid development in the productive resources in white agriculture. They were also characterized by the often unsuccessful attempts of white landlords to subsume the labour and capital resources of their tenants more directly under their own organizational control, to siphon off larger surpluses from tenant production, as well as to reduce tenants' burgeoning stockholdings. Resistance by Africans to this attempted coercion led to much displacement of African families, as they sought to maintain their productive independence.

These years were also characterized by recurrent moral panics concerning the position of the 'poor whites', the supposed degeneration of the race, and the perceived dangers implicit in the growing lumpenproletarian army of white indigents in the towns and in the countryside. The agitation against the black sharecroppers was generally focused on the supposed and ill-defined relationship between black peasant prosperity and white landlessness and impoverishment, with all that these developments allegedly meant for the structure of authority in a racially ordered society.

It is largely in these contexts too that legislation prohibiting black sharecropping tenancy should be seen. The 1913 Land Act had been preceded in the Orange Free State by Act 23 of 1908 which had also been designed to stamp out all forms of independent black tenancy. Like other similar legislation – the 1895 anti-squatting law before it and the 1913 Land Act after it – the act of 1908 served a largely symbolic, mobilizing function and was incapable of systematic implementation. In view of the approaching national convention leading to unification of the colonies, the act of 1908 was suspended as soon as it was passed.[60]

The 1913 Land Act, like the abortive 1908 act before it, was aimed at stifling the independent black tenant farmers. The major provision of the Land Act as it affected the Orange Free State was that which declared illegal any:

agreement or arrangement whereby a [black] person, in consideration of his being permitted to occupy land, renders or promises to render to any person a share of the produce thereof, or any valuable consideration of any kind whatever other than his own labour or services or the labour or services of any of his family.[61]

In short, the only legal form of rent payment by black tenants to white landlords was labour service. Second, the act prohibited all land purchases by blacks outside scheduled reserve areas – generally those areas which blacks had been able to preserve from alienation (or had purchased back) – pending the proclamation of released land for addition to the reserves.

The act also reiterated the provision in the 1895 law that only five heads of (nuclear) families could live on any one farm, a provision which had never been enforced with much vigour. But such had been the degree of subdivision of the large landholdings of the nineteenth century, and such was the extent of closer settlement by white farmers, that this provision no longer evoked much serious dissension. This was in sharp contrast to the general tenor of the anti-squatting agitation of the 1880s and 1890s which focused largely on the issue of the forced redistribution of potential labour supplies. By 1913 the focus of popular agitation was on the content of tenancy relationships, rather than on the large concentrations of 'squatter' settlement on absentee-owned land. The issue was no longer one of securing an equitable distribution of tenants on the land of white farmers, but of imposing ever more servile conditions on them.

The implementation of the act in the Orange Free State was at first based on the proposition that contracts were automatically terminated at the close of each reaping season unless otherwise specified in writing. Thus the 1913 act was not to be officially enforced before the 1914 winter harvest, since all existing tenancy agreements were left to run their course.[62] But many landlords took the opportunity in the winter and spring of 1913 of removing Africans who would not sell off excess stock or submit to landlords' authority; and when the Natives Land Commission (appointed to recommend what extra land could be bought up for addition to the reserves) visited the Orange Free State in October 1913, the effects were dramatically evident. Without the support of the authorities and notwithstanding the precise provisions of the act, the passing of the 1913 act provided many landlords with an opportunity, a justification to organize and issue ultimatums in pursuit of their own interests.

The Orange Free State evidence before the Land Commission is replete with evidence of attempts dramatically to increase labour service, of forced stock sales and summary evictions.[63] In the winter of 1913 a great flurry of ultimatums was delivered, much confrontation and recrimination echoed through the countryside and a great trekking began. The incidence of expulsions after ploughing and sowing on trifling pretexts increased greatly. Africans at the receiving end were typically the wealthier tenants who owned more stock than the landlords were willing to tolerate.

By October police reports indicated that about 150 families were leaving the Ladybrand district, allegedly because of the law.[64] The magistrate in Winburg, R. Harley, reported that thirty African heads of households who had been turned off farms had been to see him to ask advice 'as to the best way out of their present trouble'. Practically all had had large possessions. One had sixty head of cattle, 140 sheep and eleven horses, but could offer the services of only one son aged fourteen. On the farm where he had lived, his two spans of oxen had done all the ploughing. No landholder would take him: 'no one will take a native with a large number of stock where he would only get the services of one man or perhaps two', said Harley.[65]

The magistrate in Bothaville in the north of the province reported that he had attended three meetings in his subdistrict at which representatives of over 400 tenant families were present. All wished to know whether reserves were to be established for them. Complaints were made that the government was trying to 'cut the throats' of the Africans. 'It was maintained that Natives possessing considerable stock would have difficulty in obtaining places of abode without selling their stock, and if they did succeed in obtaining employment their remuneration would perforce be small.'[66] Likewise, the magistrate in Heilbron, H. Reading, reported that 450 uninvited Africans had appeared before him, urging that summary evictions would cause great hardship. 'Already boys are trekking to the Transvaal from my district in considerable numbers', said Reading. The police in the district had issued passes to forty African families in order to leave the district since the promulgation of the act, taking with them 380 head of cattle, 593 sheep and twenty-two horses.[67]

The magistrate in the neighbouring Parys district reported in August that he had received a deputation of ten Africans possessing 289 head of cattle, together with horses and small stock. They had been given notice to 'trek' as soon as the harvest had been completed. 'We have applied elsewhere', they told him, 'but are always told that natives with cattle are not required.' They wished to know what to do and where to go. 'The natives, who are typical of their class, are respectable persons – law-abiding, thrifty and comparatively high in the scale of civilization', wrote the magistrate. 'Their efforts for years have been directed to the accumulation of flocks and herds. . . . I know of one instance of a native receiving notice to quit after a tenancy of twenty-three years.'[48]

The magistrate in Vrede had actually to intervene with white farmers to prevent them from expelling Africans until they could be provided for. 'They come to me and ask: "What must we do? Where must we go?" In some cases I have written to the master and asked him to allow the boy to stay on until we receive definite instructions.'[69] E. C. Roos, a Bethlehem farmer, said in October 1913 that in his district farmers were everywhere giving notice to their tenants to reduce their stock. And a pass issuer in Thaba Nchu district, E. A. Worringham, told the Land Commission that Africans were being 'hustled about considerably' by farmers who told them that they could no longer keep all the Africans' stock. 'I am daily issuing passes to natives who I know were living in my district before the war. . . . It is rather the well-to-do native who is getting a pass to go into Basutoland or elsewhere.'[70] But as Sol Plaatje discovered on visiting the border districts in September 1913, the rate of influx of farm tenants into Basutoland was threatening seriously to affect the 'land question' there.[71] The Kroonstad magistrate, R. C. Rosenzweig, reported that he had been approached by Africans applying unsuccessfully for butchers' licences – clearly considered by harassed stockowners with entrepreneurial skills to be an answer to their dilemma.[72] Forced stock sales inevitably depressed the market and provided a lucrative business for stock speculators.

Reverend C. Stuart Franklin, Wesleyan minister of Kroonstad, testified that up to 1 October, 208 members of his church had been 'lost'. A few of them had gone to Basutoland, although they had lived in the Orange Free State for forty to sixty years; a few had gone to Bechuanaland, but the larger number had gone to Johannesburg:

> In some cases these natives have experienced considerable hardship, because they have had to leave under pressure, and have had no time to remove their effects, stock, and implements, which have been sacrificed. I wish I could make you realize the unrest and the dissatisfaction which is in the minds and hearts of the native people right throughout this district. They think that this coming year will be a year of terrible loss and deprivation to them.[73]

Similar evictions were taking place in the more advanced maize districts of the southern Transvaal, despite the fact that the provisions of the act were suspended there. From Potchefstroom it was reported that the passing of the act had 'stimulated trekking on an extensive scale from various parts of the southwestern districts, many natives with their families and stock having crossed over into Bechuanaland'.[74]

Vivid personal witness to this dispersal is contained in Sol Plaatje's classic polemic, *Native Life in South Africa*.[75] Plaatje travelled through the Orange Free State between July and September 1913, investigating the consequences of the passing of the act. He tells of nights spent with 'fugitives' on the open veld: 'Some of their cattle had perished on the journey, from poverty and lack of fodder, and the native owners ran a risk of imprisonment for travelling with dying stock.' As this great dispersal took place in the middle of winter, grazing was poor and the animals weak. He describes refugees he met in the eastern districts:

> some of them with their belongings on their heads driving their emaciated flocks attenuated by starvation and the cold. The faces of some of the children, too, are livid from the cold. It looks as if these people were so many fugitives escaping from a war, with the enemy pressing hard at their heels.[76]

Plaatje describes the fate of one such family who moved north of the Vaal in search of ground on which to settle. Having failed to get satisfactory terms from the landowners, having sold some stock on the way and losing many others from cold and starvation, they eventually worked their way back to the Bloemhof diggings on the Vaal with the remainder, selling them for anything they could fetch. The household head went to work for a digger.[77]

Africans complained that the farmers were taking advantage of the confused state of affairs and of the Africans' ignorance of the law in order to delude them as to the dimensions of the law. Blacks from Winburg petitioned the Secretary for Native Affairs, complaining that they were being told 'all sorts of unfounded stories': stock speculators tried to convince them that the act obliged them to sell off their animals; farmers told them that according to the law they now had use of the Africans' oxen and wagons free of charge and that the tenant families had now to work without wages in return for grazing.[78] The magistrate in Bothaville wrote, 'I regret to state that some farmers have been endeavouring to make contracts most advantageous to themselves and to force Natives to dispose of their stock.' One instance had been brought to his notice of a head of family being offered 2s 6d per month for the services of males and 1s per month for females.[79] Plaatje also gives evidence of this. On his arrival at Bloemhof north of the Vaal in July 1913, he heard stories of African families having passed through the town within the previous fortnight, whose landlords had demanded that their cattle be handed over free of charge. 'Then the Natives would decide to leave the farm rather than make the landlord a present of all their life's earnings, and some of them had passed through the diggings in search of a place in the Transvaal.'[80]

The expulsions in the late winter and spring of 1913, which were taking place throughout the arable districts, were frequently in breach of existing landlord–tenant agreements, as we have seen. T. M. Mapikela, secretary of the Orange Free State Natives Congress, told the Land Commission of cases in which magistrates had referred expelled African tenants to lawyers, who had in turn demanded an initial payment of £50 before going into the matter.[81] When the Secretary for Native Affairs visited Winburg, he was presented with a petition by local Africans who complained of the attitude of the police, who always told them to take their complaints to a lawyer. They appealed for the Native Affairs Department to appoint local commissioners to intercede on tenants' behalf.[82]

So, despite the polemical nature of some of it, the evidence clearly illustrates the widespread occurrence of evictions which followed the passing of the 1913 Land Act. Twenty years previously Africans who were ordered to sell stock, render more intensive labour service or hand over a larger proportion of their product would have been able to find alternative arrangements under the patronage of a large landholder whose demands were less intrusive. This was no longer possible for most. The age when capitalist farmers were often also large land barons was receding. The private labour reserves of wealthy farmers were often being sold at high prices to farmers with access to land bank loans, and being put to the plough. Much absentee-owned land and many speculation farms were gradually being sold off or leased out to whites. Land was too valuable for farmers to continue relying indefinitely and uncomplainingly on access to a supply of labourers from amongst the junior members of large, wealthy and independent tenant communities.

The land crisis was coming to a head for the black tenants in the heartland of the arable Highveld. Blacks who decided to move rather than submit to forced dispossession and impoverishment as often as not discovered that there were no choices left. It is probable that those who submitted were no worse off in the end than most of those who chose to join the army of trekkers in the winter of 1913.

What this evidence in part signifies is the break-up of large homesteads. Relations between white farmers with extensive land-holdings and the patriarchs of black settlement groups had long been breaking down. The family seniors usually suffered most. They were often too old to work, and usually controlled the multi-generational family's often very substantial herds and flocks. They found themselves in an invidious position, and were likely to be expelled sooner or later from the farm, whereas the juniors could more readily find employment which enabled them to re-establish contracts of tenancy. These developments reached a peak in 1913. Thus, as often as not, those in distress who were reported to be wandering around the districts

all the productive resources were the property of and put in
n under the organizing authority of the white employer of labour.
who were familiar with the rural areas and who were acquainted
ne contents of the law were fully aware of its impracticability. The
s has been seen, declared illegal any agreement whereby an
n paid rent by means of a share of the crop or any other 'valuable
eration', other than his and his family's labour services. A
ehem farmer, A. J. Bruwer, told the Natives Land Commission in
nat if the use of tenants' oxen was to be accounted a 'valuable
eration' and made illegal by the act, he would have to dismiss his
– and presumably also abandon farming – 'because if I cannot
ir cattle to plough I would have no use for them'. J. P. Steyl, MLA
aba Nchu, while condemning sharecropping, urged that an
tenant should be permitted 'to give his oxen as well as his
l service – to count the service of his oxen, which are to be used in
ration of his occupying the land'.[97] A. H. Maree of the same
agreed. Oxen service should be allowed:

ng as it can be proved that the service of the oxen has not been
in lieu of rent. As long as the boy gives his service and is willing
ist his employer with the help of his oxen, I do not think you can
hat as rent.[98]

government's law advisors' conciliatory and meaningless
was that oxen service was only illegal if included in the contract
ndition of tenancy.[99] But legal argument was essentially
t; the act, like so much social-engineering legislation, was a
t of ideals, a declaration of intent, a call to action by dominant
ather than a formal legal code. Legal debate was taking place in
divorced from social reality. Whatever the law advisors and in
nt years the Supreme Court might decide to be the correct
ation of one or other provision of the law, the effect on what
ening in the real world was minimal.[100]

neless, it would be quite wrong to discount the Land Act as a
factor in shaping future development of rural capitalism. For
another aspect of the act which was crucial in strengthening
on of capitalizing landlords. The act laid down that all black
ere to be defined as servants under the 1904 Masters and
Ordinance, and not just individually contracted employees
or a wage. This had considerable implications for the legal
enants and for the criminal sanctions that the farmer could
o his aid against recalcitrant or unwilling Africans on his

appealing to magistrate and missionary for aid and advice were older
men.[83]

However, land shortage was always relative. When Naphtali Pooe
was forced off the farm Berlin on which he had been sharecropping in
1913 because he refused to sell his stock, he and his brother found the
greatest difficulty finding another farm. 'They would come back to
report that one Boer had promised them a farm on which he wanted to
settle sharecroppers', says his wife:

They would then go there to see what kind of soil there was and to
assess the prospects of settling there. . . . When they arrived there they
discovered to their disappointment that it was a very poor soil area
with sour grass over – a clear indication of poor soil – which would
make it very difficult to practise sharecropping profitably.[84]

So the long search continued. It was not simply a matter of finding land
on which to settle and a landowner who would allow them to keep their
cattle and maintain their independence. It was also a matter of finding
land on which a satisfactory standard of peasant production could be
maintained. It seems, indeed, that the only landlords who would accept
the Pooes and their cattle on their own terms were those with poorer
land. Those with good arable land were those whose terms were the most
unacceptable to this prosperous sharecropping family.[85]

Ultimatums and evictions were not directly caused by the Land Act,
though. The formal prohibition of sharecropping in the act was in large
part ineffective, and indeed it was not even implemented by the
authorities – certainly not in 1913. But the act provided a catalyst to
concerted action on the part of the landlords. White farmers involved in
an intense struggle for control over resources and human labour were
not concerned with precise legal definition; for them, the passing of the
act was a catharsis, an affirmation from the highest authority of the
legitimacy of their cause and the inevitability of their victory against
their black competitors. And they acted on that perception. Legislatures
often serve broader, less tangible functions than those encompassed in
legal theory.

But what were the dimensions of the transformation being wrought
amidst all this trauma? Once the great dispersal had run its course and
black families had re-established working relationships with landlords,
new or old, how had the patterns of productive life changed? Some black
informants recall this as the time when landlords replaced a
sharecropping system with one in which the tenants worked two days on
their own fields for four in the landlord's fields – although usually still

using their own oxen and equipment.[86] No doubt more white farmers felt able to exert greater authority over production once the Land Act and the great dispersal of 1913 had provided the resolve and the incentive. White farmers benefited from a splitting of the arable in this way, in so far as they could reserve good arable land for themselves while banishing the tenants to stony or exhausted ground, or reserve manure or maize stalks for their own use.[87] The price they had to pay was far greater supervision and enforcement of work discipline.

The symbolic importance of such a transformation was not lost on contemporary observers. J. G. Keyter, MLA for Ficksburg and a major protagonist of the 1913 Land Act, expressed its essential significance thus:

> when the boy had his whole piece of ground to sow and be given a half of the crops, he was not a servant but a partner – a master. The moment you draw the line under the new law that boy becomes your servant at once. . . . As soon as you draw the line on your farm and say 'You can sow this for yourself', he is your servant.[88]

I. J. Meyer, MLA for Harrismith, said: 'The difference . . . is this, that if a Kaffir ploughs for me and ploughs again for himself he looks upon me as his master, whereas if he is working on the halves he looks upon me as his partner or his equal.'[89]

Nevertheless, splitting the arable did not necessarily imply a decline in landlords' reliance on their tenants' productive resources and skills. Deskilling only came with mechanization of peak seasonal activities, which was still a long way off. There was no widespread revolution in the productive processes, no general stripping of black tenants' means of arable production, no universal undermining of peasant skills and household labour organization, as long as tenant households continued to own the capital resources necessary for preparing the soil and planting the crop. Commonly, as we have seen, explicit sharecropping arrangements gave way to 'ploughing-and-sowing' agreements, involving the use of tenants' oxen and ploughs in landlords' fields, and often also including the use of tenants' wagons for transporting the crop.[90]

But for many landholders, splitting the arable into landlord's and tenants' fields was not a viable option, mainly because they were not able or willing to provide the sort of supervision which such an arrangement required. This clearly applied to absentee landlords. Many poor whites continued to survive on the land by hiring farms and battening on to black tenant production over which they exerted no

direct control. Many landholders saw no incent control over production, given the risks of capita lower productivity of alienated labour. Many wo Wepener farmers who at their congress in Ja opposed the abortive 1908 act on the grounds would be a curse to the landowners'.[91] As early as 1 Administration Commission had perceptively investigations that it was not possible to frame p against sharecropping which could not be evade to enforce such legislation would only drive tl subterfuge and evasive expedients'.[92] In the ever fully borne out. As the magistrate in Vredefor great idea of the natives is to plough, sow and rea The Natives Land Act has not materially alter previously existed between the European maste this respect.'[93]

In subsequent years the prohibition on sha the act was rarely enforced by the author illegality, combined with public opinion disincentive).[94] Sharecropping in its most expl practised on many farms right through to the Free State districts most affected by the evi tractor more than anything else which event ongoing importance of such relationships Grosskopf, who investigated conditions on many maize districts, he found, there were fa the 'real producers', who provided the land produce. Grosskopf reported that every atto evasion of the law in this respect. A 'reliable a certain ward of the southwestern Transv of the maize crop was produced by Africal Free State maize district he had encount tenant who owned seven spans of oxen each.[95] But sharecroppers were by no m harsher regime in the countryside after recall that it was about this time that th only a third of their crop instead of a h

*   *

The framers of the Land Act were provic future ideal, but which was as yet unattai

which
motio
Many
with t
act, a
Africa
consid
Bethel
1913 t
consid
tenants
use the
for Th
African
persona
conside
district

as lo
given
to ass
take t

The
response
as a co
irreleva
statemen
classes,
a vacuu
subseque
interpret
was happ

Nevert
powerful
there was
the positi
tenants w
Servants
working f
status of t
summon

land.[101] The *Farmer's Advocate* in an editorial in August 1913 asserted that this provision was of paramount importance. The difference made by the new law was:

> the natives declare themselves to be the servants of the farmer and not his tenants, and bring themselves thereby under the provisions of the Masters and Servants Act. . . . The work that such natives will do will consist as heretofore in ploughing on shares, but they will be nominal servants instead of nominal tenants. . . . By such means the farmers get a closer grip over the 'loose' or unattached natives to whom they may give permission to reside upon their properties.[102]

Both the African Political Organization and the OFS Natives Congress, in their petitions against the act, expressed their deep concern that the term 'farm servant' as used in the 1913 Land Act to describe all Africans resident on white-owned land, would render the wives, daughters and minor sons of African tenants 'practically slaves to the owner of the farm'. The head of the family would have 'no right to order his children to attend school, nor may he require his wife to attend to her domestic duties'. The extension of the masters-and-servants law to all tenants effectively stripped tenant families of their defences in law against the landlords.[103] Clearly this extension of legal servile status with the threat of criminal sanctions that went with it was potentially a major victory for the master class.

Of course, legal procedure in local courts constituted only the tip of the iceberg in the whole structure of social control on the farms, and, as we have seen, what happened in local courts often reflected very imperfectly the rules of legal procedure and the formal provisions of the statute book.[104] The informal face of the law in local courts was not greatly affected by the activities of the legislators. But extending the criminal law to encompass all farm tenants was an important symbolic act, provided new sources of intimidation or threat, and occasionally enabled individual farmers to enforce their will at crucial points in the transformation of productive relationships on their land by direct resort to criminal prosecution.

*   *   *

In the few years before the First World War, there was a concerted and determined effort, largely successful in the heartland of the arable Highveld, to subsume tenant production far more tightly under the organizational control of white farmers, to channel a greater proportion of the profits of their enterprise in the direction of their landlords, and to place general limits on their capacity for accumulation and self-enrichment. The most devastating immediate manifestation of these developments was the forced sale of much of their livestock, over and above those required for production and immediate subsistence (such as milk cows). The significance of the 1913 Land Act and the great spate of forced removals that it sparked off lay not in its effectiveness in abolishing sharecropping (as was the act's formal intention) but in the tighter grip which landholders were able to exert over their tenants' productive activities and the more efficient siphoning-off of their surpluses. The act had social consequences which were quite different from those which a legalistic reading of its provisions would lead one to expect. On the other hand, the act, while relatively ineffective in relation to the quite unrealistic projections of its progenitors, did provide part of the statutory framework within which future struggles over resources and control over labour could be fought.

The extension of white control over production was not directly the result of the act, but of concerted action and collusion amongst landlords – together with great pressure brought to bear on those landlords who allowed too great a degree of independence and scope for accumulation to their tenants. This combined assertiveness was not easily achieved. A crescendo of agitation, proselytizing, organizing and intimidation reached its peak with the passing of the 1913 act. The purpose was not primarily to destroy the black tenant farmers, but to harness their labour, their skills and their capital resources more fully to the profit of their landlords. The significance of the events described in this chapter is that for the first time white farmers in the arable heartland of the Highveld were able to intervene decisively to halt and to turn back the tide of black accumulation on the land in a period of rapid productive expansion. These years of crisis provided the first indication, albeit only in the most advanced heartland of the arable Highveld, of the forces that accumulating white farmers and landholders could array on their side when the circumstances were propitious for their use.

But by 1914 many of the preconditioning factors behind the rural crisis were receding. The drought which began in 1913 became more serious. More importantly, the outbreak of war brought the financial boom to an end. The land bank severely curtailed its activities, and private loan capital virtually dried up. The private banks instituted a policy of reducing their advances to the farming community as rapidly as possible. The Boer rebellion which was prompted by the government's decision to invade German South West Africa on behalf of the British Empire caused a stagnation in trade as merchants' stocks throughout the maize districts were commandeered by the rebel forces, paralyzing the credit system. One consequence was a slump in land prices – by as much as 25 per cent in some of the Highveld maize districts.[105] These developments might have resulted in a resurgence of the peasant sector. Further, when in 1916 the Natives Land Commission, appointed under the 1913 act to define extra 'released' land for addition to the scheduled reserves, published its report, nothing came of it for another twenty years. The corporate landowners were no longer as willing to dispose of their massive landholdings in the Transvaal as they had been in 1913 when prices were at a peak.

The development of rural capitalism was unsustained, cyclical and cumulative. It has also varied greatly from region to region. It would probably be wrong to claim that 1913 was a decisive watershed year, even in the heartland of the arable Highveld. But there is no doubt that in many black farmers' memories, things were never quite the same again. The sharecroppers quickly lost their social optimism and their faith in self-improvement. Sharecropping communities no longer had the self-confidence to build schools, carve desks and hire teachers. Increasingly rarely were sharecroppers able to invest in upward social mobility by sending their sons to Kilnerton Institute. Those who sought to elevate themselves or their children into the new elite found that rural production provided them less and less with a viable base. Typically, the religion of the sharecroppers of a later era was no longer Anglicanism, Methodism or Presbyterianism. Increasingly, the sharecroppers' church was a separatist one.[106]

Conclusion

The model which many recent scholars have used to interpret the transformation of rural South Africa is that of the 'Prussian path'. First used by Lenin to explain one variant of capitalist development, the analogy with east Elbian Germany was further developed by Barrington Moore in his influential comparative survey of industrialization. In analyses of South Africa, the analogy has been found useful at different times by scholars as diverse as Stanley Trapido, Martin Legassick, M. L. Morris, Stanley Greenberg and Frederick Cooper.[1] The significance of the Prussian experience lies in the transition to capitalism 'from above'. In the paradigmatic Prussian case, the feudal aristocracy itself took charge of capitalist production, forcibly turning the serfs into labourers.

The German analogy presented in this schematic way implies fundamental continuities on two levels. First, it implies an evolutionary, internal transformation of the pre-industrial white landowning class (the 'Boer Junkers' in Morris' terminology) into a class of capitalist farmers, by a sustained and self-generating process of accumulation. Second, it implies that the rise of an industrial economy and of urban markets was directly accompanied by the emergence and intensification of labour-tenancy relationships between servile black tenant and dominant white landlord, which were increasingly analogous with and merging into explicit wage labour – what has been called 'internal proletarianization'.[2] The model contains the assumption that the process of 'labour repression' was an integral aspect of the rise of commercial agriculture. As a broad generalization the model might seem at first sight to bear some superficial resemblance to what happened in South Africa over the long term. But on both counts it obscures and misrepresents the real significance of the processes involved.[3]

Were the capitalist farmers of the Highveld in the twentieth century really direct lineal descendants of the landowners of the mid-nineteenth century? Was capital accumulation self-sustaining? Did it proceed in an evolutionary trajectory? The evidence suggests the opposite. Productive capital was not generated from agricultural production itself – at least not indefinitely. The old Boer landowner and extensive pastoralist of the 1860s was more likely to be amongst the victims of the industrial revolution than amongst its beneficiaries. The progressive farmers of the early twentieth century were more likely to be new settlers of British or colonial origins than members of the old Boer landowning class. The great bulk of new capital being invested in agricultural enterprise was imported from elsewhere or was accumulated in non-agricultural pursuits. Many of the most capitalized farmers had alternative sources of income.[4] Typically, fully capitalized farming went hand in hand with entrepreneurial activities of one sort or another. Indeed, the capital-intensive farming enterprises in the early years of the century generally belonged to men who made their money in mining or mercantile enterprise or in speculation. Highly capital-intensive farms were also often thoroughly uneconomic. Capital intensity in agriculture did not guarantee profitability.[5]

During boom periods the capital base of white farming expanded rapidly, particularly as a result of injections of capital from elsewhere as new settlers moved on to the Highveld bringing capital with them. However, the bulk of white landholders did not have unlimited capital resources at their disposal for investment. Undercapitalization was the normal condition for most. Yet the old Boer landowner could not simply opt out of the spread of arable farming. Drought, disease and war devastation in the 1890s and early 1900s caused a gradual slide by white landholders into indebtedness, mainly through the bonding of landed property, aggravated by the flood of speculative capital surging through the countryside in the wake of the gold discoveries on the Witwatersrand. Older, part-time economic activities were becoming less and less viable as commercial hunting disappeared, and as trade and transport fell under the control of a professional mercantile class. Extensive pastoralism was declining in the face of fencing and the rising value of land. Moreover, the larger farms of the past were being subdivided to pay off debts or to restock, which tended to promote a shift to cultivation of the soil.

Resident white landholders who were increasingly dependent on producing grain for the market commonly turned to sharecropping relationships with black tenants, often as a supplement to their own efforts. As landholders found that arable farming was becoming more and more indispensable for their survival, they became increasingly dependent on the capital resources and skills of black tenants. This did not inevitably imply explicit sharecropping arrangements. But it did often mean use of Africans' ploughing oxen and equipment in order to get a sizeable crop in the ground. It is in the context of the uncertainties and risks involved in capital investment and the unpredictable productivity of rural resources that the prevalence of sharecropping relationships between white and black should be seen. Because of their extensive networks of kinship and the ethics of communality and reciprocity, the black tenant farmers were far more able to ride the destructive impact of natural disaster and war-induced deprivation without contracting debt than their white counterparts.

Far from being a 'quasi-feudal' relationship associated with the precapitalist past, sharecropping was a product of the early stages of South Africa's industrial revolution.[6] Sharecropping was a compromise between whites who lacked sufficient capital to acquire equipment and to secure an adequate labour force and blacks with the labour, resources and skills to take advantage of the abundance of land which whites controlled. It was the way in which black households without alternative access to land and white landholders without the skills or the capital to cultivate the soil intensively themselves, responded to the new opportunities and new pressures presented by the rise of internal markets and by the penetration of rural areas by mercantile and speculative capital. The extensive nature of land use and relative sparsity of white settlement intially gave blacks some leverage in the terms under which they entered productive relationships with white landlords. Sharecropping was thus also related to the relatively abundant land resources which characterized the interior regions of white settlement in the late nineteenth century, and the consequent weakness of the settler economy in the mobilization of labour resources from the indigenous societies.

Sharecropping on the white-settled Highveld served as a transition from a relatively peripheral colonial rural economy linked into capitalist markets through the provision of animal products to an arable hinterland feeding rapidly growing urban markets in an industrializing economy. Sharecropping was a bridge to a more explicitly capitalist agriculture in which there was no place for black household production. But this model is only valid from the vantage point of the historian. For at the time it was not objectively determined that sharecropping relationships would eventually make way for capitalist farming. There was no inevitability about the process whereby capital was generated within the white farming economy. Clearly sharecropping surpluses provided a potential base for capital accumulation for individual white landholders; but for many whites, black production meant not so much capital generation as survival on the land. It was primarily state intervention which was eventually to provide the wherewithal for undercapitalized whites to launch, however tenuously, into capitalist farming.

The 'seigneurial' stereotype of sharecropping, derived from the image of the European, Latin American or Asian great estate, where the wealthy, exploitative landowner controls a large, impoverished tenantry, is clearly not applicable to the South African case. It has often been assumed that sharecropping did not and does not exist in Africa, because of the obvious absence of the seigneurial pattern. However, recent research has shown that share contracts in fact exist fairly widely in Africa and in such cases seem to be relatively equitable relationships between small farmers by means of which scarce resources are combined in an efficient manner in order to ensure mutual survival and expanded production. Sharecropping can also be a means whereby resources are transferred within kin groups or between generations.[7] Share contracting is widely practised in Lesotho today, and even in black communities in South Africa, and in these contexts it seems to be a means of ensuring the survival of the household economy in areas which have been reduced to sources of supply of migrants to service the industrial economy of 'white' South Africa. There is little class differentiation in such relationships, which seem by and large to be determined by cyclical, generational factors.[8] On the other hand, it is not at all unusual in black areas of South Africa today for rural entrepreneurs with tractors (white as well as black) to plough the land of poor families stripped of their labour resources by the exigencies of labour migrancy, in return for perhaps four-fifths of the resultant crop.[9] The notion that the provider of land can be the economically weaker participant in the sharecropping agreement might seem strange to observers of sharecropping elsewhere in the world. But it should not surprise us when we remember what sharecropping meant for many on the white-owned farms of the Highveld in the early years of the century.

But sharecropping relationships between white and black were never regarded as legitimate in the dominant perceptions of whites. Sharecropping on the farms was largely practised outside formal civil sanctions and prescriptions (which also explains the paucity of documentary or statistical evidence on such relationships). Whites were generally very reluctant to admit that they were so 'degenerate' as to rely on 'Kaffir farmers', and dominant populist ideology was fiercely antagonistic to any form of black economic independence. This factor provided much of the impetus behind the drive to suppress black sharecropping by legislation, and the drive of various governments to pour large sums of capital into white farming. There was generally an intense desire by white farmers to establish greater control over productive activities on their land for 'cultural' reasons, quite apart from any rational calculation of costs and benefits. The ideal of the white farmer controlling production and directing black labour was propagated tirelessly in the populist agitations of the day.

There are no universal 'laws of capital' to explain why wage relationships have been generalized throughout the South African countryside, and why the sharecropping peasant eventually disappeared. The nature of agricultural enterprise is such that it is questionable whether capital investment in rural production was consistently remunerative enough to justify the risks involved, when compared with the advantages of leaving cultivation in the hands of a sharecropping tenantry, and given the fact that the technology and productive processes at the disposal of the white farmer were not yet substantially different from those employed by the black tenant household. Indeed, it is very unlikely that rational considerations of opportunity cost in a narrow economic sense had much bearing on white farmers' image of the ideal relationship between black and white. The exercise of class power imposed its own constraints and limitations on economic decision-making. The landed whites saw themselves as an emergent class, a class in the making; and their corporate self-perception was based fundamentally on a pre-existing sense of racial identity.

It is thus not surprising to discover that public perception often conflicted with private behaviour. Many who condemned black tenant farming enterprise were themselves dependent in some or other degree on the skills and capital resources of black tenants. As a perceptive observer wrote in 1908:

> One sometimes thinks that nothing could more embarrass the farmers individually than that very enforcement of the squatting laws which they are always collectively asking for. If the native squatter is so great an evil, how comes it that nine farmers out of ten are willing to put their land at his disposal.[10]

The rhetorical ideal of a fully capitalist agriculture was no less potent for being quite unattainable for most (at any rate by 1914).[11]

The Afrikaner cultural awakening in the late nineteenth century derived many of its ideas from the nationalism of nineteenth-century Europe, and took fire in the Boer republics because it met the needs of Afrikaner intellectuals in the material circumstances of the economic revolution being wrought in their midst under the auspices of an alien imperial power. Embedded in the Afrikaner cultural nationalism of the later nineteenth and early twentieth centuries were newer ideas about the need to promote racial domination in all facets of economic enterprise – ideas particularly apposite to an age of scientific racism and

European imperialism, but which took on a special resonance for a white settler people who were themselves the victims of imperialism.

Although Afrikaner agitations about the extent of land dispossession were clearly exaggerated, landownership was clearly becoming increasingly precarious for many Boer farmers as mortgage and other forms of indebtedness spread. Much land was taken over by capitalist interests during periods of bad climatic or economic conditions, such as the early 1880s, the late 1890s and the half-dozen years after the close of the Anglo-Boer War. The long-term tendency certainly seemed at the time to be toward the gradual expropriation of the Boer economy, and the increasing control of land by speculative capitalists, who were not always inclined to share populist resentment at the independent black farmers. Many absentee landowners saw black tenant production as a viable long-term option with a view to the feeding of urban markets and the filling of corporate pockets. Such factors as these lent special urgency to the drive to assert indigenous white control over productive resources on the land as the mainspring of incipient Afrikaner nationalism.

The continual influx of farmers with access to capital resources on to the Highveld provided indigenous whites with a constant model of the ideal to which they should strive. The newer settlers of British descent brought with them very definite ideas of proper class relationships in a capitalist economy, ideas which were bolstered by Lord Milner's reconstruction regime after the Anglo-Boer War with its radical social-engineering proclivities. The ideals embodied in the initial sanguine policies of Milner's administration (both in terms of the promotion of capitalized white land settlement by empire loyalists at the expense of the old burgher population, and the provision of a black labouring force) left a far deeper impression than the policies themselves, which soon proved hopelessly impractical.[12]

*   *   *

It was only on the basis of constant state support that a capitalized farming economy under white control eventually emerged and was maintained. As we have seen, by the early twentieth century the possibilities of capital accumulation by the various means available throughout the nineteenth century were becoming very limited: trade, transport, hunting and speculation were no longer readily available options for young adventurers. It was at this point that the state took over as the main generator of productive capital for white farmers. And the preservation of a viable productive base increasingly depended on continued state supports at every stage in the processes of production and marketing of produce. To an ever greater degree as the century progressed, the survival of white farmers (which did not necessarily mean consistent and cumulative profit-making) required access to fairly substantial funds from outside agricultural production, at least initially, and continual reliance on the state's resources as a cushion against climatic and market fluctuations.

State intervention on the necessary scale required a particular set of historical circumstances. The breakthrough to a generalized rural capitalism was predicated upon the rise of urban industry. In South Africa, as part of the colonial periphery in the international economy of the nineteenth century, the initial impetus behind the generalization of capitalist relationships derived from the massive importation of finance capital to exploit the rich mineral resources of the region. The establishment of heavy industry with a view to extracting raw materials for export was a necessary precondition for the capitalist trans-formation of the countryside. For in the modern world, only in an industrializing economy are markets sufficiently large and expansive to allow for the emergence of a capitalist agriculture, and only such an economy can sustain the kind of state intervention which is necessary for such a rural transformation.

But a necessary precondition does not add up to a sufficient explanation. What distinguished South Africa from other parts of Africa with rich mineral resources was that South Africa had a well-established white ruling class (both English- and Afrikaans-speaking), which was able to exploit the potential created by the influx of capital to forge a state system with the financial muscle and coercive power to support and sustain a far-reaching process of indigenous capital formation and social restructuring. This was especially so after the Anglo-Boer War, which, whatever its causes might have been, swept aside the old Boer republican regimes which had proved themselves structurally inadequate to the task of modernization and rationalization in the new industrial era. At first, the indigenous Afrikaners were largely excluded from the benefits of these developments. But the fact that they quickly regained their membership of the ruling class after the war enabled them eventually to tap and exploit the creation of new wealth. This was accomplished in large part through the mediation of the state, which in rural areas promoted a new generation of Afrikaners into the ranks of the capitalist farmers, especially from the second decade of the century onward.

One important and enduring intervention of the state was in the institutionalized provision of loan capital, thereby providing a more sympathetic, flexible and reliable alternative to resort to private capital. Land banks were established in the ex-republics in 1907–8, and were superseded by the Union Land Bank in 1912. The establishment of land banks (whose facilities were available to whites only) was an important watershed, for it marked the beginning of sustained, large-scale state financing of white farming. Their establishment also coincided with the transfer of responsible government in the ex-republics to local whites. The ministries which came to power in 1907–8 were dominated by men who had commanded Boer forces in the Anglo-Boer War. Thus the imperial power confirmed not only its commitment to a white-supremacist rural economy, but also its realization that the recently conquered Boers were bound to be a major element in the state-sponsored rural capitalism that they envisaged emerging in the future. In succeeding decades state-subsidized farmers' co-operatives, price supports and statutory marketing monopolies greatly extended white farmers' dependence on the state.[13]

The accumulation and eventual monopolization of capital resources by white farmers necessarily went hand in hand with the process whereby a black labour force, dependent on selling its labour in order to survive, was created, maintained and controlled. Equally crucial to the generalization of capitalist relations throughout the rural political economy was the stripping of productive resources from African peasants.[14] However, contrary to the trajectory implicitly suggested by the German analogy, the proletarianization of black peasants in South Africa did not proceed as a logical corollary of industrialization and urban growth. Just as there was no direct or unproblematical line of descent between the old landowning class and the new capitalist farmers, so there was a discontinuity in the process whereby the relatively independent black tenant homesteads of pre-industrial times were reduced to the rural work force of today. The one-way procession from serf to proletarian implied by the German analogy does not reflect the South African experience. Many black tenant producers were amongst the beneficiaries rather than the victims of the commercialization of agriculture on the South African Highveld, although their success was to be short-lived.[15] While it is true that demands for labour from black tenants rapidly intensified under the impact of growing markets, it is equally clear that the end of the nineteenth century saw a great spread and intensification of commercial arable farming by blacks on white-owned land, particularly, as we have seen, in sharecropping arrangements. Indeed, this was a period of rapid, albeit short-lived, accumulation of productive capital in the hands of black tenants.

There is an implicit tendency in much of the literature to overemphasize the role of state action in the decline of the black tenant farmers. But more than state power was required to take charge of the rural economy in the face of a resilient and successful black peasantry. The agencies of control, the local courts, the police and the laws they applied were never more than marginally effective in reshaping the countryside, valuable weapons though they may intermittently have been to individual white landholders. The creation of a black labour force was not the result of a single, irreversible coup. Social-engineering legislation (such as the Natives Land Act of 1913 which sought to outlaw sharecropping by black tenants and enforce labour service) never wrought the transformations intended by its sanguine progenitors.

The creation of a labour force required a determined and protracted expenditure of effort by white farmers in the day-to-day struggle to bend black tenants to their will. It also required the periodical and recurrent mobilization of racial energies in concerted drives against the independence and the productive resources of black tenants. Racial domination was not a condition but a process, constantly being undermined and constantly being reasserted and extended. The assertion and extension of racial domination came in cyclical waves. At times of financial boom and productive expansion (such as the years 1893–5, 1908–13 and again in the mid-1920s) the mobilization of white opinion and concerted action against the independent tenant farmers were at their most intense.

The level of energy that had to be expended in proselytizing and mobilizing white opinion was extraordinary, as was the effort required in extending control over the black rural economy and eventually subverting it fatally. Co-ordinated and simultaneous action together with the intimidation of landholders who were too blatant in their dependence on black sharecropping enterprise were necessary if black tenants were not to play landlords off against one another. For the intensification of white capitalist farming was accompanied by an often remarkably high level of mobility of tenant families. By the second decade of the twentieth century land was becoming a scarce resource and the threat of eviction was becoming a real weapon in landlords' hands. Tenant mobility was increasingly becoming an index of their vulnerability. Closer land settlement by black and white alike, and the ubiquitous unwillingness of landholders to allow large stockholdings on their land, lay behind the great dispersal of 1913.

The extension of white domination over rural production did not invariably coincide with the total capitalization of white farming. White landholders were able to extend control over black tenant households without necessarily expropriating black capital resources. Activities which required capital investment and which were suited to household forms of labour organization, such as ploughing and sowing, were often left in the hands of tenant households under 'ploughing-and-sowing' contracts; while more labour-intensive activities suited to the organization of work parties and requiring minimal capital investment (such as weeding and reaping) were often taken under landlord control first. The convention of 'separate fields' (rather than explicit sharecropping arrangements) required a very considerable investment in supervision and control, but enabled the white landholder to reserve good arable land, manure (for fertilization) and maize stalks (for fodder and fuel) for himself, while continuing to profit from the use of black-owned productive equipment and draught animals.

Labour tenancy – the ubiquitous emergent labour relationship on the Highveld in the first half of the twentieth century as the white farmers gained a stranglehold on productive resources – should be seen as a solution to problems of labour supervision and control in the face of black tenants' determination to maintain some kind of independent productive base. It was also consistent with some of the constraints of capital. Few farmers had the liquid capital to pay regular wages or to be able to attract labourers at short notice for specific seasonal tasks. The radical unevenness of labour requirements, the long periods of minimal labour input in arable farming, the utility of women's and children's labour, as well as the utility of black tenants' productive resources (particularly ploughing spans): all these factors made tenant household labour preferable to proletarian wage labour, quite apart from the extreme difficulty of mobilizing, controlling and supervising a forcibly dispossessed rural work force. Labour tenancy was thus a perfectly rational way of organizing labour, although many of its advantages were to wane under the impact of mechanization from the 1940s onward.[16]

By mid-century the productivity of capitalist farming was being greatly increased under the auspices of a paternalistic state. Technological innovation was decisively shifting agricultural production toward capital-intensive methods. The mechanization of white farming on the back of massive state subsidies had by the 1970s vastly extended the productive potential of the farming enterprise on the South African Highveld. These developments conclusively robbed blacks, who were denied access to state aid, of the advantages of greater relative productivity and of lower relative risk which had once enabled them to prosper as independent tenants on white-owned farms. Black productive resources and household labour became expendable to white farmers, and the seasonal intensity of labour demands on the farms was substantially reduced. At the same time as the labour requirements of the arable farmer were being greatly reduced, the mobilization and control of a labour force were also becoming far easier, given mass unemployment and marginalization of the surplus African population in resettlement slums within the reserves.[17]

The 1950s, then, saw the beginnings of the end of the labour-tenancy system (especially as tractors made tenants' ploughing oxen not only dispensable but also a nuisance) at the same time as the 'black spots', many of them farms acquired in the few years prior to the prohibition of black land purchase in 1913, have been gradually expropriated by the Nationalist government, signifying the final triumph of the political economy of white supremacy on the rural Highveld. However, these developments do not necessarily imply the take-off of white capitalist farming into an era of sustained profitability. Farmers' reliance on state aid has not subsided. If anything it has increased. And, as the drought of the 1980s has shown, capitalist farming is just as tenuous, vulnerable and dependent on massive debt contraction today as eighty years ago.

*   *   *

The principle focus in this book has been the arable districts of the southern Highveld, for it was here, in the Orange Free State, that the capitalization of agriculture had proceeded furthest and the exploitation of the soil was most intense by 1914. It was here too that rural struggle was most developed, and the drive for white supremacy at the point of production had proceeded furthest. In the western Transvaal, where intensive maize farming was a later development, sharecropping seems to have become really ubiquitous only in the 1920s and 1930s. The history of black tenant farming has varied significantly from region to region. Some informants grew up in labour tenant households in the Orange Free State, only to take to sharecropping as adults further north. The frontier of white capitalist farming has advanced sporadically and gradually. Indeed, it would not be surprising to find that it also receded at times. But even this might eventually seem too schematic a formulation; we might yet discover that local experiences were *sui generis*, and not simply variations of period. Only oral research will illuminate these issues. What is clear is that abstract, overgeneralized, schematic approaches, which talk of the 'trajectory' of capitalist development in South African agriculture, are no longer adequate to an understanding of the complexities involved.

In contrast to much revisionist writing on the emergence of modern South Africa, this book has sought to stress the contingent factors in the transformation of rural society. There was no consistent trajectory of development or inevitability either in the spread of capitalist relations in agriculture or in the assertion of white control over productive resources. The role of ideology and of self-image in providing the ongoing impetus behind the reforging of rural society has not been inconsiderable. State intervention in the generation of capital and in cushioning farmers against the recurrent destruction of capital resources characteristic of agriculture, has been of decisive importance. Revisionist interpretations of South African history have tended to stress industrial capitalism and its need for cheap labour as the central factor in the creation of the contemporary racial order. This book has focused on the rise of white rural populism and the drive to secure a white-supremacist rural economy in the face of an aggressive imperial capitalism. The drive for racial supremacy at the point of production was more a concern of the Afrikaner intelligentsia than of the financial and mining capitalists who presided over the industrial revolution. But it is also true that this drive for white supremacy in all facets of economic enterprise was a product of the age of industrial capitalism, rather than a product of an earlier age of frontier violence. The Boers had inherited a tradition of racial exclusivity in social and political spheres; but it was only in the circumstances of the new industrial imperialism which seemed to threaten the expropriation of the Boer economy, that racial monopolization of productive resources became the central tenet of indigenous white struggle. And eventually this struggle was to develop into the exclusive Afrikaner nationalism of the 1930s and 1940s.

Statistical Appendix

The following tables of statistics are drawn from the early censuses of population and agricultural production, dating from 1880, 1890, 1904 and 1911. Agricultural statistics were probably often speculative and arbitrary, particularly in the early years. Some local officials were no doubt more diligent in collecting statistics from farmers than others, and some farmers were more numerate and less vague in estimating acreages and stock numbers than others. Indeed, officials reported that farmers were often reluctant to provide estimates, fearing that these would be used for tax purposes.

The early censuses took no account of who the producers were – black or white. It can be accepted, however, that to a large degree black production on the farms was included in returns, especially as the white landholders often had an interest in the black-produced crop. The statistics for sorghum (largely an African-grown crop) suggest that returns did reflect total production on the farms.

Only Orange Free State district statistics are used, and not statistics from Highveld districts north of the Vaal River, as the earlier censuses were not comparable. Not all Orange Free State districts are included in the district tables – only the arable districts.

1 Livestock numbers, Orange Free State

	Horses	Trek oxen	Other cattle	Merino sheep	Other sheep	Angora goats	Other goats
1880	131 594	147 432	464 575	5 056 301	139 846	426 535	247 489
1890	248 878	276 037	619 026	5 916 611	703 381	627 617	230 538
1904	76 251	116 663	246 541	2 436 891	562 656	402 192	331 977
1911	220 725	368 930	917 304	7 355 052	1 232 586	545 577	502 994

Note: These figures include both white- and black-owned stock. The 1911 census distinguished between stock owned by black and white respectively, but it was conceded in the report that in practice black-owned stock had frequently been included in returns furnished by white landholders without distinction, so the figures are useless.

2 Density of livestock per square mile

	Cattle 1904	Cattle 1911	Horses 1904	Horses 1911	Sheep 1904	Sheep 1911	Goats 1904	Goats 1911	Pigs 1904	Pigs 1911
OFS	7.21	25.53	1.51	4.38	59.52	170.43	14.57	20.81	1.22	3.23
Tvl		12.13		0.81		30.93		16.04		2.74
Cape		9.80		1.21		61.86		28.71		1.83
Ntl		12.92		2.14		43.05		28.03		3.13

3 Density of livestock per square mile, Orange Free State, 1911

District	Cattle	Horses	Sheep	Goats	Pigs
Bethlehem	37.89	6.57	146.02	32.21	5.90
Bloemfontein	19.27	4.21	189.31	11.66	1.44
Ficksburg	90.94	10.68	195.96	75.95	13.89
Frankfort	35.05	5.51	148.63	15.73	6.48
Harrismith	39.13	8.63	232.81	48.07	6.01
Heilbron	33.76	4.23	166.25	7.83	5.61
Hoopstad	16.90	1.99	89.48	20.29	1.98
Kroonstad	26.30	2.65	145.34	.11.46	3.99
Ladybrand	61.54	6.47	202.39	14.19	7.29
Lindley	36.40	4.95	188.36	17.56	6.24
Rouxville	26.33	3.62	262.76	11.87	1.02
Senekal	42.90	5.82	202.15	21.09	6.66
Thaba Nchu	47.43	4.12	213.80	16.23	5.84
Vrede	28.68	9.50	183.25	42.79	4.30
Vredefort	25.82	1.74	76.51	14.77	4.35
Wepener	27.69	4.45	278.11	2.76	1.99
Winburg	27.04	3.66	178.41	18.48	3.15

4 Imported stock, 1911

	Bulls	Cows	Stallions	Rams	Ewes
OFS	279	990	251	1981	10 963
Tvl	119	450	79	467	2 448
Cape	216	766	232	850	1 573
Natal	58	77	95	347	653

5 Areas planted under different crops, 1911

	Maize (morgen)	Wheat (morgen)	Oats (morgen)	Sorghum (morgen)
Union	1 081 719	379 571	382 553	78 712
OFS	431 191	112 706	87 858	40 707
Transvaal	424 816	34 796	48 663	24 938
Cape	115 394	230 961	238 113	9 206
Natal	110 318	1 108	7 919	3 861

Note: Maize grown on the arable Highveld was more likely to be grown for sale; while that grown elsewhere was usually fed to livestock. The major wheat- and oat-growing area was in the southwestern Cape coastal belt.

6 Maize, Orange Free State

	Muids planted	Muids harvested	Yield per morgen
1880	4638	99 118	21.37 muids
1890	9780	185 585	18.98 muids

	Morgen planted	Muids harvested	Yield per morgen
1904	134 065	387 543	2.89 muids
1911	431 191	1 788 294	4.15 muids
1925	1 318 895		

Note: Yields are not as revealing as the extent of planting, as yields reflect climatic variables peculiar to the year of the census, which might render the figures unreliable as an indicator of long-term trends.

In 1911 maize accounted for 49.44 per cent of all cultivated land in the Orange Free State; by 1925, 75.47 per cent.

7 Maize, Orange Free State, by district

District	Morgen planted, 1904	Morgen planted, 1911
Bethelehem	10 802	24 231
Bloemfontein	3 369	15 638
Ficksburg	10 259	19 814
Frankfort	10 571	38 475
Harrismith	14 869	32 819
Heilbron	10 963	43 350
Hoopstad	3 463	22 626
Kroonstad	10 053	41 966
Ladybrand	9 197	38 202
Lindley	5 682	16 794
Rouxville	6 217	8 778

Senekal	8 633	26 419
Thaba Nchu	7 357	19 323
Vrede	4 388	16 447
Vredefort	5 213	22 090
Wepener	2 809	1 605
Winburg	7 025	35 984
OFS Total	134 065	431 191

Note: District figures are often not strictly comparable, as district boundaries changed over time, especially as new districts were established. Between 1904 and 1911, however, district boundaries were fairly stable.

8   Wheat, Orange Free State

	Muids planted	*Muids harvested*	*Yield per morgen*
1880	9 011	92 780	10.30 muids
1890	18 002	204 075	11.34 muids

	Morgen planted	*Harvested*		*Yield per morgen*
		Muids	Bundles	
1904	66 894	63 584	17 764	
1911	112 706	232 591		2.06 muids
1925	44 646			

9   Wheat, Orange Free State, by district

District	*Morgen planted, 1904*	*Morgen planted, 1911*
Bethlehem	7 615	13 342
Bloemfontein	932	1 233
Ficksburg	11 790	21 273
Frankfort	135	681
Harrismith	952	4 940
Heilbron	279	781
Hoopstad	220	200
Kroonstad	714	514
Ladybrand	15 768	21 271
Lindley	1 126	1 965
Rouxville	7 463	9 533
Senekal	3 005	13 195
Thaba Nchu	7 021	12 756
Vrede	136	945
Vredefort	655	293
Wepener	2 918	3 372
Winburg	3 965	4 213
OFS Total	66 894	112 706

Note: Between 1904 and 1911 acreages under wheat declined from 18 to 13 per cent of total cultivated land in the Orange Free State. By the mid-1920s, the proportion had declined to under 1 per cent.

10   Oats, Orange Free State

	Muids planted
1880	7 358
1890	16 784

	Morgen planted
1904	47 037
1911	87 858
1925	69 918

Note: Yields for oats are confusing, as they are given sometimes in muids, sometimes both in muids and bundles or pounds of oat hay.

11   Oats, Orange Free State, by district

District	Morgen planted, 1904	Morgen planted, 1911
Bethlehem	6 285	18 140
Bloemfontein	2 158	873
Ficksburg	5 076	11 055
Frankfort	829	2 554
Harrismith	5 862	12 982
Heilbron	2 017	4 032
Hoopstad	153	140
Kroonstad	871	1 246
Ladybrand	7 201	7 228
Lindley	1 482	5 301
Rouxville	3 370	2 032
Senekal	1 827	8 996
Thaba Nchu	3 634	2 899
Vrede	1 177	4 343
Vredefort	847	670
Wepener	861	762
Winburg	1 507	3 034
OFS Total	47 037	87 858

12   Sorghum, Orange Free State

	Morgen planted	Muids harvested	Yield per morgen
1904	29 212	85 270	2.92 muids
1911	40 707	191 414	4.70 muids
1925	41 737		

Note: There are no statistics before 1904, presumably because sorghum was a mainly black-grown crop.

13 Sorghum, Orange Free State, by district

District	Morgen planted, 1904	Morgen planted, 1911
Bethlehem	1 971	1 303
Bloemfontein	1 886	5 165
Ficksburg	2 362	2 764
Frankfort	743	1 144
Harrismith	2 799	2 396
Heilbron	1 310	1 649
Hoopstad	1 268	5 416
Kroonstad	2 134	2 169
Ladybrand	1 900	1 457
Lindley	1 113	1 222
Rouxville	1 562	853
Senekal	1 871	1 100
Thaba Nchu	3 555	3 048
Vrede	262	732
Vredefort	806	1 402
Wepener	510	844
Winburg	1 700	4 902
OFS Total	29 212	40 707

14 Area cultivated, Orange Free State, by district, 1911

District	Total area (morgen)	Area cultivated (all crops)	Proportion of cultivated land to total area
Bethlehem	743 750	73 927	9.94 per cent
Bloemfontein	1 330 833	31 180	2.34 per cent
Ficksburg	222 500	66 839	30.04 per cent
Frankfort	435 000	49 966	10.80 per cent
Harrismith	958 333	79 281	8.27 per cent
Heilbron	577 500	67 243	11.64 per cent
Hoopstad	1 063 750	30 537	2.87 per cent
Kroonstad	1 041 666	58 182	5.59 per cent
Ladybrand	335 416	78 859	23.51 per cent
Lindley	348 333	35 827	10.29 per cent
Rouxville	562 500	22 742	4.04 per cent
Senekal	497 916	66 540	13.36 per cent
Thaba Nchu	396 666	49 023	12.36 per cent
Vrede	666 666	30 513	4.58 per cent
Vredefort	500 000	31 935	6.39 per cent
Wepener	254 166	16 323	6.42 per cent
Winburg	1 121 666	62 161	5.54 per cent
OFS Total	15 237 074	872 073	5.72 per cent

Note: It is likely that the figures for cultivated acreages are underestimates, and in some cases very inaccurate. Given that all farming was mixed farming and given the primitive ploughing technology available, it is probably true to say that where the proportion of cultivated land exceeded 10 per cent of total area, we are dealing with a fairly intensive cash-crop economy. Moreover, certain districts (for example Hoopstad) lay only partially within the arable belt, and arable production was far greater in one part of the district than elsewhere.

According to the figures given in the censuses of 1880 and 1890, the proportion of cultivated land to the total area of the Orange Free State was 0.49 per cent and 1.05 per cent respectively. Apart from the 872 073 morgen of cultivated land in the OFS in 1911, 185 990 morgen were lying fallow. By 1925 cultivated and fallow land combined in the OFS amounted to 1 747 572 morgen.

In 1911, the proportion per cent of cultivated land to total area of each province was as follows (although of course very considerable variation was to be found in each province): OFS 5.72 per cent; Natal 4.61 per cent; Transvaal 2.86 per cent; Cape 1.16 per cent.

15   Average farm size, Orange Free State, by district

District	Number of farms	Total area (morgen)	Average size (morgen)
Bethlehem	770	743 750	965.9
Bloemfontein	1 500	1 330 833	887.2
Ficksburg	400	222 500	556.3
Frankfort	460	435 000	945.7
Harrismith	720	958 333	1331.0
Heilbron	580	577 500	995.7
Hoopstad	580	1 063 750	1834.1
Kroonstad	920	1 041 666	1132.2
Ladybrand	510	335 416	657.7
Lindley	370	348 333	941.4
Rouxville	610	562 500	922.1
Senekal	440	497 916	1131.6
Thaba Nchu	420	396 666	944.4
Vrede	420	666 666	1587.3
Vredefort	340	500 000	1470.6
Wepener	300	254 166	847.2
Winburg	940	1 121 666	1193.3
OFS Total	13 195	15 237 074	1154.8

Note: These statistics of farm size are only very general indicators. Often individually registered farms were informally subdivided amongst a number of different co-owners; less often a single farming unit comprised more than one separately registered farm. But it is clear that in the most intensely arable districts – those in the Conquered Territory – the farms were smallest, followed by the mid-Vaal maize districts.

16   Farm implements, Orange Free State

	1904	1911
One-share ploughs	14 617	19 236
Two-share ploughs	7 774	22 442
Three-share ploughs	286	1 278
Drills (sowing)	383	2 122
Harrows	6 879	14 009
Cultivators	608	5 391
Mowers	495	1 527
Hay and straw cutters	313	1 142
Reapers (ordinary)	154	876
Reapers (self-binding)	125	382
Corn strippers	146	106
Threshers	82	247
Maize cleaners and shellers	920	2 751
Corn mills (horse)	33	311
Corn mills (water)	39	39
Corn mills (wind)	18	914
Cream separators	713	6 490
Ox wagons	5 425	13 610

17   Animal products, Orange Free State

	Wool	Mohair (lb)	Butter (lb)	Cream (lb)
1880	48 665 bales			
1890	59 555 bales			
1904	11 105 553 lbs	756 057	637 148	
1911	34 288 370 lbs	1 134 264	3 826 977	6 105 946

18   Population density, Orange Free State, by district, 1911

	People per square mile	Whites per square mile	Blacks per square mile
Bethlehem	15.46	4.12	11.34
Bloemfontein	13.28	5.94	7.34
Ficksburg	31.74	7.52	24.22
Frankfort	11.28	4.65	6.63
Harrismith	15.64	2.78	12.86
Heilbron	12.71	4.60	8.11
Hoopstad	4.41	2.04	2.37
Kroonstad	10.40	3.77	6.63

Ladybrand	23.21	7.07	16.14
Lindley	13.45	4.03	9.42
Rouxville	8.88	3.84	5.04
Senekal	14.95	4.04	10.91
Thaba Nchu	21.31	2.47	18.84
Vrede	9.74	2.14	7.60
Vredefort	9.58	4.61	4.97
Wepener	9.49	3.60	5.89
Winburg	9.74	2.84	6.90
OFS Total	10.48	3.48	7.00

19   Proportion between white and black enumerated in returns of occupation under category 'Agricultural', Orange Free State, by district, 1911

	White population	Black population	Blacks per 100 whites
Bethlehem	2 160	11 980	555
Bloemfontein	2 670	7 873	295
Ficksburg	1 061	8 190	772
Frankfort	1 623	3 546	218
Harrismith	2 458	16 959	690
Heilbron	1 931	3 479	180
Hoopstad	1 905	2 736	144
Kroonstad	4 046	8 383	207
Ladybrand	2 520	5 565	221
Lindley	1 133	2 592	229
Rouxville	2 106	1 851	88
Senekal	1 887	8 738	463
Thaba Nchu	777	11 614	1495
Vrede	1 257	8 123	646
Vredefort	1 799	3 207	178
Wepener	633	1 245	197
Winburg	2 580	6 283	244
OFS Total	39 407	122 069	310

Note: There is clearly a great deal of arbitrariness in these occupational statistics, especially regarding women, who were as often as not returned as 'dependants' rather than as occupied in agriculture. Nevertheless, the proportions reveal relative density of black settlement. The heaviest concentrations were to be found in Thaba Nchu, where the remains of Moroka's Rolong chiefdom lived; in the Conquered Territory districts bordering Basutoland; and in Harrismith and Vrede, an area of dense pre-colonial settlement, where chiefly authority survived on the farms in some degree, and where blacks had never been subjected to military dispossession.

20   Ethnic origins of blacks in the Orange River Colony, 1904

Sotho	130 213
Rolong	37 998
Zulu	35 275
Mfengu	6 275
Xhosa	5 376
Tswana	5 115

21   Major religious denominations among blacks in the Orange River Colony, 1904

Wesleyan Methodist	51 576
Dutch Reformed Church	21 272
Church of England	14 782
African Methodist Episcopal	3 747

22   Urban population of major towns in the arable districts, Orange Free State

	1904		1911	
	White	*Black*	*White*	*Black*
Bloemfontein	17 588	19 993	14 720	12 205
Harrismith	4 345	3 955	3 447	3 352
Kroonstad	3 863	3 537	2 602	3 098
Ladybrand	2 334	1 528	1 924	1 399
Bethlehem	1 401	902	1 827	1 345

Note: Black population statistics are always very dubious – quite likely informed guesses in some instances. The inflated 1904 urban population figures (compared with 1911) were the result of the post-war commercial speculation, the lingering presence of the British military and the job opportunities thereby created.

23   Land occupation

	Orange Free State		Transvaal	
	1918	*1925*	*1918*	*1925*
	(proportion per cent of farming units)			
Occupied by owners	63.9	68.5	55.1	65.6
Leased	19.3	14.9	26.2	19.8
Farmed on shares (by whites)	8.1	10.6	12.0	9.3
Under manager	8.7	6.1	6.7	5.4

Note: These are the earliest statistics relating to land occupation available. The latter three categories (farms leased, worked on shares – by which is meant white share tenants – and under managers) should be treated with caution. They were probably loosely defined and overlapped to a large degree. Undoubtedly on many of these farms (possibly most) Africans were the real producers, although white occupants filling in census returns would not have revealed this. The number of farms worked on shares indicates the extent to which white lessees paid their rent in the form of a share of the crop (often grown by black sharecropping tenants rather than the nominal white lessee). Further, many a 'manager' was paid a proportion of the crop rather than a cash wage. Many of those in all three categories were probably no more than *bywoners*. Further discussion is to be found on pp. 49–50 of this book.

Sources

Table 1   OFS Censuses, 1880, 1890 (unpaginated); ORC Census, 1904, 214–15; UG 32–1912, Union Census, 1911, 1208–9.
Table 2   ORC Census, 1904, 220; UG 32–1912, 1226–7.
Table 3   UG 32–1912, 1229.
Table 4   UG 32–1912, 1230–1.
Table 5   UG 32–1912, 1296.
Tables 6, 8 and 10   OFS Censuses of 1880, 1890; ORC Census, 1904, 222–3; UG 32–1912, 1286, 1302; UG 13–1927, Agricultural Census, 1925, 104.
Tables 7, 9, 11 and 13   ORC Census, 1904, 222; UG 32–1912, 1302.
Table 12   ORC Census, 1904, 222–3; UG 32–1912, 1286, 1302; UG 13–1927, 104.
Table 14   UG 32–1912, 1254, 1260, and Report, para. 250; UG 13–1927, 104.
Table 15   ORC Department of Agriculture, Annual Report, 1907–8, 42.
Table 16   ORC Census, 1904, 229–30; UG 32–1912, 1350–1, 1354–5, 1357.
Table 17   OFS Censuses of 1880, 1890; ORC Census, 1904, 228; UG 32–1912, 1288–9.
Table 18   UG 32–1912, 62.
Table 19   UG 32–1912, 899.
Table 20   ORC Census, 1904, 3.
Table 21   ORC Census, 1904, 120.
Table 22   ORC Census, 1904, 4–5; UG 32–1912, 92.
Table 23   UG 13–1927, 104.

Notes and References

Introduction

1. The Highveld slopes from an altitude of 1800 metres (6000 feet) on its eastern margin to 1200 metres (4000 feet) in the west. Its eastern border is sharply defined by the Drakensberg and Maluti ranges, marking the escarpment. Mean annual rainfall declines from more than 800 millimetres on the escarpment as one moves westward. The western and southern boundaries of the Highveld are probably best defined for our purposes as the 500 millimetre isohyet, beyond which large-scale dryland cultivation becomes impossible. The Transvaal Highveld in the north gives way to the Bushveld roughly just north of the Witwatersrand.
2. See C. W. de Kiewiet, *A History of South Africa, Social and Economic* (London, 1941) chs 8 and 9. These images took their cue from a number of alarming investigations of rural conditions in the 1920s and 1930s. Particularly influential were UG 49-1923, *Final Report of the Drought Investigation Commission*; W. M. Macmillan, *Complex South Africa: An Economic Footnote to History* (London, 1930); Carnegie Commission, *Report on the Poor White Problem in South Africa*, 5 vols (Stellenbosch, 1932). What was being observed were the effects on dispossessed blacks and whites alike of 'primitive accumulation' on the land, rather than any stagnation of the rural economy.
3. As a sample: M. L. Morris, 'The Development of Capitalism in South African Agriculture', *Economy and Society*, 5, 3 (1976): Colin Bundy, *The Rise and Fall of the South African Peasantry* (London, 1979) 213-15, 230-6; Stanley Greenberg, *Race and State in Capitalist Development* (New Haven, 1980) ch. 4; Marian Lacey, *Working for Boroko: The Origins of a Coercive Labour System in South Africa* (Johannesburg, 1981) ch. 4; Dan O'Meara, *Volkskapitalisme: Class, Capital and Ideology in the Development of Afrikaner Nationalism, 1934-48* (Cambridge, 1983) 21-30; John W. Cell, *The Highest Stage of White Supremacy: The Origins of Segregation in South Africa and the American South* (Cambridge, 1982) 72-81; Martin Murray, 'The Formation of the Rural Proletariat in the South African Countryside: The Class Struggle and the 1913 Natives Land Act' in Edinburgh University, *Southern African Studies: Retrospect and Prospect* (Edinburgh, 1983).
4. Recent examples are D. J. Jacobs, 'Die Ontwikkeling van Landbou in die Vrystaat, 1890-1910', D.Litt. et Phil. thesis, University of South Africa, 1979; C. C. Eloff, *Oos-Vrystaatse Grensgordel: 'n Streekhistoriese Voorstudie en Bronneverkenning* (Pretoria, 1980).
5. H. J. van Aswegen, 'Die Verhouding tussen Blank en nie-Blank in die Oranje-Vrystaat, 1854-1902', *Archives Year Book for South African History*, 1971, 1 (Pretoria, 1977).
6. C. C. Eloff, *Oranje-Vrystaat en Basoetoeland, 1884-1902: 'n Verhoudingstudie* (Pretoria, 1984).

7. South Africa (unlike most African countries) has produced very few black historians equipped to bring informed Africanist perspectives to bear on historical research – a result in large part of a black educational system which remains committed to a 'white pioneer' interpretation of Africa's past.

8. A recent pioneering attempt to outline Afrikaner social history in the past hundred years still manages to account for pre-industrial Afrikaner economy and society by a series of abstract psychological characteristics: 'mobility, self-sufficiency, independence, conservatism, individualism, stubbornness, hospitality and devoutness'. F. A. van Jaarsveld, *Die Afrikaner se Groot Trek na die Stede* (Johannesburg, 1982) 138.

1 The nineteenth-century political economy of the southern Highveld

1. See P. J. van der Merwe, *Die Noordwaartse Beweging van die Boere voor die Groot Trek* (Cape Town, 1937). Two collections provide an historiographical overview: R. Elphick and H. Giliomee (eds) *The Shaping of South African Society, 1652-1820* (London, 1979) and H. Lamar and L. M. Thompson (eds) *The Frontier in History: North America and Southern Africa Compared* (New Haven, 1981).

2. R. Ross, *Adam Kok's Griqua* (Cambridge, 1976); M. Legassick, 'The Northern Frontier' in Elphick and Giliomee, *Shaping*; M. Kinsman, 'Populists and Patriarchs: The Transformation of the Griqua Captaincy, 1801-20', unpublished paper, 1984.

3. S. Trapido, 'Reflections on Land, Office and Wealth in the South African Republic, 1850-1900' in S. Marks and A. Atmore (eds) *Economy and Society in Pre-Industrial South Africa* (London, 1980); P. Delius and S. Trapido, '*Inboekselings* and *Oorlams*: The Creation and Transformation of a Servile Class' in B. Bozzoli (ed.) *Town and Countryside in the Transvaal* (Johannesburg, 1983).

4. P. Delius, *The Land Belongs to Us: The Pedi Polity, the Boers and the British in the Nineteenth Century Transvaal* (London, 1983).

5. W. Lye, 'The *Difaqane*: The *Mfecane* in the Southern Sotho Area: 1822-24', *Journal of African History*, 8,1 (1967). For a revisionist view of these events see J. Cobbing, 'The Case Against the *Mfecane*', unpublished paper, 1982.

6. T. M. O'C. Maggs, *Iron Age Communities of the Southern Highveld* (Pietermaritzburg, 1976); E. Ellenberger and J. MacGregor, *History of the Basuto: Ancient and Modern* (London, 1912); J. Kimble, 'Towards an Understanding of the Political Economy of Lesotho', M.A. thesis, National University of Lesotho, 1978; P. Sanders, *Moshoeshoe, Chief of the Sotho* (London, 1975); and L. M. Thompson, *Survival in Two Worlds: Moshoeshoe of Lesotho* (Oxford, 1975).

7. W. Lye, 'The Distribution of the Sotho Peoples after the *Difaqane*', in L. M. Thompson (ed.) *African Societies in Southern Africa* (London, 1969); P. Sanders, 'Sekonyela and Moshoeshoe: Failure and Success in the Aftermath of the *Difaqane*', *Journal of African History*, 10,3 (1969); H. J. van Aswegen, 'Die Verhouding tussen Blank en nie-Blank in die Oranje-Vrystaat, 1854-1902', *Archives Year Book for South African History*, 1971, vol. 1 (Pretoria, 1977) Part II.

8. See C. Murray, 'Land, Power and Class in the Thaba Nchu District, 1884–1983', *Review of African Political Economy*, 29 (1984).
9. On the Ndebele, see K. Rasmussen, *Migrant Kingdom: Mzilikazi's Ndebele in South Africa* (London, 1978).
10. J. S. Galbraith, *Reluctant Empire* (Berkeley, 1963) ch. 11; W. W. Collins, *Free Statia* (1907, reprinted Cape Town, 1965) ch. 4.
11. G. D. Scholtz, *Die Konstitusie en Staatsinstellings van die Oranje-Vrystaat, 1854–1902* (Amsterdam, 1937).
12. Collins, *Free Statia*, 84–5; Ross, *Adam Kok's Griqua*, ch. 5.
13. Perhaps the most important example in the middle years of the century were the Mosenthals. D. Fleischer and A. Caccia, *Merchant Pioneers: The House of Mosenthal* (Johannesburg, 1983).
14. H. Green wrote in 1853: 'Bloemfontein . . . was supported . . . by the Port Elizabeth and Cape Town merchants to whom the houses of many of the inhabitants, most of whom were engaged in trade, were mortgaged as security for the capital advanced them'. Cape Archives, GH 20/2, H. Green to Government Clerk, 1 November 1855. See also Collins, *Free Statia*, 43.
15. On land prices, see Collins, ibid, 182–3. On speculative landownership see S. van der Horst, *Native Labour in South Africa* (London, 1942) 55; Galbraith, *Reluctant Empire*, 271; K. N. Bell and W. P. Morrell, *Select Documents on British Colonial Policy, 1830–60* (Oxford, 1928) 531–3.
16. E. H. D. Arndt, *Banking and Currency Development in South Africa, 1652–1927* (Cape Town, 1928) ch. 8.
17. J. F. W. Grosskopf, *Rural Impoverishment and Rural Exodus*, vol. 1 of the Carnegie Commission, *The Poor White Problem in South Africa*, 5 vols (Stellenbosch, 1932) 142; K. J. de Kok, *Empires of the Veld* (Durban, 1904) *passim*.
18. See R. Ross, 'Capitalism, Expansion and Incorporation on the South African Frontier' in Lamar and Thompson (eds) *The Frontier in History*.
19. De Kok, *Empires of the Veld*, 100 and 111: 1s 6d was paid for a wildebeest hide and 2s for a blesbok hide. See also J. L. Hattingh, 'Die Trekke uit die Suid-Afrikaanse Republiek en die Oranje-Vrystaat, 1875–95', Ph.D. thesis, Pretoria, 1975, 399–400; E. F. Sandeman, *Eight Months in an Ox-wagon: Reminiscences of Boer Life* (London, 1880, reprinted Johannesburg, 1975) 106.
20. De Kok, *Empires of the Veld*, 94–5, 97 and 109.
21. Ibid, 46 and 205.
22. See T. Keegan, 'White Settlement and Black Subjugation on the South African Highveld: The Tlokoa Heartland in the Northeastern Orange Free State, 1850–1914' in W. Beinart and P. Delius (eds) *Putting a Plough to the Ground* (Johannesburg and London, 1986). There had always undoubtedly been relations of clientage and dependence amongst Boers as well, usually involving stock-loan systems. There were always poor Boers just as there were wealthy notables. The democracy of property owners which is a common later image of the early burgher community is clearly a false one. From the start of expansion in the interior of the Cape many Boers did not own land of their own. This will be discussed in the next chapter.
23. P. Delius, 'Abel Erasmus: Power and Profit in the Eastern Transvaal' in Beinart and Delius (eds) *Putting a Plough to the Ground*; S. Trapido,

'Landlord and Tenant in a Colonial Economy: The Transvaal, 1880–1910', *Journal of Southern African Studies*, 5,1 (1978).

24. Van Aswegen, 'Die Verhouding tussen Blank en nie-Blank', 20.
25. Ibid, 250–2; Collins, *Free Statia*, 155–6; J. M. Orpen, *Reminiscences of Life in South Africa from 1846 to the Present Day* (Cape Town, 1964) 303–24; De Kok, *Empires of the Veld*, 172–81; E. Murray, *Young Mrs Murray Goes to Bloemfontein* (Cape Town, 1954) 56. Much information on this trade in captives is contained in P. Bonner, *Kings, Commoners and Concessionaires: The Evolution and Dissolution of the 19th Century Swazi State* (Cambridge, 1983).
26. Wesleyan Methodist Missionary Society, 315/5/4, J. Cameron to General Secretary, WMS, 21 February 1842; GH 20/2, H. Green, 1853. See also J. H. Malan, *Die Opkoms van 'n Republiek* (Bloemfontein, 1929) 270.
27. Delius and Trapido, *'Inboekselings'*.
28. Interview, M. Sauls.
29. The relationship survived far longer in pastoral districts, where there were no tenant communities. 'A peculiar feature', wrote the superintendent of the Springfontein refugee camp in 1901, 'is the presence among the families in camp of "adopted" or "apprenticed" little coloured children', whom he described as 'virtually slaves'. CS 1460/01, 10 May 1901.
30. *SANAC*, 1903–5, 5 vols (Cape Town, 1905) vol. 4 (para. 37 923, evidence of J. G. Fraser).
31. C. F. J. Muller, *Die Oorsprong van die Groot Trek* (Cape Town, 1974) ch. 3.
32. Kimble, 'Political Economy of Lesotho', 98; see S. Newton-King, 'The Labour Market of the Cape Colony, 1807–28' in Marks and Atmore, *Economy and Society*.
33. De Kok, *Empires of the Veld*, 151–2.
34. Kimble, 'Political Economy of Lesotho', 183–4.
35. Ibid, 186.
36. Ibid, 98 and 173–4.
37. Ibid, 98 and 175.
38. Van Aswegen, 'Verhouding tussen Blank en nie-Blank', 248–50 and 253–6. A 10s poll tax was imposed on all Africans in 1866. Ibid, 257–60.
39. See Kimble, 'Political Economy of Lesotho', 94–7; R. C. Germond (ed.) *Chronicles of Basutoland* (Morija, 1967) 266–7.
40. Germond, ibid, 441.
41. *Grahamstown Journal*, 29 November 1846, quoted in Kimble, 'Political Economy of Lesotho', 96.
42. Cited in Kimble, ibid, 95; also see Germond, *Chronicles*, 451.
43. D. J. Jacobs, 'Landbou en Veeteelt in die Oranje-Vrystaat, 1864–88', *Archives Year Book for South African History*, 1969, I (Pretoria, 1969) 161. In 1859, grain to the value of £8000 was imported from the Transvaal. This intra-Boer trade is well described by S. P. Engelbrecht, *Geskiedenis van de Nederduits Hervormde Kerk in Zuid-Africa* (Amsterdam and Pretoria, 1920) vol. 1, Annexure L.
44. Germond, *Chronicles*, 266–7.
45. *Friend*, 30 December 1864. The extent to which Free State exports were dependent on wool is indicated by the estimates of 1868–9. Of £265 000 worth of exports in that year, £230 000 was accounted for by wool. The rest

was made up of feathers, skins, cattle and horses. G. J. Lamprecht, 'Die Ekonomiese Ontwikkeling van die Vrystaat, 1870–99', D.Phil thesis, Stellenbosch, 1954, 130. It was also in the 1860s that a currency crisis caused the Free State to print its 'bluebacks', which very quickly depreciated in value and led to a standstill in trade. Arndt, *Banking and Currency*, ch. 4; Lamprecht, 'Ekonomiese Ontwikkeling', ch. 1.

46. Germond, *Chronicles*, 267.
47. Sanders, *Moshoeshoe*, 294–5.
48. See Kimble, 'Political Economy of Lesotho', 175–8; Van Aswegen, 'Verhouding tussen Blank en nie-Blank', 260–1.
49. 'Ladybrand (Conquered Territory)', *Friend*, 7 October 1869. The colonization of higher lands towards the Maluti mountains and the more intensive cultivation of the lowlands together with the increasing use of mountainous areas for grazing meant that land pressures were not immediately felt by the Sotho. Kimble, 'Political Economy of Lesotho', 225.
50. Ibid, 256. For evidence of the very high cost of produce on urban markets in the 1870s, see Lamprecht, 'Ekonomiese Ontwikkeling', 44–5 and 32; C. A. Payton, *The Diamond Diggings of South Africa* (London, 1872) 152. On the boom generally see Lamprecht, 32–3, 94–6 and 122–4.
51. Kimble, 'Political Economy of Lesotho', 252–66; and van der Horst, *Native Labour*, chs 5 and 6.
52. Kimble, ibid, 275–85; P. Delius, 'Migrant Labour and the Pedi, 1840–80' in Marks and Atmore, *Economy and Society*. G. Tylden estimates that nearly a quarter million guns entered Basutoland between 1870 and 1880. *The Rise of the Basuto* (Cape Town and Johannesburg, 1950) 156.
53. See A. Atmore and S. Marks, 'The Imperial Factor in South Africa in the Nineteenth Century: Towards a Reassessment', *Journal of Imperial and Commonwealth History*, 3, 1 (1974); N. Etherington, 'Labour Supply and the Genesis of South African Confederation', *Journal of African History*, 20, 2 (1979).
54. Germond, *Chronicles*, 320–1.
55. Ibid, 320–6; Tylden, *Rise of the Basuto*, 117–18.
56. Jacobs, 'Landbou en Veeteelt', 161. The missionary F. Maeder reported in 1873 that the Sotho were witnessing the 'daily influx in their midst of crowds of people, who do nothing else but buy the wheat and other food crops, with the object of selling them again to the mines'. Germond, *Chronicles*, 323.
57. Kimble, 'Political Economy of Lesotho', 200.
58. 'The State of Trade', *Friend*, 29 March 1883. Transport-riding was an important way in which the sons of landowners set up as independent farmers.
59. 'Jottings from Wepener', *Friend*, 9 October 1873.
60. 'Agricultural Prospects of the Conquered Territory', *Friend*, 3 August 1876.
61. Jacobs, 'Landbou en Veeteelt', 171.
62. Grosskopf, *Rural Impoverishment*, 53.
63. Van der Horst, *Native Labour*, 141; Hattingh, 'Trekke', 393.
64. De Kok, *Empires of the Veld*, 8; M. C. E. van Schoor and J. C. Moll, *Edenburg: Grepe uit die Geskiedenis van die Dorp en Distrik* (Bloemfontein, 1963) 99.

65. 'Harrismith', *Friend*, 25 February 1875; 'Local and General News: Winburg', *Friend*, 10 April 1873.
66. Jacobs, 'Landbou en Veeteelt', 171. Jacobs cites several such petitions from the border districts.
67. The purpose of such legislation, as *The Friend* put it, was 'to compel Old Free State farmers, who live from their wool, and not from their grain, to buy from New Free State farmers, who can't grow wool, but can grow grain, so as to keep money in the State, and benefit each other generally' (17 August 1874).
68. Jacobs, 'Landbou en Veeteelt', 171–2.
69. See Kimble, 'Political Economy of Lesotho', 263–4; Collins, *Free Statia*, 302–4.
70. Kimble, 'Political Economy', 263–4.
71. 'One Who Wants a Good Servant' to editor, *Friend*, 29 June 1871; De Kok, *Empires of the Veld*, 180.
72. See pp. 131–2; also van Aswegen, 'Verhouding tussen Blank en nie-Blank', 265–7.
73. Van Aswegen, 'Verhouding', 268–9.
74. Ibid, 271.
75. Ibid, 263–5, 271–4 and 280–2.
76. See Keegan, 'Tlokoa Heartland', for a local analysis.
77. See pp. 57–9.
78. See J. G. Fraser, *Episodes of My Life* (Cape Town, 1922).
79. 'Legislative Assembly', *Friend*, 1 July 1908; also O. Jensen to editor, *Friend*, 10 November 1908.
80. C. G. W. Schumann, *Structural Changes and Business Cycles in South Africa, 1806–1936* (London, 1938) ch. 3(4).
81. Economic repercussions were aggravated for the Sotho by the Gun War (1880–1) and the civil war in Basutoland (1882–4).
82. 'The State of Trade', *Friend*, 29 March 1883. Cf. the comments of Gustav Baumann, land surveyor: 'the collapse of 1882 was dragging us into the mire of financial despair. There was no money in the land; farmers got next to nothing for their produce. I had to take oxen, sheep and mealies in payment for the work I did'. G. Baumann and E. Bright, *Lost Republic: The Biography of a Land Surveyor* (London, 1940) 95.
83. Germond, *Chronicles*, 470; see 469–71 for evidence of the decline of the Sotho economy during these years.
84. Jacobs, 'Landbou en Veeteelt', 170.
85. The 'discovery' of gold was unlikely to have been fortuitous. It is likely that it was related to the immediate requirements of international finance and industrial capital at a particular conjuncture in its development.
86. See Baumann and Bright, *Lost Republic*, 134–5, 141–7 on financial speculation and prospecting on land in the Free State; also 84–5 on the speculative boom of 1880–1.
87. See pp. 41–9.
88. S. F. Malan, *Politieke Strominge onder die Afrikaners van die Vrystaatse Republiek* (Durban, 1982) 165–70.
89. 'Free State Produce at Johannesburg', *Friend*, 21 November 1888; 'The Johannesburg Market', *Friend*, 10 January 1893; 'Free State Trade with the

Transvaal', *Friend*, 27 March 1894; 'Transvaal Imports', *Friend*, 19 April 1895; 'Trade Returns', *Friend*, 6 March 1896; 'Transvaal Trade', *Friend*, 10 December 1897.

90. An indication of this was provided in 1892, a year when crops were devastated by locusts and when many Sotho sold their maize to traders for 5–6s per bag immediately after harvest, perhaps because of an accumulation of store debts in the preceding period. In October of that year it was reported that many Sotho were faced with starvation, and many were giving young heifers in exchange for a bag of maize or sorghum, which fetched some 35s per bag. The British authorities in Maseru offered to buy grain from Free State traders to relieve the situation. Maize was reconsigned from Kimberley to meet the need ('Crops in the Conquered Territory', *Friend*, 11 October 1892; 'Farming Prospects in the Grain Districts', *Friend*, 18 October 1892; 'Jottings from Leeuwrivierdrift', *Friend*, 4 November 1892). When the new wheat harvest came in toward the end of the year, Masupha and other chiefs, in an attempt to recoup losses, ordered their people not to sell any grain whatever to traders unless the latter were prepared to pay 30s per bag. The traders were content to wait, confidently expecting the Sotho to 'cave in', as they soon did. The lesson of this episode was that the dependence of the Sotho producers on the credit of the traders was far too great for them to dictate the prices for their produce. 'Notes from Ladybrand and District', *Friend*, 21 February 1893.

91. VR 378, 1–8, 53–72, 102–4, 1893; VR 384, 63–133, 156–75, 1894 (comprising thirty-seven petitions from all parts of the Free State, referring to the fear of Sotho competition and glutting). At Ladybrand in October 1895, Free State wheat was quoted at 16s 6d to 20s, and Basutoland wheat at 9s to 12s 6d. 'Ladybrand', *Friend*, 11 October 1895.

92. VR 384, 115–18, fifty-two burghers of Onderwittebergen, Winburg, 1894.

93. VR 380, 167–93; VR 381, 99–146 (twenty-nine petitions signed by 1687 burghers), 1894.

94. VR 380, 181–3, fifty-one burghers of Dewetsdorp, May 1894; VR 380, 189–90, thirty-five burghers of Bethlehem, April 1894. Also see *Volksraadsnotule*, 26 October 1896, 141 (C. R. de Wet); 28 October 1896, 166 (J. P. Roux).

95. VR 380, 191–3. Another aspect of this competition between Basutoland producers and the burghers was the agitation, also evident in bumper years, most notably in 1893 and 1894, against Sotho transport riders who rode much of the Sotho grain to the mills and stores across the border. In 1896 the *Volksraad* passed a law levying a road tax on 'foreign' Africans. Anxiety about the allegedly unhygienic condition of black-owned stock accompanied the spread of rinderpest in 1896–7, with the result that a succession of enactments proscribed Africans travelling with stock (other than that of their masters) in any part of the state. Thus blacks and their livestock became the scapegoats for disease, and disease was used as a legitimation for the suppression of black economic enterprise – in much the same way as the influenza epidemic a few years later spurred widespread urban segregationist measures. 'Is rinderpest liable only to be carried by native people?' asked a black Wesleyan minister from Harrismith, 'Cannot a white man carry it as well?' W. G. Thembu to editor, *Friend*, 25 December

1896; also see, for example, VR 381, 26–31 and 59–61, April 1894; *Volksraadsnotule*, 23 April 1895, 247, 249, etc.; VR 412, 183–4, 1896; 'Rinderpest', *Friend*, 1 June 1897.

96. Report in VR 381, 225–8.
97. See 'The Supply of Wheat', *Friend*, 28 September 1894; 'Notes from Ladybrand', *Friend*, 12 July 1895.
98. 'Populism' is used to refer to the movement of mass mobilization amongst rural whites in pursuit of indigenous capital formation and white supremacy, spurred by the encroachment of big capital and the expansion of the black economy which accompanied the rise of urban markets. Populism was anti-imperialist and anti-capitalist in its rhetoric and Afrikaans in its cultural symbolism. The ideological pacemakers were the small-town Afrikaner petty bourgeoisie (for example, the teachers and churchmen), and the readiest response came from the small men amongst the rural whites – those on the edge of respectability who were most vulnerable in the face of middlemen, financiers and speculators. On the other hand, the most marginalized poor whites were often likely to resist these cultural interventions; and the more prosperous landed whites with sources of income from other economic sectors were similarly unlikely to be responsive to populist agitation.
99. This term enjoyed wide currency at the time. See G. Stedman Jones, *Outcast London: A Study in the Relationship between Classes in Victorian Society* (Harmondsworth, 1976) 11.

2 Transformations in Boer society

1. See J. F. W. Grosskopf, *Rural Impoverishment and Rural Exodus*, vol. I of the Report of the Carnegie Commission, *The Poor White Problem in South Africa*, 5 vols (Stellenbosch, 1932) 37–9; G. Baumann and E. Bright, *Lost Republic: The Biography of a Land Surveyor* (London, 1940) *passim*.
2. See S. Trapido, 'Reflections on Land, Office and Wealth in the South African Republic' in S. Marks and A. Atmore (eds) *Economy and Society in Pre-Industrial South Africa* (London, 1980); S. Trapido, 'Landlord and Tenant in a Colonial Economy: The Transvaal, 1880–1910', *Journal of Southern African Studies*, 5,1 (1978); T. Keegan, 'White Settlement and Black Subjugation on the South African Highveld: The Tlokoa Heartland in the Northeastern Orange Free State, 1850–1914', in W. Beinart and P. Delius (eds) *Putting a Plough to the Ground* (Johannesburg and London, 1986).
3. See the evidence of P. J. G. Theron, MLA, in SC 9–1913, *Select Committee on European Employment and Labour Conditions*, Evidence, 577–9.2
4. Grosskopf, *Rural Impoverishment*, 38 and 125. The term *bywoner* has a long history, though. See, for example, P. J. van der Merwe, *Trek: Studies oor die Mobiliteit van die Pioniersbevolking aan die Kaap* (Cape Town, 1945) 48.
5. It seems to have been common to distinguish between *bewoners* (residents) and *bywoners* in the terminology of the day. The former seem to have been

relations of the landowner – often adult sons and sons-in-law. In a petition from the male white residents of fourteen farms of the *wyk* Midden Modderrivier in 1897, fourteen signatories were listed as owners, twenty-nine as *'bewoners'* (most of them with the same names as the landowners) and nine as *'bywoners'*. VR 425, 143–5, March 1897.

6. See J. Hattingh, 'Die Trekke uit die Suid-Afrikaanse Republiek en die Oranje-Vrystaat, 1875–95', Ph.D. thesis, University of Pretoria, 1975, 556–7.

7. The Minister of Lands in the Smuts government in 1924, Deneys Reitz, who had been brought up in the Orange Free State (his father was president between 1888 and 1895) alleged that 'in republican days' landowners had been satisfied to exact a tenth of a *bywoner's* crop as against at least a third by the 1920s. 'Agriculture in the Past', *FW*, 13 February 1924, 2283.

8. P. J. de Vos, 'Die "Bywoner": 'n Sosiologiese Studie oor die Bywonerskap in sekere Hoë en Middelvelddistrikte in die Transvaal en Vrystaat', M.A. thesis, University of Pretoria, 1937, 18–19.

9. Grosskopf, *Rural Impoverishment*, 125. See also 'Poor Whites', *Friend*, 11 April 1895.

10. H. Giliomee, 'Processes in the Development of the South African Frontier' in H. Lamar and L. M. Thompson (eds) *The Frontier in History* (New Haven, 1981) 80; L. Guelke, 'The White Settlers, 1652–1780' in R. Elphick and H. Giliomee (eds) *The Shaping of South African Society, 1652–1820* (London, 1979). Colin Bundy nails the myth that white poverty in the Cape only emerged in the 1890s in 'Vagabond Hollanders and Runaway Englishmen: White Poverty in the Cape before Poor Whiteism' in Beinart and Delius (eds) *Putting a Plough to the Ground*. The best source of evidence on the Boer economy of the early Cape interior is to be found in the books of P. J. van der Merwe, *Trek* and *Die Trekboer in die Geskiedenis van die Kaapkolonie, 1657–1842* (Cape Town, 1938).

11. Grosskopf, *Rural Impoverishment*, 140.

12. See Bundy, 'Vagabond Hollanders', for a discussion of the context in which 'poor whiteism' became a political and moral issue at this time.

13. In the South African Republic the *Volksraad* budgeted £15 000 in 1896 for needy *Voortrekkers*. (A. N. Pelzer, 'Die "Arm-Blanke" Verskynsel in die Suid-Afrikaanse Republiek tussen die jare 1882–1899: 'n Sosiaal-Historiese Studie', M.A. thesis, Pretoria, 1937, 73–5. See Grosskopf, *Rural Impoverishment*, 37–9; R. W. Wilcocks, *The Poor White, Psychological Report*, vol. 2 of the Carnegie Commission, *The Poor White Problem*, 10; and Pelzer, 'Arm-Blanke', *passim*.

14. Hattingh, 'Trekke', 569–9.

15. For example, in 1904 J. Rorich and Company of Fauresmith petitioned the government to stay construction of the Springfontein–Jagersfontein railway on the grounds that transport-riding was the only occupation for hundreds of Boers who had acquired wagons from the Repatriation Boards. After construction was completed it was reported that 100 transport wagons always in use previously had been 'obliged to move elsewhere'. CS 2988/04, 27 April 1904; CS 9135/04, 28 November 1904.

16. 'Frankfort Notes', *Friend*, 2 June 1909. See also J. M. McCalman,

Belladale, Frankfort, to editor, *Friend*, 12 June 1909, for an opposite perspective. The line reached Frankfort in 1914.

17. See pp. 98–100.
18. Grosskopf, *Rural Impoverishment*, 43–4. A fencing law was first passed in 1890. See 'Harrismith Notes', *Friend*, 4 September 1894. A *Friend* editorial described in 1892 one marginal entrepreneurial activity which soon ceased to be viable:

> A certain number of people in this free and independent State are in the habit of hunting game of all descriptions in season and out of season. It is far more enjoyable employment and easier of accomplishment than chopping down one's neighbours' trees and carrying the wood to the market, which is being resorted to when everything else fails. The *modus operandi* is to drive all the game against a farmer's fence and then shoot them down, regardless of the cost of the fence. When fencing is more general, however, the *bywoners* will have to make tracks or give up their favourite pastimes ('What Fencing is Good for', *Friend*, 1 April 1892).

19. *De Express*, 12 March 1889, cited in S. F. Malan, *Politieke Strominge onder die Afrikaners van die Vrystaatse Republiek* (Durban, 1982) 190. Basic literacy for Bible-reading was general among Boers, however.
20. 'Looking Forward', *Friend*, 6 January 1891; 'Burning Quetions', *Friend*, 22 March 1898. On traditional Boer artisanal skills, see Grosskopf, *Rural Impoverishment*, 142.
21. This is evident in the detailed family histories provided by Grosskopf, *Rural Impoverishment*, 100–104.
22. See pp. 43–4. Also pp. 64–8 on black sharecropping on absentee-owned land.
23. See pp. 57–61 on the context and periodization of these anxieties. Also see H. J. van Aswegen, 'Die Verhouding tussen Blank en nie-Blank in die Oranje-Vrystaat, 1854–1902', *Archives Year Book for South African History*, 1971, 1 (Pretoria, 1977) ch. 14; Hattingh, 'Trekke', 464.
24. A sampling: VR 349, 10–24, 1891; VR 376, 122–61, 1893; VR 383, 92–8, 1894. See *Volksraadsnotule*, 1 May 1896, 262–4. For the Dutch Reformed Church's view see VR 395, 21–3, G. Radloff, Scriba, NGK, 16 May 1895. Compulsory education was introduced in urban schools in 1895. Educational reformists coupled these initiatives with a drive to promote the Dutch language as the compulsory medium of instruction in the face of an influx of foreigners and foreign capital. The development of ethnic consciousness as a response to incorporation into the international capitalist economy as a dependent periphery is a common phenomenon best described in Tom Nairn's book, *The Break Up of Britain* (London, 1977). The ethnicization of struggle against foreign domination emerged after the Anglo-Boer War in the independent 'Christian-national' school system, in response to the anglicizing policies of the Milner regime. For a romantic and teleological view of these developments, see F. A. van Jaarsveld, *Die Afrikaners se Groot Trek na die Stede* (Johannesburg, 1982) 50–6.
25. Child labour amongst Boers was also a cause for much populist anxiety. See Hattingh, 'Trekke', 460–1.

26. 'Clouds Looming', *Friend*, 18 November 1892.

27. See VR 339, 35–7, sixty-four burghers of Bloemfontein district, 1890.

28. A. N. Grundlingh, *Die 'Hensoppers' en 'Joiners': Die Rasionaal en Verskynsel van Verraad* (Pretoria, 1979) 234; Hattingh, 'Trekke', 568 and 574.

29. VR 339, 33–4, 1890; VR 353, 119–35, 1891; VR 403, 129–95, 1896; VR 404, 25–39, 1896. Also see Malan, *Politieke Strominge*, 241–3.

30. 'The Gloomy Future', *Friend*, 17 August 1897; also 'A Gloomy Outlook', *Friend*, 4 December 1896.

31. 'The Problem of the Future', *Friend*, 10 December 1897; also 'The Drought and the Future', *Friend*, 7 January 1898.

32. 'Rinderpest and its Effects', *Friend*, 27 August 1897.

33. 'Town Council', *Friend*, 24 December 1897; 'Picknicking Poor People', *Friend*, 10 December 1897; K. Schoeman, *Bloemfontein: Die Ontstaan van 'n Stad, 1846–1946* (Cape Town, 1980) 136–7.

34. 'Ficksburg Jottings', *Friend*, 21 September 1897; 'Ficksburg Notes', *Friend*, 28 December 1897.

35. 'A Poor Burgher' to editor, *Friend*, 10 September 1897; *Volksraadsnotule*, April 1898, 39, 151–4 and 156–70.

36. *Volksraadsnotule*, 29 April 1898, 224–8; see VR 427, 5–29, 1898 for petitions; 'The Drought and the Farmers', *Friend*, 7 January 1898; 'Customs Notice', *Friend*, 15 March 1898.

37. See adverts, *Friend*, 25 and 28 January 1898; also 'Basutoland Affairs', *Friend*, 15 March 1898.

38. VR 425, 66–71; VR 427, 50–79; VR 433, 22–4; VR 438, 138–59. See also Grosskopf, *Rural Impoverishment*, 194 and 226; J. P. Kotze, 'Die Runderpes in die Transvaal en die onmiddelike gevolge daarvan, 1896–99', M.A. thesis, Rand Afrikaans University, 1974, chs 6 and 7; C. van Onselen, 'Reactions to Rinderpest in Southern Africa, 1896–97', *Journal of African History*, 12, 3 (1972).

39. CS 1620/02, P. J. Blignaut, 2 June 1902.

40. CS 6164/03, RM Vredefort, 24 August 1903.

41. CS 1184/04, RM Vredefort, 16 February 1904. For evidence of extreme distress amongst landless whites after the war see the district reports in CO 224/12, Alleged Distress among Boers in Certain Districts, 12 October 1903.

42. Grundlingh, *'Hensoppers' en 'Joiners'*, 7–9.

43. T. Pakenham, *The Boer War* (London, 1979) 568 and 571.

44. Grundlingh, *'Hensoppers' en 'Joiners'*, 232–40; see also D. Denoon, *A Grand Illusion: The Failure of Imperial Policy in the Transvaal Colony during the Period of Reconstruction, 1900–05* (London, 1973) 17–18.

45. Quoted in G. B. Beak, *The Aftermath of War* (London, 1906) 43.

46. E. F. Knight, *South Africa after the War* (London, 1903) 197; also CS 1783/04, RM Edenburg, 15 March 1904: 'the innate distrust of the Boer for his fellow countryman in Office is pronounced'.

47. CO 529/1, petition of P. D. de Wet and other burghers, 6 February 1903; see also Beak, *Aftermath*, 58 and 131. A Volunteer Repatriation Department was set up to provide for those ex-burghers who had served on the British side. The British also instituted a special land-settlement scheme for landless 'Loyal Dutch'. Grundlingh, *'Hensoppers' en 'Joiners'*,

ch. 8; Beak, *Aftermath*, 65–7. The ORC Settlers Association was formed by officers of the Burgher Scouts to secure land for Boers who had served under them.

48. See Lt.Governor H. Goold-Adams' comments in CS 2829/03, 30 March 1903. Also, Beak, *Aftermath*, 43.
49. Beak, *Aftermath*, 42–7, 153–4 and 194; A. P. J. van Rensburg, 'Die Ekonomiese Herstel van die Afrikaner in die Oranjerivier-Kolonie, 1902–07', *Archives Year Book for South African History*, 1967, II (Pretoria, 1967) 278–9.
50. CS 7362/03, RM Ficksburg, 12 October 1903; CS 7580/03, RM Smithfield, 24 October 1903.
51. CS 7125/03, RM Hoopstad, 3 October 1903.
52. CS 1389/04, RM Wepener, 17 February 1904.
53. CS 3195/04, D. Holbech, 5 May 1904.
54. CS 5113/02, 10 November 1902.
55. Beak, *Aftermath*, 68–9 and 187–9.
56. CS 8046/03, H. Pilkington, O/C SAC, 5 October 1903.
57. CS 300/04, 15 January 1904. Government relief payments were finally halted in June 1904. Beak, *Aftermath*, 186.
58. See S. Marks and S. Trapido, 'Lord Milner and the South African State', *History Workshop Journal*, 9 (1980) 70.
59. CS 5113/02, E. H. M. Legget, 10 November 1902.
60. On P. de Wet see Grundlingh, *'Hensoppers' en 'Joiners'*, 240–51. See pp. 33–5 on 'back-to-the-land' schemes.
61. See de Vos, 'Die Bywoner', 26 and 71–3.
62. 'The Passing of the Bywoner', *FA*, May 1913, 491–3.
63. SC 9–1913, 581 (para. 4118).
64. See de Vos, 'Die Bywoner', 71–3.
65. J. Barraclough, Aankom, Roodewal, OFS, to editor, *Friend*, 26 February 1911.
66. T. Matsetela, 'The Life Story of Nkgono Mma-Pooe: Aspects of Sharecropping and Proletarianization in the Northern Orange Free State, 1890–1930' in S. Marks and R. Rathbone (eds) *Industrialization and Social Change in South Africa* (London, 1982) 225–6.
67. See pp. 76–9.
68. See, for example, KRS 7/9, 10–11, State *v.* S. J. Fischer, 9 January 1894; KRS 7/9, 248–52, State *v.* Anna S. Cloete, 2 April 1897 for a case of assault on the *bywoner*'s wife by the landlord's as a result of the former's refusal to allow her daughter to work in the homestead after being ill-treated by the latter.
69. See J. B. Adams, The Grange, Parys, to editor, *FW*, 20 November 1912, 880; evidence of J. J. Bouwer of Bethlehem in *NLC*, 56; and that of J. M. van Reenen, *SANAC*, vol. 4, para. 38 752.
70. See Grosskopf, *Rural Impoverishment*, 126–7; SC 9–1913, 119–20, evidence of Rev. B. P. J. Marchand.
71. A. W. Barlow, Brereton, to editor, *FW*, 16 August 1911.
72. ORC, *Natives Administration Commission*, 1908 (Pretoria, 1911) 9. G. W. Edmunds, Colesberg, to editor, *FW*, 8 November 1911, 313; O. Naude Haarhoff, Strydpoort, Bethulie, to editor, *FW*, 13 December 1911, 521; Z.

J. Senekal, Zwartlaagte, Kroonstad, to editor, *FW*, 29 November 1911, 437. A typical wage for a white *bywoner* was £3 to £4 a month plus food. SC 9–1913, 578 (4091), P. J. C. Theron, MLA for Heilbron.

73. 'Legislative Assembly', *Friend*, 22 July 1908. See also 'What is Wrong with Our Boys', *FW*, 23 October 1912, 563; 'South African Boys', *Friend*, 16 September 1912; 'Country Day by Day', *Friend*, 18 February 1911. See van Jaarsveld, *Trek na die Stede*, 145–59 for a sampling of such perceptions drawn from newspapers.

74. CS 6320/08, J. L. Pretorius, Klipfontein, 6 July 1908.

75. See Grosskopf, *Rural Impoverishment*, 170–3; and Wilcocks, *Poor White*, ch. 6.

76. W. F. Dugmore, to editor, *Friend*, 18 August 1908. See also 'Closer Settlement', *FW*, 10 May 1911, 6.

77. 'Farmers' Congress', *Friend*, 24 November 1906. ORC, *Commission of Enquiry into the Position and Circumstances of Poor Whites in the Orange River Colony* (Bloemfontein, 1908) 3–5.

78. G. J. van Riet to editor, *Friend*, 8 August 1908. A correspondent from Thaba Nchu returned to the subject in 1912 when the provincial banks were about to be replaced by a Union Land Bank:

   Now is the time for the Government to endeavour to settle many white people who are not landowners, so that they may be ready to start in time for wheat ploughing . . . . It is the individual who has no stock or ploughing plant that will require more assistance, but in helping him you are putting him on his feet – to make a living, to find money to educate his family, to save them from a downward path ('Pro Patria', Thaba Nchu, to editor, *Friend*, 7 February 1912).

79. See ORC *Legislative Assembly Debates*, 1907–8, cols 1303–24. The capital of the bank was eventually fixed at £500 000.

80. UG 34–1913, *Land and Agricultural Bank of South Africa, Report for the Period 1 October–31 December 1912*, 19–20.

81. 'Union Parliament', *Friend*, 17 May 1912. See also E. R. Roper, 'The Advantages and Disadvantages of the Establishment of Land Banks with Special Relation to South Africa', *Journal of the Institute of Bankers of South Africa* April 1912, 62. For complaints of the uselessness of the bank for non-landowners see: 'A True-Hearted South African' to editor, *Friend*, 1 May 1911; 'Land Banks and Their Uses', *FA*, February 1912, 373; W.G.A., Clocolan, to editor, *Friend*, 23 March 1911; JUS 1/401/10, Annual Report, 1910: Reitz. The experiences of the Repatriation Department after the war, when a similar system of sureties in relation to repatriation loans was operated, were much the same. See ORC, *Report of a Commission Appointed to Enquire into the Question of Repatriation Debts*, 1908, 22–4; Transvaal, *Report of the Committee of Enquiry on Repatriation Debts*, TG 32–1908, 35 and 37. See also Transvaal, *Report of the Land Bank Commission*, 1907, evidence of J. C. Smuts, 150–1.

82. UG 13–1914, *Land and Agricultural Bank of South Africa. Report for the Period 1 January 1913 to 31 December 1913*, 16.

83. E. R. Roper, 'The Land Bank Bill', *The State*, June 1912, 501–2. See pp. 168–9 below on the broader significance of the Land Bank.

84. See I. Hofmeyr, 'Building a Nation from Words: Afrikaans Language, Literature and "Ethnic" Identity, 1902–24', unpublished paper, 1984.
85. See R. Krut, 'Maria Botha and her Sons: The Making of a White South African Family in the Twentieth Century', unpublished paper, 1984.
86. T. R. H. Davenport, 'The South African Rebellion of 1914', *English Historical Review*, 78, 306 (1963).
87. On state policies, see R. H. Davies, *Capital, State and White Labour in South Africa, 1900–1960* (Brighton, 1979).
88. See Wilcocks, *Poor White*, ch. 2. On white sharecropping in the 1910s and 1920s, see W. M. Macmillan, *The South African Agrarian Problem and Its Historical Development* (Johannesburg, 1919, reprinted Pretoria, 1974) 75–8; W. M. Macmillan, *Complex South Africa* (London, 1930) 95; and de Vos, 'Die Bywoner'.
89. See pp. 68–72.
90. See Grosskopf, *Rural Impoverishment*, 118–23, 143 and 148. See also T. Clynick, 'The Lichtenburg Alluvial Diamond Diggers, 1926–29', unpublished paper, 1984. Thus it was reported from Ficksburg in January 1908 that whites from the non-arable Boshof district in the west of the colony were arriving in wheat-growing areas and finding employment at a rate of a bucket of wheat for every load of sheaves delivered at the stacks. These might well have been landless men – possibly sons of landowners – whose major (and diminishing) source of income was transport-riding.
91. Once urbanized, many such families continued to invest their income in accumulating stock in anticipation of a return to the land. See Macmillan, *Complex South Africa*, 95; also D. Welsh, 'The Growth of Towns' in M. Wilson and L. M. Thompson (eds) *Oxford History of South Africa*, vol. 2 (Oxford, 1971) 206.
92. See C. van Onselen, 'The Main Reef Road into the Working Class' in C. van Onselen, *Studies in the Social and Economic History of the Witwatersrand, 1886–1914*, vol. 2, *New Nineveh* (London, 1982); J. J. Fourie, *Afrikaners in die Goudstad, 1886–1924*, ed. E. L. P. Stals (Cape Town and Pretoria, 1978) 33–4. For comparative perspectives on nineteenth-century British capitalism, see R. Samuel, 'The Workshop of the World', *History Workshop Journal*, 3 (1977).
93. Statistics on white urbanization are to be found in the *Report of the Commission of Enquiry into European Occupancy of Rural Areas* (Pretoria, 1960) ch. 6.
94. See B. Bozzoli, 'Marxism, Feminism and South African Studies', *Journal of Southern African Studies*, 9,2 (1983) 152–4. On the Afrikaans women workers who dominated the garment, textile and confectionery industries, see Grosskopf, *Rural Impoverishment*, 214–29; E. Brink, '" Maar 'n Klomp 'Factory' Meide": The Role of Female Garment Workers in the Clothing Industry, Afrikaner Family and Community on the Witwatersrand during the 1920s', unpublished paper, 1984; Solly Sachs, *Rebel's Daughter* (London, 1957). The socialist culture of these women proved very difficult for the Afrikaner nationalists of the 1930s to subvert. See also Krut, 'Maria Botha', for an insight into the struggles of urban Afrikaner women, often family heads, to survive in a hostile environment. For a general survey of Afrikaner employment in urban areas, see S. Pauw, *Die Beroepsarbeid van die Afrikaner in die Stad* (Stellenbosch, 1946).

95. See D. O'Meara, *Volkskapitalisme: Class, Capital and Ideology in the Development of Afrikaner Nationalism, 1934–48* (Cambridge, 1983).

96. Editorial, *Friend*, 12 May 1906.

97. F. Schimper to editor, *Friend*, 13 June 1893.

98. 'Take It From Me', Frankfort, to editor, *FW*, 20 November 1912, 880.

99. Ross suggests that the tendency of the Boer family toward regular fission and continual expansion of colonial settlement in the pre-Trek Cape had much to do with the early age of marriage of Boer women – most seem to have been married by the age of twenty (82 per cent in early Potchefstroom, according to one source) – and the very large families which they bore. But Ross's argument becomes circular when he suggests that rapid population increase 'to a considerable extent ... was encouraged by the presence of the frontier'. He adds that as the frontier 'closed', the age of marriage went up, and presumably families declined in size. This interesting speculation, however, is not backed up by convincing evidence. R. Ross, 'Capitalism, Expansion and Incorporation on the South African Frontier' in Lamar and Thompson (eds) *Frontier in History*, 217–19.

100. See, for example, E. H. Burrows, *The Moodies of Melsetter* (Cape Town, 1954) 105–7 and chs 6–8; 'The Free State and Mashonaland', *Friend*, 16 June 1891, 28 July 1891; 'Mashonaland', *Friend*, 22 January 1892; 'The Bethlehem District Trek', *Friend*, 22 March 1892; 'Mashonaland Development', *Friend*, 24 May 1892; 'The Adendorff Trek', *Friend*, 10 June 1892; 'The Bethlehem Trek', *Friend*, 15 July 1892, etc. See Hattingh, 'Trekke', for a detailed treatment of the trek movements of these years. R. Hodder-Williams tells of continual immigration of Boer 'younger sons and *bywoners*' into Rhodesia – often squatting illicitly – and the efforts of the company officials to keep them out. 'The British South Africa Company and the Search for "Suitable" White Immigrants', unpublished paper, 1980. See also M. P. K. Sorrenson, *Origins of European Settlement in Kenya* (London, 1968) 65–6 and 229–30. Also G 199/07, High Commissioner, Johannesburg, 18 November 1907; CO 224/26, 27 July 1908; CO 224/27, 26 October 1908; CO 224/28, 23 July 1908 (latter three comprising correspondence from W. A. Boyd-King, Kestell, concerning a planned trek by farmers in the neighbourhood to East Africa).

101. Few farms were to be had in the older-established areas, and the *Volksraad* had enforced a Fencing Act in 1890 with which the poorer landowners were unable to comply, according to the report. In consequence of this influx into Vryburg district, the speculators who owned the land were selling it off at rapidly inflating prices ('Bechuanaland', *Friend*, 19 August 1892). Certain areas such as the northwestern and northern Cape, the far northern and southwestern Transvaal, saw massive population increases and rapid land subdivision and capital development in the early decades of this century. *The Annual Reports of the Department of Justice* (magistrates' annual reports) for 1910 and succeeding years are very revealing regarding the development of such districts. See also 1921 *Census Report*, UG 37–1924, Part 4; Grosskopf, *Rural Impoverishment*, ch. 3.

102. See *Farm List, ORC, by Districts* (Bloemfontein, 1902). See also VR 389, 80–1, from four van der Walts, 1894, re Randfontein, owned by fourteen heirs in undivided portions. The ORC *Poor Whites Commission* of 1908

saw this as a major factor in impoverishment: see the evidence of the magistrate in Boshof, 10. See also de Vos, 'Die Bywoner'. It was for these reasons that, for example, the Afrikaner Bond in the Cape in 1895 discussed the introduction of a law of primogeniture to prevent land being split up and falling in the hands of strangers as a result of impoverishment. 'The Law of Inheritance', *Friend*, 15 January 1895; *idem*, 18 January 1895; 'Jottings from Senekal', *Friend*, 1 February 1895.

103. See TG 13–1908, *Transvaal Indigency Commission*, Evidence, 141 (para. 3419) figs I, J, K (between 192 and 193), Report, 66, 68–71 and 85. Cases of excessive fragmentation and overcrowding, for example in such Transvaal districts as Potchefstroom, Rustenburg and Marico, were to be found in irrigable areas, where each owner had access to permanent water supplies. This explains the elongated configuration of such plots, designed to ensure each owner has a frontage on the river. Grosskopf, *Rural Impoverishment*, 112 and 118–21.

104. TG 13–1908, 184 (paras 4340–1).

105. De Vos, 'Die Bywoner', 23.

106. Grosskopf, *Rural Impoverishment*, 42; Wilcocks, *Poor White*, ch. 3 on 'overcrowding' on farms; SC 6–1914, *Report of the Select Committee on Removal of Restrictions under Wills Bill*, 64–5; SC 5–1913, *Report of the Select Committee on Fidei-Commissary Bequests*, 7; TG 13–1908, 182 (para. 4268).

107. Thus in 1893 the ten sons and sons-in-law of P. J. Engelbrecht of Kleinzevenfontein, Caledon River district, petitioned that their children could not possibly all make a living on the farm in future years. VR 372, 27–9.

108. VR 418, 138–44, G. A. Hill, 10 April 1897.

109. See H. J. S. Weideman, 'Die Geskiedenis van die Ekonomiese Ontwikkeling van die Oranje-Vrystaat met verwysing na die Ontstaan van die Armblankedom, 1830–70', M.A. thesis, University of South Africa, 1946, 44–5.

110. 'A Johannesburg Opinion', *Friend*, 8 April 1892; 'Landed Property', *Friend*, 21 March 1893; also 'A Tell-Tale', *Friend*, 1 April 1892; 'The Problem of the Future', *Friend*, 10 December 1897. Amongst internal sources of mortgage funds was the Bloemfontein Board of Executors and Trust Company, Ltd, which regularly advertised that it had up to £50 000 available for loans on first mortgage of landed properties in the Orange Free State. H. Klynveld, a lawyer in Bethulie, advertised in 1891 and 1892 that he had £100 000 available for loans at 5 per cent interest on Free State farms. *Friend*, 16 June 1891, 13 September 1892, 13 April 1897, 25 September 1891, 23 August 1892. An indication of the rise in bonding of property is given here:

	Bonds Passed £	Bonds Cancelled £
1888–9	271 655	—
1889–90	291 382	—
1890–1	401 817	226 453
1891–2	505 570	231 878
1892–3	607 976	229 552

Of this £607 976, £246 321 was due to companies and others outside of the state. In the three years 1890–3 cancellations of old bonds amounted to only 45.5 per cent of new bonds passed (37.5 per cent in 1892–3). *Annual Report of the Registrar of Deeds, 1892–3* (Bloemfontein, 1893).

111. VR 382, 104–17, 1894.
112. VR 382, 107–9, 12 April 1894. In June 1894 the Administrator of Funds reported that the government held 924 mortgage bonds on land worth £282 543, an average of £305 each. 'Government Funds', *Friend*, 1 June 1894.
113. 'Free State Mining Products', *Friend*, 30 July 1895; 'Heilbron District', *Friend*, 13 August 1895; 'Mining and Farming', *Friend*, 16 August 1895; 'More Options', *Friend*, 13 September 1895; 'The Concession Mania', *Friend*, 13 September 1895; 'Free State Minerals', *Friend*, 21 February 1896; 'Options', *Friend*, 21 April 1896.
114. 'Another Diamond Mine', *Friend*, 20 May 1898.
115. See W. Bleloch, *The New South Africa* (London, 1901) 218; also the evidence of W. Findlay before the Transvaal *Land Bank Commission*, 1907, 208.
116. J. J. Oberholster and M. C. E. van Schoor (eds) *President Steyn aan die Woord* (Bloemfontein, 1953) 36–8; 'A Retrograde Movement', *Friend*, 19 June 1896; see also Malan, *Politieke Strominge*, 238–40.
117. See Malan, *Politieke Strominge*, 260–2. In 1896 147 Ficksburg residents petitioned the government to close the civil courts, as their creditors were threatening to ruin them. VR 416, 21–3.
118. See pp. 66–7, 240n.47.
119. It is almost impossible to speculate on what proportion of the land was owned by absentees in the nineteenth century and whether this proportion was higher or lower by 1900 than it had been in 1860. In 1918 64 per cent of farms in the Orange Free State were occupied by their owners, but this is not necessarily an indication of the situation thirty or fifty years earlier. No doubt the extent of absentee speculative landownership varied with economic conditions, and the land registers indicate a high turnover of property throughout the republican period. Much speculatively-owned land was taken up by new influxes of white settlers from the Cape and Natal colonies from the 1870s; but speculative interest in land acquisition increased greatly in the 1880s and especially the 1890s.
120. CS 6164/03, RM Lindley, 24 August 1903; CS 5116/04, RM Frankfort, 9 July 1904; JUS 1/401/10, Annual Report: Bethulie, 1910.
121. See magistrates' reports on 'distress amongst Boers', CO 224/12, 12 October 1903.
122. CS 800/04, RM Smithfield, 1 February 1904; CS 6164/03, RM Smithfield, 24 August 1903.
123. When the government acquired the 40 000-morgen estate of Charles Newberry between Thaba Nchu and Ladybrand for £90 000, the sale was negotiated by Sugden, Newberry's agent. Sugden was immediately approached by the Land Settlement Board with a view to purchasing other farms in the colony for them. Sugden was subsequently charged with having deliberately inflated values in order to strike a 'generous bargain' for his 'employer' (CO 224/25, Sir Gilbert Parker, MP, 2 May 1907). Sugden toured the concentration camps in order to buy up Boer land, and

The Friend argued in 1905 that the land had been bought 'on the notorious "brass band" system of enquiry, at, in many cases, double its proper value' (*Friend*, 4 November 1905). The government also bought other large estates, such as 8135 morgen from J. G. Keyter, lawyer and *Volksraad* member for Ficksburg for the very high sum of 65*s* per morgen. *Friend*, 22 July 1908; CS 1294/02, 25 April 1905.

124. CS 1424/02, J. A. Sugden, 17 May 1902. These syndicates were generally based in Johannesburg and consisted of up to a dozen men, each of whom would provide a certain sum, say £100, to form the working capital. Agents were then sent out to persuade impoverished landowners to grant options for the purchase of their land. £50 was paid for the option, and absurdly high purchase prices promised. The options were then passed on to speculators in London to have companies floated to acquire the ground at 'some outrageous figure'. The ORC General Agency of Bloemfontein dealt in 1901 on behalf of 'several' London firms interested in acquiring properties with mineral rights in the Heilbron district (CS 4162/01, 14 November 1901). 'A great amount of capital is now invested in options over an enormous number of farms in the ORC by Johannesburg capitalists waiting for a favourable opportunity for entering the Colony' (*The Orange River Colony: Its Resources and Development* (Bloemfontein, 1906) 77). An example of corporate land purchase after the war was the purchase of 38 000 morgen in the Vredefort district by the Transvaal and Orangia Property Trust, Ltd. CS 1876/03, 10 March 1903.

125. Editorial, *Friend*, 20 January 1908.

126. CO 224/26, Governor Goold-Adams, 27 July 1908.

127. CO 224/26, Governor Goold-Adams, 17 August 1908.

128. CS 2813/04, RM Heilbron, 20 April 1904; Transvaal, *Report of the Land Bank Commission*, 162 and 208 (evidence of M. Mulder and W. Findlay).

129. CS 1708/04, RM Vrede, 10 March 1904; CS 3221/04, RM Rouxville, 2 May 1904.

130. CS 4521/04, RM Bloemfontein, 21 June 1904.

131. CS 8964/04, ORC CFU, 18 November 1904.

132. The largely government-owned National Bank of the ORC (which before the war had a monopoly of banking business in the republic) extended credit facilities to farmers after the war well in excess of banking prudence. Its monopoly was abolished in 1902, and the Standard Bank in particular became an important source of mortgage capital to farmers (a line of business which commercial banks had previously shunned, preferring to keep their assets more liquid). The general manager of the bank said in 1907 that after the war the bank had 'done more to encourage advances to farmers than has been done in the history of the country previously' – to the value of £1 000 000 on the security of mortgage bonds throughout South Africa. A 15–1907, *SC on Agricultural Credit Bank Bill*, 61. See also, 'Chamber of Commerce', *Friend*, 29 March 1907; C. R. Serfontein to editor, *Friend* 14 April 1908; CO 224/26, Governor Goold-Adams, 27 July 1908; and CO 224/26, Colonial Treasurer's Budget Statement, 17 August 1908.

133. CS 8356/04, W. J. Pienaar, 1 November 1904; CS 8536/04, J. Pienaar, 2 November 1904.

134. Transvaal, *Land Bank Commission*, 103.

135. Editorial, *Friend*, 13 July 1908.

136. 'Dingaan's Day', *Friend*, 17 December 1912. The Day of the Covenant, commemorating the vow to God taken by the Natal Voortrekkers before the decisive battle of Blood River against the Zulus in 1838, was itself a late nineteenth-century innovation, replete with a cultural symbolism apposite to the populist struggle. See also the report of the Central Farmers' Congress in *Friend*, 7 February 1908, and the report of ex-President Steyn's speech on the 'battle against unscrupulous capital' in *Friend*, 26 February 1907.

137. Macmillan, *Complex South Africa*, 93.

138. J. de Swardt and J. C. Neethling, *Report of an Economic Investigation into Farming in Four Maize Districts of the Orange Free State, 1928–30*, Department of Agriculture, Economic Series, 22 (Pretoria, 1937).

139. UG 13–1927, *Agricultural Census*, 8, 1924–5. See Appendix, pp. 217–18.

140. UG 37–1924, *1921 Census*, 182.

141. Grosskopf, *Rural Impoverishment*, 97–9.

142. UG 37–1924, Part 4; Grosskopf, *Rural Impoverishment*, ch. 3.

143. *Report of the Commission of Enquiry into European Occupancy of Rural Areas* (Pretoria, 1960) 15.

3 Black tenant production and white accumulation

1. The earliest reference found to Griqua sharecropping is in James Backhouse, *A Narrative of a Visit to the Mauritius and South Africa* (London, 1844) 433. For early cases of sharing arrangements between Boers, see *Reports of the Cases Decided in the High Court of the Orange Free State in the Years 1874 and 1875*, J. N. Eagle (ed.) (Philippolis, 1879) 9–10.

2. As an example of evidence of this, see VR 393, 7–9, 12–24, thirty-eight burghers of Wepener, March 1895.

3. Of his family's decision to leave Basutoland one informant recalls: 'They did not want to stay under the chiefs. They saw no progress. They were called to work in the fields without remuneration' (Interview, Daniel Makiri, 2). In the late nineteenth and early twentieth centuries there was a steady expansion of settlement into the sparsely populated mountainous areas of Basutoland, previously used for grazing. But at the same time population growth was exhausting further oportunities for expansion and led to greater stability of settlement as young men sought to secure rights to land virilocally. Movement into the Orange Free State should be seen in this light (Colin Murray, *Families Divided: The Impact of Migrant Labour in Lesotho* (Cambridge, 1981) 105; see also R. C. Germond (ed.) *Chronicles of Basutoland* (Morija, 1967) 414, 417, 426–30). A considerable efflux from Basutoland in the early 1880s was caused by the civil war then consuming the kingdom. See C. C. Eloff, 'Die Verhouding tussen die Oranje-Vrystaat en Basoetoland, 1878–84', *Archives Year Book for South African History*, 1980, 2 (Pretoria, 1983) ch. 6.

4. Interview, Ndae Makume, I, 3 and 8; II, 2 and 3.

5. Interview, R. C. Manaba, 1–5.

6. Interview, K. Phalime, 2–5.

7. Interview, Petrus Pooe, 6–8. The sharecroppers were archetypal representatives of a whole stratum of free-floating people found throughout southern Africa who were created by the *Difaqane*, who moved intermittently between chiefdom, mission station, colonial employment and tenancy on farms, and who were particularly susceptible to new ideas and values. The Mfengu of the eastern Cape, who surely formed the model for Colin Bundy's image of the atomized peasant in *The Rise and Fall of the South African Peasantry* (London, 1979) are also representative of the type. See also P. Delius, *The Land Belongs to Us: The Pedi Polity, the Boers and the British in the Nineteenth Century Transvaal* (London, 1983). A vivid depiction of the social base from which many of the Highveld sharecroppers derived is to be found in Brian Willan, *Sol Plaatje: A Biography* (London, 1984). The significance of Christianity is elaborated in the third section of this chapter.

8. *Volksraadsnotule*, 28 June 1898, 733 (M. Heyns, Onderwittebergen, Winburg); CS 7536/03, Commandant SAC, 23 October 1903. It was also widely believed that white residents of the border districts bought farms with cash supplied by Sotho chiefs, who effectively owned these farms, with the whites acting as proxies. *Friend*, 14 October 1908.

9. 'Native Labour', *Friend*, 26 February 1892. See C. Murray, 'The Land of the Barolong: Annexation and Alienation, 1884–1900', unpublished paper, 1983.

10. See pp. 64–7.

11. *Volksraadsnotule*, 29 April 1895, 331; also 28 June 1898, 733.

12. Interview, A. Mokale, 8–9.

13. T. Matsetela, 'The Life Story of Nkgono Mma-Pooe' in S. Marks and R. Rathbone (eds) *Industrialization and Social Change in South Africa* (London, 1982) 215–19.

14. Interview, J. Moiloa, 7–8 and 10–11.

15. Interview, E. M. Pooe, I, 2.

16. For example, petitions containing some 1200 signatures are to be found in VR 381, 1894.

17. See Chapter 6.

18. See pp. 13–15.

19. See H. J. van Aswegen, 'Die Verhouding tussen Blank en nie-Blank in die Oranje-Vrystaat, 1854–1902', Ph.D. thesis, University of the Orange Free State, 1969, 564–9 and 581–95. The provisions of the law are to be found in T. R. H. Davenport and K. S. Hunt (eds) *The Right to the Land* (Cape Town, 1974) 56–7.

20. *Volksraadsnotule*, 26 April 1897, 214; see also 29 April 1895, 311; 29 May 1896, 525 and 28 June 1898, 520.

21. See, for example, VR 428, 65–7, sixty-three burghers of Korannaberg ward, 1898; VR 436, 27–9, fifty-one burghers of Korannaberg, 1899.

22. See, for example, *Volksraadsnotule*, 29 May–1 June 1896, 522–34; 2 July 1896, 878–89, etc.

23. See pp. 21, 29–32, 227n.7.

24. See, for example, VR 381, 69–72, 109 burghers of the Ficksburg district, 1894; VR 393, 123–25, twenty-four burghers of the Ficksburg district,

1895; VR 393, 7–9 and 12–14, two petitions, thirty-eight burghers of the Wepener district, March 1895.

25. VR 372, 71–4, two petitions, 111 burghers of Kromellenboog ward, 24 April 1893; see also, for example, *Volksraadsnotule*, 17 May 1894, 124; 28 April 1897 (J. P. Janse, Kromellenboog).

26. VR 381, 49–52, seventy burghers of Vechtkop ward, Heilbron, 1894.

27. *Volksraadsnotule*, 17 May 1894, 127. See also VR 381, 7–12, 101 burghers of the Ficksburg and Ladybrand districts, April 1894, who declared that it was 'impossible for the white grain farmer to rival the blacks, and this even in our own country!'.

28. VR 433, 121–2, sixty-three burghers of Ficksburg and Ladybrand districts, March 1898; *Volksraadsnotule*, 28 June 1898, 732–3.

29. Germond, *Chronicles*, 522–33.

30. CO 417/297, Resident Commissioner, Basutoland, to Secretary of State, 12 September 1900. See in general for the experiences of the Sotho during the war, P. Warwick, *Black People and the South African War* (Cambridge, 1983) ch. 3.

31. CO 417/297, Resident Commissioner, 12 September 1900.

32. CO 417/297, Resident Commissioner, 12 September 1900; CO 417/328, 15 April 1901, 10 May 1901, 11 October 1901; CO 417/355, 14 March 1902, 28 October 1902.

33. G. B. Beak, *The Aftermath of War* (London, 1905) 25–9.

34. Annual *Basutoland Colonial Reports* (British Command Papers); also CO 417/455, Resident Commissioner, 20 July 1908.

35. *SANAC*, 1903–5, vol. 4, *passim*.

36. See S. B. Spies, *Methods of Barbarism* (Cape Town, 1977) on the devastation of the Boer capital base in the scorched-earth policy. See also A. P. J. van Rensburg, 'Die Ekonomiese Herstel van die Afrikaner in die Oranjerivier-Kolonie, 1902–07', *Archives Year Book for South African History*, 1967, 2 (Pretoria, 1967).

37. See especially Chapter 6.

38. See p. 114.

39. CO 224/16, Sir J. Swinburne, 20 May 1904.

40. Mrs Peeters claimed to have earned from these families £1500 per year on the basis of a half-share of the crop before the war – £75 per tenant family on average. The Africans' dwellings were 'mostly good ones', and fallowing was practised. Many of the tenant families had lived on the farms for some fifteen to twenty years, and were described by Mrs Peeters as 'diligent' (On Peeters' land, see CS 3304/04, RM Parys, 6 May 1904). Mrs Peeters' husband had been an eminent Smithfield attorney and member of the Free State *Volksraad*. In 1893 he tried unsuccessfully to persuade the *Raad* to declare one of the farms a township – a proposal which promised great profits for the owner of the land.

Sol Plaatje, travelling between Ladybrand and Wepener along the Basutoland border in 1913 found that many of the farms he passed were owned by 'Germans, Jews, Russians and other continentals'. 'Some of the proprietors do not reside on the farms at all; they are either Hebrew merchants or lawyers, living in the towns and villages away from the farms.' These were all sharecropping landlords (S. Plaatje, *Native Life in*

South Africa (1916, reprinted New York, 1969) 104). Cf. the case of A. D. Macaskill, clerk to the firm of Ross and Co. of Ficksburg at a salary of £25 per month, who bought a farm at £6 per morgen in 1913, passing a bond for £2000. The balance of £900 was raised by the sale of his wife's town property (SBA, Annual Inspection Reports, Ficksburg, 1914). Such cases were common and reflect the high premium placed on landownership amongst even the most humble of white town dwellers.

41. See J. L. Hattingh, 'Die Trekke uit die Suid-Afrikaanse Republiek en die Oranje-Vrystaat, 1875–95', Ph.D. thesis, University of Pretoria, 1975, 526–34.

42. See SBA, Annual Inspection Reports, Heidelberg, various years.

43. *NLC*, Evidence, 289.

44. See evidence of J. van der Walt, MLA, Pretoria District (South), *NLC*, 267.

45. 'A History of Tenant Production on the Vereeniging Estates, 1896–1920' in W. Beinart and P. Delius (eds) *Putting a Plough to the Ground* (Johannesburg and London, 1986).

46. On which see C. van Onselen, 'Randlords and Rotgut, 1886–1903' in C. van Onselen, *Studies in the Social and Economic History of the Witwatersrand, 1886–1914*, vol. 1, *New Babylon* (London, 1982).

47. In Carolina district in the eastern Transvaal there were also black sharecroppers on farms owned by the Lewis and Marks company. Marks' private landholdings amounted to over ninety farms, mostly in the western Transvaal. He was also associated with a syndicate in 1892–3 which took over land belonging to A. H. Nellmapius, and which under Wernher–Beit leadership was formed into the Transvaal Consolidated Land and Exploration Company (Trapido, 'Vereeniging Estates'. See also J. S. Preddy, Carolina District, *NLC*, 321). Abraham Mokale, once a tenant on the Estates, tells us that Marks 'would go around selling wine and brandy to the Boers. Because cash was scarce some took it on credit from him and some pawned their lands'. This interesting bit of local folklore might contain more than a grain of truth. Interview, Abraham Mokale, II, 18.

48. CS 3203/06, ANA, 16 July 1906.

49. Trapido, 'Vereeniging Estates'; SAIRR, *A Community Man* (Johannesburg, 1983) 2; Matsetela, 'Life Story', 225–6.

50. See pp. 29–33.

51. 'Progress', Kroonstad, to editor, *Friend*, 19 July 1911. See also Trapido, 'Vereeniging Estates'. Four sharecroppers of Gelukfontein, were fined £2 each or two weeks' imprisonment by the Resident Justice of the Peace in Bothaville in July 1900 under the new British military regime for refusing to allow John Wallace, a landlord's agent, to take the landlord's (one Pieters') share of the crop. The Africans' reason for adopting this attitude was that Pieters had sent a policeman after the sharing ceremony the previous year to search their huts. KRS 7/9, 339, State *v.* Thomas *et al*, 13 July 1900.

52. See R. Seggie, 'Squatting and Ploughing on Shares', *FW*, 8 May 1912.

53. 'Wepener Congress', *Friend*, 27 January 1909. See Abraham Mokale's description of a sharing ceremony on the Vereeniging Estates in Trapido, 'Vereeniging Estates'; also Matsetela, 'Life Story', 221.

54. CO 417/394, Basutoland Reports, 21 November 1904.

55. A. Mohwerane noted (interview, 23):

> It was not only a matter of sharing the bags but there was another snag – when the plough broke it became my expense to fix it; the yoke broke – my expense too, all these things, grease for the wagons, that all rested on my shoulders.

56. See, for example, VR 381, 26–8, thirty-five burghers from Onder Valschrivier, Kroonstad, 13 April 1894; ibid, 29–31, thirty-six burghers from Onder Renosterrivier, Kroonstad; 59–61, ninety-eight burghers from Midden Valschrivier, Kroonstad. Also VR 597, 146, G. J. B. de Wet, JP, wyk Midden Liebenbergsvlei, Bethlehem, to Labour Commission.

57. G 441/1/08, Acting Governor R. D. Allason, 28 August 1908.

58. 'Taxation and Registration of Stallions', *FW*, 19 April 1911, 5.

59. NAB 8, Encl. 6, F. A. S. Schimper, 1 August 1905; *NLC*, Evidence, 40.

60. 'Farmers' Associations: Petrus Steyn', *FW*, 12 November 1924, 909.

61. Interview, K. Phalime, 28.

62. VR 381, 76–8, thirty-four burghers from Hoopstad, 24 April 1894. See also *NLC*, Evidence, 70, for the case of Major Gent, farmer of Kroonstad, who hired farms in the northwestern Zandveld on which to settle sharecropping tenants.

63. Interviews, J. Molete, 3; and T. Manoto, 35.

64. NAB, vol. 8, Encl. 10, J. M. McCalman, Belladale, Frankfort, 9 October 1905.

65. See the evidence of Archdeacon Hill, Springs, in UG 22–1932, *Report of the Natives Economic Commission*, 199–200.

66. LPA 1/7, Kromellenboog Farmers' Association to RM Vredefort, 6 July 1904. An example in the vicinity was Mrs G. W. Peeters' two farms mentioned earlier (pp. 64–5) on which lived Cornelis Smuts and Jan Nel as her representatives. LPA 1/7, W. C. Peeters to RM Vredefort, 17 May 1904.

67. Interview, J. Molete.

68. Interview, N. Makume, I, 5 and 24–5. It is probable that a proportion of the 36 per cent of farms in the Orange Free State in 1918 that were absentee-owned and which were leased by whites (either for a fixed rental or a share of the crop) or worked under a white manager, according to census returns of that year, were in fact worked primarily by blacks under some form of sharing contract such as described in this section. See Appendix for details, pp. 217–18.

69. See Chapter 1, note 98.

70. See Native Labour Circulars in CS 5775/01, 15 December 1902; CS 1477/03, 23 February 1903; CS 8384/03, 3 December 1903; and CS 2682/04, 19 April 1904.

71. CS 3218/02, J. M. Kok, 11 August 1902; CS 314/03, 13 January 1903; CS 3913/01, 25 October 1901.

72. CS 4566/02, 23 October 1902; CS 3557/02, RM Heilbron, 1 September 1902.

73. CS 4979/04, RM Heilbron, 5 July 1904; CS 7490/04, 29 September 1904. For the similarly fruitless struggle to disperse the sharecropping tenantry on Mrs Peeters' land, see CS 1894/03, W. C. Peeters, 4 March 1903; CS

5407/03, W. C. Peeters, 24 July 1903; LPA 1/7, W. C. Peeters to RM Parys, 29 March 1904; ibid, 17 May 1904; CS 3303/04, RM Parys, 6 May 1904. The capitulation of the administration in 1904 in the face of resistance from the big sharecropping landlords elicited a predictable outcry from local farmers. LPA 1/7, Kromellenboog Farmers' Association to RM Vredefort, 6 July 1904; ibid, 12 August 1904.

74. See T. J. Keegan, 'The Restructuring of Agrarian Class Relations in a Colonial Economy: The Orange River Colony, 1902–1910', *Journal of Southern African Studies*, 5, 2 (1979) 243–5 for the case of Sir John Swinburne, member of the British parliament and landowner in Harrismith district.

75. See Matsetela, 'Life Story', 227–8; SAIRR, *A Community Man*, 2–3 and 6–7 for the testimony of Emelia Pooe and Barney Ngakane about sharecropping in the mid-Vaal area prior to 1914, both of whom stress the skills and diligence of the sharecroppers. Both relate vivid testimony of the awe and jealousy evoked locally by their large crops and the inability of the *bywoners* to compete with them.

76. Interview, Petrus Pooe, 15; GS 806, 8–10, *landdros*, Ladybrand, to GS, 22 June 1893; interview, Emelia Molefe Pooe, II, 33; interview, Marobane Ngakane, 7–8; interview, Dinah Molope Pooe, 14.

77. See, for example, *NLC*, Evidence, passim; *BBNA*, 1910, 153, 178, etc.; SC 3–1910, *Select Committee on Native Affairs*, 1910, 136.

78. This is indicated in much of the oral testimony. See, for example, interview, E. M. Popane.

79. Interviews, P. Pooe, 3–4, 23 and 24; A. Mokale, I, 16; E. Pooe, II, 7 and 12; Trapido, 'Vereeniging Estates'.

80. *BBNA*, 1910, 53, 153–5 and 149; Trapido, 'Vereeniging Estates'; interviews, A. Mokale, I, 5, II, 1, III, 17; Petrus Pooe, 3; K. Phalime, 2; M. Ngakane, 6 and 9; Matsetela, 'Life Story', 227.

81. Trapido, 'Vereeniging Estates'; interview, A. Mokale, I, 12, and III, 8 and 12; interview, E. Pooe, II, 5; SAIRR, *A Community Man*, 7; interview, D. Molope Pooe, 12.

82. Interview, J. Moiloa, 7; E. M. Pooe, II, 15–16; M. Ngakane, 6–7; K. Phalime, 16.

83. See GS 588, 173–4, H. Edwards to *landdros*, Heilbron, 22 October 1892.

84. See Rev. Mpela, *SANAC*, 1903–5, vol. 4, 371.

85. Interview, A. Mokale, I, 12; Trapido, 'Vereeniging Estates'.

86. Interview, K. Phalime, 2–4.

87. Interview, N. Makume, II, 37–8.

88. *A Community Man*, 2; interview, P. Pooe, 1; Matsetela, 'Life Story', 221–2.

89. Interview, E. M. Pooe, II, 7.

90. Interview, A. Mokale, I, 13, III, 16; Trapido, 'Vereeniging Estates'; interview, M. Ngakane, 9; also interview, J. Molete, 5.

91. Interview, Dinah Molope Pooe, 6.

92. Interview, E. M. Pooe, II, 19; Matsetela, 'Life Story', 219.

93. Interview, E. M. Pooe, II, 6; Matsetela, 'Life Story', 222; interview, J. Moiloa, 5.

94. Interviews, E. M. Pooe, II, 24; J. Moiloa, 6–7; J. Masina, 12. A farmer complained in January 1912, during the bumper winter cereal harvest of that year, of the system he called 'reaping with beer':

A native gives notice that he is about to reap and will kill a sheep and supply unlimited Kaffir beer. It is astonishing to see the crowd that collects in no time, and the ease with which his crops come off. But the poor farmer when he gets up finds his boys missing, off to the beer drink. They turn up the next day, muddled and useless ('Our Weekly Causerie', *FW*, 31 January 1912).

Clearly there is something of the relationship of employer and employee being described here.

95. See, for example, interview, L. Nqandela.
96. Matsetela, 'Life Story', 231.
97. White resentment against this form of social mobility amongst the blacks led to much harassment of black church-goers and teachers. The pass laws were used to prevent blacks from attending church. For example, GS 583, 135–6, Harmon to Rev. J. Scott, 29 July 1890. Of course, there were different forms of Christianity. The sharecropping elite was more likely to be Protestant, most notably Methodist. Other mission denominations such as the Afrikaans churches and the Catholics were likely to discourage pretensions to social betterment and probably attracted the poorer and less sophisticated tenants. The separatist African Methodist Episcopal church does not yet seem to have had much attraction for the upwardly mobile, as it had later. (See p. 195.)
98. *Presbyterian Churchman*, November 1914. See pp. 176–8 on this purchase of land in 1910–12.
99. Interview, Rev. A. Poho.
100. Interview, E. M. Pooe, II, 26 and 30; see also Petrus Pooe, 5 and Dinah Molope Pooe, 7.
101. *A Community Man*, 4, 9–12 and *passim*.
102. Interview, P. Pooe, 18; see also Dinah Pooe, 12.
103. Interview, E. M. Pooe, II, 26–7.
104. Interview, J. Molete, 3, 5 and 16.
105. Interview, P. Pooe, 20.
106. Many of the larger stockowners forced off the farms in the great dispersal of 1913 were older men who had lost control of the labour of juniors and were thus of little utility to landlords. See pp. 188–9.
107. Interviews, J. Moiloa, 22; K. Phalime, 14; T. Manoto, 20.
108. R. Seggie, 'Squatting and Ploughing on Shares', *FW*, 8 May 1912, 574; also see A. J. Boshof, Lisbon, Heilbron, to editor, *FW*, 16 October 1912, 436.
109. *NLC*, Evidence, 49 (Senator H. Potgieter), 5 (H. J. Vivier, Winburg), 58 (Rev. Obed Mokhosi). See interview, K. Phalime, 18. Of course, it is likely that the most prosperous tenants kept cash reserves, even perhaps bank accounts, although evidence on this is lacking.
110. For example, interview, J. Masina, 4.
111. See pp. 173–5.
112. See, for example, p. 78.
113. See Murray, *Families Divided*, 127–8, for a brief review of historical evidence on Sotho bridewealth usages.
114. Interviews, K. Phalime, 19; J. Moiloa, 18; N. Makume, II, 15.
115. *BBNA*, 1910, 192.
116. Ibid, 127–9, 192, and 275; also *NLC*, Evidence, 27. There was no serious

problem of storage amongst the Africans whose craft industry had solved this problem far more effectively than had the white farmers. The traditional woven grain baskets (*sesiu*) were common on the farms, and Kodisang Phalime, who was a boy at the time of the Jameson Raid (1895) and who was born into a sharecropping family, remembers his family weaving storage baskets in the evenings. He remembers the British searching the stores for hiding Boers during the war, and expressing surprise at how watertight the granaries were. Interview, K. Phalime, 12–13. See also interviews, T. R. Mmolotsi, 34; V. R. C. Manaba, 10.

117. See T. Keegan, 'White Settlement and Black Subjugation on the South African Highveld: The Tlokoa Heartland in the Northeastern Orange Free State, 1850–1914' in Beinart and Delius (eds) *Putting a Plough to the Ground*.

118. For details of land occupancy, see Appendix, pp. 217–18.

119. As was seen earlier, access to loan capital and credit did not necessarily increase the productive capital of white farmers, as funds were so often drained off in unproductive expenditure, such as land purchase. See pp. 38–49.

120. *Volksraadsnotule*, 28 April 1897, 240 (C. van der Wath, Moroka).

121. Ibid.

122. Enclosure in CO 224/27, Lord Harris to Secretary of State, 21 September 1908.

123. 'Talis Qualis', Lower Vet River, to editor, *Friend*, 29 October 1913.

124. Interviews, K. Phalime, 3; E. M. Pooe, II, 6; J. Moiloa, 5; Matsetela, 'Life Story', 222.

125. JUS 5/262/13, C. C. Chase to RM Heilbron, 17 August 1913.

126. *NLC*, Evidence, 71.

127. Ibid, 15.

128. 'Free State Farming', *FW*, 27 December 1911; also Jill Johnson, *South Africa Speaks* (Johannesburg, 1981) 24; CS 5880/04, RM Bloemfontein, 4 April 1904; LHS 165, J. P. Paist, Brakvallei, to RM Harrismith, 15 August 1905.

129. *NLC*, Evidence, 55 and 16.

130. 'A Settler' to editor, *FA*, July 1912, 669.

131. *BBNA*, 1910, 154.

132. 'No Compulsion', Thaba Nchu, to editor, *FW*, 11 December 1912.

133. See Trapido, 'Vereeniging Estates', on the massive losses incurred by John Fowler and Co. of Leeds, who leased land from Lewis and Marks, when they introduced steam-powered ploughs on to their land. Similarly, R. Seggie of Kroonstad was involved in 1915 in a suit against the sellers of a traction engine for ploughing which had been a 'complete failure'. The action cost some £2000. SBA, Inspection Reports, Kroonstad, 1915.

134. ORC, *Natives Administration Commission*, 1908 (Cape Town, 1911) 9. Cf. J. K. Rennie, 'White Farmers, Black Tenants and Landlord Legislation: Southern Rhodesia, 1890–1930', *Journal of Southern African Studies*, 5,1 (1978).

135. See the following cases for an indication of the pitfalls awaiting landlords who separated the arable into the landlord's and the tenant's fields without supervising the work on the land: KRS 7/9, 5–7, State *v.* Afrika, 11

December 1893. (In this case A. J. van Coller discovered that the tenant had entrusted the ploughing on the landlord's land to two boys of twelve and thirteen, had wasted the seed, and then complained that his oxen were lame and could not finish the job.) Also ibid, 212–27, State *v.* Willem Plaatje, 28 September 1896; and 193–7, State *v.* Magone, 5 May 1896.

136. *BBNA*, 1910, 154; see also *NLC*, Evidence, 16 (E. C. Roos, Bethlehem); ibid, 30 (RM Harrismith, who reported in 1913 that Africans had complained to him on several occasions that their oxen had been 'ploughed to death').

137. Interview, N. Makume, II, 25–6. See also for a similar case, 'Law Problems on the Farm', *FW*, 3 September 1924, 2562.

138. Interview, K. Phalime, 21.

139. 'What Hoe!' to editor, *FW*, 25 September 1918, 390.

4 Interventions of the capitalist state and the development of the arable Highveld

1. Many of the smaller storekeepers were recent immigrants from eastern Europe, who arrived in successive waves in the later nineteenth century and early twentieth century. As with so many of the trader-immigrants elsewhere in Africa, their trading and credit linkages were very much based on networks of ethnicity and kinship. They depended largely on doing business with white *bywoners* and black tenants. (See P. J. de Vos, ' "Die Bywoner": 'n Sosiologiese Studie oor die Bywonerskap in sekere Hoë en Middelvelddistrikte in die Transvaal en Vrystaat', M.A. thesis, Pretoria, 1947, 57–63; on the Jewish immigrants see C. van Onselen, 'Randlords and Rotgut, 1886–1903' in C. van Onselen, *Studies in the Social and Economic History of the Witwatersrand, 1886–1914*, vol. 1, *New Babylon* (London, 1982). The early years of the century also saw expulsions of Indian traders from the Orange Free State, as their trading licences were systematically withdrawn.

2. 'Boettie Boett', Winburg, to editor, *Friend*, 21 January 1896.

3. See JUS 1/401/10, Annual Reports, 1910: Frankfort, Harrismith; JUS 1/566/11, Annual Reports, 1911: Hoopstad. See also H. S. Frankel, *Co-operation and Competition in the Marketing of Maize in South Africa* (London, 1926) 24 and 25.

4. See Editorial, *Friend*, 24 November 1908; 'Government Granaries', *FW*, 19 February 1913, 20; J. Burtt-Davy, *Maize: Its History, Cultivation, Handling and Uses* (London, 1914) 582.

5. A Ficksburg farmer wrote in 1913: 'I have watched this maize market for many years, and I see that maize increases in value quite 50 per cent between harvest and the New Year regularly' ('Government Granaries', *FW*, 19 February 1913, 20). Governor Selborne wrote in February 1906 that the price of maize was then 12*s* a bag in Johannesburg and was expected to rise to 18*s* as there was none left on the market: 'The foreigner will get the advantage of the enhanced price of mealies, not the ORC farmer, because the latter long ago parted with all his mealies at the ruinous price of 5*s* to 7*s* 6*d* a bag'. CS 981/06, Selborne, 14 February 1906. See also evidence of E.

W. Hunt, Transvaal *Land Bank Commission*, 1907, 158; 'Over-Production and Under-Demand', *FA*, December 1913, 203. This phenomenon is well illustrated in the regular reports on the maize trade in the town of Heilbron during the year 1909 in *The Friend*, 'Heilbron Notes' and 'Heilbron News'.

6. See T. Keegan, 'Seasonality, Prices and Markets: The South African Maize Trade in the Early Twentieth Century', *Collected Seminar Papers on the Societies of Southern Africa*, Institute of Commonwealth Studies, London, vol. 10 (1981) for an attempt to grapple with some of these problems at a very abstract level.

7. Report, *Friend*, 28 April 1905.

8. 'Spoon-Feeding the "Backbone of the Country"', *FA*, May 1914, 539. See also Editorial *Friend*, 14 February 1908; O. Thomas, *Agricultural and Pastoral Prospects of South Africa* (London, 1904) 60–1.

9. D. J. Jacobs, 'Die Ontwikkeling van Landbou in die Vrystaat', D.Litt. et Phil. thesis, University of South Africa, 1979, 80.

10. 'A Branch Grain Line', *Friend*, 15 June 1897.

11. Jacobs, 'Ontwikkeling van Landbou', 91.

12. CS 8009/03, Inhabitants of Ficksburg Town and District, 17 November 1903.

13. *Annual Report, ORC Public Works Department, 1905–06* (Bloemfontein, 1906). In that year £23 553 was expended on road- and bridge-building in the ORC. Petitions for road- and bridge-building were frequently to be found in letters to government and in resolutions. See, for example, 'Senekal Show', *Friend*, 9 March 1909; CS 8829/04, R. A. Luck, Harrismith, 17 November 1904, for a description of the main road into Natal.

14. Editorial, *Friend*, 15 September 1891. *The Daily Express* (11 June 1895) contended that it cost 9*d* per bag to transport grain from Australia to South Africa, whereas it cost 2*s* 6*d* to carry a bag of grain forty miles by ox wagon. Cited in Jacobs, 'Ontwikkeling van Landbou', 90.

15. 'The Terrible Drought', *Friend*, 21 October 1912. In December 1912 it was reported from Blaauwbosch that because of the scarcity of riders, the rate to the railhead was 2*s* per 100 lbs as against 1*s* a few months previously. 'Country Day By Day: Blaauwbosch', *Friend*, 14 December 1912. Very heavy crops and a very high demand for transport could also cause a sharp increase in rates. See 'Country Day By Day: Edenburg', *Friend*, 30 December 1911.

16. 'Goods for Jagersfontein', *Friend*, 22 May 1891. See also 'A Gloomy Outlook', *Friend*, 4 December 1896; 'Farmer' to editor, *Friend*, 23 June 1896; 'Our Transport', *Friend*, 5 February 1897; 'The Trial of the Traction Engine', *Friend*, 9 February 1897.

17. 'Country Day By Day: Koffyfontein', *Friend*, 5 January 1911; 'Parliament', *Friend*, 4 April 1913.

18. See 'Country Day By Day: Koffyfontein', *Friend*, 22 March 1913.

19. CS 3625/02, D. Fraser, Wepener, 5 September 1902; CS 8009/03, Inhabitants of Ficksburg Town and District, 17 November 1903.

20. Enclosure in CO 417/297, High Commissioner, 27 December 1900; also CO 224/3, 20 February 1901; CS 2949/02, Messrs Fraser, Mafeteng, 28 July 1902.

21. CS 4690/02, Superintendent, Natives Refugee Department, Harrismith, 30

October 1902. The Transvaal Chamber of Mines urged as a consequence that a special railway rate for imported maize be introduced. CS 233/03, 7 January 1903.

22. CS 2766/02, 23 July 1902; CS 3276/02, 18 August 1902. The ORC Natives Refugee Department bought 12 000 bags of maize from Basutoland traders in May 1902. CO 224/7, Report of Civil Administration since September 1901, 30 May 1902.

23. CS 3386/02, Messrs Fraser, Wepener, 20 August 1902.

24. Immediately after the war many oxen were in the hands of the Repatriation Department, which loaned them to farmers for ploughing.

25. CS 3518/02, Wepener Repatriation Board, 12 August 1902 (emphasis in original).

26. CS 3374/02, Resolutions of a public meeting in Bethlehem, 18 August 1902.

27. See also CS 2654/04, Ficksburg Farmers' Association, 18 April 1904.

28. By mid-1913 there were in the Orange Free State 550 miles of rail on the largely arable eastern side of the main Port Elizabeth–Johannesburg line, and 185 on the largely pastoral western side. The lines on the west were those in the maize districts of the northwest, the line linking Bloemfontein to Kimberley, and the line to the diamond-mining centre of Jagersfontein. See 'Correspondence', *Friend*, 31 May 1913.

29. See Chapter 6.

30. CS 361/4/08, petition from residents of Frankfort district, 1908.

31. See 'Parliament', *Friend*, 3 June 1913; CS 1112/04, RM Hoopstad, 14 February 1904; 'New Lines', *Friend*, 4 June 1912.

32. 'The Bothaville District', *Friend*, 20 July 1912.

33. UG 40–1912, *Report of the Board of the South African Railways on Proposed New Lines of Railway*, 6. A correspondent wrote in 1912 that before the war the Bothaville district 'grew very little grain, carried but few stock, no forestry, and was considered of little value . . . today you have fenced farms in all directions, mealie-growing, cattle-raising and tree-planting on a large scale' ('The Bothaville District', *Friend*, 20 July 1912). The farms of the Pilgrims Mining, Estate and Exploration Company Ltd in the district were amongst the most capitalized farming enterprises in the colony: see p. 115. See also 'Country Day By Day: Bothaville', *Friend*, 12 May 1913. On neighbouring Hoopstad district see JUS 1/566/11, Annual Reports, 1911: Hoopstad; 'The Middle Veld', *Friend*, 18 May 1912; 'Neglected West', *Friend*, 22 May 1912.

34. C. Stevens, Schutte's Draai, to editor, *Friend*, 28 June 1905. This flooding of markets was equally felt in centres which were traversed by the railway such as Harrismith. CS 774/04, RM Harrismith, 5 February 1904. On overproduction in Vrede district see A. A. Willis, Success, to editor, *Friend*, 6 May 1905 and 14 June 1905; reports in *Friend*, 12 and 22 April 1905.

35. Report in *Friend*, 23 June 1905.

36. 'The Kimberley Line', *Friend*, 27 November 1905.

37. See 'Thaba Nchu East Farmers' Association', *Friend*, 21 July 1904; 'Springfontein Farmers' Association', *Friend*, 14 August 1905.

38. Report in *Friend*, 14 September 1905.

39. Report in *Friend*, 28 June 1905.

40. Report in *Friend*, 28 July 1905. There were other factors as well. The low

bulk of South African exports meant that ships returning from South African ports to Europe had to carry ballast in their holds. In order to make the South African services pay, therefore, freight rates on cargo to South Africa were considerably higher than, say, to Australia. So there were pressing reasons why commercial and industrial interests in South Africa were intent on promoting an agricultural export trade. See CS 1358/08, Prime Minister, Pretoria, 21 September 1908; Editorial, *Friend*, 20 March 1911.

41. See Burtt-Davy, *Maize*, 511–13. In 1908 the London price was as much as 29s a quarter. 'Maize Export', *Friend*, 17 March 1909.

42. 'Central Farmers' Union', *Friend*, 5 February 1908.

43. Burtt-Davy, *Maize*, 521–4, and 531–57; Natal Government Railways, *Maize Cultivation and Export in South Africa* (Durban, 1909); *Central South African Railways, General Manager's Report, 1907* (Pretoria, 1908) 14 and 36; *Report of the ORC Agricultural Department, 1907–8* (Bloemfontein, 1908) 19–20; *Friend*, 27 January 1908. Evidence on the working of the export trade in maize is to be found in Keegan, 'Maize Trade'.

44. *Natal Agricultural Journal*, October 1907, 1185; also see 'Country Day By Day', *Friend*, 18 February 1911.

45. 'Durban Maize Trade', *FA*, March 1914, 427–9.

46. See 'The South African Grain Rate', *FA*, March 1907, 315. High rail rates on local grain had long been a source of dissatisfaction. See Jacobs, 'Ontwikkeling van Landbou', 92, for the representations of the Free State Chamber of Commerce in 1894.

47. See Editorial, *Friend*, 18 September 1911.

48. See 'Agriculture in Parliament', *FW*, 26 April 1911, 18; Burtt-Davy, *Maize*, 501 and 564.

49. Editorial, *Friend*, 18 September 1911.

50. Ibid; 'Mealie Export', *Friend*, 30 November 1912. During the drought year of 1912 when maize was in very short supply after the export season and stock were dying of hunger in large numbers, a strong agitation against precipitate and ill-considered exportation of maize arose. See 'Does it pay to Sell Grain?', *FA*, December 1912, 175–7; N. A. P. Molteno to editor, *FA*, December 1912, 199; 'Mealies on Hoof and in Bag', *FA*, August 1912, 735–7; 'Importing Stock and Exporting Mealies', *FW*, 18 September 1912.

51. 'Reduced Railway Rates', *FA*, October 1911, 73.

52. Editorial, *Friend*, 18 September 1911.

53. Editorial, *Friend*, 25 September 1911; 'Reduced Railway Rates', *FA*, October 1911, 73; 'Maize Industry', *FW*, 20 September 1911, 64; 'Mielie Vrachtprijzen', *FA*, October 1911, 64; 'Een Ander Protest', *FA*, October 1911, 127.

54. D. and D. H. Fraser's mills at Wepener handled 45 000 bags of wheat in 1909, of which 35 000 came from Basutoland; in 1910, 28 000 bags out of 44 000 milled came from Basutoland. JUS 1/401/10, Annual Reports, 1910: Wepener.

55. Wheat production in the Orange Free State was very unsure on account of the uncertainties of spring rain, hail damage, the wheat louse and rust. Wheat yields per morgen were generally relatively low, and decreased over time.

56. UG 42–1919, *Report of the Departmental Committee on Wheat Growing,*

21–2 and 89–93; *Handbook for Agricultural Statistics, 1904–50* (Pretoria, 1961) 54. The number of wheat-reaping machines in the Orange Free State dropped from 1258 in 1911 to 979 in 1926, if census statistics are to be believed. *Handbook for Agricultural Statistics*, 14.

57. *Volksraadsnotule*, 4 May 1893, 60–5; ibid, 12 July 1898, 831; 11 April 1899, 92; Jacobs, 'Ontwikkeling van Landbou', ch. 4.
58. See S. Marks and S. Trapido, 'Lord Milner and the South African State', *History Workshop Journal*, 9 (1980).
59. Interview, T. R. Mmolotsi.
60. See pp. 28–9.
61. See pp. 72–4.
62. There were also considerations of a demographic nature, related to electoral calculations. South Africa could only be made to favour the Empire, it was thought, by overwhelming the Boers numerically. The zeal with which the British approached the task of reconstruction is evident in the policy that Dutch titles and terminology should be abolished (CS 894/02, Colonial Secretary, ORC, 25 March 1902). Most republican officials were replaced by pro-Empire loyalists.
63. See ORC, *Annual Report of the Department of Agriculture, 1903–04* (Bloemfontein, 1904).
64. CO 224/30, Report of the Land Settlement Board, 1908–9, 22 November 1909. By 1906, when land purchases had virtually stopped, the ORC administration had bought 1 109 081 acres at £846 184. Including state land inherited from the republican regime, 1 457 541 acres had been allotted to settlers by the end of 1909. Ibid; CO 224/23, Report of the Land Settlement Board, 1905–6, 7 January 1907.
65. See Annual Reports cited in previous footnote, as well as CO 224/26, 17 August 1908.
66. CO 224/30, Report of the Land Settlement Board, 1908–9, 22 November 1909. (The words are those of Governor Goold-Adams.)
67. See CO 224/18, Departmental Reports, 1904–5, 30 October 1905.
68. See CO 224/28, W. D. Drew, October 1908. Drew, former editor of *The Friend*, wrote that many had failed because their land was overvalued (a major complaint after the slump in land values from 1904) and because 'they wasted their money on tillage which in this colony is at best speculation, and for stock their farms were too small and too dear'.
69. CO 224/7, 29 April 1902; CO 224/22, T. A. Hill, 20 June 1906; CO 224/31, A. P. Francis, 2 February 1909; CO 224/33, Governor Goold-Adams, 24 January 1910.
70. CO 224/13, Sir H. Goold-Adams, 15 May 1903; 'The Westminster Estate', *FA*, September 1908, 47.
71. CO 224/13, ISAA, 13 July 1903, 9 November 1903; CO 224/16, ISAA, 5 February 1904; CO 224/23, Departmental Reports, Year ending 30 June 1906.
72. Colonial Office officials in London with their more prosaic visions than the social imperialists were never as convinced of their capacity to reforge the world. See CO 224/13, ISAA, 11 November 1903.
73. More on the significance of the Land Bank is found on pp. 168–9.
74. See *Men of the Times: Old Colonists of the Cape Colony and the Orange River Colony* (Cape Town, 1906) 631–2. By the time of his death in 1925, Gradwell

owned 40 000 morgen and had 2000 beasts in his prize Afrikander herd as well as over 10 000 merino sheep. Obituary in *South Africa*, 20 February 1925, 331.

75. H. W. Stockdale who farmed near Clocolan advertised in 1895–6 that he would make his threshing machines available to any company of farmers who could guarantee that their grain would be gathered at one place. 'Boettie Boett', Arcadia, Winburg, to editor, *Friend*, 3 January 1896.

76. 'Important to Free State Farmers', *Friend*, 9 June 1891; 'Jottings from the Conquered Territory', *Friend*, 6 April 1894; 'Chips from Moroka', *Friend*, 4 September 1891; 'Notes from Ladybrand and District', *Friend*, 15 December 1893.

77. In January 1891 a report vividly described the daily sight of eighty to 100 wagons outspanned at Robertson's mills, loaded with wheat in the ear waiting their turn at the threshing machine, while others waited with loads of threshed grain to be put through the mill. 'Chips from Thaba Nchu', *Friend*, 13 January 1891.

78. On the Prynnsberg estate, see 'Jottings from the Conquered Territory', *Friend*, 16 March 1894; 'Chips from Moroka', *Friend*, 15 April 1892; 'Opening of the new Leeuw River Mills', *Friend*, 1 August 1893; 'Notes from Ladybrand and District', *Friend*, 18 August 1893; F. J. Harper, Platkop, to editor, *FA*, December 1912, 193; CS 4873/07, Director of Agricuture, 19 July 1907.

79. Evidence regarding these booms and land transactions in the Cape, especially that found in the Cape Colonial Annual Blue Books, is too voluminous to be listed in detail here. See K. W. Smith, *From Frontier to Midlands: A History of the Graaff-Reinet District, 1786–1910* (Grahamstown, 1976).

80. Thus J. A. Sugden, inspector for the Land Settlement Department, estimated in 1908 that six post-war immigrants into the Bethlehem district (Ross, Hall, Woodgate, the Andersons, the Woods and Harding) had brought in over £40 000 in cash and stock. CO 224/26, 17 August 1908. Generally, see SBA, Branch Inspection Reports, *passim*.

81. On Nourse, see *Dictionary of South African Biography*, vol. 3 (Pretoria, 1977) 659–60; *Men of the Times: Pioneers of the Transvaal and Glimpses of South Africa* (Johannesburg, 1905) 28–9. Nourse owned the Nourse mine and owned 25 000 acres in Harrismith district on which his brother farmed. On this estate, 1040 acres were cultivated in 1906, and the land supported 1065 head of cattle, 3683 sheep, 377 pigs and 255 horses (NAB 861/07, J. B. Gedye, 27 August 1907). Bailey's farm, Zeekoevlei, in Vrede district, was 13 327 acres in extent; he also headed a syndicate which owned twenty-one farms (100 000 acres) near Colesberg south of the Orange river on which 65 000 merino sheep grazed in 1910. 'Free State: Our Production and Possibilities', *Friend*, 20 January 1911; E. Rosenthal, *Other Men's Millions* (Cape Town, n.d.) 178. On Marks' and Lewis's farming activities, see *Dictionary of South African Biography*, vol. 1 (Pretoria, 1968) 515–18; 'A Great Property', *FA*, October 1907, 85–90.

82. DA 1915/2/09, G. H Daw, Karree Stn, 24 June 1909; CS 3832/04, PME Co., 26 May 1904; ORC, *Report of Committee on Leasing of Government Farms* (Bloemfontein, 1904) 35–6.

83. 'Another Diamond Mine', *Friend*, 20 May 1898; 'The Steam Plough',

Friend, 3 May 1898; 'Mr Minter's Steam Plough', *Friend*, 20 May 1898; 'A Rare Chance', *Friend*, 27 May 1898; G. Baumann and E. Bright, *Lost Republic: The Biography of a Land Surveyor* (London, 1940) 141–52.

84. A. P. Cartwright, *The First South African: The Life and Times of Sir Percy Fitzpatrick* (Cape Town, 1971) 119–20; advertisement, *FW*, 9 April 1913, 314. On the transformation of the 'political economy of hunting', see S. Trapido, 'Poachers, Proletarians and Gentry in the Early Twentieth Century Transvaal', unpublished paper, 1984. Charles Newberry imported four sable antelopes and an eland from Rhodesia in 1908 (G 198/07, 7 November 1907). More spectacularly, Karl Wolff of Mosenthal, the giant merchant house in Port Elizabeth, received official approval in 1907 for his plans to establish a 100-square-mile game reserve in the north of the Boshof district. He had inherited 40 square miles of land in this undeveloped region from his father-in-law, Emanuel Fichardt, and the rest was owned by the government, by W. Barlow and by H. Klynveld, a wealthy Bethulie lawyer (CS 4797/07, H. Mosenthal, 22 June 1907; CS 5151/07, de Villiers and Brebner, 28 November 1907). Many landowners earned an income from charging hunting fees on their land. See CS 717/03, A. Ranger and C. W. Malcomess, East London, 26 January 1903.

85. 'Mr S. G. Vilonel at De Rust', *FA*, March 1908, 371–3.

86. 'Farmers of Orangia', *FA*, April 1908, 413–15; 'African Farms Ltd', *FA*, June 1908, 573; 'Our Weekly Causerie', *FW*, 10 July 1918, 2099. Similarly, Grant's Farming Company was launched with subscribed capital of £16 000 in London in 1899 under the chairmanship of Miles Miley for the working of the farm Baviaankranz of 10 000 acres in the Orange Free State. CO 224/9, 23 September 1902; CS 593/03, 24 January 1903.

87. Baumann and Bright, *Lost Republic*, 141–52; S. Trapido, 'A History of Tenant Production on the Vereeniging Estates, 1896–1920' in W. Beinart and P. Delius (eds) *Putting a Plough to the Ground* (Johannesburg and London, 1986); SBA, Inspection Reports, Kroonstad: 1915.

88. R. Seggie, Holfontein, to editor, *Friend*, 22 February 1912.

89. DA 1997/1/09, Sir P. Fitzpatrick, 14 June 1909. On the Westminster Estate, steam ploughing was computed to cost 5s 5d per acre, allowing for the employment of a blacksmith at £15 per month, two engineers at £30 per month, eight black workers at £12, and 25 tons of coal at £37 10s per month. On the other hand, the steam plough ploughed to a depth of 14 inches and turned 14 acres of soil a day. Ibid.

90. See Jacobs, 'Ontwikkeling van Landbou', 336–9.

91. See pp. 23, 24–5.

92. See, for example, S. J. de Swardt and J. C. Neethling, *Report on an Economic Investigation into Farming in Four Maize Districts of the Orange Free State, 1928–30*, Economic Series no. 22, Department of Agriculture (Pretoria, 1937).

5 The making of a servile tenantry

1. See pp. 86–95.

2. K. R. Macaskill to editor, *Friend*, 16 November 1911. See also NAB 8,

Encl. 7, J. N. B. Beyers, Wydgelegen, to RM Harrismith, 10 September 1905.

3. 'Kleinspeen' to editor, *FW*, 30 August 1911.
4. See A. D. J. Taylor, Aberfeldy, Harrismith, to editor, *FW*, 16 August 1911.
5. 'No Compulsion', Thaba Nchu, to editor, *FW*, 15 January 1913.
6. 'Legislative Assembly', *Friend*, 1 July 1908.
7. See pp. 124–8.
8. See pp. 132–40.
9. Cd. 1897, *Transvaal Labour Commission*, 1903–4, Evidence, 687 (para. 10 663).
10. For example, see *BBNA*, 1910, 256; UG 37–1912, *Annual Report of the Department of Justice*, 209.
11. Inevitably conflict often resulted from the failure of the crops, for the tenant then felt cheated of the rewards of his services. See comments of RM Reitz, *BBNA*, 1910, 252; also interviews, J. Masina, 13; J. Moiloa, 33–4.
12. NAB 8, Encl. 10, J. M. McCalman, JP, 9 October 1905; *BBNA*, 1910, 154 (RM Harrismith).
13. See SAIRR, *Farm Labour in the Orange Free State* (Johannesburg, 1939) 17–18.
14. *The Orange River Colony: Its Resources and Development* (Bloemfontein, 1906) 30; *Volksraadsnotule*, 11 May 1898, 335 (C. van der Wath, Moroka); J. A. Bosch, *Ladybrand, 1867–1967* (Bloemfontein, 1967) 111; F. A. S. Schimper, Winburg, to editor, *Friend*, 24 December 1894; SC 3A–1912, *Select Committee on Native Affairs*, 95–6 (W. Robertson, RM Bethlehem); LBD, 4/4, 276, State *v.* September, 20 February 1897.
15. F. Blersch, *Handbook of Agriculture for South Africa* (Cape Town, 1906) 119.
16. GS 795, 63–6, D. Scott, February 1889.
17. *NLC*, Evidence, 11; *SANAC*, 1903–5, vol. 4, para. 38 786.
18. LBD 4/3, 29–36, State *v.* Pikinien, 22 January 1891.
19. See 'Notes from Ladybrand and District', *Friend*, 12 January 1894.
20. *Volksraadsnotule*, 28 April 1897, 242 (J. P. Roux, wyk Wepener). The difficulties of procuring seasonal labour from Basutoland were gravely aggravated by the rinderpest regulations in 1896–7 which restricted the movement of Africans across the border, causing forty Ladybrand farmers to petition the president to establish a fumigation station to facilitate the passage of 'disinfected' Sotho on to the farms to reap. GS 814, 132–5, F. Johnson, 5 December 1896.
21. W. Milligan to editor, *Friend*, 6 June 1893.
22. 'Jottings from Senekal', *Friend*, 9 November 1894; see also *Volksraadsnotule*, 26 April 1897, 213; 29 April 1895, 313; 8 May 1895, 410 (P. de Wet, Bethlehem); Editorial in *Friend*, 19 October 1911.
23. See 'Senekal Jottings', 12 December 1893; 'Notes from Basutoland and the Conquered Territory', 11 December 1894; 'Ladybrand', 6 December 1895, all in *Friend*. Imports of agricultural implements into the Orange Free State increased from £13 000 to £19 400 between 1892 and 1893. The value of grain bags imported increased by 50 per cent. 'The Trade of the State', *Friend*, 16 March 1894. On 1911 see JUS 1/566/11, Annual Reports, 1911: Thaba Nchu, Rouxville, Zastron, Smithfield, Lindley, Ficksburg; and

'Country Day By Day' column in *Friend*, 7 October, 3 November, 2 December, 8 December, 14 December 1911; 'Our Weekly Causerie' column in *FW*, 27 December 1911, 625, 14 February 1912, 985; DA 2221/16/11, Manager, Bestersput, 19 October 1911; 'The Wheat Crop', *Friend*, 16 December 1911. Reaping machines could clear some 7 to 15 acres in a day, and they cost £18–25. Blersch, *Handbook*, 121.

24. H. G. Stuart to editor, *FA*, September 1912, 25.
25. See UG 42–1919, *Report of the Departmental Committee on Wheat Growing; Native Farm Labour Committee*, 1937–9 (Pretoria, 1939) 53–4. See pp. 107–8.
26. See *Volksraadsnotule*, 26 April 1897, 233.
27. J. Burtt-Davy, *Maize: Its History, Cultivation, Handling and Uses with Special Reference to South Africa* (London, 1914) 461; interview, J. Moiloa, 34 and 40–1.
28. 'A Maize Reaper and Binder', *FA*, September 1911, 33.
29. H. D. Leppan and G. J. Bosman, *Field Crops in South Africa* (Johannesburg, 1923) 253.
30. Ibid, 92–3.
31. JUS 1/401/10, Annual Report, 1910; see also Burtt-Davy, *Maize*, 451–2.
32. But see *NLC*, 288 (A. J. Kerslake, JP, Standerton) and 323 (W. G. van E. Schuurman, RM Bethal).
33. See CS 5116/04, RM Frankfort, 9 July 1904. Of course, harvest labour requirements were not inconsiderable for maize, especially as acreages became more and more extensive. Rev. F. A. Amor of Kroonstad vividly described the nature of this seasonal labour force in 1929:

> Just now . . . we have come to the 'slump' period of Free State mission work. Congregations are about half what they might be . . . church life is as dead as the frostbitten grass of the Veld . . . . Hardly a day has gone by during the past month without a request for a letter of commendation. 'Where to?' and the answer always is 'To the farms for the Harvest'. And so the congregation goes: first the older women, then the younger; near the end of term begins a huge exodus from the school; all going off to the farms, ten, twenty, thirty miles away, or even further, to help gather in the maize harvest . . . . The farmer provides them with bags to stuff the cobs into and pays them so much per bag filled . . . . When all the lands have been reaped they will present themselves at the farmer's office and in return for their chits will receive the payment due them. If it is still early on in the season they may trek off to another farm, but generally they return to town, settle up their debts, buy new clothes, look a little better fed; and then church life begins again.

United Society for the Propagation of the Gospel Archives, Series E, Missionary Reports, Rev. F. A. Amor, Kroonstad, 17 June 1929.

34. Interview, T. R. Mmolotsi, 35–7, also 33 and 44.
35. See pp. 76–9.
36. See, for example, interview, K. Phalime, 3, 10, 13, 14.
37. E. Webb to editor, *Friend*, 4 October 1911.
38. It should be reiterated here that the 'labour tenantry' did not constitute a discrete group on the farms in contradistinction to the sharecroppers.

Many families moved regularly from one form of tenancy to another. Strategies of survival and accumulation changed according to circumstances. Often sharecropping arrangements were combined with obligations on junior family members to render some labour service. Most tenant families experienced cycles of accumulation and dispossession. Apart from a Christian elite, who perhaps had greater access to off-farm income, the often considerable differentiation between tenant households tended often to be transient and contingent. Chapter 3 provides the background to this discussion. Further, labour tenancy was not incompatible with considerable prosperity as commercial producers, especially on very extensive landholdings. See interviews, N. Makume; D. Thukwe.

39. See M. Nkadimeng and G. Relly, 'Kas Maine: The Story of a Black South African Agriculturalist' in B. Bozzoli (ed.) *Town and Countryside in the Transvaal: Capitalist Penetration and Popular Response* (Johannesburg, 1983) for an example of one such farmer.

40. T. Matsetela, 'The Life Story of Nkgono Mma-Pooe' in S. Marks and R. Rathbone (eds) *Industrialization and Social Change in South Africa* (London, 1982) 21; see also interview, J. Molete, 9.

41. See K. R. Macaskill, Ruilplaats, Clocolan, to editor, *Friend*, 16 November 1911.

42. See VR 597 and VR 598, evidence before the Labour Commission, 1895, *passim*.

43. It did, however, provide ineffectively for *pro deo* representation of Africans suing in civil courts for unpaid wages. The law is to be found in ch. CXI of the *Orange Free State Law Book* (Bloemfontein, 1901).

44. For a sampling, see: LBD 4/3, 146, State *v.* Thae, 12 May 1891; KRS 7/9, 257–61, State *v.* Piet and September, 20 May 1890; LFI 1/1/4/1/1, 213, State *v.* Matoane, 7 September 1895; ibid, 124, State *v.* Jack, 30 December 1892. See pp. 142–9 on the function of local courts.

45. Matsetela, 'Life Story', 231–2. See also interviews, D. Thukwe, 2; K. Phalime, 10–11; J. Moiloa, 12; T. Mmolotsi, 37; GS 806, 56, J. A. Collins, *landdros*, Ladybrand, 28 August 1893.

46. Interview, J. Molete, 6.

47. See LBD 4/3, 29–36, State *v.* Pikinien, 22 January 1891; LBD 4/4, 275–80, State *v.* September, 20 February 1897; LFI 1/1/4/1/1, 210–11, State *v.* Mousa, 9 October 1897; GS 1272, 220–47, J. A. Collins, *landdros*, Ladybrand, to Assistant Commissioner, Maseru, 13 October 1893.

48. Interview, N. Makume, II, 24–6 and 31; also Matsetela, 'Life Story', 224; LFI 1/1/4/2/1, 360–2, State *v.* Klaas, 27 August 1895. See also interview, D. Makiri, 9, for another case of a landlord providing new tenants with a wagon and oxen for the move.

49. Interview, N. Makume, II, 26.

50. K. R. Macaskill, Ruilplaats, Clocolan, to editor, *Friend*, 16 November 1911. A Thaba Nchu farmer wrote in 1911 of the 'pernicious' practice of hiring Africans without any documents: 'The consequence is that we are the victims frequently of these natives, who are really roamers, and in many cases worthless individuals'. E. D. Holmes, Thaba Nchu, to editor, *FW*, 8 November 1911, 313; also A. D. J. Taylor, Aberfeldy, Harrismith, to

editor, *FW*, 16 August 1911, 13; Jim Human, Welgelegen, to editor, *FW*, 5 February 1913, 1874, for advocacy of testimonials.

51. LHS 181, R 886/09, R. J. Hall, 22 December 1909.
52. T. Newton, Pittani, Tiger River Station, to editor, *FW*, 13 December 1911. For revealing cases of desertion of sons at earlier times see LFI 1/1/4/2/1, 247–8, State *v.* Lilo, 22 February 1894; LFI 1/1/4/1/1, 259–60, State *v.* Kanon, 24 December 1897; KRS 7/9, 104–6, State *v.* Willem, 4 September 1895.
53. S. F. Papenfus, Harrismith, to editor, *FW*, 18 October 1911. See Abram Mofulu's evidence before *NLC*, 58; he had three or four children who ran away, as a consquence of which he was driven from the farm.
54. Interview, J. Moiloa, 19–20 and 22.
55. KRS 7/9, 124–30, State *v.* Jonas, 18 November 1895. See also the similar case in KRS 6/12, State *v.* Swartbooi, 26 May 1894.
56. KRS 7/9, 116–17, State *v.* Armoed, 2 November 1895.
57. LHS 171, R 538/09, R. A. Luck, 15 June 1909; LHS 171, R 476/09, R. A. Luck, 21 June 1909. In another case, Achem considered it necessary in disputing J. G. Berry's claim to the labour of his son, to inform the *landdrost*'s court in Ladybrand that 'I bought the accused's mother and paid for her' (LBD 4/4, 279, State *v.* September, 20 February 1897). Generational conflict could be infused with competition between white employers of labour as well. See LIN 1/4, 11, Captain Cagney, 25 February 1904.
58. Interview, R. Mogoai, 2–7.
59. VR 598, 156 and 237 (M. H. Steyn, Heilbron); *Legislative Council Debates*, 25 January 1906, 41; also CS 7816/04, ORC Central Farmers' Union, 11 October 1904; 'Bethlehem Native Affairs Congress', *Friend*, 6 November 1908.
60. NA 2626/1912/126, Orange Free State Native Fund. On the other hand the Eastern Natives Vigilance Association in 1913 proposed that children working on farms should receive due wages as a reward for their toil. *NLC*, Appendix X, 1–2.
61. Interview, J. Moiloa, 48–50.
62. LBD 4/4, 470–2, State *v.* April, 5 November 1898.
63. See W. Burns-Thompson, *Legislative Council Debates*, 25 January 1906, 41, on attitudes of black heads of families, who, he said, preferred their women to have to carry passes.
64. ORC, *Natives Administration Commission*, 1909 (Cape Town, 1911) 10. The witness recommended that only unmarried girls should have to carry passes, 'which would render it less easy for them to desert from service and run away to the town'.
65. J. Wells, 'Why Women Rebel: Women's Resistance in Bloemfontein, 1913, and Johannesburg, 1958', *Journal of Southern African Studies*, 10, 2 (1984).
66. Art. 3, Law 4–1895. See KRS 7/9, 261–2, State *v.* Sara and three others, 25 June 1897.
67. VR 598, 227; see VR 597 and VR 598 for evidence before the commission; also VR 343, 233–6, ninety-three Winburg burghers, April 1890; VR 393, 16–18, 119 burghers of wyk Kaalspruit, 21 November 1895.
68. VR 598, 240.

69. See, for example, VR 597, 107, F. H. Becker, Winburg; various petitions in VR 381, 1895.

70. VR 597, 88, D. M. Botha, *vrederechter*, Meriba, 1892.

71. For example, VR 339, 38–9, eighteen burghers of Vrede, February 1890. For debate on the issue, see *Volksraadsnotule*, 10 June 1890, 447–51 and 21 May 1892, 236–8.

72. VR 598, 187, C. G. Radloff, Ficksburg, 1 February 1893; VR 598, 160, J. Robertson, *landdros*, Ficksburg, 19 January 1893.

73. VR 597, 100, J. A. Collins, December 1892.

74. See LFI 1/1/4/2/1, 144, State *v.* Januari, 9 February 1893, for a case in which a *landdros* dismissed a charge of desertion from service on the grounds that Januari (a sharecropper) was a 'contractor' not a servant.

75. VR 597, 148, G. J. B. de Wet, wyk Midden Liebenbergsvlei, Bethlehem, 14 January 1893; VR 597, 79, A. P. Cronje, Welgelegen, Winburg, 22 December 1892.

76. Art. 20, Law 4–1895. On the law, see pp. 57–9.

77. The law of 1904 also applied to white workers for the first time, although they were treated separately, and were excluded from the wide-ranging criminal sanctions imposed on blacks, which were taken over in their entirety from the republican law.

78. *Cases on Review and Appeal, 1903–06* (Bloemfontein, 1907) 85. See also cases of C. Bookholane, P. Pgonyama, and J. Bangisane, ibid, 75. See remarks of J. G. Keyter, MLA, *NLC*, Evidence, 50–1.

79. ORC Law Department, *Codified Circular Instructions* (Bloemfontein, 1906) 43–4.

80. LHS 172, R 139/10, E. Cameron, Bughtie, 3 March 1910. The importance of this issue for white farmers is revealed in the evidence of J. F. van Iddekinge, RM Bethlehem, SC 6A–1917, *Report of the Select Committee on Native Affairs*, 431–46. Provision was made in the 1913 Natives Land Act to extend the Orange Free State masters-and-servants law to all tenants, thereby resurrecting the provisions included in Law 4 of 1895. See pp. 192–3.

81. *Landdrosts* (magistrates) and resident *vrederechters* (JPs) were salaried officials without legal training – the latter resident in smaller centres away from the district town where the *landdros* would hold court. The *vrederechters* were likely to be local landed notables whose judicial functions took up only a small portion of their time. *Landdrosts* were full-time administrators as well as court officials. The sixty cases heard in 1899 by the resident *vrederechter* in Reitz, a small court which was less patronized than many, probably gives a typical breakdown: twenty-six cases of *landlopery* (i.e. pass laws), twelve masters-and-servants cases, five cases of improper clothing, three breaches of the peace, three assaults, three thefts, two of drunkenness, and six involving municipal regulations.

82. For an example of acquittal of a farmer charged with assault, see LBD 4/4, 202–3, State *v.* J. H. Krynauw, 12 January 1896. Krynauw admitted assault, but argued that it was justified as Kleinbooi (a sharecropper) appeared late when called upon to work for him. The court agreed.

83. These conclusions are based on a detailed perusal of a number of record books of various *vrederechters* and *landdrosts* in Bothaville, Viljoensdrift, Ladybrand, Ficksburg and Kroonstad in the 1890s (including minutes of

evidence). Given the fact that so little of this type of material survives, it is impossible to say to what extent these conclusions can be generalized.

84. LBD 4/4, 275–80, State *v.* September, 20 February 1897; also the similar case in KRS 6/12, State *v.* Zwartbooi, 26 May 1894 in which a law agent, M. L. Beukes, also appeared for the convicted African on appeal.

85. KRS 7/9, 86, State *v.* Krisjan, 15 April 1895.

86. *Volksraadsnotule*, 29 April 1895, 299. Specific instances are found in LFI 1/1/4/2/1, 367–8, State *v.* Pekoe, 25 and 27 September 1895; *Cases on Review and Appeal*, 73, R. *v.* J. Matsi. It was for this reason both the Masters and Servants Ordinance (7–1904, Art. 43) and the Pass Laws Amendment Ordinance (9–1906, Art. 10) protected servants against prosecution for desertion or under the pass laws if they had been denied a pass to enable them to lay a charge against their masters.

87. GS 800, 128–9, J. Bothma, 16 January 1891.

88. LFI 1/1/4/2/1, 3, State *v.* Kleingeld, 2 September 1891; also see ibid, 222, State *v.* Lena, 10 November 1893.

89. The resident magistrates appointed to take over civil administration after the war were for the most part British, many of them ex-army officers, who were unfamiliar with local conditions and unable to communicate in Afrikaans. JPs were drawn from the local notables, prominent farmers, commercial agents and even police officers – mainly persons 'of a certain amount of leisure and private means' in the words of the Attorney General. However, the colonial administration after the war ensured that appointees were loyalists. *Legislative Council Debates*, 21 February 1907, 51.

90. *Conference of Resident Magistrates* (Bloemfontein, 1906) 9.

91. *Legislative Council Debates*, 27 January 1903, 35 (Ord. 6–1903). At first only ten 'Special' JPs were appointed and 173 'Honorary' JPs (usually 'landowners and local magnates' without judicial functions).

92. See Attorney General's remarks in *Legislative Council Debates*, 21 February 1907, 51–2; also 13 January 1905, 10–12.

93. See *Codified Circular Instructions*, 24–5.

94. A sample is to be found in *Remarks of the Judges of the High Court in Quashing and Altering Sentences of RMs and Special JPs* (Bloemfontein, 1903–04) vol. 1, 20 and 30–2; vol. 2, 5 and 8–9; vol. 3, 23–4. See also 'High Court', *Friend*, 12 December 1904; 'Quashed Sentences', *Friend*, 23 November 1905.

95. For example, *Cases on Review*, 41.

96. Ibid, 82. An effort in 1919 to amend the ORC Masters and Servants Ordinance so as to define all Africans on farms up to the age of 21 as minors was rejected. The Labour members in the Union parliament condemned the proposal as a return to slavery. 'Agriculture in Parliament', *FW*, 26 February 1919, 2855. The OFS Agricultural Union in 1924 called for a law to make the head of the family responsible for the whole family in contracts of tenancy. 'Free State Congress', *FW*, 20 August 1924, 2364.

97. *Cases on Review*, 83.

98. CS 3652/04, RM Ficksburg, 25 June and 16 May 1904. See also CS 3829/04, RM Bethlehem, 14 August 1904. C. Newberry of Clocolan wrote in May 1904 that the country people suffered great inconvenience as a

result: 'Many small grievances between masters and servants which could be satisfactorily dealt with by such JPs are now suffered rather than journey to the towns perhaps more than once to get them attended to'. He added that there were 'good, just and experienced' men who could safely be entrusted with this function. CS 3422/04, C. Newberry, 6 May 1904. See also CS 7816/04, ORC Central Farmers' Union, 11 October 1904; CS 3837/04, ORC CFU, 28 May 1904, for an indication of the strength of farmers' feelings on this matter. As late as 1913, farmers still looked back to the republican period as a golden age when the authorities were at their disposal for the enforcement of their will. See 'Masters and Servants', *FA*, May 1913, 481.

99. *Legislative Council Debates*, 23 July 1908, 92. See also *Conference of Resident Magistrates*, 8 and 18 for the suggestion that unpaid men be appointed as SJPs to overcome the fiscal restraints involved, a proposal shot down by the Chief Justice as subversive of judicial standards.

100. *Legislative Council Debates*, 18 June 1908, 302 and 305.

101. Ibid, 90–3.

102. 'Native Association Congress', *Friend*, 27 February 1909.

103. See pp. 163–5.

104. 'A Warning', *Friend*, 12 February 1895; 'Feeling among the Basutos', *Friend*, 19 February 1895.

105. LHS 168, R 869/07, Cpl, SAC, Bughtie, 31 August 1907; LHS 154, R 303/11, N. Parry, 21 July 1911. See also J. M. Theunissen, *Volksraadsnotule*, 29 April 1895, 299. The SAIRR investigation in the 1930s noted that debt bondage was very widespread on the farms – typically £10 per worker. It was common for employers to state on passes the indebtedness of the bearer in order to deter other farmers from employing him/her. *Farm Labour in the Orange Free State*, 39.

106. VR 597, Labour Commission, 109–10, Z. J. de Beer, Harrismith, 7 January 1893; ibid, 41–2, *vrederechter*, Moroka; VR 598, 175, *landdros*, Boshof; ibid, 231–2, J H. Meiring.

107. On the other hand it was not uncommon for a difference of opinion to arise over the duration of a contract. The complaint by white farmers that Africans interpreted a year to mean ten months reflected the duration of a full productive cycle in arable farming, from ploughing to reaping. African tenants wishing to move attempted to do so as soon as the harvest was in, in about June. See LHS 169, R 491/08, W. Newton, Newton Dale, Harrismith, 12 June 1908. See also *Volksraadsnotule*, 29 April 1895, 298 and 24 April 1895, 276. An example of conflict over the duration of contracts and non-payment of wages is found in KRS 7/9, 141–2, State *v.* C. S. Roberts (Civil Case), 24 January 1968.

108. LHS 160, H. Mundy, Somersby, 8 September 1911 and 21 September 1911; LHS 159, X 139/04, H. Mundy, 12 August 1909. See also LHS 160, R 661/08, J. A. Schoeman, Bergvliet, 17 July 1908; LHS 169, R 969/07, RM to George Liddell, 7 August 1907; ibid, G. Liddell to RM, 9 August 1907.

109. See also LHS 170, R 378/09, A. D. J. Taylor, Aberfeldy Station, 13 May 1909.

110. LHS 159, X 51/07, H. Mundy, 21 February 1907.

111. LHS 169, R 551/08, G. Robinson, 8 June 1908.

112. 'Bethlehem Native Affairs Congress', *Friend*, 6 November 1908; ORC, *Natives Administration Commission*, 10; KRS 7/9, 117–18, State *v.* G. Heath, 2 November 1895.

113. LHS 162, R 164/04, J. N. van der Bosch, 1904. See also LHS 154, R 113/11, R. A. Luck, 17 March 1911; ibid, R 132/11, R. A. Luck, 29 March 1911; R 155/11, R. A. Luck, 17 April 1911; R 306/11, B. G. Oosthuyse, 24 July 1911.

114. See VR 393, 10–11, four burghers of wyk Midden Liebenbergsvlei, Bethlehem, 1895; 'Burgher', Kaallaagte, to editor, *Friend*, 21 May 1895; LIN 1/4, B. J. de Lange, Reitz, 20 December 1904.

115. CS 8632/04, ORC Central Farmers' Union, 10 November 1904; Circular 8632/04, in LHS 137, A 364/04. See also ORC, *Natives Administration Commission*, 10; CS 3400/4/04, J. A. Sugden, 11 April 1907; 'Take It From Me', Frankfort, to editor, *FW*, 16 October 1912, 437.

116. 'Fair Play', Winburg, to editor, *Friend*, 12 March 1897.

117. SAIRR, *A Community Man* (Johannesburg, 1983) 8.

118. Ibid; also see 'Police Irregularities', *Friend*, 24 April 1894.

119. VR 333, 152, Opgaaf der manschappen . . . 28 February 1890; 'Stock Thefts', *Friend*, 6 December 1892; *Volksraadsnotule*, May 1893, 257–65, and January 1894, 36–43 and 75–6; 'The Mounted Police', *Friend*, 22 February 1898. As a result of the *Diensmacht*'s activities, in 1894–5 3825 persons were punished, 2782 of them under the pass laws, and 147 blacks under the masters-and-servants law. It is probable that whereas the *Diensmacht* were well-placed to indulge in mass arrests of Africans under the pass laws, masters generally went straight to the nearest court with recalcitrant servants, which would explain this discrepancy. A more accurate reflection is provided by statistics that a couple of thousand masters-and-servants cases came before the courts annually under colonial rule. *OVS Oranjeboek, 1895: Rapport van den Kommandant de Rydende Diensmacht* (Bloemfontein, 1895); *ORC Police, Report of the Commissioner, 1908* (Bloemfontein) 7.

120. A. P. J. van Rensburg, 'Die Ekonomiese Herstel van die Afrikaner in die Oranjerivier-Kolonie, 1902–07', *Archives Year Book for South African History*, 1967, 2 (Pretoria, 1967) 193–5.

121. *Offisieël Verslag van die Brandfort-kongres* (Bloemfontein, 1905) 68–71.

122. LHS 159, X 27/07, Cpl W. Culling, Aberfeldy Station, 8 February 1907.

123. See C. J. P. le Roux, 'Die Verhouding tussen Blank en nie-Blank in die Oranjerivier-Kolonie, 1900–10', D.Litt. thesis, Rand Afrikaans University, 1980.

124. This decision was confirmed in 1910, when it was laid down that the pass law 'is merely directed against vagrancy and does not apply to natives who have a fixed abode, and are merely on a visit to neighbouring farms'. Quoted in SC 8–1914, *Report of the Select Committee on Native Affairs*, Appendix A, xii. The judicial history of the pass laws was summarized by J. G. Keyter in a speech in 1914 urging that the original intentions of the law be reconfirmed in statute. *House of Assembly Debates*, 1914, cols 903–5 and generally cols 903–21.

125. 'Industries Commission: Evidence by Free State Farmers', *FW*, 1 July 1911, 16. See also 'Disgusted Farmer', Senekal, to editor, *Friend*, 24 February 1909.

126. See M. Lacey, *Working for Boroko: The Origins of a Coercive Labour System in South Africa* (Johannesburg, 1981) chs 4 and 5.

127. See 'A Warning', *Friend*, 12 February 1895; 'Feeling Among the Basotho', *Friend*, 19 February 1895; 'South Africa Today', *Friend*, 5 March 1906. It is perhaps significant that in one expression of popular folklore, there was 'no government' in republican days. 'You were in the hands of whichever Boer was around', maintains Philip Masike, born in Thaba Nchu in 1889. Further, there were no jails before the Anglo-Boer War, he asserts. If an African did wrong, he was killed or thrashed, and those responsible were never prosecuted. 'If you were lashed with the *kats*, you knew they felt pity for you; you might have been punished by the *veldcornet*. . . . People were shot and there was no court case.' Masike's interpretation of the Peace of Vereeniging in 1902 was that the British agreed to hand the blacks back to the control of the Boers, with the provision that the latter stop killing and thrashing them. Lord Kitchener, recounts Masike, 'said that he would build a jail for people who violated the laws and regulations. If a person was found guilty of an offence, he would be sent to jail'. Interview, P. M. Masike, 12–13, 15 and 19. See pp. 145–7 on British judicial reform in relation to the suppression of corporal punishment.

128. Interview, N. Makume, I, 13–15. Much the same story of life in Harrismith district before 1912 is told by Josiah Moloi, interview, 29–30; also E. Moloko, 23–4; and P. M. Masike, 12–13.

129. LHS 172, deposition of J. Odendaal, JP, 3 March 1910.

130. *SANAC*, 1903–5, vol. 4 (para. 39 035); 'Agricola' to editor, *FW*, 16 August 1911, 12; 'Onlooker', Bethlehem, to editor, *FW*, 13 December 1911, 522; 'Organize' to editor, *FW*, 13 November 1912, 788; Horatio P. Long, P. O. Rustig, to editor, *FW*, 25 June 1919, 2095; CS 4322/04, RM Ladybrand, 10 June 1904; see also Colonel J. J. Byron's revealing speech to the Legislative Council in *Friend*, 25 August 1908.

131. J. D. Spence, Good Hope, Bethlehem, to editor, *FA*, May 1907, 509. Zulu labour may have been more amenable after the suppression of the Bambatha rebellion in 1906; also see CS 242/1/08, E. Buttemer, Good Hope, Harrismith, 10 and 23 April 1908; Cd. 1897, 688 (paras 10 681–2, General Olivier, Lindley district).

132. A farmer in the eastern Orange Free State discovered that an 'educated' tenant worker on his farm was wilfully loosening bolts on farming implements in order to cause delays in the work. J. W. Goodes, Westminster, to editor, *FW*, 28 April 1920, 1149. See also 'Work or Starve' to editor, *FW*, 12 February 1913, 1972.

133. See B. Blenkinsop to editor, *FW*, 15 November 1908, 347; 'Pure-Bred Frieslands', *FW*, 15 March 1911, 19; G. Martin to editor, *FW*, 25 October 1911, 231; 'Hand-Feeding of Calves', *FA*, September 1911, 41; 'Legislative Council', *Friend*, 25 August 1908 (Colonel J. J. Byron); CS 1422/02, J. K. Hill, 17 May 1902.

134. 'A Maize Reaper and Binder', *FA*, September 1911, 33; 'Handicaps to Farming', *Friend*, 25 May 1912; 'The Ploughing Season', *FA*, September 1914, 20.

135. See Editorial, *Friend*, 19 October 1911; also H. Wolfe, *Main Problems in the Economics of Agricultural Production in South Africa*, Industries Bulletin Series (Pretoria, 1919) 4 and 34.

136. See C. van Onselen, 'The Witches of Suburbia: Domestic Service on the Witwatersrand, 1890–1914' in C. van Onselen, *Studies in the Social and Economic History of the Witwatersrand, 1886–1914*, vol. 2, *New Nineveh* (London, 1982); T. O. Ranger, 'The Invention of Tradition in Colonial Africa' in E. Hobsbawm and T. O. Ranger (eds) *The Invention of Tradition* (Cambridge, 1983). The almost desperate striving to maintain the traditions of gentility amongst settler women is reflected in women's writings of the day. See A. von Kotze, 'Teutonic Ladies and Their "Savages": Thoughts on Women Writers and Their Image of the Black Population of Colonial South West Africa, 1900–14', unpublished paper, 1984.

137. See Anna Davin, 'Imperialism and Motherhood', *History Workshop Journal*, 5 (1978). See also F. E. Huggett, *Life Below Stairs* (London, 1977) on the nature of housework and domestic relations in Victorian Britain.

138. 'Puzzled', OFS, to editor, *FW*, 4 October 1911, 116; also see Mrs Fred Strauss, Zevenfontein, Colesberg, to editor, *FW*, 20 December 1911, 568; C. G. B. to editor, *FW*, 31 December 1912; Mrs H. S. Viljoen, Greenlands, OFS, to editor, *FW*, 31 December 1912.

139. See pp. 5–6. See also *Farm Labour in the OFS*, 33; Olive Schreiner, *Thoughts on South Africa* (London, 1923, reprinted Johannesburg, 1976) on the nature of Boer paternalism.

140. 'A Family Poisoned', *Friend*, 10 December 1897; 'A "*Taai*" Afrikaner', *Friend*, 16 November 1897; HG 1/1/4/34, Case 1; LFI 1/1/5/1/1, 1–2, 6 February 1892.

141. 'Cattle Poisoning', *Friend*, 27 February 1909.

142. CS 7187/03, RM Fauresmith, 2 October 1903.

143. 'Incendiarism on Farms', *Friend*, 21 February 1912. Also GS 803, 100–4, J. A. Collins, *landdros*, Ladybrand, 17 March 1891: April, sentenced to 5 years and sixty strokes in 1888 for burning Piet Jordaan's wheat crop, swore to fellow prisoners that on release he would take revenge by poisoning Jordaan's cattle.

144. CS 1223/2/06, Commandant, SAC, 11 September 1907.

145. CS 1261/04, Colonel Pilkington, 24 February 1904.

146. J. W. Goodes, Westminster, to editor, *FW*, 28 April 1920, 1149.

147. W. T. Woods, Rietfontein, Winburg, to editor, *FW*, 8 November 1911, 312.

148. 'Observer' to editor, *FA*, January 1916, 277. See also *Farm Labour in the OFS*, 32: stock theft was 'almost certainly due to the absence of a meat ration or to downright hunger, and some farmers close their eyes to it provided it is not on too large a scale'. One farmer visited was content to lose up to twenty sheep a year. Also J. Dalrymple to editor, *Friend*, 16 March 1911.

149. See Russell Harding, Kimberley, to editor, *FW*, 2 October 1912, 274. Also 'Low Country Farmer' to editor, *FW*, 5 February 1919, 2437: 'The natives are past-masters in killing sheep and goats. Among their tricks are smothering them, driving a needle into the heart or the brain or inserting a pointed stick underneath the tail'. Also see 'Farm, Veld and Town', *FW*, 30 July 1924, 2067; HG 1/1/1/4, 292–6, State *v.* Zwartbooi, 17 April 1893, convicted of killing a sheep by inserting a needle in the base of its head; his landlord, G. P. Kemp, had lost ninety-five sheep in suspicious

circumstances and had always given the carcasses to his tenants for meat. See *FW*, 5 March 1924, 2590 for a similar case.

150. 'Zwaartland', Transvaal, to editor, *FW*, 13 February 1924, 2251. See also 'Farm, Veld and Town', *FW*, 17 September 1924, 82, for a case of prosecution of a farmer who wounded an African after taking this advice. Also 'A Peculiar Hanging Case', 26 March 1897; 'The Recent Hanging Case', 2 April 1897; 'Farm Thefts', 6 April 1897, all in *Friend*.

151. 'Notes from the Northern Cape', *FW*, 29 January 1913, 1807. See also *SANAC*, 1903–5, vol. 4 (para. 37 857); *NLC*, Evidence, 32 (RM Vrede); NAB 8, Encl. 10, J. M. McCalman, Belladale, Frankfort, 9 October 1905.

152. 'JB' to editor, *Friend*, 24 November 1905.

153. In 1894 'Sixpence' received ten lashes with the *kats* at the order of the *landdros* in Ladybrand for having urged young hirelings of one Basson, his employer, to desert as Basson was apparently in the habit of not paying his workers. LLA 4/4, 54, State *v.* Sixpence, 17 October 1894. See also A. D. J. Taylor, Aberfeldy, Harrismith, to editor, *FW*, 16 August 1911.

154. J. A. T. Jorissen, 'The Native Labour Problem', *FW*, 5 July 1911, 16.

155. 'Our Weekly Causerie', *FW*, 24 January 1912, 823.

156. CS 2385/3/10, RM Parys, 26 April 1910.

157. Interview, Dinah Pooe, 9.

158. SC 6a–1917, *Report of the Select Committee on Native Affairs*, 416–31 and 433.

159. 'Farm, Veld and Town', *FW*, 8 March 1921, 3415.

160. See, for example, the work of Helen Bradford on the Industrial and Commercial Union in the 1920s: '"A Taste of Freedom": Capitalist Development and Response to the I.C.U. in the Transvaal Countryside' in B. Bozzoli (ed.) *Town and Countryside in the Transvaal*.

6 Years of crisis, 1908–14

1. UG 34–1913, *Land and Agricultural Bank of South Africa, Report for Period 1 October to 31 December 1912*, 19, 20. See pp. 34–5.

2. JUS 1/401/10, Annual Reports, 1910: Bethlehem, also Edenburg, Heilbron.

3. SBA, Inspection Reports, 1912: Ficksburg; JUS 1/566/11, Annual Reports, 1911: Fouriesburg; JUS 1/401/10, Annual Reports, 1910: Ficksburg, Smithfield.

4. JUS 1/566/11, Thaba Nchu, Kroonstad; JUS 1/401/10, Parys.

5. JUS 1/566/11, Vrede.

6. G. T. Amphlett, *History of the Standard Bank of South Africa* (Glasgow, 1914) 58.

7. SBA, Inspection Reports, 1911: Heilbron.

8. See H. G. Hardy, 'Agricultural Land Banks', *Journal of the Institute of Bankers of South Africa*, November 1907, 265.

9. J. A. Henry, *The First Hundred Years of the Standard Bank* (London, 1963) 157.

10. See *Annual Reports of the Department of Justice* (magistrates' reports) for years 1910–14, *passim*. Standard Bank Inspection Reports from all districts bear testimony to this rapid inflation.

11. Again Standard Bank Inspection Reports for these years from many districts refer to the influx of new 'progressive' farmers, and the frequent sales and subdivision of land. Cf. a comment from Potchefstroom district: 'It is quite remarkable to find how rapidly the aspect of the district is changing, many of the old Dutch farmers having disposed of their holdings to more progressive agriculturists who have come in from the Cape Province and elsewhere.' 'Our Weekly Causerie', *FW*, 23 April 1913, 607.

12. See Senate SC 6–1910–11, *Senate Select Committee on Closer Land Settlement*. The issues of land settlement and subsidized immigration became bones of great political contention between 1910 and 1914. Populist interests, led by General Hertzog, saw in these schemes an attempt to make South Africa safe for 'foreign capital' and to force unskilled Afrikaners into the reserve army of labour. See T. Keegan, 'Black Peril, Lapsed Whites and Moral Panic', unpublished paper, 1978.

13. See UG 13–1914, *Land and Agricultural Bank of South Africa, Report for Period 1 January 1913 to 31 December 1913*, 22; UG 20–1915, *Land and Agricultural Bank of South Africa, Report for Year Ended 31 December 1914*, 23 and 24.

14. Thus the Lewis and Marks partnership in 1913 formed the Union Land Settlement Company Limited, to which they transferred 1 319 866 acres of land for the low price of £750 000 (mostly in the Transvaal), with the specific purpose of effecting improvements and leasing the land to white settlers with an option to purchase after a short period. See Prospectus in *FW*, 17 September 1913, 216–18. See also the evidence of William Pott, chairman of the Transvaal Land Owners' Association and general manager of Henderson Estates, SC 3–1910, *Select Committee on Native Affairs*, 385–6; also *NLC*, 300–2. Cf. Paul Rich, 'African Farming and the 1913 Natives Land Act: Toward a Reassessment' in University of York, *Collected Papers on Southern Africa*, vol. 4 (York, 1978).

15. Extensive reserves had long been demarcated in the Cape and Natal colonies, and in the Orange Free State there was precious little undeveloped land which could be added to the existing small reserves. In the Transvaal, on the other hand, very little land had been defined as reserve land, and much of the land communally inhabited by blacks was crown land and speculatively-owned land away from the Highveld. It was in the Transvaal where most of the extra 'released' land earmarked for addition to existing reserves was located, and the big land companies stood to gain from the extension of reserves there – by the sale of their land at inflated prices to African syndicates and chiefs, and epecially to the state. The Transvaal Land Owners' Association represented the owners of 4 326 000 morgen in the Bushveld and 602 800 on the Highveld. Whites (649 in all) leased 459 947 morgen, almost exclusively on the Highveld. The rest was occupied solely by blacks (some 1200 farms in all). Of the Transvaal Consolidated Land and Exploration Company's 707 farms (3 368 730 acres) only 110 were occupied by whites. 'Farmer George', Roodepoort, to editor, *FW*, 23 April 1913, 561; evidence of C. A. Madge, Senate SC 6–1910–11, 136–40.

16. See UG 9–1912, *Orange Free State, Land and Agricultural Loan Fund. Report for the Period Ended 31 March 1911*, 2. All loans carried an interest rate of 5 per cent.

17. The Poor Whites Commission estimated the extent of mortgage indebtedness on land in the Orange Free State at £3 580 000 in 1908. Further, repatriation debts (most of which were secured by promissory notes) still amounted to £401 663 (owed by some 5260 debtors). ORC, *Report of a Commission of Enquiry into the Position and Circumstances of Poor Whites in the Orange River Colony* (Bloemfontein, 1908) 36; ORC, *Report of a Commission appointed to enquire into the Question of Repatriation Debts* (Bloemfontein, 1909) 14.

18. UG 34–1913, 19 and 20; UG 13–1914, 22.

19. See pp. 45–9.

20. See pp. 57–61.

21. CS 4502/07, Director of Land Settlement, 28 March 1907. See also Emelia Pooe's comment, p. 131.

22. JUS 1/401/10, Annual Reports, 1910: Lindley.

23. J. A. Jorissen to editor, *FW*, 8 May 1912, 557.

24. 'Spes Bona' to editor, *FW*, 30 August 1911, 30; also 'Progress', Kroonstad, to editor, *FW*, 19 July 1911.

25. See pp. 140–2.

26. H. S. Viljoen, Florence, Fouriesburg, to editor, *Friend*, 23 September 1911.

27. 'Death-Knell to Kaffir-Farming', *FA*, September 1913, 39; also Edgar I. Webb to editor, *Friend*, 4 October 1911; S. F. Papenfus, Harrismith, to editor, *FW*, 25 October 1911; JUS 1/401/10, Annual Reports, 1910: Winburg; J. G. Keyter, MLA, Ficksburg, *NLC*, 51–2.

28. For evidence of the burgeoning stockholdings of black tenants, see *NLC*, Evidence, *passim*; *BBNA*, 1910, 178.

29. See R. Pell Edmonds to editor, *FW*, 13 September 1911; J. A. Jorissen to editor, *FW*, 5 July 1911; K. R. Macaskill, Clocolan, to editor, *FA*, February 1907, 295.

30. SBA, Inspection Reports, 1909: Ladybrand; ibid, 1913: Bethlehem.

31. *NLC*, Evidence, 2, 12, 38, 39–40. See also 'Natives and Land', *FA*, October 1913, 73.

32. Senator H. G. Stuart, Winburg, *NLC*, 54 and 56. See also 'Young Farmer' to editor, *FW*, 26 July 1911, 11; A. D. J. Taylor, Harrismith, to editor, *FW*, 16 August 1911.

33. 'Puzzled' to editor, *FW*, 4 October 1911. Concern over the consequences of allowing African stockholdings to proliferate was reflected in the widespread fear that black-owned stock was peculiarly susceptible to disease – an ideological intervention paralleled by the 'sanitation syndrome' which provided the context for the introduction of segregationist measures in towns. See M. W. Swanson, 'The Sanitation Syndrome: Bubonic Plague and Urban Native Policy in the Cape Colony, 1900–1909', *Journal of African History*, 18, 3 (1977); cf. Chapter 1, note 95. See 'The Cattle-Owning Native', *FA*, June 1912, 633, for an example.

34. See 'Taxation and Registration of Stallions', *FW*, 19 April 1911, 5.

35. For example, interview, L. Nqandela.

36. Interview, N. Makume, II, 16–17; also interviews, D. Makiri, 9–10; J. Molete, 7; J. Moiloa, 15.

37. In about 1912, Fanie Cronje of Vlakplaas, Vereeniging, issued an ultimatum to the tenant families either to sell off their cattle other than the

trek oxen and four cows for milking, or to share the increase of all their livestock with him (SAIRR, *A Community Man: An Oral History of Barney Ngakane* (Johannesburg, 1983) 4). Some charged their tenants for grazing rights, for example a shilling a month for a cow or a horse (R. Pell Edmonds to editor, *FW*, 13 September 1911). But presumably few tenants were prepared to submit to such exactions without fierce resistance.

38. G. Behrens, *NLC*, Evidence, 333.
39. *BBNA*, 1910, 340; also H. Rose-Innes, *NLC*, 271–2.
40. G. Behrens, *NLC*, 333.   .
41. Interview, P. Pooe, 5–7.
42. Ibid, 9; T. Matsetela, 'The Life Story of Nkgono Mma-Pooe' in S. Marks and R. Rathbone (eds) *Industrialization and Social Change in South Africa* (London, 1982) 236.
43. Interview, P. Pooe, 6. There is evidence from another source of Chief Darius Mogale (of the same chiefly lineage) visiting the Orange Free State from the Transvaal in 1906 with a view to collecting money – £6 10s per head – from his 'subjects', which was apparently intended to pay for the expenses of litigation (NAB 471/06, D. Moore, Wesleyan Minister, Heilbron, 1906). A Mokale, interview, I, 2–4, says that a Chief Mogale moved in the nineteenth century from Magaliesberg to Basutoland where he was given land and established a village called Bakoena for his followers.
44. Interview, P. Pooe, 8. See also T. Matsetela, 'Rural Change among Africans in the Ventersdorp District, 1910–35: A Case Study of Bakwena-Ba-Ga-Mokgopa', M.A. thesis, University of London, 1981.
45. Interview, Dinah M. Pooe, 1.
46. This subject is pursued more fully in Keegan, 'White Settlement and Black Subjugation on the South African Highveld: The Tlokoa Heartland in the Northeastern Orange Free State, 1850–1914' in W. Beinart and P. Delius (eds) *Putting a Plough to the Ground* (London and Johannesburg, 1986). The Reverend Abner Poho of Heilbron, whose father declined in 1914 to join the move to Mogopa, still identifies himself today as one of the 'Bakoena-ba-Mogopa', even though his forebears came from Botswana, and he has never lived at Mogopa. His father, like so many of those who did settle at Mogopa, had resided amongst Moshoeshoe's Sotho before moving into the northern Orange Free State. Interview, A. R. Poho.
47. Interview, E. Moloko. See UG 23–1918, *Report of the Natives Land Committee, Western Transvaal*, 35–7, on the farms Quaggaslaagte and Dunbar, bought under the auspices of the Koena chief Serobatse.
48. *Community Man*, 5; interviews, M. Ngakane, 16–18; A. M. Motsuenyane.
49. C. Griffith, RM Wakkerstroom, *NLC*, 296. One such from the Harrismith district was Josiah Moloi's father. See interview, J. Moloi; Keegan, 'White Settlement and Black Subjugation'. The minute books of the Native Farmers' Association are deposited in the African Studies Institute, Johannesburg.
50. Interview, E. M. Pooe.
51. J. de V. de Beer, attorney of Pretoria, *NLC*, 282–3; also A. G. E. Pienaar, RM Ermelo, *NLC*, 306–7.
52. E. C. Dower, *NLC*, 235–6.

53. It was no coincidence that 1912–13 saw a dramatic upsurge in 'black peril' scares in urban areas – reflecting no doubt a greater sense of moral crisis amongst whites rather than any absolute increase in the incidence of sexual assaults by blacks on white women. See Keegan, 'Black Peril, Lapsed Whites and Moral Panic'; C. van Onselen, 'The Witches of Suburbia: Domestic Service on the Witwatersrand, 1890–1914' in C. van Onselen, *Studies in the Social and Economic History of the Witwatersrand, 1886–1914*, vol. 2, *New Nineveh* (London, 1982).

54. CS 1325/1/09, D. J. van Zyl, Langkloof, 14 January 1909. See also CS 617/09, L. D. J. Erasmus, Parys, 26 March 1909; 'A Working Farmer', Westminster, to editor, *Friend*, 27 September 1911; 'Pro Patria', Thaba Nchu, to editor, *Friend*, 7 February 1912.

55. 'A Sympathiser', Bloemfontein, to editor, *Friend*, 9 May 1911; also DA 72, 2065/1/10, L. M. B. Honge, Zuikerkop, Clocolan, 4 April 1910.

56. *Community Man*, 3–4; also interview, M. Ngakane, 13.

57. 'A Mutual Bond', *Friend*, 1 November 1912; 'Country Day By Day: Frankfort', *Friend*, 4 February 1913; 'Boerenbond Congress', *Friend*, 19 and 20 February 1913.

58. See, for example, 'Bethlehem Native Affairs Congress', *Friend*, 6 November 1908; 'Bethlehem Native Affairs Congress', *Friend*, 29 January 1909; 'Wepener Congress', *Friend*, 27 January 1909.

59. See, for example, *Die Hertzogtoesprake*, vol. 2, March 1910–March 1913 (Pretoria, 1977) *passim*.

60. There was a clear relationship between this act and that establishing the ORC Land Bank enacted in 1909 (although first debated in 1908); for, as J. G. Keyter, MLA for Ficksburg, said in the Assembly in August 1908, now that the government had prohibited 'ploughing on the halves' by Africans, white farmers had to be helped to acquire oxen and equipment 'to enable them to do that which the natives had hitherto done for them'. *Friend*, 21 August 1908.

61. Section 7(3) of Act 27 of 1913. The original intention of the act was to suspend all action against black tenants until extra land had been demarcated for addition to the scheduled reserves. But this *quid pro quo* did not apply in the case of the Orange Free State, where it was intended that black sharecropping should become illegal immediately. This exemption was due to pressures brought to bear by General Hertzog and his Orange Free State followers in parliament, and is explained by the fact that in the Orange Free State the capitalization of agriculture had been longest developing, and rural crisis and competition were most intense. The Orange Free State was also relatively free of the countervailing interests of the big corporate landowners. But, as we shall see, these legislative arrangements are of marginal interest in an analysis of the significance and consequences of the act. Details of the complex legislative history of the act are found in P. L. Wickens, 'The Natives Land Act of 1913: A Cautionary Essay on Simple Explanations of Complex Change', *South African Journal of Economics*, 49,2 (1981); P. Dickson, 'The Natives Land Act, 1913: Its Antecedents, Passage and Reception', M.A. thesis, University of Cape Town, 1969.

62. JUS 5/262/13, E. Dower to Apthorpe, 12 August 1913. As the editor of the *Farmer's Advocate* noted in October 1913 ('Natives and Land', 73):

As a matter of fact, no owner or occupier has yet been compelled, under the Act, to get rid of squatting natives, or natives ploughing on shares, because it is held by the law officers that contracts which were in force when the Act came into operation, must be allowed to run out. . . . [This ruling] virtually postpones the operation of the Act until next July, most of the contracts being annual.

63. *NLC*, Evidence, 11.
64. *NLC*, Appendix XI, 5.
65. *NLC*, 1–4.
66. *NLC*, Appendix XI, 4.
67. *NLC*, 35–6.
68. JUS 5/262/13, Natives Land Act, 1913: Opinions re position in the Orange Free State.
69. *NLC*, Evidence, 32. Also see evidence of Rev. Xopa Meshac, *NLC*, 33–4; also 76.
70. *NLC*, 16 and 21.
71. Sol T. Plaatje, *Native Life in South Africa* (London, 1916, reprinted New York, 1969, Johannesburg, 1983) 103. Page references are to 1969 edition.
72. *NLC*, 10 and 12.
73. *NLC*, 70–1.
74. *FW*, 29 October 1913, 866. See also evidence of Barnard Bahane and T. M. Dambuza, *NLC*, 291–2.
75. See also R. W. Msimang, *Natives Land Act, 1913* (Johannesburg, ca. 1914) 18–32. Msimang was deputed by the South African Natives National Congress to collect evidence of evictions under the act. Both Plaatje's and Msimang's testimony is highly polemical and thus must be treated with care. Plaatje's outrage at the fate of so many of the sharecroppers was not fortuitous; many of them shared Plaatje's social origins, his commitment to education and self-improvement, and his optimism. For men like Plaatje the great dispersal of 1913 more than any other development undermined their faith in the ultimate efficacy of personal initiative and diligence. See Brian Willan, *Sol Plaatje: A Biography* (London, 1984).
76. Plaatje, *Native Life*, 68, 105–6.
77. Ibid, 60; see also, 68–71, 75–6, 78–80, 102–3.
78. JUS 5/262/13, Natives Land Act, 1913: Opinions re position in the Orange Free State.
79. Ibid, RM Bothaville, 29 August 1913.
80. Plaatje, *Native Life*, 58–9.
81. *NLC*, 45.
82. JUS 5/262/13, Natives Land Act, 1913.
83. See *NLC*, 12 and *passim*.
84. Matsetela, 'Life Story', 224.
85. Cf. the comment in 1913 of a farmer from Winburg district where much of the soil was 'turf' and too stony for cultivation: 'many farmers living on farms with this kind of soil cannot get natives. The first thing the native asks is "where are your lands?" and if you have no lands for sowing, off he goes'. *NLC*, 5.
86. See evidence of Archdeacon Hill of Springs on a company-owned farm in the southern Transvaal:

> In 1913 or soon afterwards the farmers [white lessees] called the Natives together and told them that the half share system had come to an end, and if they wished to remain on the farm they would be given a few morgen to plough for themselves, but that they must now plough the rest of the lands for the farmers with their own ploughs and oxen and that for the pasturage of their cattle they must be prepared to do the transport of the produce to the market (UG 22–1932, *Report of the Natives Economic Commission, 1930–32*, 199–200).

87. See interview, T. Manoto, 18.
88. *NLC*, 52–3.
89. *NLC*, 59.
90. See pp. 93–4.
91. 'Wepener Congress', *Friend*, 27 January 1909.
92. ORC, *Natives Administration Commission*, 1908 (Pretoria, 1911) 9.
93. UG 36–1919, *Annual Report of the Department of Justice, 1918*, 33.
94. Matsetela, 'Life Story', 224–5. Plaatje tells us that he passed through a few farms where the landholders were visibly sympathetic toward the harried Africans, and some were accepting them as tenants on their farms as sharecroppers (*Native Life*, 73, 81–90). Prosecutions were few in succeeding years. In December 1917 it was reported that a farmer in the Bloemfontein district had been fined £10 for entering sharecropping arrangements with black tenants (*FW*, 12 December 1917, 1503). So presumably, although such cases were rare, they were not unknown. Prosecutions were instituted probably only in cases of incessant complaint by neighbours.
95. J. F. W. Grosskopf, *Rural Impoverishment and Rural Exodus*, vol. 1 of Carnegie Commission, *The Poor White Problem in South Africa*, 5 vols (Stellenbosch, 1932) 168. See also SAIRR, *Farm Labour in the Orange Free State* (Johannesburg, 1939) 34–5.
96. Interview, Petrus Pooe, 5; see also interviews, M. Ngakane, 21; D. Makiri, 12–14; P. M. Masike, 11; T. Manoto, 12. Not surprisingly, not all of these can put a precise date to this changeover to third shares.
97. *NLC*, Evidence, 17 and 19; also Appendix X, 1 (RM Bethlehem).
98. *NLC*, 29.
99. JUS 5/262/13, RM Parys, 29 July 1914; also *NLC*, 28 and 35.
100. Supreme Court decisions were less placatory than the law advisors'. See 'Law Problems on the Farm', *FW*, 7 April 1926, 388 and 15 October 1924, 472; 'Ban on Lease of Land to Natives', *FW*, 5 March 1930, 2535.
101. See pp. 140–2 on the masters-and-servants legislation.
102. 'The Native Bill: Its Probable Effects', *FA*, August 1913, 665–7.
103. CS 1278/2/08, Colonial Secretary's Office, 1908; G 444/1/08, Governor to Secretary of State, 28 August 1908. This provision was not extended to Natal and the Transvaal until 1926, when a Masters and Servants Amendment Bill was passed.
104. See pp. 142–8.
105. UG 20–1915, *Land and Agricultural Bank of South Africa, Report for Year Ended December 1914*, 23–4. SBA, Inspection Reports from any number of

districts on the Highveld for 1914–15 provide rich evidence on these developments.

106. These conclusions are based on a mass of interview evidence.

Conclusion

1. Barrington Moore, *The Social Origins of Dictatorship and Democracy: Lord and Peasant in the Making of the Modern World* (Boston, 1966); Stanley Trapido, 'South Africa in a Comparative Study of Industrialization', *Journal of Development Studies*, 7, 3 (1971); Martin Legassick, 'South Africa: Capital Accumulation and Violence', *Economy and Society*, 3, 3 (1974); M. L. Morris, 'The Development of Capitalism in South African Agriculture: Class Struggle in the Countryside', *Economy and Society*, 5, 3 (1976); Stanley Greenberg, *Race and State in Capitalist Development* (New Haven, 1980); Frederick Cooper, 'Peasants, Capitalists and Historians: A Review Article', *Journal of Southern African Studies*, 7, 2 (1981) 300–1. For other attempts at comparison, see Cristobal Kay, 'Comparative Development of the European Manorial System and the Latin American Hacienda System', *Journal of Peasant Studies*, 2, 1 (1974); Jonathan M. Wiener, 'Class Structure and Economic Development in the American South, 1865–1955', *American Historical Review*, 84, 4 (1979).

2. David Goodman and Michael Redclift, *From Peasant to Proletarian: Capitalist Development and Agrarian Transitions* (Oxford, 1981) 102.

3. It is only fair to say that at least some of these writers escape in practice the limitations inherent in the model.

4. Mosley tells us that many early agricultural settlers in Southern Rhodesia were prospectors, or alternated periods on the land with periods in retailing or government employment. In Kenya 'most' early settlers had alternative sources of income, like cutting wood for the railways (Paul Mosley, *The Settler Economies: Studies in the Economic History of Kenya and Southern Rhodesia, 1900–63* (Cambridge, 1983) 186). These observations prompt wider comparisons with the incomplete forms of accumulation typical of some black rural economies in Africa. What has been called 'straddling' has been common amongst Africa's black farmers: the process whereby money earned in the wage sector is ploughed back into rural production (John Iliffe, *The Emergence of African Capitalism* (London, 1983) 31; Frederick Cooper, 'Africa and the World Economy', *African Studies Review*, 24 (1981) 42–4). Kitching describes in detail the way in which in Kenya black rural accumulators with larger landholdings and who increasingly employed members of poorer families for wages were usually also better-educated men with white-collar clerical or teaching jobs as well as trading interests, and hence greater access to non-agricultural income. Similarly, Beinart shows that in Pondoland, the initial extension of rural production was made possible by and accompanied the generalization of labour migrancy, thus contradicting Bundy's assertion that mass labour migrancy was a function of the decline of peasant production. (Of course, the process did not proceed very far in Pondoland, which was eventually to degenerate into a labour reserve.) (Gavin Kitching, *Class and Economic Change in Kenya: The*

Making of an African Petite-Bourgeoisie (New Haven, 1980) esp. 364–72; William Beinart, *The Political Economy of Pondoland, 1860–1930* (Cambridge, 1983); Colin Bundy, *The Rise and Fall of the South African Peasantry* (London, 1979).) Underdevelopment theorists tend to see the farmer–worker primarily as subsidizing the capitalist sector through rural household production, but the phenomenon can perhaps be better understood historically by looking at the dynamics of the rural economy rather than at the requirements of capital.

5. Cf. the experiences of Lord Delamere, Kenya's leading capitalist farmer, who soon discovered that his traction engine was not nearly so satisfactory as 'Boer methods' of ploughing (Mosley, *The Settler Economies*, 187). In a situation of 'cheap labour, dear capital and high risk' the use of outdated or improvised equipment and labour-intensive methods were highly appropriate, asserts Mosley.

6. The spread of sharecropping in non-European parts of the world not uncommonly accompanied or followed integration into international markets. Sharecropping is entirely compatible with rural capitalism and is often found in economies in which market production is generalized and predominant. See the several contributions in T. J. Byres (ed.) *Sharecropping and Sharecroppers* (London, 1983).

7. A. F. Robertson, 'On Sharecropping', *Man*, 15, 3 (1980); *idem*, 'Abusa: the Structural History of an Economic Contract', *Journal of Development Studies*, 18, 4 (1982).

8. Colin Murray *Families Divided: The Impact of Migrant Labour in Lesotho* (Cambridge, 1981) 75–85; A. D. Spiegel, 'Rural Differentiation and the Diffusion of Migrant Labour Remittances in Lesotho' in P. Mayer (ed.) *Black Villagers in an Industrial Society: Anthropological Perspectives on Labour Migration in South Africa* (Cape Town, 1980) 131–2 and 145–6.

9. For example, interview, M. Ngakane.

10. Editorial, *Friend*, 4 February 1908; also evidence of E. R. Grobler before *NLC*, 81.

11. On some of the indigenous historical roots of the capitalist ideal see R. Ross, 'The First Two Centuries of Colonial Agriculture in the Cape Colony: A Historiographical Review' in P. Delius and W. Beinart (eds) *Putting a Plough to the Ground* (Johannesburg and London, 1986).

12. See Shula Marks and Stanley Trapido, 'Lord Milner and the South African State', *History Workshop Journal*, 9 (1980).

13. See Francis Wilson, 'Farming, 1866–1966' in M. Wilson and L. M. Thompson (eds) *The Oxford History of South Africa*, vol. 2 (London, 1971). By 1934 white farmers owed the Land Bank £15m – mostly in the former Boer republics. UG 16–1934, *Report of the Commission to Enquire into Co-operation and Agricultural Credit, 1932–34*, 153–4.

14. Amongst those who were excluded in the process were, of course, many whites, including very large numbers of the old Boer population, ex-landowners as well as those who had never owned land. But, unlike the black tenants, 'poor whites' of the twentieth century were not on their way to becoming a rural proletariat. They were gradually absorbed into the urban areas, where they were provided with protected employment.

15. This is no longer a novel observation of course: see Bundy, *The Rise and Fall of the South African Peasantry*.

16. See Alan Richards, 'The Political Economy of Gutswirtschaft: A Comparative Analysis of East Elbian Germany, Egypt and Chile', *Comparative Studies in Society and History*, 21, 4 (1979) for comparative perspectives on labour tenancy emphasizing its utility in situations of incomplete control over labour.

17. On these developments see, for example, M. de Klerk, 'Seasons that will Never Return: The Impact of Farm Mechanization on Employment, Incomes and Population Distribution in the Western Transvaal', *Journal of Southern African Studies*, 11, 1 (1985). By 1985 farmers' debts exceeded R8000m.

Bibliography

Archival Sources 272

Published Collections of Documents 273

Government Publications 274

Periodicals and Newspapers 277

Primary Sources 277

Secondary Sources 279

Unpublished Theses and Papers 288

Oral Testimony 290

ARCHIVAL SOURCES

Public Record Office, London

CO 224, vols 4–33, Orange River Colony, 1900–10.
CO 417, vols 297, 328, 355, 375, 394, 426, 439, 455, Africa South: Original Correspondence (Basutoland).
CO 529/1, Secretary of State's Tour, 1902–3: Original Correspondence.
CO 596, vols 1–5, Acts, 1902–10.
CO 598/1, Blue Book of Statistics, ORC, 1905–6.
CO 599, vols 1–19, Sessional Papers, ORC, 1902–10.

Orange Free State Archives, Bloemfontein

Archive of the Secretary of the *Volksraad* (VR) vols 286–442, *Bylae tot Volksraadsnotule*, 1886–99; vols 597–8, Evidence, Land Commission, 1892–5.
Archives of the Government Secretary (GS) Incoming Correspondence, various, mainly vols 457–69, Ficksburg, 1891–7; vols 565–607, Heilbron, 1879–97; vols 724–60, Kroonstad, 1890–7; vols 761–816, Ladybrand, 1870–97; vols 817–37, Moroka, 1880–97; vols 942–60, Wepener, 1885–97; vols 1263–73, Basutoland, 1868–97.
Archive of the State President (P) vols 1–12, Incoming Correspondence, 1854–99.
Archive of the Supreme Court (HG) individual volumes consulted, 1870–99.
Archive of the Colonial Secretary, Orange River Colony (CS) vols 1–1030, Incoming Correspondence, 1901–11.

Archive of the Department of Agriculture, ORC (DA) vols 1–94, 1903–13.
Archive of the Governor, ORC (G) vols 1–145, 1907–10.
Archive of the Native Affairs Branch, ORC (NAB) vols 1–43, 1902–11.
Archive of the South African Police, Orange Free State (FSP) vols 1–12, 1900–25.
District Archives, miscellaneous, mainly criminal and civil court records and correspondence files from Bothaville (LBD), Ficksburg (LFI), Harrismith (LHS), Kroonstad (KRS), Ladybrand (LLA), Lindley (LIN), Parys (LPA).

Union Archives, Pretoria

Archive of the Native Affairs Department (NA) Correspondence Files, 1910–14.
Archive of the Department of Justice (JUS) Correspondence Files, 1910–14.

Standard Bank Archives, Johannesburg

Inspection Reports from district branches, 1903–18.

Barclays Bank Archives, Johannesburg

Minute Books of the National Bank of the Orange Free State, 1890–1914.

Archives of the United Society for the Propagation of the Gospel, London

Series E, Missionary Reports, 1890–1914.

PUBLISHED COLLECTIONS OF DOCUMENTS

BELL, K. N. and MORRELL, W. P. (eds) *Select Documents on British Colonial Policy, 1830–60* (Oxford, 1928).
DAVENPORT, T. R. H. and HUNT, K. S. (eds) *The Right to the Land* (Cape Town, 1974).
GERMOND, R. C. (ed.) *Chronicles of Basutoland* (Morija, 1967).
HEADLAM, C. (ed.) *The Milner Papers* (London, 1931–2) 2 vols.
HOUGHTON, D. H. and DAGUT, J. (eds) *Source Material on the South African Economy, 1860–1970* (Cape Town, 1972–3) 3 vols.
OBERHOLSTER, J. J. and VAN SCHOOR, M. C. E. (eds) *President Steyn aan die Woord* (Bloemfontein, 1953).
SPIES, F. J. du T., KRUGER, D. W. and OBERHOLSTER, J. J. (eds) *Die Hertzogtoesprake* (Johannesburg, 1977) vols 1–3.

GOVERNMENT PUBLICATIONS

Orange Free State

Census van den Oranjevrijstaat, 31 Maart 1880.
Census, 1890, Report of a Census taken on 31 March 1890.
Notulen der Verrichtingen van den Hoogedelen (Volksraadsnotule, annual, 1870–99.
Rapport van den Administrateur der Fondsen, annual, 1882–5.
Rapport van den Arbeids Commissie (1894).
Rapport van den Kommandant der Rijdenden Dienstmacht, annual, 1892–5.
Rapport van den Registrateur van Acten, annual, 1892–8.
Rapport van den Weesheer en Meester der Insolvente Boedelkamer, annual, 1884–98.
Rijdenden Dienstmacht, Rapport van den Commissaris van Politie, OVS, annual, 1896–8.
Runderpest, Rapport van de Commissie aangesteld bij Volksraad besluit van 14 October 1896 (1896).
Wetboek van den Oranjevrijstaat (1891).

Orange River Colony

Census of the Orange River Colony, 17 April 1904.
Codified Circular Instructions of the Law Department of the Orange River Colony to 31 December 1906 (1907).
Conference of Resident Magistrates of the Orange River Colony (1906).
Department of Agriculture, Annual Reports, 1904–10.
Department of Public Works, Annual Reports, 1902–10.
Farm List, ORC, by Districts (1902).
Law Reports: Reports of Cases Decided in the High Court, annual, 1904–7.
The Laws Relating to the Powers and Duties of Field Cornets (1908).
List of Farms Owned by the Late Orange Free State, including those recently purchased by the Orange River Colony Administration, with areas and other particulars (1902).
Minutes of the Proceedings of the Legislative Assembly, annual, 1903–10.
The Powers and Duties of Justices of the Peace in the Orange River Colony (1904).
Remarks of the Judges of the High Court in Dealing with Cases on Review and Appeal during the Years 1903 to 1906 (1906).
Report of a Commission Appointed to Consider and Report upon and Make Suggestions for Modifying or Amending Laws with Regard to Natives and Native Administration within the Orange River Colony (Natives Administration Commission) 1908 (Pretoria, 1911).
Report of the Commission Appointed by the Government of the Orange River Colony to Enquire into and Report on the Desirability of Establishing a Labour Colony or Taking other Measures for the Employment of Impoverished White Inhabitants (1908).
Report of a Commission Appointed to Enquire into the Question of Repatriation Debts (1908).

Report of a Commission of Enquiry into the Position and Circumstances of Poor Whites in the Orange River Colony (1908).

Report of the Committee on the Leasing of Government Farms (1903).

Report of the Industrial Commission (1904).

Remarks of the Judges of the High Court in Quashing and Altering Sentences of Resident Magistrates and Special Justices of the Peace, (1903–4) 3 vols.

Statute Law of the Orange River Colony, ed. C. L. Botha (1901).

Statute Law of the Orange River Colony, eds P. L. Lefebre and B. B. L. Jackson (1906).

Union of South Africa, Parliamentary Papers

Annual Report, Department of Agriculture, UG 54–1912; UG 47–1913; UG 2–1915.

Annual Report, Department of Justice, UG 35–1911; UG 56–1912; UG 44–1913; UG 28–1915; UG 39–1917; UG 36–1918.

Annual Report, Land and Agricultural Bank of South Africa, UG 34–1913; UG 13–1914; UG 20–1915; UG 12–1916.

Census of Agricultural and Pastoral Production, UG 53–1919; UG 20–1920; UG 12–1921; UG 13–1927.

House of Assembly Debates, 1910–14.

Population Census, Final Report, 1911, UG 32–1912; 1918, UG 56–1920; 1921, UG 37–1924.

SC 3–1910, *Select Committee on Native Affairs.*

SC 3A–1912, *Select Committee on Native Affairs.*

SC 5–1913, *Select Committee on Fidei-Commissary Bequests.*

SC 9–1913 *Select Committee on European Employment and Labour Conditions.*

SC 6–1914, *Select Committee on Removal of Restrictions under Wills Bill.*

SC 8–1914, *Select Committee on Native Affairs.*

SC 3–1916, *Select Committee on Drought Distress Relief.*

SC 6A–1917, *Select Committee on Native Affairs.*

SC 1–1919, *Report of the Select Committee on the Cost of Living Commission Report.*

Senate SC 6–1910–11, *Senate Select Committee on Closer Land Settlement.*

UG 17–1911, *Blue Book on Native Affairs for 1910.*

UG 23–1911, *Department of Agriculture, OFS, Report for 1909–10.*

UG 26–1911, *Director of Irrigation, Annual Report.*

UG 43–1911, *Report on Storage and Handling of Grain.*

UG 9–1912, *Orange Free State, Land and Agricultural Loan Fund, Report for the Period Ended 31 March 1911.*

UG 10–1912, *Report of the Trade and Industries Commission.*

UG 40–1912, *Report of the Board of the South African Railways on Proposed New Lines of Railway.*

UG 9–1913, *Trade and Industries Commission, Evidence.*

UG 33–1913, *Report of the Native Affairs Department for 1913.*

UG 64–1913, *Government Agriculturist, OFS, Report for 1912–13.*

UG 26–1915, *Report on Agricultural Education.*

UG 19–1916, *Report of the Native Land Commission.*

UG 22–1916, *Natives Land Commission, Evidence.*

UG 42–1916, *Judicial Commission of Inquiry into the Causes and Circumstances relating to the Recent Rebellion in South Africa, Minutes of Evidence.*

UG 16–1918, *Report of the Cost of Living Commission.*

UG 22–1918, *Report of the Natives Land Committee, Orange Free State.*

UG 23–1918, *Report of the Natives Land Committee, Western Transvaal.*

UG 31–1918, *Majority Report of the Natives Land Committee, Eastern Transvaal.*

UG 3–1919, *Report of the Commission on Taxation of Farmers' Income.*

UG 42–1919, *Report of the Departmental Committee on Wheat Growing.*

UG 17–1922, *Report of the Unemployment Commission.*

UG 41–1922, *Report of the Inter-Departmental Committee on the Native Pass Laws.*

UG 49–1923, *Final Report of the Drought Investigation Commission.*

UG 22–1932, *Report of the Natives Economic Commission, 1930–32.*

UG 16–1934, *Report of the Commission to Enquire into Co-operation and Agricultural Credit, 1932–4.*

Union of South Africa, Miscellaneous

DE SWARDT, J. and NEETHLING, J. C., *Report of an Economic Investigation into Farming in Four Maize Districts of the Orange Free State, 1928–30*, Department of Agriculture, Economic Series, 22 (Pretoria, 1937).

Handbook for Agricultural Statistics, 1904–50 (Pretoria, 1961).

McKELLAR, D. W., *Cost of Production of Maize: Report on the Investigation for the Season 1923–4*, Department of Agriculture, Science Bulletin, 52 (Pretoria, 1926).

Native Farm Labour Committee, 1937–9 (Pretoria, 1939).

NEETHLING, B. A., *An Economic Investigation of Farms in the Maize Districts of the Orange Free State, 1927–8*, Department of Agriculture, Economic Series, 12 (Pretoria, 1930).

PARISH, E., *Report on the Cost of Production of Maize Investigation for the Season 1921–2*, Department of Agriculture, Science Bulletin, 33 (Pretoria, 1924).

Report of the Commission of Enquiry into European Occupancy of Rural Areas (Pretoria, 1960).

WOLFE, H., *Main Problems in the Economics of Agricultural Production in South Africa*, Industries Bulletin Series (Pretoria, 1919).

Other

British Parliamentary Papers (BPP), Cds 1551, 1552, 1553, 1895, 2104, 2482, 2563, 3028, 3526, 3528, *Papers Relating to the Transvaal and Orange River Colony*, 1903–7.

BPP, Cd. 1896, 1897 *Transvaal Labour Commission, Report and Minutes of Proceedings.*

Cape of Good Hope, A 15–1907, *Select Committee on Agricultural Credit Bank Bill.*

Cape of Good Hope, C 3–1906, *Report of the Select Committee on Labour Settlements for Indigent Whites.*

Central South African Railways, General Manager's Report, annual, 1902–9 (Pretoria).

Inter-Colonial Irrigation Commission, Final Report (Pretoria, 1908).

Natal Government Railways, *Maize Cultivation and Export in South Africa* (Durban, 1909).

South African Native Affairs Commission, 1903–5, (Cape Town, 1905) 5 vols.

Transvaal Colony, *Report of the Land Bank Commission* (Pretoria, 1907).

Transvaal Colony, TG 11–1908, *Transvaal Indigency Commission, Minutes of Evidence.*

Transvaal Colony, TG 13–1908, *Report of the Transvaal Indigency Commission.*

Transvaal Colony, TG 32–1908, *Report of the Committee of Enquiry on Repatriation Debts.*

Transvaal Colony, TG 16–1910, *Native Affairs Department, Annual Report for the Year ended 30 June 1909.*

PERIODICALS AND NEWSPAPERS

Agricultural Journal of the Union of South Africa, monthly, 1910–14.
De Fakkel, fortnightly, Bloemfontein, 1903–9.
Farmer's Advocate, monthly, Bloemfontein, 1904–20.
Farmer's Weekly, Bloemfontein, 1911–14, 1919–24.
Farming in South Africa, monthly, Pretoria, 1926–30.
Friend, The, daily, Bloemfontein, 1903–13.
Friend of the Free State, The, twice weekly, Bloemfontein, 1890–8.
Journal of the Institute of Bankers in South Africa, monthly, 1904–14.
Natal Agricultural Journal, individual issues consulted.
Presbyterian Churchman, individual issues consulted.
South Africa, London, individual issues consulted.

PRIMARY SOURCES

BACKHOUSE, J., *A Narrative of a Visit to the Mauritius and South Africa* (London, 1844).

BALFOUR, A. B., *Twelve Hundred Miles in a Waggon* (London, 1895).

BAUMANN, G. and BRIGHT, E., *Lost Republic: The Biography of a Land Surveyor* (London, 1940).

BEAK, G. B., *The Aftermath of War: An Account of the Repatriation of Boers and Natives in the Orange River Colony, 1902–1904* (London, 1906).

BLELOCH, M., *The New South Africa: Its Value and Development* (London, 1901).

BLERSCH, F., *Handbook of Agriculture for South Africa* (Cape Town, 1906).

BOURDILLON, E., *Farming in the Orange River Colony* (Bloemfontein, 1901).

BRYCE, J., *Impressions of South Africa* (London, 1897).

BURTT-DAVY, J., *Maize: Its History, Cultivation, Handling and Uses* (London, 1914).

CARNEGIE COMMISSION, *Report on the Poor White Problem in South Africa*, (Stellenbosch, 1932) 5 vols.

COLLINS, W. W., *Free Statia, or Reminiscences of a Lifetime in the Orange Free State* (Bloemfontein, 1907).

DE KOK, K. J., *Empires of the Veld* (Durban, 1904).

EAGLE, J. N. (ed.) *Report of the Cases Decided in the High Court of the Orange Free State in the Years 1874 and 1875* (Philippolis, 1879).

FRANKEL, H. S., *Co-operation and Competition in the Marketing of Maize in South Africa* (London, 1926).

FRASER, J. G., *Episodes in My Life* (Cape Town, 1922).

GROSSKOPF, J. F. W., *Rural Impoverishment and Rural Exodus*, vol. 1 of Carnegie Commission, *Report on the Poor White Problem in South Africa* (Stellenbosch, 1932).

HARDY, H. G., 'Agricultural Land Banks', *Journal of the Institute of Bankers of South Africa* (November 1907).

JEWELL, G. W., *The National Guide to Transvaal and the ORC* (London, 1903).

JINGOES, S. J., *A Chief is a Chief by the People*, ed. J. and C. Perry (London, 1975).

JOHNSON, J., *South Africa Speaks* (Johannesburg, 1981).

KNIGHT, E. F., *South Africa After the War: A Narrative of Recent Travel* (London, 1903).

LEPPAN, H. D. and BOSMAN, G. J., *Field Crops in South Africa* (Johannesburg, 1923).

McCRAE, J. F. (ed.) *The Orange Free State: Its Pastoral, Agricultural and Industrial Resources* (London, 1912).

MACDONALD, J. R., *What I Saw in South Africa* (London, 1902).

MARKHAM, V., *The New Era in South Africa* (London, 1904).

MARKS, A. E., 'Agricultural Co-operation in South Africa', *Monthly Bulletin of Economic and Social Intelligence*, 45 (September 1914).

Men of the Times: Old Colonists of the Cape Colony and the Orange River Colony (Cape Town, 1906).

Men of the Times: Pioneers of the Transvaal and Glimpses of South Africa (Johannesburg, 1905).

MSIMANG, R. W., *Natives Land Act, 1913: Specific Cases of Evictions and Hardships* (Johannesburg, ca. 1914).

MURRAY, E., *Young Mrs Murray Goes to Bloemfontein* (Cape Town, 1954).

NOBLE, J., *Descriptive Handbook of the Cape Colony: Its Condition and Resources* (Cape Town, 1875).

Offisieël Verslag van der Verrichtingen van het Nasionaal Kongres gehouden te Brandfort op 1 en 2 Desember 1904 (Bloemfontein, 1905).

The Orange River Colony: An Illustrated, Historical, Descriptive and Commercial Review (London, 1905).

The Orange River Colony: Its Resources and Development (Bloemfontein, 1906).

ORPEN, J. M., *Reminiscences of Life in South Africa from 1846 to the Present Day* (Cape Town, 1964).

PAYTON, C. A., *The Diamond Diggings of South Africa* (London, 1872).

PLAATJE, S. T., *Native Life in South Africa* (London, 1916, reprinted New York, 1969, Johannesburg, 1983).

ROPER, E. R., 'The Advantages and Disadvantages of the Establishment of

Land Banks with Special Relation to South Africa', *Journal of the Institute of Bankers of South Africa* (April 1912).

ROPER, E. R., 'The Land Bank Bill', *The State* (June 1912).

SACHS, S., *Rebel's Daughter* (London, 1957).

SANDEMAN, E. F., *Eight Months in an Ox-Wagon: Reminiscences of Boer Life* (London, 1880, reprinted Johannesburg, 1975).

SAUL SOLOMON & CO., *The South African Directory for 1883-4* (Cape Town, 1883).

SAUNDERS, A. R., *Maize in South Africa* (Johannesburg, 1930).

SCHREINER, O., *Thoughts on South Africa* (London, 1923, reprinted Johannesburg, 1976).

S. W. Silver and Co's Handbook to South Africa, including the Cape Colony, Natal, the Diamond Fields, the Trans-Orange Republics etc. (London, 1876).

SOUTH AFRICAN INSTITUTE OF RACE RELATIONS, *A Community Man: An Oral History of Barney Ngakane* (Johannesburg, 1983).

SOUTH AFRICAN INSTITUTE OF RACE RELATIONS, *Farm Labour in the Orange Free State* (Johannesburg, 1939).

SOUTH AFRICAN NATIVE RACES COMMITTEE, *The Natives of South Africa: Their Economic and Social Condition* (London, 1901).

SOUTH AFRICAN NATIVE RACES COMMITTEE, *The South African Natives: Their Progress and Present Condition* (London, 1908).

TAYLOR, H., *Doctor to Basuto, Boer and Briton, 1877-1906: Memoirs of Dr Henry Taylor*, ed. P. Hadley (Cape Town, 1972).

THOMAS, O., *Agricultural and Pastoral Prospects of South Africa* (London, 1904).

TROLLOPE, A., *South Africa* (London, 1878) 2 vols.

Twentieth Century Impressions of the Orange River Colony and Natal: Their History, People, Commerce, Industries and Resources (Natal, 1906).

WILCOCKS, R. W., *The Poor White, Psychological Report*, vol. 2 of Carnegie Commission, *Report on the Poor White Problem in South Africa* (Stellenbosch, 1932).

WILLCOCKS, W., *Report on Irrigation in South Africa* (1901).

WORSFOLD, W. B., *The Reconstruction of the New Colonies under Lord Milner* (London, 1913) 2 vols.

SECONDARY SOURCES

ADAM, H. and GILIOMEE, H., *The Rise and Crisis of Afrikaner Power* (Cape Town, 1979).

AMPHLETT, G. T., *History of the Standard Bank of South Africa* (Glasgow, 1914).

ARNDT, E. H. D., *Banking and Currency Development in South Africa, 1652-1927* (Cape Town, 1927).

ATMORE. A. and MARKS, S. 'The Imperial Factor in South Africa in the Nineteenth Century: Towards a Reassessment', *Journal of Imperial and Commonwealth History*, 3, 1 (1974).

BANAJI, J., 'Modes of Production in a Materialist Conception of History', *Capital and Class*, 3 (1977).

BEINART, W., *The Political Economy of Pondoland, 1860–1930* (Cambridge, 1982).

BEINART, W. and DELIUS, P. (eds) *Putting a Plough to the Ground: Accumulation and Dispossession in Rural South Africa, 1850–1930* (Johannesburg and London, 1986).

BERMAN, B. and LONSDALE, J., 'Crises of Accumulation, Coercion and the Colonial State: the Development of the Labour Control System in Kenya, 1919–29', *Canadian Journal of African Studies*, 14, 1 (1980).

BERNSTEIN, H., 'Notes on Capital and Peasantry', *Review of African Political Economy*, 10 (1977).

BERNSTEIN, H., 'African Peasantries: A Theoretical Framework', *Journal of Peasant Studies*, 6, 4 (1979).

BONNER, P., *Kings, Commoners and Concessionaires: The Evolution and Dissolution of the Nineteenth Century Swazi State* (Cambridge, 1983).

BOSCH, J. A., *Ladybrand, 1867–1967* (Bloemfontein, 1967).

BOZZOLI, B., *The Political Nature of a Ruling Class: Capital and Ideology in South Africa, 1890–1933* (London, 1981).

BOZZOLI, B., 'Marxism, Feminism and South African Studies', *Journal of Southern African Studies*, 9, 2 (1983).

BOZZOLI, B. (ed.) *Town and Countryside in the Transvaal: Capitalist Penetration and Popular Response* (Johannesburg, 1983).

BRADFORD, H., '"A Taste of Freedom": Capitalist Development and Response to the ICU in the Transvaal Countryside' in B. Bozzoli (ed.) *Town and Countryside in the Transvaal* (Johannesburg, 1983).

BRENNER, R., 'The Origins of Capitalist Development: A Critique of Neo-Smithian Marxism', *New Left Review*, 104 (1977).

BROOKES, E. H., *The History of Native Policy in South Africa from 1830 to the Present Day* (Cape Town, 1924).

BUNDY, C., *The Rise and Fall of the South African Peasantry* (London, 1979).

BUNDY, C., 'Vagabond Hollanders and Runaway Englishmen: White Poverty in the Cape before Poor Whiteism' in W. Beinart and P. Delius (eds) *Putting a Plough to the Ground* (Johannesburg and London, 1986).

BURROWS, E. H., *The Moodies of Melsetter* (Cape Town, 1954).

BYRES, T. J. (ed.) *Sharecropping and Sharecroppers* (London, 1983).

CARTWRIGHT, A. P., *The First South African: The Life and Times of Sir Percy Fitzpatrick* (Cape Town, 1971).

CELL, J. W., *The Highest Stage of White Supremacy: The Origins of Segregation in South Africa and the American South* (Cambridge, 1982).

COLLINS, J. A., *The Struggles of an Infant State* (Cape Town, 1925).

COOPER, F., *From Slaves to Squatters: Plantation Labour and Agriculture in Zanzibar and Coastal Kenya, 1890–1925* (New Haven, 1980).

COOPER, F., 'Africa and the World Economy', *African Studies Review*, 24, 2/3 (1981).

COOPER, F., 'Peasants, Capitalists and Historians: A Review Article', *Journal of Southern African Studies*, 7, 2 (1981).

DANZIGER, C., *A Trader's Century: The Story of Frasers* (Cape Town, 1978).

DAVENPORT, T. R. H. 'The South African Rebellion of 1914', *English Historical Review*, 78 306 (1963).

DAVENPORT, T. R. H., *South Africa, A Modern History* (London, 1977).

DAVIES, R., KAPLAN, D., MORRIS, M. and O'MEARA, D. 'Class Struggle and the Periodization of the State in South Africa', *Review of African Political Economy*, 7 (1976).

DAVIES, R. H., *Capital, State and White Labour in South Africa, 1900–1960* (Brighton, 1979).

DAVIN, A., 'Imperialism and Motherhood', *History Workshop Journal*, 5 (1978).

DE KIEWIET, C. W., *A History of South Africa, Social and Economic* (London, 1941).

DE KLERK, J. C., *A Century of Merino Sheep Farming in the Orange Free State* (Pretoria, 1952).

DE KLERK, M., 'Seasons that will Never Return: The Impact of Farm Mechanization on Employment, Incomes and Population Distribution in the Western Transvaal', *Journal of Southern African Studies*, 11, 1 (1985).

DE KOCK, M. H., *Selected Subjects in the Economic History of South Africa* (Cape Town, 1924).

DE KOCK, M. H., *The Economic Development of South Africa* (London, 1936).

DELIUS, P., 'Abel Erasmus: Power and Profit in the Eastern Transvaal' in W. Beinart and P. Delius (eds) *Putting a Plough to the Ground* (Johannesburg and London, 1986).

DELIUS, P., *The Land Belongs to Us: The Pedi Polity, the Boers and the British in the Nineteenth Century Transvaal* (London, 1983).

DELIUS, P., 'Migrant Labour and the Pedi, 1840–80' in S. Marks and A. Atmore (eds) *Economy and Society in Pre-Industrial South Africa* (London, 1980).

DELIUS, P. and TRAPIDO, S., *'Inboekselings* and *Oorlams*: The Creation and Transformation of a Servile Class' in B. Bozzoli (ed.) *Town and Countryside in the Transvaal* (Johannesburg, 1983).

DENOON, D., *A Grand Illusion: The Failure of Imperial Policy in the Transvaal Colony During the Period of Reconstruction, 1900–1905* (London, 1973).

DOBB, M., *Studies in the Development of Capitalism* (London, 1946).

DUBOW, S., *Land, Labour and Merchant Capital: The Experience of the Graaff Reinet District in the Pre-Industrial Rural Economy of the Cape, 1852–72* (Cape Town, 1982).

ELLENBERGER, E. and MACGREGOR, J. C., *History of the Basuto, Ancient and Modern* (London, 1912).

ELOFF, C. C., *Oos-Vrystaatse Grensgordel: 'n Streekhistoriese Voorstudie en Bronneverkenning* (Pretoria, 1980).

ELOFF, C. C., *Oranje-Vrystaat en Basoetoeland, 1884–1902: 'n Verhoudingstudie* (Pretoria, 1984).

ELOFF, C. C., 'Die Verhouding tussen die Oranje-Vrystaat en Basoetoeland, 1878–84' in *Archives Year Book for South African History*, 1980, 2 (Pretoria, 1983).

ELPHICK, R. and GILIOMEE, H. (eds) *The Shaping of South African Society, 1652–1820* (London, 1979).

ENGELBRECHT, S. P., *Geskiedenis van de Nederduits Hervormde Kerk in Zuid-Afrika* (Amsterdam and Pretoria, 1920) vol. 1.

ENNEW, J., HIRST, D. and TRIBE, K., '"Peasantry" as an Economic Category', *Journal of Peasant Studies*, 4, 4 (1977).

ERASMUS, D. F., *Heilbron, 1873–1973* (Heilbron, 1973).

ETHERINGTON, N., 'Labour Supply and the Genesis of South African Confederation', *Journal of African History*, 20, 2 (1979).

FAURE, C., *Agriculture et Capitalisme: Essai sur les Rapports de Production et Agriculture* (Paris, 1978).

FLEISCHER, D. and CACCIA, A., *Merchant Pioneers: The House of Mosenthal* (Johannesburg, 1983).

FOURIE, J. J., *Afrikaners in die Goudstad, 1886–1924*, ed. E. L. P. Stals (Cape Town and Pretoria, 1978).

FREDRICKSON, G., *White Supremacy: A Comparative Study in American and South African History* (New York, 1981).

FRIEDMANN, H., 'World Market, State and Family Farm: Social Bases of Household Production in the Era of Wage Labour', *Comparative Studies in Society and History*, 20, 4 (1978).

FRIEDMANN, H., 'Household Production and the National Economy: Concepts for the Analysis of Agrarian Formations', *Journal of Peasant Studies*, 7, 1 (1977).

GALBRAITH, J. S., *Reluctant Empire: British Policy on the South African Frontier, 1834–1854* (Berkeley, 1963).

GILIOMEE, H., 'Processes in the Development of the South African Frontier' in H. Lamar and L. M. Thompson (eds) *The Frontier in History* (New Haven, 1981).

GOODFELLOW, D. M., *A Modern Economic History of South Africa* (London, 1931).

GOODMAN, D. and REDCLIFT, M., *From Peasant to Proletarian: Capitalist Development and Agrarian Transitions* (Oxford, 1981).

GREENBERG, S., *Race and State in Capitalist Development: South Africa in a Comparative Study of Industrialization* (New Haven, 1980).

GRUNDLINGH, A. N., *Die 'Hensoppers' en 'Joiners': Die Rasionaal en Verskynsel van Verraad* (Pretoria, 1979).

GUELKE, L., 'The White Settlers, 1652–1780' in R. Elphick and H. Giliomee (eds) *The Shaping of South African Society, 1652–1820* (London, 1979).

HENRY, J. A., *The First Hundred Years of the Standard Bank* (London, 1963).

HERRMAN, L., *A History of the Jews in South Africa, from the Earliest Times to 1895* (London, 1930).

HOOPS, O. W. A., *Bothaville, 1891–1966: Seventy-five Years of Progress* (Bothaville, 1966).

HORWITZ, R., *The Political Economy of South Africa* (London, 1967).

HOUGHTON, D. H., *The South Africa Economy* (Cape Town, 1967).

HUGGETT, F. E., *Life Below Stairs* (London, 1977).

ILIFFE, J., *The Emergence of African Capitalism* (London, 1983).

JACOBS, D. J., 'Landbou en Veeteelt in die Oranje-Vrystaat, 1864–88' in *Archives Year Book for South African History* 1969, 1 (Pretoria, 1969).

JACOBS, D. S., 'Abraham Fischer in sy Tydperk, 1850–1913' in *Archives Year Book on South African History*, 1965, 2 (Pretoria, 1965).

JONES, J. Stedman, *Outcast London: A Study in the Relationship between Classes in Victorian Society* (Harmondsworth, 1976).

KAY, C., 'Comparative Development of the European Manorial System and the Latin American Hacienda System', *Journal of Peasant Studies*, 2, 1 (1974).

KEEGAN, T. J., 'The Restructuring of Agrarian Class Relations in a Colonial

Economy: The Orange River Colony, 1902–1910', *Journal of Southern African Studies*, 5, 2 (1979).

KEEGAN, T. J., 'Seasonality, Price and Markets: The South African Maize Trade in the Early Twentieth Century', *Collected Seminar Papers on the Societies of Southern Africa in the Nineteenth and Twentieth Centuries*, Institute of Commonwealth Studies, University of London, 10 (1981).

KEEGAN, T. J., 'The Sharecropping Economy, African Class Formation and the Natives Land Act of 1913 in the Highveld Maize Belt' in S. Marks and R. Rathbone (eds) *Industrialization and Social Change in South Africa* (London, 1982).

KEEGAN, T. J., 'The Sharecropping Economy on the South African Highveld in the Early Twentieth Century', *Journal of Peasant Studies*, 10, 2/3 (1983).

KEEGAN, T. J., 'Crisis and Catharsis in the Development of Capitalism in South African Agriculture', *African Affairs*, 84, 336 (1985).

KEEGAN, T. J., 'Trade, Accumulation and Impoverishment: Mercantile Capital and the Economic Transformation of Lesotho and the Conquered Territory, 1870–1920', *Journal of Southern African Studies*, 12, 2 (1986).

KEEGAN, T. J., 'White Settlement and Black Subjugation on the South African Highveld: The Tlokoa Heartland in the Northeastern Orange Free State, 1850–1914' in W. Beinart and P. Delius (eds) *Putting a Plough to the Ground* (London and Johannesburg, 1986).

KEEGAN, T. J., 'The Dynamics of Rural Accumulation in South Africa: Historical and Comparative Perspectives', *Comparative Studies in Society and History*, 28, 4 (1986).

KEEGAN, T. J., 'Dispossession and Accumulation in the South African Interior: The Boers and the Batlhaping of Bethulie, 1833–61', *Journal of African History*, 27, 3 (1986).

KESTELL, J. D., *Christiaan de Wet: 'n Lewensbeskrywing* (Cape Town, 1920).

KIRK, T., 'The Cape Economy and the Expropriation of the Kat River Settlement, 1846–53' in S. Marks and A. Atmore (eds) *Economy and Society in Pre-Industrial South Africa* (London, 1980).

KITCHING, G., *Class and Economic Change in Kenya: The Making of an African Petite-Bourgeoisie* (New Haven, 1980).

LACEY, M., *Working for Boroko: The Origins of a Coercive Labour System in South Africa* (Johannesburg, 1981).

LAMAR, H. and THOMPSON, L. M. (eds) *The Frontier in History: North America and Southern Africa Compared* (New Haven, 1981).

LEGASSICK, M., 'South Africa: Capital Accumulation and Violence', *Economy and Society*, 3, 3 (1974).

LEGASSICK, M., 'The Frontier Tradition in South African History' in S. Marks and A. Atmore (eds) *Economy and Society in Pre-Industrial South Africa* (London, 1980).

LIPTON, M., 'South Africa: Two Agricultures?' in F. Wilson, A. Kooy and D. Hendrie (eds) *Farm Labour in South Africa* (Cape Town, 1977).

LONSDALE, J. and BERMAN, B., 'Coping with the Contradictions: The Development of the Colonial State in Kenya, 1895–1914', *Journal of African History*, 20, 4 (1979).

LOUDON, J. B., *White Farmers and Black Labour-Tenants* (Cambridge, 1970).

LYE, W., 'The *Difaqane:* The *Mfecane* in the Southern Sotho Area, 1822–24', *Journal of African History*, 8, 1 (1967).

LYE, W., 'The Distribution of the Sotho Peoples after the *Difaqane*' in L. M. Thompson (ed.) *African Societies in Southern Africa* (London, 1969).

LYE, W. and MURRAY, C., *Transformations on the Highveld: The Tswana and Southern Sotho* (Cape Town, 1980).

MACMILLAN, W. M., *The South African Agrarian Problem and Its Historical Development* (Johannesburg, 1919, reprinted Pretoria, 1974).

MACMILLAN, W. M., *Complex South Africa: An Economic Footnote to History* (London, 1930).

MAGGS, T. M. O'C., *Iron Age Communities of the Southern Highveld* (Pietermaritzburg, 1976).

MALAN, J. H., *Die Opkoms van 'n Republiek* (Bloemfontein, 1929).

MALAN, S. F., *Politieke Strominge onder die Afrikaners van die Vrystaatse Republiek* (Durban, 1982).

MARAIS, A. H., 'Die Ontstaan en Ontwikkeling van Partypolitiek in die Oranjerivier-Kolonie, 1902–12' in *Archives Year Book for South African History*, 1970, 2 (Pretoria, 1970).

MARAIS, J. S., *The Fall of Kruger's Republic* (Oxford, 1961).

MARKS, S., 'Natal, the Zulu Royal Family and the Ideology of Segregation', *Journal of Southern African Studies*, 4, 2 (1978).

MARKS, S. and ATMORE, A. (eds) *Economy and Society in Pre-Industrial South Africa* (London, 1980).

MARKS, S. and RATHBONE, R. (eds) *Industrialization and Social Change in South Africa: African Class Formation, Culture and Consciousness, 1870–1930* (London, 1982).

MARKS, S. and TRAPIDO, S., 'Lord Milner and the South African State', *History Workshop Journal*, 9 (1980).

MATSETELA, T., 'The Life Story of Nkgono Mma-Pooe: Aspects of Share-cropping and Proletarianization in the Northern Orange Free State, 1890–1930' in S. Marks and R. Rathbone (eds) *Industrialization and Social Change in South Africa* (London, 1982).

MOODIE, T. D., *The Rise of Afrikanerdom: Power, Apartheid and the Afrikaner Civil Religion* (Berkeley, 1975).

MOORE, B., *The Social Origins of Dictatorship and Democracy: Lord and Peasant in the Making of the Modern World* (Boston, 1966).

MORRIS, M. L., 'The Development of Capitalism in South African Agriculture', *Economy and Society*, 5, 3 (1976).

MORRIS, M. L., 'State Intervention and the Agricultural Labour Supply Post-1948' in F. Wilson, A. Kooy and D. Hendrie (eds) *Farm Labour in South Africa* (Cape Town, 1977).

MOSLEY, P., *The Settler Economies: Studies in the Economic History of Kenya and Southern Rhodesia, 1900–1963* (Cambridge, 1983).

MULLER, C. F. J., *Die Oorsprong van die Groot Trek* (Cape Town, 1974).

MURRAY, C., *Families Divided: The Impact of Migrant Labour in Lesotho* (Cambridge, 1981).

MURRAY, C., 'Land, Power and Class in the Thaba Nchu District, Orange Free State, 1884–1983', *Review of African Political Economy*, 29 (1984).

MURRAY, M., 'The Formation of the Rural Proletariat in the South African

Countryside: The Class Struggle and the 1913 Natives Land Act' in Edinburgh University, *Southern African Studies: Retrospect and Prospect* (Edinburgh, 1983).

NAIRN, T., *The Break-Up of Britain: Crisis and Neo-Nationalism* (London, 1977).

NEUMARK, S. D., *Economic Influences on the South African Frontier* (Stanford, 1957).

NEWTON-KING, S., 'The Labour Market of the Cape Colony, 1807–28' in S. Marks and A. Atmore (eds) *Economy and Society in Pre-Industrial South Africa* (London, 1980).

NIENABER, P. J., *Dr J. D. Kestell, Vader van die Reddingsdaad* (Bloemfontein, 1946).

NIMOCKS, W., *Milner's Young Men: The 'Kindergarten' in Edwardian Imperial Affairs* (Durham, North Carolina, 1968).

NKADIMENG, N. and RELLY, G., 'Kas Maine: The Story of a Black South African Agriculturalist' in B. Bozzoli (ed.) *Town and Countryside in the Transvaal* (Johannesburg, 1983).

OBERHOLSTER, J. J., *Wepener, 1869–1969* (Wepener, 1969).

OBERHOLSTER, J. J. and STEMMET, J., *Senekal se Eerste Honderd Jaar* (Senekàl, 1977).

ODENDAAL, A., *Vukani Bantu! The Beginnings of Black Protest Politics in South Africa to 1912* (Cape Town, 1984).

O'MEARA, D., *Volkskapitalisme: Class, Capital and Ideology in the Development of Afrikaner Nationalism, 1934–1948* (Cambridge, 1983).

PAKENHAM, T., *The Boer War* (London, 1979).

PALMER, R. and PARSONS, Q. N. (eds) *The Roots of Rural Poverty in Central and Southern Africa* (London, 1977).

PAUW, S., *Die Beroepsarbeid van die Afrikaner in die Stad* (Stellenbosch, 1946).

POLLOCK, N. C. and AGNEW, S., *An Historical Geography of South Africa* (London, 1963).

RANGER, T. O., 'Growing from the Roots: Reflections on Peasant Research in Central and Southern Africa', *Journal of Southern African Studies*, 5, 1 (1978).

RANGER, T. O., 'The Invention of Tradition in Colonial Africa' in E. Hobsbawn and T. O. Ranger (eds) *The Invention of Tradition* (Cambridge, 1983).

RASMUSSEN, K., *Migrant Kingdom: Mzilikazi's Ndebele in South Africa* (London, 1978).

RENNIE, J. K., 'White Farmers, Black Tenants and Landlord Legislation: Southern Rhodesia, 1890–1930', *Journal of Southern African Studies*, 5, 1 (1978).

RICH, P., 'African Farming and the 1913 Natives Land Act: Toward a Reassessment', *Collected Papers on Southern Africa*, University of York, 4 (1978).

RICHARDS, A., 'The Political Economy of Gutswirtschaft: A Comparative Analysis of East Elbian Germany, Egypt and Chile', *Comparative Studies in Society and History*, 21, 4 (1979).

ROBERTSON, A. F., 'Abusa: The Structural History of an Economic Contract', *Journal of Development Studies*, 18, 4 (1982).

ROBERTSON, A. F., 'On Sharecropping', *Man*, 15, 3 (1980).

ROSENTHAL, E., *Other Men's Millions* (Cape Town, n.d.).

ROSS, R., *Adam Kok's Griquas: A Study in the Development of Stratification in South Africa* (Cambridge, 1976).

ROSS, R., 'Capitalism, Expansion and Incorporation on the South African Frontier' in H. Lamar and L. M. Thompson (eds) *The Frontier in History* (New Haven, 1981).

ROSS, R., 'The First Two Centuries of Colonial Agriculture in the Cape Colony: A Historiographical Review' in W. Beinart and P. Delius (eds) *Putting a Plough to the Ground* (London and Johannesburg, 1986).

SAMUEL, R., 'The Workshop of the World', *History Workshop Journal*, 3 (1977).

SANDERS, P., *Moshoeshoe, Chief of the Sotho* (London, 1975).

SANDERS, P., 'Sekonyela and Moshoeshoe: Failure and Success in the Aftermath of the *Difaqane*', *Journal of African History*, 10, 3 (1969).

SARON, G. and HOTZ, L., *The Jews in South Africa: A History* (Cape Town, 1955).

SCHOEMAN, K., *Bloemfontein: Die Ontstaan van 'n Stad, 1846–1946* (Cape Town, 1980).

SCHOLTZ, G. D., *Die Konstitusie en Staatsinstellings van die Oranje-Vrystaat, 1854–1902* (Amsterdam, 1937).

SCHUMANN, C. G. W., *Structural Changes and Business Cycles in South Africa, 1806–1936* (London, 1938).

SEMMEL, B., *Imperialism and Social Reform* (London, 1960).

SHANIN, T. (ed.) *Peasants and Peasant Societies* (London, 1971).

SHANIN, T., 'Defining Peasants: Conceptualisations and De-Conceptualisations Old and New in a Marxist Debate', *Peasant Studies*, 8, 4 (1979).

SLATER, H., 'Land, Labour and Capitalism in Natal: The Natal Land and Colonisation Company, 1860–1948', *Journal of African History*, 16, 2 (1975).

SLATER, H., 'The Changing Pattern of Economic Relationships in Rural Natal, 1838–1914' in S. Marks and A. Atmore (eds) *Economy and Society in Pre-Industrial South Africa* (London, 1980).

SMITH, K. W., *From Frontier to Midlands: A History of the Graaff-Reinet District* (Grahamstown, 1976).

SORRENSON, M. P. K., *The Origins of European Settlement in Kenya* (London, 1968).

SPIEGEL, A. D., 'Rural Differentiation and the Diffusion of Migrant Labour Remittances in Lesotho' in P. Mayer (ed.) *Black Villagers in an Industrial Society: Anthropological Perspectives on Labour Migration in South Africa* (Cape Town, 1980).

SPIES, S. B., *Methods of Barbarism? Roberts and Kitchener and Civilians in the Boer Republics, January 1900–May 1902* (Cape Town, 1977).

STEYTLER, F. A., *Die Geskiedenis van Harrismith* (Bloemfontein, 1932).

SWANSON, M. W., 'The Sanitation Syndrome: Bubonic Plague and Urban Native Policy in the Cape Colony, 1900–1909', *Journal of African History*, 18, 3 (1977).

TATZ, C., *Shadow and Substance: A Study in Land and Franchise Policies Affecting Africans, 1910–60* (Pietermaritzburg, 1962).

THOM, H. B., *Die Geskiedenis van die Skaapboerdery in Suid-Afrika* (Amsterdam, 1936).

THOMPSON, L. M. (ed.) *African Societies in Southern Africa: Historical Studies* (London, 1969).

THOMPSON, L. M., *Survival in Two Worlds: Moshoeshoe of Lesotho* (Oxford, 1975).

TRAPIDO, S., 'South Africa in a Comparative Study of Industrialization', *Journal of Development Studies*, 7, 3 (1971).

TRAPIDO, S., 'South Africa and the Historians', *African Affairs*, 71, 285 (1972).

TRAPIDO, S., 'Landlord and Tenant in a Colonial Economy: The Transvaal, 1880–1910', *Journal of Southern African Studies*, 5, 1 (1978).

TRAPIDO, S., ' "The Friends of the Natives": Merchants, Peasants and the Political and Ideological Structure of Liberalism in the Cape, 1854–1910' in S. Marks and A. Atmore (eds) *Economy and Society in Pre-Industrial South Africa* (London, 1980).

TRAPIDO, S., 'Reflections on Land, Office and Wealth in the South African Republic, 1850–1900' in S. Marks and A. Atmore (eds) *Economy and Society in Pre-Industrial South Africa* (London, 1980).

TRAPIDO, S., 'A History of Tenant Production on the Vereeniging Estates, 1896–1920' in W. Beinart and P. Delius (eds) *Putting a Plough to the Ground* (London and Johannesburg, 1986).

TYLDEN, G., *The Rise of the Basuto* (Cape Town, 1950).

VAN ASWEGEN, H. J., 'Die Verhouding tussen Blank en nie-Blank in die Oranje-Vrystaat, 1854–1902' in *Archives Year Book for South African History*, 1971, 1 (Pretoria, 1977).

VAN DEN HEEVER, C. M., *General J. B. M. Hertzog* (Johannesburg, 1943).

VAN DER HORST, S., *Native Labour in South Africa* (London, 1942).

VAN DER MERWE, P. J., *Die Noordwaartse Beweging van die Boere voor die Groot Trek* (Cape Town, 1937).

VAN DER MERWE, P. J., *Die Trekboer in die Geskiedenis van die Kaapkolonie, 1657–1842* (Cape Town, 1938).

VAN DER MERWE, P. J., *Trek: Studies oor die Mobiliteit van die Pioniersbevolking aan die Kaap* (Cape Town, 1945).

VAN DER POEL, J., *Railway and Customs Policies in South Africa, 1885–1910* (London, 1933).

VAN JAARSVELD, F. A., *Die Afrikaner se Groot Trek na die Stede* (Johannesburg, 1982).

VAN ONSELEN, C., 'Reactions to Rinderpest in South Africa', *Journal of African History*, 12, 3 (1972).

VAN ONSELEN, C., *Studies in the Social and Economic History of the Witwatersrand, 1886–1914*, vol. 1, *New Babylon*, vol. 2, *New Nineveh* (London, 1982).

VAN ONSELEN, C., 'The Witches of Suburbia: Domestic Service on the Witwatersrand, 1886–1914' in C. van Onselen, *Studies in the Social and Economic History of the Witwatersrand, 1886–1914*, vol. 2, *New Nineveh* (London, 1982).

VAN RENSBURG, A. P. J., *Die Geskiedenis van Bethlehem, 1864–1964* (Bethlehem, 1964).

VAN RENSBURG, A. P. J., 'Die Ekonomiese Herstel van die Afrikaner in die Oranjerivier-Kolonie, 1902–07' in *Archives Year Book for South African History*, 1967, 2 (Pretoria, 1967).

VAN RHYN, P. H. and KLOPPER, A. H., *Die Geskiedenis van Ficksburg, 1867–1967* (Senekal, 1967).

VAN SCHOOR, M. C. E. and MOLL, J. C., *Edenburg: Grepe uit die Geskiedenis van die Dorp en Distrik* (Bloemfontein, 1963).

WALTON, J., *Father of Kindness and Father of Horses: A History of Frasers Limited* (Wepener, 1958).

WARWICK, P., *Black People and the South African War* (Cambridge, 1983).

WATSON, R. L., 'The Subjection of a South African State: Thaba Nchu, 1880–4', *Journal of African History*, 21, 3 (1980).

WELLS, J., 'Why Women Rebel: Women's Resistance in Bloemfontein, 1913, and Johannesburg, 1958', *Journal of Southern African Studies*, 10, 2 (1984).

WELSH, D., 'The Growth of Towns' in M. Wilson and L. M. Thompson (eds) *The Oxford History of South Africa*, vol. 2 (Oxford, 1971).

WELSH, D., *The Roots of Segregation: Native Policy in Natal, 1845–1910* (Cape Town, 1971).

WICKENS, P. L., 'The Natives Land Act of 1913: A Cautionary Essay on Simple Explanations of Complex Change', *South African Journal of Economics*, 49, 2 (1981).

WIENER, J. M., 'Class Structure and Economic Development in the American South, 1865–1955', *American Historical Review*, 84, 4 (1979).

WILLAN, B., *Sol Plaatje: A Biography* (London, 1984).

WILSON, F., 'Farming, 1866–1966' in M. Wilson and L. M. Thompson (eds) *The Oxford History of South Africa*, vol. 2 (Oxford, 1971).

WILSON, F., KOOY, A. and HENDRIE, D. (eds) *Farm Labour in South Africa* (Cape Town, 1977).

WILSON, M. and THOMPSON, L. M. (eds) *The Oxford History of South Africa*, 2 vols (Oxford, 1969, 1971).

UNPUBLISHED THESES AND PAPERS

BEINART, W. and DELIUS, P. '"The Family" and Early Migrancy in Southern Africa', paper presented to African History Seminar, Institute of Commonwealth Studies, London, 1979.

BESTER, J. J. H., 'Die Ekonomiese Ontwikkeling van die Oranje-Vrystaat, 1888–99', M.A. thesis, University of South Africa, 1946.

BRAND, S. S., 'The Contribution of Agriculture to the Economic Development of South Africa since 1910', D.Sc. thesis, University of Pretoria, 1969.

BRINK, E., '"Maar 'n Klomp 'Factory' Meide": The Role of Female Garment Workers in the Clothing Industry, Afrikaner Family and Community on the Witwatersrand during the 1920s', paper presented to the History Workshop Conference, University of the Witwatersrand, 1984.

CLYNICK, T., 'The Lichtenburg Alluvial Diamond Diggings, 1926–29', paper presented to the History Workshop Conference, University of the Witwatersrand, 1984.

COBBING, J., 'The Case Against the *Difaqane*', unpublished paper, 1982.

DE KLERK, M., 'Technological Change and Employment in South African Agriculture: The Case of Maize Harvesting in the Western Transvaal, 1968–81', M. A. thesis, University of Cape Town, 1983.

DE VOS, P. J., 'Die "Bywoner": 'n Sosiologiese Studie oor die Bywonerskap in sekere Hoë en Middelvelddistrikte in die Transvaal en Vrystaat', M.A. thesis, University of Pretoria, 1937.

DICKSON, P., 'The Natives Land Act, 1913: Its Antecedents, Passage and Reception', M.A. thesis, University of Cape Town, 1969.

HATTINGH, J. L., 'Die Trekke uit die Suid-Afrikaanse Republiek en die Oranje-Vrystaat, 1875–95', Ph.D. thesis, University of Pretoria, 1975.

HODDER-WILLIAMS, R., 'The British South Africa Company and the Search for "Suitable" White Immigrants', paper presented to Africa Seminar, University of Cape Town, 1980.

HOFMEYR, I., 'Building a Nation from Words: Afrikaner Language, Literature and "Ethnic" Identity, 1902–24', paper presented to the History Workshop Conference, University of the Witwatersrand, 1984.

JACOBS, D. J., 'Die Ontwikkeling van Landbou in die Vrystaat, 1890–1910', D.Litt. et Phil. thesis, University of South Africa, 1979.

KEEGAN, T. J., 'Black Peril, Lapsed Whites and Moral Panic: A Study of Ideological Crisis in Early Twentieth Century South Africa', paper presented to South African History Conference, Danbury Park, Essex, 1980.

KEEGAN, T. J., 'The Transformation of Agrarian Society and Economy in Industrializing South Africa: The Orange Free State Grain Belt in the Early Twentieth Century', Ph.D. thesis, University of London, 1981.

KIMBLE, J., 'Towards an Understanding of the Political Economy of Lesotho: The Origins of Commodity Production and Migrant Labour, 1830–ca. 1885', M.A. thesis, National University of Lesotho, 1978.

KINSMAN, M., 'Populists and Patriarchs: The Transformation of the Griqua Captaincy, 1801–20', paper presented to the African Studies Seminar, University of the Witwatersrand, 1984.

KOEN, H. B., 'Die Geskiedenis van Reitz en Distrik tot 1910', M.A. thesis, University of the Orange Free State, 1979.

KOTZE, J. P., 'Die Runderpes in die Transvaal en die Onmiddelike Gevolge Daarvan, 1896–99', M.A. thesis, Rand Afrikaans University, 1974.

KRUT, R., 'Maria Botha and her Sons: The Making of a White South African Family in the Twentieth Century', paper presented to Seminar on the Societies of Southern Africa, Institute of Commonwealth Studies, London, 1983.

LAMPRECHT, G. J., 'Die Ekonomiese Ontwikkeling van die Vrystaat, 1870–99', D.Phil. thesis, University of Stellenbosch, 1954.

LEGASSICK, M., 'The Making of South African "Native Policy", 1903–23: The Origins of Segregation', paper presented to Institute of Commonwealth Studies seminar, London, 1972.

LE ROUX, C. J. P., 'Sir Hamilton John Goold-Adams se Rol in die Oranjerivier-Kolonie, 1901–10', M.A. thesis, Rand Afrikaans University 1977.

LE ROUX, C. J. P., 'Die Verhouding Tussen Blank en nie-Blank in die Oranjerivier-Kolonie, 1900–10', D.Litt. thesis, Rand Afrikaans University, 1980.

MATSETELA, T., 'Rural Change Among Africans in the Ventersdorp District, 1910–35: A Case Study of Bakwena-Ba-Ga-Mokgopa', M.A. thesis, University of London, 1981.

MORRELL, R. G., 'Rural Transformations in the Transvaal: The Middelburg District, 1919–30', M.A. thesis, University of the Witwatersrand, 1983.

MURRAY, C., 'The Land of the Barolong: Annexation and Alienation, 1884–1900', paper presented to the Seminar on the Societies of Southern Africa, Institute of Commonwealth Studies, London, 1983.

PELS, J. M., 'The History of Transport Development in the Orange Free State from 1903 to 1936', M.Com. thesis, University of South Africa, 1937.

PELZER, A. N., 'Die "Arm-Blanke" Verskynsel in die Suid-Afrikaanse Republiek tussen die Jare 1882–99: 'n Sosiaal-Historiese Studie', M.A. thesis, University of Pretoria, 1937.

REDLINGHUIS, A. C., ''n Histories-Geografiese Oorsig van die Ontwikkeling van Landbou in die Oranje-Vrystaat Sedert die Begin van Blanke Vestiging tot 1969', M.A. thesis, University of the Western Cape, 1974.

SWANEPOEL, J., 'Landbou-ontwikkeling in Suid-Afrika, 1652–1954, met Spesiale Verwysing na Staatsoptrede in Hierdie Opsig', D.Com. thesis, Potchefstroom University, 1958.

SWANEPOEL, J. M., 'Spoorweë in die Republiek van die Oranje-Vrystaat: 'n Histories-Ekonomiese Studie met Spesiale Verwysing na die Dekade 1890–99', M.Com. thesis, University of Natal, 1953.

TRAPIDO,. S., 'Poachers, Proletarians and Gentry in the Early Twentieth Century Transvaal', paper presented to the African Studies Seminar, University of the Witwatersrand, 1984.

VAN ASWEGEN, H. J., 'Die Verhouding tussen Blank en nie-Blank in die Oranje-Vrystaat, 1854–1902', D.Phil. thesis, University of the Orange Free State, 1969.

VAN ASWEGEN, J., 'Verhandeling oor die Opkoms van die Landbou in die Oranjerivier-Kolonie vanaf 1902 tot Unie', M.A. thesis, University of South Africa, 1932.

VAN NIEKERK, P. J., 'Die Ekonomiese Gevolge van die Ontdekking van Diamante vir die Oranje-Vrystaat ten tyde van President Brand', M.A. thesis, University of South Africa, 1936.

VON KOTZE, A., 'Teutonic Ladies and their "Savages": Thoughts on Women Writers and their Image of the Black Population of Colonial South West Africa, 1900–14', paper presented to the History Workshop Conference, University of the Witwatersrand, 1984.

WEIDEMAN, H. J. S., 'Die Geskiedenis van die Ekonomiese Ontwikkeling van die Oranje-Vrystaat met Verwysing na die Ontstaan van die Armblankedom, 1830–70', M.A. thesis, University of South Africa, 1946.

ORAL TESTIMONY

(All tapes and transcripts are housed in the Oral History Project, African Studies Institute, University of the Witwatersrand, unless otherwise stated.)

BOHLOKO, Daniel Sefatsa, Sandfontein, 27 February 1980.

LEREFUDI, Makoto Tshonoko, Lichtenburg, 26 August 1982.

MAKIRI, Daniel, Evaton, 20 November 1980.

MAKUME, Ndae, Viljoensdrift, 10 June 1982, 10 August 1982.

MANABA, Ramakatu Chebase, Evaton, 16 July 1981.
MANOTO, Tolo, Heilbron, 24, 26 February 1980.
MASIKE, Philip Mokgong, Viljoenskroon, 24 February 1980.
MASINA, Jacob, Ledig, 27 November 1979.
MMOLOTSI, Tshwene, Viljoenskroon, 13–14 April 1980.
MOGOAI, Rebecca Mmamoipone, Potchefstroom, 6 November 1979.
MOHWERANE, Andries, Sandfontein, 27 February 1980.
MOILOA, Johannes, Koppies, 11 April 1980.
MOKALE, Abraham, Evaton, 21 November 1980, 2 April 1982, 12 May 1982.
MOKHACHANE, Molefe Job, Klerksdorp, 28 November 1979.
MOLETE, Jameson, Kroonstad, 26 February 1980.
MOLOI, Josiah, Daggakraal, 31 August 1983.
MOLOKO, Ezekiel Motshubelwe, Boons, 20 November 1979.
MOSINA, John Mohlalefi, Heilbron, 8 April 1980.
MOTSUENYANE, Aaron Molefe, Randfontein, 6 March 1984.
NGAKANE, Morobane, Soweto, 6 September 1979.
NTAMBO, Jewel, Ledig, 23 November 1979.
NQANDELA, Lucas, Ledig, 4 January 1983.
PHALIME, Kodisang Petrus, Heidelberg, 18 November 1980.
POHO, Rev. Abner Rebaitsile, Heilbron, 16 April 1980.
POOE, Dina Molope, Mogopa, 28 August 1980.
POOE, Emelia Molefe, Soweto, 29 August 1979, 29 October 1979.
POOE, Petrus, Mogopa, 28 August 1980.
POPANE, Elias Molefe, Heilbron, 15 April 1980.
SAULS, Mrs M. M., Potchefstroom, 3 December 1979.
THUKWE, Daniel, Nietverdiend, 18 October 1982 (South African Institute of
    Race Relations, Oral Archive).

Index

African Farms Ltd   117
African Methodist Episcopal Church
   243n.97
African Political Organization
   193
Allason, R. D.   69
Amor, Rev. F. A.   253n.33
Amphlett, G. T.   167
Anglo–Boer War
   and Basutoland   61–3
   and Boer treason/desertion   25,
      27, 229–30n.47
   and compensation   109
   and devastation   26–7
   and impoverishment   60, 61–3,
      83–4, 128–9, 171
   and spread of indebtedness   44–5,
      197
   and transport   100–1
animal disease   22, 45, 49, 108, 174,
   197, 264n.33
   in 1890s   60, 109
   post-Anglo–Boer War   46–8
   see also rinderpest
Antwerp   105
apprenticeship system   5–6, 222n.29
   see also Oorlamsches
Archibald Brothers   113
Argentina   101, 104, 105
Australia   101

'back-to-the-land' schemes   33–5,
   231n.78
Badenhorst, W. J.   59
Bailey, Sir Abe   115, 250n.81
Bakubung   178
Ballantine, D.   161
banking   3
   and boom of 1908–14   167–8
   and depression of 1904–8   46, 194
   National Bank   168, 236n.132
   Standard Bank   167–8, 236n.132
Barlow, Alfred   33

Basutoland   2, 223n.49, 237n.3
   in Anglo–Boer War   61–3
   annexation by Britain   8–9
   Chamber of Commerce   101
   emigration of Sotho from   52–5,
      74, 80, 125–7, 237n.3
   export trade   8, 10–13, 16, 17–18,
      57, 98–9, 100–1, 104, 107,
      223n.56, 225n.90, 247n.22,
      248n.54
   grain trade taxed   12–13, 224n.67
   immigration into   53, 80, 177, 178,
      186, 265nn. 43, 46
   land alienation   7, 8–9
   rinderpest in   61
   sharecropping in   52, 199
Bauman, William   146
Bauman, A. M.   164
Bechuanaland   186
Beinart, William   270n.4
Berlin   88
Berry, J. C.   143
Bethanie   177–8
Bethlehem   22, 38, 90, 101, 102, 140,
   152, 158, 161, 167, 171, 174, 180,
   182, 186, 192, 250n.80
Bethulie   45
Beukes, M. J.   139
Blignaut, P. J.   26
Bloemfontein   3, 11, 15, 26, 28, 33,
   46, 99, 101, 113, 115, 118, 119,
   125, 172, 221
Bloemhof   187
Boerenbond   182
Boons   178
Borckenhagen, Carl   44
Botha, L. J.   41
Botha, General Louis   181
Botha, Colonel P. S. J.   164
Bothaville   65, 85, 103, 135, 136, 143,
   185, 187
Bothma, J. C.   143
Bothma, Johannes   144

Bourke, T. 115
Brand, J. H. 4
Brandfort Congress 154
Brandsdrift 113
British Settlement of South Africa
   Ltd 111
British South Africa Company
   39–40
Brits 177
Bruwer, A. J. 192
Buckland Downs 116, 118
Burger, Andries 15, 122
Burgher Land Settlements 29
Burns-Thompson, W. 137
bywoners 21–3, 25, 26, 27–9, 29–33,
   36, 109, 226–7n.5, 227n.7,
   228n.18, 231n.72
   on absentee-owned land
      69–72
   attitudes to work 32–3
   and black tenant competition
      57–9, 67, 180–1
   and household labour 30–1
   and land banks 34–5
   and land loss 39–40, 48–9

capitalization of white farming
   113–20, 196–7
   and black sharecropping 86–95,
      118, 170, 198
   and boom of 1908–14 166
   and capital constraints 87–8, 108,
      205
   and Department of Agriculture
      110
   and education 118–19
   and forms of partnership with
      blacks 93–5, 118, 189–91,
      197–8, 205
   and land banks 170
   and land speculation 114
   and marketing constraints 96–107
   and mechanization 117–18,
      126–7, 170, 205–6, 270n.5
   and off-farm income 113–17,
      196–7, 250n.80, 269n.4
   and reconstruction regime 109–11
   and state supports 107, 108–12,
      198, 201–3, 205–6

Carroll, Francis 89
Cathcart, Governor 8
Central Farmer's Union, ORC 46
Chamber of Commerce, ORC 104
Chamberlain, Joseph 27
Chase, C. C. 89, 92
Chebase, Motiapi 53
Chinese on mines 103
Clocolan 64, 97, 114, 121
coal mines 12, 17, 54–5, 66–7, 115,
   118
Colesberg 100
Collins, James 140
Commissions
   Labour Commission, 1878 13–14
   Labour Commission, 1892–5 139,
      140–1, 150
   Natives Administration
      Commission, 1908 32, 91,
      152, 191
   Natives Land Commission, 1916
      176, 184–6, 188, 192, 195
   Poor Whites Commission, 1908
      34, 46, 264n.17
   Trade and Industries Commission,
      1912 155
   Transvaal Labour Commission,
      1903 123
Conquered Territory
   annexation of 8–9
   entrepreneurship in 113–14
   farming in 11, 12–13, 15, 53–4,
      107
   grain trade in 98–9, 101–2
   and wheat farming 107–8, 125–7,
      248–9n.55
Cooper, Frederick 196
co-operative societies 44, 107, 118
courts of law 133, 135–6, 140–2,
   142–9, 151–2, 153, 155–6, 173,
   193, 204, 256n.81, 257nn.83, 89,
   91, 258n.98, 260n.127
Cronje, A. P. 141
Cronje, Andries 137
Cronje, Fanie 67, 77, 78, 178, 181
Customs Union 18

Daggakraal 179
dairies 110, 111

dam-making 36, 54, 110
Day of the Covenant 48, 237*n.136*
De Beer, Z. J. 150
De Beers Ltd 114, 115
De Express 44
De Jager, L. 143
De Kiewiet, C. W. xv
De Kok, K. J. 12
Department of Agriculture, ORC
   110, 174
Depressions
   1860s 8, 41, 223*n.45*
   1880s 15–16, 224*nn.81, 82*
   1904–8 45–9, 166
   1930s 36, 50
De Rust 116
De Villiers, A. J. B. 143
De Villiers, C. J. 5
De Villiers, D. J. 167
De Wet, General Christiaan 29, 55,
   60–1
De Wet, General Piet 29
Dewetsdorp 60
diamond fields 9–12, 15–16, 114, 154
diamond-prospecting 36
Difaqane 2, 6, 53, 80, 85–6
Dower, E. E. 179
Driefontein 179
Driepan 179
drought 22, 45, 49, 56, 100, 108, 197
   1863 8
   1890s 25, 26, 60
   post-Anglo–Boer War 45–8, 64
   1932–3 120
   1980s 206
Du Brill, Danie 133
Du Plessis, C. J. 161
Du Preez, Paul 151
Durban 3, 105
Dutch Reformed Church 26, 34, 48

East Anglia 112
Easton, C. N. 179
Eaton Hall 112
Edenburg 12
education, black 79–80, 137–8, 195
education, Boer 23, 24–5, 26, 32,
   118–19, 181, 228*nn. 19, 24*

and reconstruction regime 110,
   228*n.24*
Eloff, C. C. xvii
Emanuel, L. V. 43
Erasmus, Jan 138
Ermelo xiii
erosion 119–20
Europe 104, 105
Evans, J. K. 115
Evaton 80, 179
exportation of maize 104–5, 248*n.40*

Farmer's Advocate 118
farmers' associations 119
Farmer's Weekly 119, 172
Farrar, Sir George 106, 115
Fauresmith 3, 227*n.15*
fencing 20, 23, 36, 54, 100, 109, 110,
   170, 175, 197, 228*n.18*, 233*n.101*
Fendick, William 47
Ferreira, I. S. 58
Ficksburg 26, 44, 48, 60, 64, 99, 101,
   144, 147, 161, 167, 190, 232*n.90*,
   236*n.123*, 240*n.40*
Fischer, Abram 180
Fitzpatrick, Sir Percy 115, 116, 118
Fouriesburg 85, 90, 167, 173
Fowler, John, & Company 117,
   244*n.133*
Francistown 66
Frankfort 22, 39, 45, 71, 103
Franklin, C. Stuart 186
Fraser, D. and D. H. 97, 115,
   248*n.54*
Fraser, Sir John 15
Friend Publishing Company 119

Geldenhuis, J. J. A. 135
Germany 196
Germond, P. 16
Gill, H. F. 104
Goold-Adams, Sir Hamilton 29, 46,
   104
Graaff, Loot-Jan 72
Graaf Reinet 106
Gradwell, W. B. 113, 250*n.74*
Grant's Farming Company 251*n.86*
Great Dispersal, 1913 184–91, 204,
   267*n.75*, 268*n.94*

Great Trek 1
Green, Henry 8, 221*n.14*
Greenberg, Stanley 196
Griffith, C. 179
Griqua 1, 2
Griqualand West *see* diamond fields
Grobelaar, Piet 151
Grootvlei 119
Grosskopf, J. F. W. 21, 22, 23, 191
Grundlingh, A. M. 27

Hall, R. J. 133
Hamburg 105
Harley, R. 174, 185
Harrismith 3, 5, 22, 64, 85–6, 102,
    121, 133, 135, 136, 137, 150, 151,
    152, 156, 179, 190
Heidelberg 65
Heilbron 22, 31, 43, 46, 65, 73, 77,
    80, 89, 111, 127, 131, 164, 168,
    185, 236*n.124*
Help Mekaar 44
Hertzog, General J. B. M. 35, 147,
    182
hides, trade in 3, 4, 5
Highveld, definition of xii–xiii,
    219*n.1*
Hill, Colonel T. A. 111
historiography xv–xviii, 196, 204,
    207, 220*nn. 7, 8*
Hobson, G. R. 101
Hoopstad 28, 99–100, 103, 144
hunting, by Boers 4, 113
    decline of 22, 25, 30, 197, 228*n.18*
    as sport 116, 251*n.84*
hunting, by blacks 5

Imperial South Africa Association
    112
impoverishment, amongst blacks
    62–*3, 128*–9, 184–91
impoverishment, amongst Boers
    18–19, 20–50, 57–9, 59–61, 63, 87,
    108, 112, 119, 197, 227*n.13*,
    271*n.14*
inheritance practices, Boer 38–41,
    234*n.102*
irrigation 26, 28, 108–9, 110, 111
ivory 2, 113

Jagersfontein 11, 100, 227*n.15*
Jameson Raid 43, 44
Jammerberg Drift 97, 113
Jensen, Otto 113
Jeppe, Julius 117
Johannesburg 17, 25, 37, 43, 115,
    116, 154, 186
    see also Witwatersrand
Jorissen, J. A. 172

Kaalvallei 43
Kamtombwe, Nomwola 156–7
Karoo 49–50
Kenya 269*n.4*, 270*n.5*
Kestell, Rev. J. D. 48
Keyter, J. G. 64, 167, 190, 236*n.123*,
    259*n.124*, 266*n.60*
Khoisan 1, 5
Kholokoe 86
Kilnerton Institute 80
Kimberley 10, 11, 12, 64, 66, 97, 114,
    115, 116, 125
Kitching, Gavin 269*n.4*
Klerksdorp 103, 179
Klipgat 178
Knight, E. F. 27
Koena 53, 55, 177, 178
Koffyfontein 100
Koppies 70, 138
Korana 2
Korannaberg 58
Kriel, Rev. 26
Kromellenboog 59
Kroonstad 43, 65, 81, 89, 117, 167,
    182, 186, 253*n.33*

labour, black, on farms 5–9, 51,
    121–65
    and boom of 1908–14 170–3,
        189–90
    and capital constraints 121–7, 205
    and contracts 130–9, 140–2,
        149–50, 151, 157–8, 171–2,
        189–90, 258*n.107*
    and housework 123, 159
    of juniors 123, 132–8, 146, 157,
        255*nn.57, 60*
    and mechanization 205–6

and migrancy from farms   13, 51, 121, 123–4, 130, 134–5
and migrancy to farms   6–7, 121, 124–8, 129, 149–50
and ploughing-and-sowing agreements   93–5, 121, 189–90, 192, 197–8, 205, 245*n.135*, 268*n.86*
and reaping   12
and resistance   157–9, 160–5, 205, 260*n.132*, 261nn.143, *148*, 262*nn.149*, *153*
and tenancy   121–30, 204–6, 254*n,38*
and violence   156–7, 160–2
and wage payments   121–4, 125, 149–50, 252*n.11*
white agitations *re*   13–15, 24, 59, 170–3, 204
and white undercapitalization   86–95, 121–4
of women   123, 125, 127, 134, 138–40, 146, 156–7, 159, 255*n.64*
see also sharecropping, sharecroppers, tenant communities
Ladybrand   9, 15, 23, 26, 28, 38, 55, 58, 60, 87, 99, 101, 111, 122, 125, 140, 143, 144, 162, 174, 185
land, mortgaging of   3, 15, 16, 36, 41, 197, 234–6*n.110*, 235*n.112*, 264*n.17*
and boom of 1890s   42
and boom of 1908–14   166–7, 168–9, 169–70
and depression of 1904–8   46–9
and entails on land   41
and inheritance   39
post-Anglo–Boer War   45, 101
and post-Union booms   49–50
resistance to   44–5
by Rolong   114
land, options on   43, 45, 46, 236*n.124*
land, prospecting rights on   43
land, speculation in   2, 3, 4, 5, 16, 24, 41, 197, 201, 235*n.119*, 239–40*n.40*, 240*n.47*
and boom of 1890s   42–4

and boom of 1908–14   168–9, 195, 263*n.15*
and capitalized farming   114, 115, 116–17, 251*n.86*
in mid-Vaal region   54
in Moroka's territory   114
post-Anglo–Boer War   45, 236*n.124*
and post-Union booms   49–50
and sharecropping   54–5, 57–9, 64–74, 171, 201, 241*n.68*
land, subdivision of   20, 38–41; 197, 234*n.103*
and boom of 1908–14   166, 184, 188, 204, 263*n.11*
post-Anglo–Boer War   45, 102–3
and post-Union booms   49–50
land banks   44, 49
ORC Land Bank   34–5, 112, 166–7, 169–70, 203, 231*n.79*
Union Land and Agricultural Bank   34–5, 112, 170, 194, 203, 231*n.78*
land-settlement schemes
post-Anglo–Boer War   45, 64, 72–3, 109–12, 168, 229–30*n.47*, 235–6*n.123*, 249*nn.62*, *64*, *68*
post-Union   168–9, 263*n.12*
landlessness, Boer   20–2, 23
and black tenant farming   57–9
and indebtedness   41–2, 45–9, 201, 235*n.117*
and inheritance practices   38–41, 234*n.103*
and land banks   34–5, 169
landownership, black   175–80, 183–4, 206, 238*n.8*
landownership, Boer   4, 20–1
and black productive resources   86–95
and booms   49–50, 167
and inheritance   38–41
and labour supplies   14
servitudes on   40–1, 234*n.107*
and subdivision   38–41
threatened by indebtedness   16, 35–6, 38–9, 41–9
and trading   12, 113
see also land speculation

Leary, A. 150
Leeds 117
Leeuw River 97, 114
Legassick, Martin 196
Legget, Major E. H. M. 29
legislation
  entails on land 41
  fencing 109, 170, 228*n.18*
  inheritance laws 39
  land bank laws 34–5, 168–9,
    266*n.60*
  Land Settlement Act, 1912 168–9
  masters-and-servants laws 13,
    131–2, 137, 139, 140–2, 142–9,
    150, 164, 173, 192–3, 256*n.77*,
    257*n.96*, 259*n.119*
  pass laws 7–8, 13, 139, 144, 151–5,
    160, 243*n.97*, 259*n.124*
  'squatting' laws 7–8: Ordinance
    7–1881 14, 58, 70–1;
    Ordinance 4–1895 57–8,
    70–1, 72–3, 141, 183–4; Act
    23–1908 183, 266*n.60*
  taxing Basutoland grain 12–13,
    224*n.67*
  see also Natives Land Act, 1913
Lenin, V. I. 196
Leribe 62
Lewis & Marks 17, 44, 66, 115,
    240–7, 244*n.133*, 263*n.14*
Lindley 44, 52, 53, 55, 71, 112, 123,
    156, 172
Lloyd, J. 113
London 105, 147
Lovat, Lord 112
Lovedale 114
Luck, Reginald 136
Luckhoff 161

Macaskill, A. D. 240*n.40*
Macaskill, K. R. 121
McKechnie, G. 116–17
McLaren, J. A. 117
Macmillan, W. M. xv, 48–9
Mafeteng 61
Magaliesberg 55
Makume family 52, 133
Makume, Ndae 52, 71–2, 77, 133,
    156, 175

Mamogale 177
Mapikela, T. M. 187–8
Maree, A. H. 192
Marico 104
marketing 96–107
  annual cycle 97–8, 245–6*n.5*
  and co-operatives 44, 107
  and credit system 97–8
  and exportation 104–5, 248*n.40*
  and immobility 98–103, 246*nn.13*,
    14, 15
  and marketing boards 107, 203
  and railway construction 100–3
  and railway rating policy 105–7
  and speculation 97–8
Marks, Samuel 66, 70, 240*n.47*
Marquard 126, 135
Maseru 61
Masike, Philip 260*n.127*
Mathopestad 178
merchants 2, 3–4, 22–3, 26, 96–8,
    104, 197, 245*n.1*
  in Basutoland 11, 101, 104, 115,
    225*n.90*
  and black sharecroppers 76
  Boer opposition to 44
  and boom of 1908–14 167, 186,
    195
  and capitalized farming 113–14,
    115
  and credit system 97–8, 221*n.14*
  and speculation in produce 97–8,
    107
  as threat to landownership 41, 49
Meyer, I. J. 190
Mfengu 53
military system, Boer 3, 4–5, 25
  and 1914 rebellion 35
milling
  in Basutoland 11
  in Conquered Territory 18, 99,
    100, 113–14, 248*n.54*, 250*n.77*
Milner, Lord Alfred 29, 64, 72, 155,
    168, 201
Minter, Tom 43, 115, 117
Mitchell, Thomas 113
Mmolotsi, Tshwene 109
Mogale, Chief 265*n.43*
Mogoai, Rebecca 137

Mogopa 80, 176–8, 265*n.46*
Mohale's Hoek 61
Mohwerane, A. 241*n.55*
Moiloa, Johannes 55–6, 82, 84, 88
Mokale, Abraham 75, 78, 240*n.47*
Mokale, Tloaele 55, 76
Molefe, Emelia *see* Pooe, Emelia
Molefe, Rankwane 55
Molenspruit 113
Molete, Jameson 70, 71, 81, 132
Moletsane 2
Moloko, Ezekiel 178
Molote 178
moneylending 85, 167
Mooi Valley 163
Moore, Barrington 196
More, Petrus 177
Moroka, Chief 2, 53, 111, 114
Moroka, Samuel 66
Morris, M. L. 196
Moshoeshoe 2, 7, 53, 177, 178
Mosley, Paul 269*n.4*, 270*n.5*
Motsuenyane family 179
Mpondo 53, 270*n.4*
Msimang, R. W. 267*n.75*
Muller, Gert 76–7
Muller, Jan 181
Mundy, Harry 151

Natal 63, 86, 102, 114, 158
National Scouts 27
Native Affairs Department, ORC
    154
Native Farmers' Association of South
    Africa 179
Native Vigilance Committee 164
Natives Land Act, 1913 xv, 58, 169,
    179, 182–4, 188, 189, 190–1,
    192–3, 194, 195, 204, 266*n.61*,
    267*n.62*, 268*n.94*
Ndebele 2, 53, 80, 178
Nel, P. W. A. 143
Nellmapius, A. H. 240*n.47*
Newberry, Charles 26, 64, 97, 99,
    111, 114, 115, 235*n.123*
Newberry, John 114, 115
Newberry, Mrs E. M. 114
New York 101
Ngakane, Barney 80, 153, 180–1

Ngakane family 75–6, 80, 178–9
Ngakane, Morobane 78, 178
Ngakane, Paulus 77
Ngwato 55
Nicholson, F. T. 47–8
Nourse, Henry 115, 250*n.81*

Oberholzer, J. H. 87
Oberholzer, J. O. 90
Odendaal, Johanna 156–7
Odendaal, W. J. 144
Olivier, P. 70
Olivier, General P. 123
Oorbietjiesfontein 67, 76
Oorlamsches 6, 54, 159–60
Orange Free State Natives Congress
    188, 193
Orange Free State Republic
    economy 3–5, 222–3*n.45*
    independence recognized 2–3
    state system xiii, 3
Orange River Sovereignty 2–3, 6
ORC General Agency 236*n.124*
ORC Natives Association 148
ORC Volunteers 27
Orangia Unie 154
Ostrich feathers, trade in 4, 114

Pact government, 1924 35
Pakenham, Thomas 27
Palmer, W. J. 104
Parry, Natalie 150
Parys 88, 164, 167, 178, 185
paternalism 157–60
Peeters, Mrs G. W. 64–5, 239*n.40*
petitions
    re black economic independence
        24, 59
    re black tenant farming and white
        impoverishment 58–9
    re compulsory education 24–5
    re entails on land 41
    re interest rates 42
    re options on land 43
    re railway construction 17, 99, 101
    re relief from rent payments 26
    re Sotho competition on Rand
        produce markets 17–18
    re squatting 13

re suppression of black
  sharecropping   60–1
re war compensation   27–8
Petrus Steyn   70
Phalime, Kodisang   53, 70, 76–7,
  82–3, 84
Phuting   53, 177
Pienaar, J.   47
Pienaar, W. J.   47
Pilgrims Mining, Estate and
  Exploration Company   115,
  247*n.33*
Pilkington, Colonel J.   162
Plaatje, Sol T.   186–7, 239*n.40*,
  267*n.75*, 268*n.94*
Platrand   164
Poho, Abraham   80, 265*n.46*
police   149–50, 153–4, 155–6, 188,
  204, 259–119
Pooe, Dinah Molope   78, 178
Pooe, Emelia   31, 56, 78, 79, 131, 132
Pooe family   67, 76, 79, 80, 88, 177
Pooe, Naphtali   31, 77, 80, 81, 177,
  179, 189
Pooe, Petrus   75, 77, 80–1, 82, 176–8
populism, Boer   17–19, 207,
  237*n.136*
  and black tenant farming   57–9,
    63–4, 72, 92, 171, 180–2, 194,
    199–201, 204
  and boom of 1908–14   180–2
  and Brandfort Congress   154
  and the capitalist ideal   91–2, 121,
    199–201, 204
  defined   226*n.98*
  and education   24–5, 32–3,
    228*n.24*
  and land banks   34–5
  and land loss   48, 201
  and land speculation   43–4, 57–9,
    171
  and squatting   14–15
Potchefstroom   104, 137, 186,
  263*n.11*
Potchefstroom Convention   17
Presbyterian Church   80, 195
Pretoria   66, 178
'Prussian path'   196, 203
Prynnsberg   114

Rabie, Christi/
railway const
  after Anglo–b...
  to Conquered Terri...
    99, 101–2
  consequences of   102–4, 167,
    247*n.33*
  to Kimberley   16
  as means of relief   26, 102
  to mid-Vaal districts   103, 228*n.16*
  opposition to by Boers   12, 17, 22,
    227*n.15*
railway rates   26, 247*n.21*
  and maize trade   104–7, 248*nn.46*,
    50
Ramoloko, Chief   178
Rampa, John   164
Reading, H.   185
Realty Trust Company   179
reaping   52, 57, 107, 123, 124–8,
  161–2, 163, 205, 232*n.90*, 249*n.56*,
  252*nn.20, 23*, 253*n.33*
rebellion, Boer, 1914   35, 194–5
reconstruction regime, policies of
  27–9, 72–4, 109–11, 112, 141–2,
  145–8, 154–5, 201, 249*nn.62*,
  72
Reineke, Roelf   55
Reitz   22, 182
relief works after Anglo–Boer War
  28
Repatriation Department   28, 47,
  231*n.81*
repatriation of Boers after
  Anglo–Boer War   27–9, 227*n.15*
Rhodesia   39, 233*n.100*
Rietgat   43, 115
rinderpest 1896–7
  in Basutoland   61, 252*n.20*
  and black sharecropping   55–6,
    60, 83, 173
  and black transport-riding
    225–6*n.95*
  and impoverishment   25, 26, 44,
    58, 59, 60–1, 141, 171
  and transport   99, 100
Robertson, James   97, 99, 113,
  250*n.77*
Robertson, W.   90

...inson, G.   152
...olong   2, 53, 54, 64, 66, 114, 179
Roman–Dutch law   39
Rondeberg   113
Roos, E. C.   186
Rorich, J., & Company   227n.15
Roseberry Plain   64–5
Rosenzweig, R. C.   186
Ross, Robert   233n.99
Rosslein, E. B.   47
Rouxville   41, 46
Rustenburg   78, 175–6

Saltberry Plain   64–5
Schimper, Frans   39, 69–70
Schnehage, Mrs   47
Schuttesdraai   113
Scotland   112
Scott, David   113, 125
Scottish Sharpshooters' Association
   111
Seggie, Robert   83, 117, 244n.133
Sekonyela   2
self-government, ORC   xiv, 112, 203
Seme, Pixley   178, 179
Senekal   53, 116
Sephton, T. H.   114
Serfontein, N. W.   182
sharecroppers, black   74–86
   black and white compared   30–2,
      67, 242n.75
   and bridewealth   84
   and Christianity   53, 54, 74, 75,
      79–80, 84, 195, 243n.97
   and differentiation   74–5, 79,
      243n.94, 254n.38
   and education   79–80, 195
   and indebtedness   85
   and kinship system   60, 76–9,
      80–3, 198, 243n.106
   and labour organization   31, 76–9
   motivation of   55–6
   and obstacles to accumulation
      83–5
   and off-farm income   56, 79, 81–3,
      174
   and settlement patterns   30
   social origins   52–6, 80, 238n.7
   and stockownership   83–4, 173–5

and technology   74, 75–6,
      244n.116
sharecropping by blacks   12, 16–17,
      51–6, 140, 197–200, 203–4, 205–6
   on absentee-owned land   52, 54–5,
      56, 567–9, 64–74, 171, 239n.40
   and Anglo–Boer War   63
   in Basutoland   52
   and boom of 1908–14   171, 189–91
   and conflict   67–8, 240n.51,
      241n.55
   in Conquered Territory   53–4
   in contemporary southern Africa
      199
   and fixed rentals   67, 85–6
   on Griqua land   51–2
   in mid-Vaal region   54–5
   in partnership with poor whites
      36, 69–72, 190–1, 241n.68
   and rinderpest   55–6, 60–1
   by Rolong   54
   and white undercapitalization
      86–95, 118, 170, 197–8, 205–6
sharecropping by Boers   21, 22, 49,
      52, 67
shearing   52
Smartt syndicate   115
Smith, Sir Harry   2
Smithfield   3, 45, 167
Sotho
   and Anglo–Boer War   61–3
   on diamond fields   10, 223n.52
   in *Difaqane*   2
   in Harrismith/Vrede districts
      85–6
   migration into Orange Free State
      52–5, 61, 63, 74, 125–7, 149–50,
      237n.3
   reapers   125–7
   and rinderpest   61
   sharecroppers   51–6
   tenancy on farms   7–9, 12
   wars, 1860s   8
   see also Basutoland, labour
South African Constabulary   154
South African Mutual Trust
      Company   47
Southampton   105
Sowden, J.   26

Spence, J. D. 157–8
Staten, O. W. 65
steam ploughing 115, 117–18,
 244n.*133*, 251n.*89*, 270n.*5*
Stevens, Charles 104, 113
Steyl, J. P. 192
Steyn, President M. T. 43–4
Stockdale, H. W. 250n.*75*
stock-loan systems, Boer 21, 51,
 221n.*22*
Stofberg, G. 113
stratification, social, amongst Boers
 21–2, 23, 221n.*22*
 and Anglo-Boer War 27–8
 and boom of 1893–5 57–9
 and depression of 1904–8 46–9
 and education 119
 and inheritance 39–40
 and ORC Land Bank 34–5
 and rebellion of 1914 35
Stuart, H. G. 126
Sugden, J. A. 45, 171, 235–6n.*123*,
 250n.*80*
survival, strategies of amongst Boers
 36–8, 228n.*18*
 and black sharecropping on
  absentee-owned land 69–72
Swart, H. B. 164
Swartr and *see* Mogopa
Swinburne, Sir John 64

Taaiboschspruit 59
Taung 2, 52
taxation policy 106–7
tenant communities, black 7–8, 9,
 13–15, 24, 52–6, 57–9, 74–86,
 121–4, 128–30, 130–40, 188–9
 see also sharecroppers,
  sharecropping, labour
Thaba Nchu 2, 34, 53, 54, 60, 63, 66,
 89, 90, 101, 111, 122, 167, 186, 192
Theron, P. J. G. 30
Theunissen, J. M. 144
threshing 36, 76, 113, 250n.*75*
Tigerskloof 22
Tlokoa 86
Top Location 179
trade, by Boers 3–4, 8, 11–12, 18, 97,
 197, 222n.*43*, 223n.*56*

traders *see* merchants
transport-riding
 by blacks 76, 225–6n.*95*
 by Boers 3, 11–12, 18, 30, 33, 113,
  223n.*58*, 227n.*15*
 decline of 22–3, 30, 36, 97, 197,
  232n.*90*
 and marketing constraints 99,
  100–1, 246nn. *14, 15*
Transvaal Agricultural Union 48
Transvaal and Orangia Property
 Trust 236n.*124*
Transvaal Consolidated Land and
 Exploration Company 240n.*47*,
 264n.*15*
Transvaal Gold Mining Estates 115
Transvaal Land Owners' Association
 264n.*15*
Trapido, Stanley 66, 196
Trekboer economy 23, 233n.*99*
 decline of 30, 38
Treks, organized 39–40
Trompsburg 32
Tweespruit 111, 119, 130
Tylden, George 87, 92

Unification of South Africa xiv
Union Land Settlement Company Ltd
 263n.*14*
urbanization, black 81–2
urbanization, Boer 25–6, 35–8,
 232n.*91*
 gender differentiation 37–8
USA 104

Van Aswegen, H. J. xvii, xviii
Van der Bosch, J. N. 152
Van der Wath, C. 60–1
Van Iddekinge, J. F. 164
Van Onselen, Charles 37
Van Reenen, C. D. D. 150
Van Reenen, J. M. 125
Van Riet, G. J. 34, 89
Van Zyl, D. J. 180
Vecht, H. 43
Vechtkop 59
Ventersdorp 80, 176
Vereeniging 67, 77, 80, 178, 179

Vereeniging Estates 17, 54, 55, 59, 66–7, 73–4, 75, 76, 77, 78, 85, 117–18
Vierfontein 103, 115
Viljoen, H. S. 173
Vilonel, S. G. 116
Vincent, Charles 97
Vlakplaas 67, 75, 77, 78, 80
Volksraad 15
Von Berg, Albert 161
Voortrekkers 1
Vrede 46, 76, 84, 85–6, 138, 167, 185
Vredefort 26, 65, 191, 236*n.124*
Vryburg 40, 233*n.101*

Wakkerstroom 179
Warden line 7
Webb, Edgar 130
Weideman, A. J. 161
Wepener 97, 99, 101, 107, 115, 182, 191
Wesleyan Methodist Church 80, 186, 195, 243*n.97*
Wessels, Theuns 82, 84, 135
Westminster, Duke of 111–12, 117
Westminster Estate 111–12, 251*n.89*
Wildebeespan 179

Wildebeestfontein 116–17
Winburg 17, 39, 42, 82, 84, 85, 97, 135, 141, 148, 161, 162, 164, 174, 187, 188
Witsieshoek 53, 121
Witwatersrand
  corporate land 66
  grain trade to 16–18, 96, 98, 101–3, 104, 109, 113, 114
Wolwehoek 164
women Boer 37–8, 232*n.94*, 233*n.99*
Wonderkop 114
wood trade 12, 36
wool 3, 114, 222–3*n.45*
  in Basutoland 8, 11
Worringham, E. A. 186

Xhosa 53

Zaaiplaas 78
Zandveld 99–100, 103
Zastron xiii
Zeerust xiii
Zulu, in OFS 86, 158, 172, 260*n.131*
Zululand 53